Penguin Education

Design of Jobs

Edited by Louis E. Davis and James C. Taylor

Penguin Modern Management Readings

General Editor
D. S. Pugh

Advisory Board
H. C. Edey
R. L. Edgerton
T. Kempner
T. Lupton
D. T. Marquis
B. J. McCormick
P. G. Moore
R. W. Revans
F. J. Willett

To Bob
from Bill

Design of Jobs

Selected Readings

Edited by Louis E. Davis and James C. Taylor

Penguin Books

Penguin Books Ltd, Harmondsworth,
Middlesex, England
Penguin Books Inc, 7110 Ambassador Road,
Baltimore, Md 21207, USA
Penguin Books Australia Ltd,
Ringwood, Victoria, Australia

First published 1972
This selection copyright © Louis E. Davis and James C. Taylor, 1972
Introduction and notes copyright © Louis E. Davis and
James C. Taylor, 1972
Copyright acknowledgement for items in this volume
will be found on page 467.

Made and printed in Great Britain by
Cox & Wyman Ltd,
London, Reading and Fakenham
Set in Monotype Times

Contents

Introduction

Overview

The major purpose of this book is to show that the concepts and requirements for the design of jobs have changed in recent years. That the issue of how jobs are designed has become a central concern for highly developed societies becomes evident when we realize that most job designs are no longer socially evolved but are quite consciously created, at a point in time, and often by someone other than the person who will perform them. Georges Friedmann, referring to the organization of work, said that we are now in a *milieu technique* as distinct from the older *milieu naturel* (see Reading 5 for further discussion). Hence we are faced with a new and serious responsibility for appropriately developing jobs and organizations, and linking them to the larger society. The requirement now is to design jobs and roles in a context having few external referents and in which all must be designed: the jobs, roles, and the technological and social systems that will provide meaning for individuals and institutions in the larger society.

The readings included here start from the styles and models of job design in the industrial era. Some small attention is paid to the differences between the pre-industrial or craft era, and the industrial era. The values and assumptions behind current job design are considered and are shown to reflect the lasting influence of the industrial era. The remainder of the book emphasizes the recent theoretical work in the area of jobs or work roles, and the emerging empirical support for these new positions. It concludes on the note that what we know about the nature of jobs and work is not enough to predict job design in the future – that we must also recognize the new forces in society at large.

The onset of the industrial revolution saw the disruption of a long historical evolution in the nature of jobs. The new train of development, whose beginnings were signalized by the work of Charles Babbage, moved from a natural or tradition-guided structure of jobs and role relationships to man-made, ordered, rationalized (in mechanical or economic terms) structures and relationships. At the height of this development (1890–1920), F. W. Taylor and F. Gilbreth laid down the rule that any natural or tradition-guided development was to be viewed with suspicion, and that its existence was, in itself, reason enough to change it. We have been unequal to the task thus imposed on us to design jobs and roles that appropriately relate man, with his needs and unique capabilities, to technology: to modify and design technology to permit effective social system design; to retain and support the social fabric in which work is done; and to meet man's needs as an individual and as a member of society. What we have seen is the rationalization of man, inappropriately called the rationalization of work, and in the 1960s, the rationalization of systems. Throughout the twentieth century the Taylor thesis was expanded into a pseudo-science of work and dutifully taught to engineers, personnel managers, and business, industrial and government managers. It was supported by an ideology and a positivist philosophy of American psychology, which can be epitomized as the robot model of man (von Bertalanffy, 1967, p. 7). All this was in accord with the social ideology of the industrial era and was enshrined as social policy in such governmentally issued pronouncements as the *U.S. Dictionaries of Occupational Titles*.

Technology and work: a difference between jobs and work roles

Not so long ago tasks, jobs and work were the blue-collar equivalent of occupations and professions. They were terms depicting a man's relationship to his labors. They could be thought of as static, well-delineated entities, differing only in the inclusiveness of their referents. The task was the basic molecular unit.[1] Tasks were the elements of jobs, and jobs were the components of work. But jobs and work, viewed in this way, include only the relationship of man to his product. Work in this sense may be said to implicitly include the worker's relationship to his tools and his relationships to other persons in the performance of work. However, explicit concern with the technical and social components of jobs and work is of more recent origin.

1. Individual movements and motions, although smaller units than tasks, came in as specialized terms of time and motion study, and not as part of the common language.

In the early era of simple technology, the classical time and motion study did expressly include the worker's tools, but considered the worker as a machine – sometimes a complicated, unreliable and recalcitrant machine. The more recent notion in mass production, that of man as a physical extension of the machines he works with (or for), has perpetuated this particular man–machine relationship to the present day. But technology continues to develop, and now, in many settings of modern technology, man has ceased to be an extension of the machine and has become its supervisor instead.

By technology we mean the complex or combination of techniques used to alter materials or information in some specified or anticipated way to get a desired end result. The term 'modern technology' has been used in at least two very different ways. One use refers to sophistication and newness in the production system or process – automation is the archetype here. The second use refers to sophistication and newness in the product – such as electronics. Both of the applications are correct. The new production process is new technology: a familiar product is created in a new way. A new product such as electronics is also a new technology if it in turn is a device or technique for transforming something else in a new way. Strictly speaking, plastics, frequently referred to as a modern technology, are not a new technology, but are the *product* of a new technology – a new product of new methods.

Our definition of sophisticated or modern technology is confined to advances in the techniques of production rather than to the development of new products *per se*. The impact of technology on job design has always been strong. However, the implications of evolving sophisticated technology for job design are considerable. That more sophisticated production technology can provide a whole new work definition is a real possibility.

It is clear that what is described as a more sophisticated technology can actually result in a much smaller and simpler job. 'Job', here defined, is that portion of the employee's work role that deals with his direct activities in relation to the object undergoing transformation. In sophisticated technologies, man's role shifts from the tool and its use or guidance to the system and its maintenance, regulation and control.

As technology has been defined, man uses tools and techniques to effect change in some third object. From these three elements three technological relationships can be expressed: machine–product, man–product, and man–machine. In sophisticated or modern technology the first two of these three relationships completely define the production process. The first, the machine–product relationship, defines that portion of the process that is under automatic control. The second, the man–product relationship, defines that portion of the production process that the machine presently cannot perform; it is, in effect, the residuum of the first relationship. This second relationship defines the employee's 'job'. The third relationship, the man–machine, describes primarily a maintenance function (role- rather than job-relevant). To the degree that advanced technology, as we define it, exists in the elements of sophistication of material and complexity of machines, the machine–product relationship predominates in the production process – necessity for human intervention is minimal or nonexistent. To the degree that sophistication of technology exists in the control feedback process, there is continued, albeit diminished, inclusion of the man–product relationship. Even though the operator needs to continue to act on the more sophisticated feedback, his 'job', the man–product relationship, becomes simpler under more complex feedback systems. He need not wonder or wait under these conditions: the evaluative information comes quickly, unambiguously, correctly via a direct process in addition to his own senses.

It follows that the more sophisticated the machine–product dimension, the more limited the man–product relationship. Since the man–product relationship has been traditionally thought of as the 'job', what happens to the worker under conditions of sophisticated technology, i.e. minimal man–product relationship? One option, of course, is that his 'role' (defined as a set of rules and expectations from the employee as well as the organization, which direct all of his occupational or 'at work' behavior) diminishes and disappears with his 'job' – that is, he either is displaced, or continues working at the 'non-job' until he retires or quits. Another option might be that the worker's role enlarges as his 'job' diminishes – that is, the role enlarges vertically as the worker takes or is given responsibility for production supervision, quality control, maintenance supervision and as he comes into contact with more members of the organization to get things done. His role, then, becomes more complex, more demanding, as his 'job' becomes simpler. This involvement via 'role enlargement' is exactly the reverse of the kind of involvement included in 'horizontal job enlargement' where the worker undertakes more, rather than fewer, of the man–product functions.

The notion of occupational role is a current rather than an historical concept. It explicitly includes man's *work-relation associations* with others on the job. Although in a formal sense these particular social relations have always been a part of work, they have been ignored in traditional job design theories. This is understandable for at least two reasons. First, man-as-machine theories of time and motion study had no reason to be concerned with the cooperation among workers when the emphasis was on the saving of time through efficient movement. Second, the nature of the technology between 1910 and 1950 reduced the need for coordination by workers since that coordination was built into the process or work flow with the residuum being taken care of by management. The notion of role has, however, come into prominence and is displacing 'job' as a central concept in the 'at work' relationship. This concept of role can be seen to originate from at least two sources. First is the general human relations concern in industrial study – a parallel but unrelated movement to job design, which has developed over the past forty years. The second factor is the change in technology that has demanded closer coordination and cooperation among workers and has therefore brought the social component into prominence.

In the genealogy of work design, which follows, three current trends are identified, job rationalization, job content, and role content. It is important to note that few of the readings included in the present volume explicitly use the role concept. The notion of role is essentially our category of clarification in the development of work design. If the reader finds it useful in understanding the readings, or in thinking about the future of work design, the concept will be justified.

Genealogy of work design

The origins of modern work design are presented here as a family tree (see Figure 1) of significant intellectual and research in-

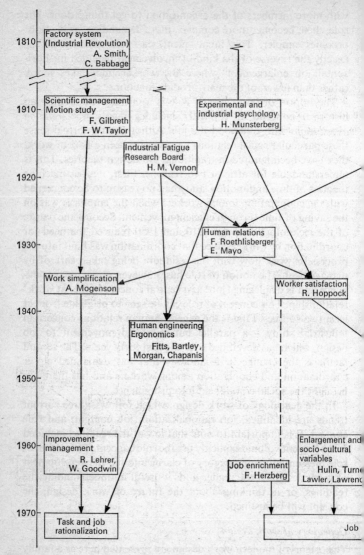

Figure 1 Genealogy of work design

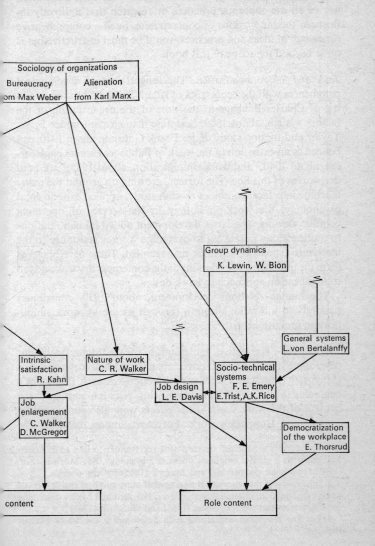

Sociology of organizations

Bureaucracy
from Max Weber

Alienation
from Karl Marx

Group dynamics
K. Lewin, W. Bion

General systems
L. von Bertalanffy

Intrinsic
satisfaction
R. Kahn

Nature of work
C. R. Walker

Socio-technical
systems
F. E. Emery
E.Trist, A.K.Rice

Job enlargement
C. Walker
D. McGregor

Job design
L. E. Davis

Democratization
of the workplace
E. Thorsrud

content

Role content

novations, which have *directly* contributed to the present state of development. Obviously, it is not a history of each innovation nor of all the concepts, practices or research that indirectly influenced the innovations of concern here. Such a comprehensive genealogy of ideas and practices would be most instructive but is quite beyond the scope of this book.

Task and job rationalization. The longest line of development commences with the economics of Adam Smith and the engineering of Charles Babbage at the time of the organization of the factory system, about 1800. Scientific management under F. W. Taylor and motion study under Frank Gilbreth, about 1910, can be seen as an extension of the work of Babbage. Human engineering, about 1940,[2] and work simplification, about 1935,[3] are both derivatives of this line. The former, growing up around the man–machine interface, combines motion study, applied experimental psychology, the work-physiology in the service of operating complex devices. The latter development added human relations to motion study in seeking to overcome worker resistance to the mechanistic goals of scientific management. These developments form the underlying foundations of the contemporary task and job rationalization approach to work design.

The human relations development, about 1930, contributes passively to job rationalization through its use by work simplification practitioners.

Job content. The active contribution of the human relations development was to rediscover man in formal organizations (Mayo); it stimulated worker satisfaction research (Hoppock), beginning about 1935.[4] However, this research excluded the content of the work itself. Other effects were also stimulated by Mayo's and Hoppock's work. Foremost among these was the

2. Ergonomics is a British development very similar to human engineering, but with a greater emphasis on work physiology. See Morgan *et al.* (1963) for human engineering, and Murrell (1965) for ergonomics.

3. Improvement management is a somewhat more comprehensive form of work simplification, retaining its objectives. For germinal papers describing these developments see Mogenson (1963) and Goodwin (1968).

4. For key references concerning each development see list of Further Reading.

interest in intrinsic job satisfaction at the University of Michigan's Institute for Social Research, about 1950, which contributed the concept of job enlargement, about 1955. In addition, the influence of C. R. Walker's nature-of-work studies on the development of job enlargement is powerful and direct. The job enlargement development focused on providing more and varied tasks or duties as a means of countering the extreme fractionation of jobs promulgated by the job rationalization school of work design.

An unintended and independent effect of work satisfaction research brought Frederick Herzberg and others to the conclusion that the content and structure of jobs rather than the conditions surrounding them were the significant influences on performance, satisfaction and motivation. By 1960 Herzberg evolved job enrichment as an approach to the development of job content and structure by adding planning, regulation and control activities (vertical enrichment) to the individual job.

About 1960, there developed a concern with socio-cultural and psychological characteristics of work, which also evolved from job enlargement research. The concern centers on the characteristics of workers' upbringing and cultural exposure, and their consequent need structure, which condition the workers' reactions to the type of job, whether fractionated, enlarged or enriched.

Role content. The third cluster of developments includes job design, about 1955, and socio-technical systems, about 1950. Job design, an American development, had its origins in the attempts at comprehensive work systems design including the social systems within which the work systems are embedded. Since the early 1960s, this development has been closely interacting with the socio-technical systems development of the Tavistock Institute in London, and now can be taken as inseparable from it.

Socio-technical systems derived partly from the research on small groups by W. R. Bion and Kurt Lewin, and from the work of Ludwig von Bertalanffy in developing open systems theory from general systems.

The contribution of socio-technical systems to work design is in the conception of autonomous group structure as appropriate to sophisticated modern technology. Autonomous groups are effectively leaderless teams of employees working together in the completion of the group's primary task. By definition, *occupational roles* are more central to the work process than are *jobs* in autonomous groups. The self-coordination and cooperation required among members, and the use of multiple (and even redundant) skills, as well as formation of composite teams, makes role content rather than job content the central concern of socio-technical systems.

The socio-technical systems development is relatively recent compared with the other two clusters of developments. Its British origins and youth make its contribution to work design better known in Europe than in North America.

At present, the three strands of development described in this introduction exist concurrently. Since we live in a society that is organized partly on industrial and partly on post-industrial models, it is not inappropriate that all three strands should co-exist. However, given the accelerating changes in technology and the social environment, it is probable that appropriate applications of the task and job rationalization strand will diminish in the future, and that it will become increasingly dysfunctional. Disturbingly, while the trend toward post-industrial organization is growing, the task and job rationalization mode is being imported with untutored disregard into the service sector – to that sector's considerable peril.

It is one of the purposes of this volume to clarify the technological and societal matrix underlying the design of jobs, by whatever mode; and to point out the relationships between the nature of the organization, its supporting social system, and the mode of job design appropriate to it.

References

ARGYRIS, C. (1957), *Personality and Organization*, Harper & Row.

BARTLEY, S. H., and CHUTE, E. (1947), *Fatigue and Impairment in Man*, McGraw-Hill.

BION, W. R. (1955), 'Group dynamics: a review', in M. Klein, P. Heimann and R. E. Money-Kyrle (eds.), *New Directions in Psycho-Analysis*, Tavistock.

CARROLL, B. (1969), *Job Satisfaction*, Industrial and Labor Relations Library, Cornell University, Key Issues Series, no. 3.

DAVIS, L. E., and CANTER, R. R. (1955), 'Job design', *Journal of Industrial Engineering*, vol. 6, no. 1, p. 3.

FITTS, P. M., and JONES, R. E. (1947), *Psychological Aspects of Instrument Display*, Report TSEAA-694-12A, US Air Force Air Material Command.

FRIEDMANN, G. (1961), *The Anatomy of Work*, Heinemann Educational Books, Free Press, 1964.

GILBRETH, F. B. (1911), *Motion Study*, Van Nostrand.

GOODWIN, H. F. (1968), 'Improvement must be managed', *Journal of Industrial Engineering*, vol. 19, pp. 538–45.

HERZBERG, F. (1966), *Work and the Nature of Man*, Harcourt, Brace & World.

HOPPOCK, R. (1935), *Job Satisfaction*, Harper and Row.

HULIN, C. L., and BLOOD, M. R. (1968), 'Job enlargement, individual differences, and worker responses', *Psychological Bulletin*, vol. 69, February, pp. 44-55.

KAHN, R. L., and MORSE, N. C. (1951), 'The relationship of productivity to morale', *Journal of Social Issues*, vol. 7, no. 3, pp. 8–17.

LAWLER, E. E. (1969), 'Job design and employee motivation', *Personnel Psychology*, vol. 22, Winter, pp. 426-35.

LEHRER, R. N. (1957), *Work Simplification*, Prentice-Hall.

LEWIN, K. (1947), 'Frontiers in group dynamics', *Human Relations*, vol. 1, pp. 5–41.

LIKERT, R. (1961), *New Patterns of Management*, McGraw-Hill.

MCGREGOR, D. (1960), *The Human Side of Enterprise*, McGraw-Hill.

MARX, Karl (1967), *Economic and Philosophical Manuscripts of 1844*, Foreign Languages Publishing House.

MAYO, E. (1933), *The Human Problems of an Industrial Civilization*, Macmillan.

MOGENSON, A. H. (1963), 'Work simplification – a program of continuous improvement', in H. B. Maynard (ed.), *Industrial Engineering Handbook*, 2nd ed., McGraw-Hill, pp. 10; 183–91.

MORGAN, C. T., COOK, J. S., CHAPANIS, A., and LUND, M. W. (1963), *Human Engineering Guide for Equipment Design*, McGraw-Hill.

MUNSTERBERG, H. (1913), *The Psychology of Industrial Efficiency*, Houghton Mifflin.

MURRELL, K. F. H. (1965), *Ergonomics: Man and His Working Environment*, Chapman Hall.

ROETHLISBERGER, F. J., and DICKSON, W. J. (1939), *Management and the Worker*, Harvard University Press.

SMITH, Adam, (1970), *Wealth of Nations*, Penguin.

THORSRUD, E., and EMERY, F. E. (1969), *Moten Ny Bedriftsorganisasjon*, Tanum Press (English edition to be published (1972).

TURNER, A. N., and LAWRENCE, R. R. (1965), *Industrial Jobs and the Worker*, Harvard University Press.

U.S. Employment Service (1965), *Dictionary of Occupational Titles*, 3rd rev. ed., U.S. Department of Labor, Manpower Administration, Bureau of Employment Security.

VERNON, H. M. (1921), *Industrial Fatigue and Efficiency*, Routledge & Kegan Paul.

VON BERTALANFFY, L. (1950), 'The theory of open systems in physics and biology', *Science*, vol. 3, pp. 23-8.

VON BERTALANFFY, L. (1967), *Robots, Men and Minds*, George Braziller.

WALKER, C. R., and GUEST, R. H. (1952), *The Man on the Assembly Line*, Harvard University Press.

WEBER, M. (1946), Essays in Sociology (translated by H. H. Gerth and C. Wright Mills), Oxford University Press.

Part One
Evolution of Job Designs in Industrial Society

The concept of the design of jobs is historically of recent origin, beginning with man's roles in the technical world rather than in the world of nature. The history of the origins of jobs has a powerful grip on the present, for this historical residue is the present conventional wisdom in the world of work. From the present perspective the crucial early developments can be examined in terms of the societal values of the then-emerging industrial era. We wish to emphasize the often-neglected point that neither social and technological developments, nor theoretical constructs, can be understood without knowledge of the fundamental values underlying them.

The industrial era began with the catalytic discovery that machines are more than devices and that by combining them with particularly conceived tasks for men a potent new social means was at hand for overcoming the historical specter of scarcity. This was clearly seen by Babbage. The history of jobs and their designs derived from this evolving social technology and in the following positivistic, optimistic era of technological determinism. The consequences, in material terms, were enormous. In social terms the consequences were the development of work performed under social compulsion and regimentation, and so organized that men are the spare parts. The central question of the industrial era has remained unanswered: how to develop organizations, and their work systems, that provide for society's needs as well as the needs of its members so that work is not dehumanizing.

Babbage identified the core concept of the social technology. Taylor operationalized it in the name of science, providing a powerful mechanistic philosophy of social organization that reinforced the evolving bureaucratic one. This machine theory of organization has proven to be the most pervasive ideology of the industrial era. As Bell indicates in his paper (Reading 3), 'The significance of Taylorism lies in its attempt to enact a social physics.' This ideology is best understood by looking back from today's perception of social systems. In this context scientific management can be seen as designing and operating production systems by means of the operating units approach described by Boguslaw (Reading 4). This approach was supported by societal values made explicit by economists of the era who provided specious explanations of human behavior, which unfortunately still persist.

Touraine (Reading 5) characterizes the technology that directed the evolution of the machine theory of man in the industrial era. The association between technology and work is cast into an evolutionary model, beginning with the pre-industrial or craft period, through the industrial period, to the emerging post-industrial period.

1 Charles Babbage

On the Economy of Machinery and Manufactures

Excerpts from Charles Babbage, *On the Economy of Machinery and Manufactures*, Charles Knight, fourth edition enlarged, 1835,* chapters 13 and 19, pp. 119–22, 172–90.

If the *maker* of an article wish to become a *manufacturer*, in the more extended sense of the term, he must attend to other principles besides those mechanical ones on which the successful execution of his work depends; and he must carefully arrange the whole system of his factory in such a manner, that the article he sells to the public may be produced at as small a cost as possible. Should he not be actuated at first by motives so remote, he will, in every highly civilized country, be compelled, by the powerful stimulus of competition, to attend to the principles of the domestic economy of manufactures. [. . .]

Perhaps the most important principle on which the economy of a manufacture depends, is the *division of labour* amongst the persons who perform the work. The first application of this principle must have been made in a very early stage of society; for it must soon have been apparent, that a larger number of comforts and conveniences could be acquired by each individual, if one man restricted his occupation to the art of making bows, another to that of building houses, a third boats, and so on. This division of labour into trades was not, however, the result of an opinion that the general riches of the community would be increased by such an arrangement; but it must have arisen from the circumstance of each individual so employed discovering that he himself could thus make a greater profit of his labour than by pursuing more varied occupations. Society must have made considerable advances before this principle could have been carried into the workshop; for it is only in countries which have attained a high degree of civilization, and in articles in which there is a great competition amongst the producers, that the most perfect system of the

* *Reprints of Economic Classics*, Augustus M. Kelly, New York, 1965.

division of labour is to be observed. The various principles on which the advantages of this system depend, have been much the subject of discussion amongst writers on Political Economy; but the relative importance of their influence does not appear, in all cases, to have been estimated with sufficient precision. It is my intention, in the first instance, to state shortly those principles, and then to point out what appears to me to have been omitted by those who have previously treated the subject.

Of the time required for learning. It will readily be admitted, that the portion of time occupied in the acquisition of any art will depend on the difficulty of its execution; and that the greater the number of distinct processes, the longer will be the time which the apprentice must employ in acquiring it. [. . .]

Of waste of materials in learning. A certain quantity of material will, in all cases, be consumed unprofitably, or spoiled by every person who learns an art; and as he applies himself to each new process, he will waste some of the raw material, or of the partly manufactured commodity. But if each man commit this waste in acquiring successively every process, the quantity of waste will be be much greater than if each person confine his attention to one process; in this view of the subject, therefore, the division of labour will diminish the price of production.

Another advantage resulting from the division of labour is, *the saving of that portion of time which is always lost in changing from one occupation to another.* When the human hand, or the human head, has been for some time occupied in any kind of work, it cannot instantly change its employment with full effect. [. . .]

Change of tools. The employment of different tools in the successive processes is another cause of the loss of time in changing from one operation to another. [. . .]

Skill acquired by frequent repetition of the same processes. The constant repetition of the same process necessarily produces in the workman a degree of excellence and rapidity in his particular department, which is never possessed by a person who is obliged to execute many different processes. This rapidity is still further increased from the circumstance that most of the operations in factories, where the division of labour is carried to a considerable extent, are paid for as piece-work. It is difficult to estimate in numbers the effect of this cause upon production. In nail-making, Adam Smith has stated, that it is almost three to one; for, he observes, that a smith accustomed to make nails, but whose whole business has not been that of a nailer, can make only from eight hundred to a thousand per day; whilst a lad who had never exercised any other trade, can make upwards of two thousand three hundred a day. [. . .]

The division of labour suggests the contrivance of tools and machinery to execute its processes. When each process, by which any article is produced, is the sole occupation of one individual, his whole attention being devoted to a very limited and simple operation, improvements in the form of his tools, or in the mode of using them, are much more likely to occur to his mind, than if it were distracted by a greater variety of circumstances. Such an improvement in the tool is generally the first step towards a machine. [. . .]

When each process has been reduced to the use of some simple tool, the union of all these tools, actuated by one moving power, constitutes a machine. [. . .]

Such are the principles usually assigned as the causes of the advantage resulting from the division of labour. As in the view I have taken of the question, the most important and influential cause has been altogether unnoticed, I shall re-state those principles in the words of Adam Smith: 'The great increase in the quantity of work, which, in consequence of the division of labour, the same number of people are capable of performing, is owing to three different circumstances: first, to the increase of dexterity in every particular workman; secondly, to the saving of time, which is commonly lost in passing from one species of work to another; and, lastly, to the invention of a great number of machines which facilitate and abridge labour, and enable one man to do the work of many.' Now, although all these are important causes, and each has its influence on the result; yet it appears to me, that any explanation of the cheapness of manufactured articles, as consequent upon the division of labour, would be incomplete if the following principle were omitted to be stated.

That the master manufacturer, by dividing the work to be executed into different processes, each requiring different degrees of skill or of force, can purchase exactly the precise quantity of both which is necessary for each process; whereas, if the whole work were executed by one workman, that person must possess sufficient skill to perform the most difficult, and sufficient strength to execute the most laborious, of the operations into which the art is divided.*

* I have already stated that this principle presented itself to me after a personal examination of a number of manufactories and workshops devoted to different purposes; but I have since found that it had been distinctly pointed out, in the work of Gioja, *Nuovo Prospetto delle Scienze Economiche*, Milano, 1815, vol. 1, ch. 4.

2 Frederick W. Taylor

The Principles of Scientific Management

Excerpts from F. W. Taylor, *The Principles of Scientific Management*, Harper & Row, 1911, Preface and chapters 1 and 2, pp. 9–144.

In the preface to the joint edition, the editor states:

'The Principles of Scientific Management', published uniform with this book, is simply an argument for Mr Taylor's Philosophy of Human Labor, – an outline of the fundamental principles on which it rests. In 'Shop Management', however, the effort is made to describe the organization and some of the mechanisms by means of which this philosophy and these principles can be made effective in the workshop, or on the market place. [. . .]

The body of this paper will make it clear that, to work according to scientific laws, the management must take over and perform much of the work which is now left to the men; almost every act of the workman should be preceded by one or more preparatory acts of the management which enable him to do his work better and quicker than he otherwise could. And each man should daily be taught by and receive the most friendly help from those who are over him, instead of being, at the one extreme, driven or coerced by his bosses, and at the other left to his own unaided devices. [. . .]

Under scientific management the 'initiative' of the workmen (that is, their hard work, their good-will, and their ingenuity) is obtained with absolute uniformity and to a greater extent than is possible under the old system; and in addition to this improvement on the part of the men, the managers assume new burdens, new duties, and responsibilities never dreamed of in the past. The managers assume, for instance, the burden of gathering together all of the traditional knowledge which in the past has been possessed by the workmen and then of classifying, tabulating, and reducing this knowledge to rules, laws, and formulae which are immensely helpful to the workmen in doing their daily work. In addition to developing a *science* in this way, the management take on three other types of duties which involve new and heavy burdens for themselves.

These new duties are grouped under four heads:

First. They develop a science for each element of a man's work, which replaces the old rule-of-thumb method.

Second. They scientifically select and then train, teach, and develop the workman, whereas in the past he chose his own work and trained himself as best he could.

Third. They heartily cooperate with the men so as to insure all of the work being done in accordance with the principles of the science which has been developed.

Fourth. There is an almost equal division of the work and the responsibility between the management and the workmen. The management take over all work for which they are better fitted than the workmen, while in the past almost all of the work and the greater part of the responsibility were thrown upon the men.

[. . .]

Perhaps the most prominent single element in modern scientific management is the task idea. The work of every workman is fully planned out by the management at least one day in advance, and each man receives in most cases complete written instructions, describing in detail the task which he is to accomplish, as well as the means to be used in doing the work. And the work planned in advance in this way constitutes a task which is to be solved, as explained above, not by the workman alone, but in almost all cases by the joint effort of the workman and the management. This task specifies not only what is to be done but how it is to be done and the exact time allowed for doing it. And whenever the workman succeeds in doing his task right, and within the time limit specified, he receives an addition of from 30 per cent to 100 per cent to his ordinary wages. These tasks are carefully planned, so that both good and careful work are called for in their performance, but it should be distinctly understood that in no case is the workman called upon to work at a pace which would be injurious to his health. The task is always so regulated that the man who is well suited to his job will thrive while working at this rate during a long term of years and grow happier and more prosperous, instead of being overworked. Scientific management consists very largely in preparing for and carrying out these tasks. [. . .]

[No] one workman [has] the authority to make other men cooperate with him to do faster work. It is only through *enforced* standardization of methods, *enforced* adoption of the best implements and working conditions, and *enforced* cooperation that this faster work can be assured. And the duty of enforcing the adoption of standards and of enforcing this cooperation rests with the *management* alone. The *management* must supply continually one or more teachers to show each new man the new and simpler motions, and the slower men must be constantly watched and helped until they have risen to their proper speed. All of those who, after proper teaching, either will not or cannot work in accordance with the new methods and at the higher speed must be discharged by the *management*. The *management* must also recognize the broad fact that workmen will not submit to this more rigid standardization and will not work extra hard, unless they receive extra pay for doing it. [. . .]

The science which exists in most of the mechanic arts is, however, far simpler than the science of cutting metals. In almost all cases, in fact, the laws or rules which are developed are so simple that the average man would hardly dignify them with the name of a science. In most trades, the science is developed through a comparatively simple analysis and time study of the movements required by the workmen to do some small part of his work, and this study is usually made by a man equipped merely with a stopwatch and a properly ruled notebook. [. . .] The general steps to be taken in developing a simple law of this class are as follows:

First. Find, say, ten or fifteen different men (preferably in as many separate establishments and different parts of the country) who are especially skilful in doing the particular work to be analyzed.

Second. Study the exact series of elementary operations or motions which each of these men uses in doing the work which is being investigated, as well as the implements each man uses.

Third. Study with a stop-watch the time required to make each of these elementary movements and then select the quickest way of doing each element of the work.

Fourth. Eliminate all false movements, slow movements, and useless movements.

Fifth. After doing away with all unnecessary movements, collect into one series the quickest and best movements as well as the best implements.

This one new method, involving that series of motions which can be made quickest and best, is then substituted in place of the ten or fifteen inferior series which were formerly in use. This best method becomes standard, and remains standard, to be taught first to the teachers (or functional foremen) and by them to every workman in the establishment until it is superseded by a quicker and better series of movements. In this simple way one element after another of the science is developed. [. . .]

With this explanation it will be seen that the development of a science to replace rule of thumb is in most cases by no means a formidable undertaking, and that it can be accomplished by ordinary, every-day men without any elaborate scientific training; but that, on the other hand, the successful use of even the simplest improvement of this kind calls for records, system, and co-operation where in the past existed only individual effort. [. . .]

Perhaps the most important law belonging to this class, in its relation to scientific management, is the effect which the task idea has upon the efficiency of the workman. This, in fact, has become such an important element of the mechanism of scientific management, that by a great number of people scientific management has come to be known as 'task management'.

There is absolutely nothing new in the task idea. Each one of us will remember that in his own case this idea was applied with good results in his school-boy days. No efficient teacher would think of giving a class of students an indefinite lesson to learn. Each day a definite, clear-cut task is set by the teacher before each scholar, stating that he must learn just so much of the subject; and it is only by this means that proper, systematic progress can be made by the students. The average boy would go very slowly if, instead of being given a task, he were told to do as much as he could. All of us are grown-up children, and it is equally true that the average workman will work with the greatest satisfaction, both to himself and to his employer, when he is given each day a definite task which he is to perform in a given time, and which constitutes a proper day's work for a good workman. This furnishes the workman with a clear-cut standard, by which he can throughout the day measure his own progress, and the accomplishment of which affords him the greatest satisfaction. [. . .]

Now, when through all of this teaching and this minute instruction the work is apparently made so smooth and easy for the workman, the first impression is that this all tends to make him a mere automaton, a wooden man. As the workmen frequently say when they first come under this system, 'Why, I am not allowed to think or move without someone interfering or doing it for me!' The same criticism and objection, however, can be raised against all other modern subdivision of labor. [. . .]

It will doubtless be claimed that in all that has been said no new fact has been brought to light that was not known to someone in the past. Very likely this is true. Scientific management does not necessarily involve any great invention, nor the discovery of new or startling facts. It does, however, involve a certain *combination* of elements which have not existed in the past, namely, old knowledge so collected, analyzed, grouped, and classified into laws and rules that it constitutes a science; accompanied by a complete change in the mental attitude of the working men as well as of those on the side of the management, toward each other, and toward their respective duties and responsibilities. Also, a new division of the duties between the two sides and intimate, friendly cooperation to an extent that is impossible under the philosophy of the old management. And even all of this in many cases could not exist without the help of mechanisms which have been gradually developed.

It is no single element, but rather this whole combination, that constitutes scientific management, which may be summarized as:

Science, not rule of thumb.
Harmony, not discord.
Cooperation, not individualism.
Maximum output, in place of restricted output.
The development of each man to his greatest efficiency and prosperity.

3 Daniel Bell

Three Technologies: Size, Measurement, Hierarchy

Excerpts from Daniel Bell, *Work and Its Discontents*,
Beacon Press, 1956, ch. 2., pp. 3–10.

The contemporary enterprise was set up to obey three peculiar technologics: the logic of size, the logic of 'metric' time and the logic of hierarchy. Each of the three, the product of engineering rationality, has imposed on the worker a set of constraints, with which he is forced to wrestle every day. These condition the daily facts of his existence.

For the man whose working day is from eight in the morning to five in the afternoon, the morning begins long before the time he is to arrive at his place of work. After a hasty wash and a quick breakfast, he is off in his car or on the streetcar, bus or subway; often he may have to spend an hour or more in getting to the plant. (There seems to be a law, as Bertrand Russell has noted, that improvements in transportation do not cut down traveling time but merely increase the area over which people have to travel.)

Although this is the most obvious fact about modern work, few writers have concerned themselves with it, or with the underlying assumption: that large masses of human labor should be brought to a common place of work. The engineer believes that concentration is technologically efficient: under one roof there can be brought together the source of power, the raw materials, the parts and the assembly lines. So we find such huge megaliths as Willow Run, now used by General Motors, a sprawling shed spanning an area two-thirds of a mile long and a quarter of a mile wide; or such roofed-over, mile-long pavements as the Boeing plant in Wichita, Kansas. [. . .]

The introduction of electric power and electric motors opened the way to greater flexibility; and within the plant these opportunities were taken. Newer work-flow designs have avoided the antiquated straight-line shafts and aisles of the older factory. Yet the outward size of the factory remained unchallenged. Why? In part because the engineer conceives of efficiency in technological terms alone; and he is able to do so because a major cost – the travel time of the worker – can be discounted. But the question can be posed: should large masses of persons be brought to a common place of work? Which is cheaper to transport: working men twice daily, or materials and mechanical parts, let us say, twice a week? Yet the question is rarely considered, for few industries pay directly for their workers' travel time. Calculations in terms of market costs alone do not force the enterprise to take into account such factors as the time used in going to and from work, or the costs of roads and other transport to the factory site, which are paid for by the employee or by the community as a whole out of taxes.

In his travel to and from work the worker is chained by time. Time rules the work economy, its very rhythms and motions. . . .

One of the prophets of modern work was Frederick W. Taylor, and the stop watch was his bible. If any such social upheaval can ever be attributed to one man, the logic of efficiency as a mode of life is due to him. With 'scientific management', as enunciated by Taylor, we pass far beyond the old rough computations of the division of labor; we go into the division of time itself. [. . .]

The stop watch itself was not new. Before Taylor, work had been timed; but only for the entire job. What Taylor did was to split each job into its component operations and take the time of each. This, in essence, is the whole of scientific management: the systematic analysis and breakdown of work into the smallest mechanical component and the rearrangement of these elements into the most efficient combination. Taylor gave his first lectures to American engineers in 1895 (the year, one might note wryly, that Freud and Breuer published their *Studies in Hysteria*, the 'breakthrough' of psychoanalysis). But it was in 1899 that Taylor achieved fame when he taught a Dutchman named Schmidt to shovel forty-seven tons instead of twelve-and-a-half tons of pig iron a day. Every detail of the man's job was specified: the size of the shovel, the bite into the pile, the weight of the scoop, the distance to walk, the arc of the swing and the rest periods that Schmidt should take. By systematically varying each factor, Taylor got the optimum amount of barrow load. By exact calculation, he got the correct response.

But Taylor also knew what such a mechanical regimen would do to a man or, rather, what sort of man could fit into this strait jacket. 'One of the very first requirements for a man who is fit to handle pig iron as a regular occupation,' he wrote, 'is that he shall be so stupid and so phlegmatic that he more nearly resembles an ox than any other type.'[1]

The logic of Taylorism was obvious: each man's work could be measured by itself; the time in which an operation could be performed could be established 'without bargaining' as an impersonal 'standard time'; pay could then be computed on the basis of the amount of work done and the time taken to do it.[2] In the modern economy, shading of time is so important (as Benjamin Franklin, the prototype of Max Weber's ethical protestant, remarked, 'time is money') that a large company like General Motors contracts with its workers on a six-minute basis. (For purposes of payroll calculation, General Motors divides the hour into ten six-minute periods and, except for the guarantee of three-hours 'call-in' pay, the worker is paid by the number of tenths of an hour he works.)

The significance of Taylorism lies in its attempt to enact a social physics. Once work was scientifically plotted, Taylor felt, there could be no disputes about how hard one should work or the pay one should receive for labor. 'As reasonably might we insist on bargaining about the time and place of the rising and setting sun,' he once said. For a managerial class which at the turn of the century had witnessed the erosion of its old justificatory mystique of 'natural rights', the science of administration *per se* provided a new foundation for its moral authority.

While Taylor analyzed the relations of work to time, another engineer, Frank Gilbreth (1868–1924), carried the process one

1. Taylor was not the first to understand such consequences. One hundred and fifty years earlier, Adam Smith wrote: 'The understandings of the greater part of men are necessarily formed by their ordinary employments. The man whose life is spent in performing a few simple operations . . . has no occasion to exert his understanding. . . . He generally becomes as stupid and ignorant as it is possible for a human creature to become' (1937, p. 734).

2. Which is why the 'protestant' industrial economy cannot adopt the system of 'family wage', to be found in Italy and other countries where Catholic social doctrine applies, whereby a man with children receives more wages than the one who has none, though both do the same work.

step further: he detached human movement from the person and made of it an abstract visualization. Not only could the pattern of machine work be broken down into elements, but human motion, too, could be 'functionalized', and the natural movements of arms and legs could be ordered into a 'one best way' of usage. [. . .] And, from the analysis of [motion] combinations, Gilbreth came to his principles of 'motion economy'. [. . .] The penalty for violating these rules is waste.[3]

There was one further step in the exorable logic of rationalization. While Taylor systematized factory operations and Gilbreth sought to reduce waste motion, Charles Bedeaux sought to combine these into a unit measurement of human power, not unsurprisingly called a 'B', which would correspond to the 'dyn', or the unit in physics of mechanical power. So defined, 'a B is a fraction of a minute of work plus a fraction of a minute of rest always aggregating unity but varying in proportion according to the nature of the strain'. Using this detailed calculus, Bedeaux formulated a complicated but mathematically neat system of wage payments which took into account not only the work done but the varying fractions of nonwork or rest required in different operations, and increased or decreased payments correspondingly.[4]

The fragmentation of work, although atomizing the worker, also created a dependency and a hierarchy in work, for inherent in the division of labor is what Marx called 'the iron law of proportionality'. Thus, in the manufacturing process, the ratios between different numbers of workers required in different work processes are ordered by technological complexities. Marx cited an example in type manufacture: one founder could cast 2000 type an hour, the breaker could break up 4000 and the polisher could finish 8000 in the same time; thus to keep one polisher busy the enterprise needed two breakers and four founders, and units were hired

3. A complete elaboration of Taylor's and Gilbreth's methodologies as currently applied is to be found in texts on 'motion and time study', of which Barnes (1969) is illustrative [Ed.].

4. At the height of its use the Bedeaux system was used in the United States by 720 corporations, employing 675,000 workers. During the Second World War, charges against Bedeaux of collaboration with Vichy, plus the bitter hostility of the unions to this method of mechanical wage calculations, brought the system into disuse here.

or discharged, therefore, in multiples of seven. In many other operations, notably an assembly line, similar inflexible ratios are established, and the hiring and firing of numbers of workers is dictated by the multiples of those ratios. But such dependency presupposes coordination, and with such coordination the multiplication of hierarchies.

The logic of hierarchy, the third of the logics created by modern industry, is, thus, not merely the sociological fact of increased supervision which every complex enterprise demands, but a peculiarly technological imperative. In a simple division of labor, for example, the worker had a large measure of control over his own working conditions, i.e. the set-up and make-ready, the cleaning and repairing of machines, obtaining his own materials, and so on. Under a complex division of labor, these tasks pass out of his control and he must rely on management to see that they are properly done. This dependence extends along the entire process of production. As a result, modern industry has had to devise an entire new managerial superstructure which organizes and directs production. This superstructure draws in all possible brain work away from the shop; everything is centered in the planning and schedule and design departments. And in this new hierarchy there stands a figure known neither to the handicrafts nor to industry in its infancy – the technical employee. With him, the separation of functions becomes complete. The worker at the bottom, attending only to a detail, is divorced from any decision or modification about the product he is working on.

These three logics of size, time and hierarchy converge in that great achievement of industrial technology, the assembly line: the long parallel lines require huge shed space; the detailed breakdown of work imposes a set of mechanically paced and specified motions; the degree of coordination creates new technical, as well as social, hierarchies.[5]

5. It is remarkable how recent is the assembly line, both as a mode of operation and as a linguistic term. Oliver Evans developed a continuous production line for milling grain in 1800, and the packinghouse industry in the 1870s had adopted the use of overhead conveyors for the processing of slaughtered animals. But the assembly line as a modern achievement owes its success largely to Henry Ford and the establishment of an auto line at Highland Park, Michigan, in 1914. And only in 1933 did the Oxford English

References

BARNES, R. M. (1969), *Motion and Time Study*, Wiley.
SMITH, A. (1937), *The Wealth of Nations*, Modern Library.

Dictionary legitimatize the term when its supplement in that year added the contemporary meaning of the word. See Siegfried Giedion, *Mechanization Takes Command*.

4 Robert Boguslaw

Operating Units[1]

Excerpts from R. Boguslaw, *The New Utopians*, Prentice-Hall, 1965,
ch. 1, 2, 4 and 5, pp. 1–126.

Utopia is a place that seems to belong either to the past or to the
future, and we tend to think of utopians as being either starry-eyed
philosophers or wild-eyed reformers. But there is a new breed of
utopians afoot, threatening to rush down all the exciting pathways
and blind alleys frequented by utopians since the days of Plato.
These are the people who are known by such titles as system
engineer, computer manufacturer, operations researcher, computer programmer, data processing specialist, or, more simply,
system designer.

This book deals with some of the problems confronting these
new utopians – the social engineers of our times. But, perhaps much
more to the point, it deals with some of the problems they are in
the process of preparing for the rest of us. [. . .]

Different system designers characteristically begin their work
not only with queries about system functions but with different
answers to questions such as the following: What is the problem
you are trying to solve? Why are you trying to solve it? What *kind*
of solution would you accept as satisfactory? How much time and
effort are you prepared to devote to the enterprise? How enduring
must your solution be?

Differences in the approach to system design involve implicit
if not explicit differences in these answers. They also imply gross
differences in methodology and technique. We may distinguish four
approaches to system design used by both the classical and the new
utopians. They are the Formalist Approach, the Heuristic

1. The assumptions and implicit value premises underlying the design of
the work organizations are revealed in the issues, raised by Boguslaw, for
development of computer (automated) systems [Ed.].

Approach, the Operating Unit Approach, and the Ad Hoc Approach. [. . .]

In explicating the operating unit approach to system design, it seems only fair to warn readers that this seems to be the chosen approach for many technically illiterate, would-be roboteers – and for many technically qualified misanthropes as well. [. . .]

The operating unit approach begins neither with models of the system nor with selected principles. It begins with people or machines carefully selected or tooled to possess certain performance characteristics. The system or organization or utopia that ultimately unfolds will incorporate solutions that these units provide.

It is obvious that the various systems that get developed through the use of this approach are, to a considerable extent, based upon the range of flexibility possessed by the operating units. It is becoming increasingly apparent that flexibility in this sense is much more than a simple distinction between man and machine. Man may be inflexible, machines may be flexible – or vice versa. Under some conditions, it may be highly desirable to limit the range of operating unit flexibility to insure reliability and predictability of system performance. Under other conditions, the reverse may be true.

Thus, in B. F. Skinner's (1948) fictional utopia, called *Walden Two*, it is clear that the flexibility of the human operating units is drastically limited to suit the requirements of the system as seen by its designer, an experimental psychologist named Frazier. The behavior of these units (people) is highly reliable, although no one has attempted to specify the situations in which they are to perform. One might almost postulate an infinity of possible system designs that might in fact emerge, and conceivably an infinity of principles or heuristics to which these systems could be required to adhere. Reliability in performance is achieved through conditioning the components to behave in a 'reasonable' fashion.

Walden Two has been called an 'ignoble utopia', because it urges men to be something less than human (Heilbroner, 1953). 'Human' in this context apparently refers to the properties of free choice or the wide range of possible responses that hopefully characterizes the unconditioned human being. It is perhaps a significant commentary on contemporary psychological and social science that its efforts often appear directed toward making men less than human through the perfecting of behavioral control techniques, while contemporary physical science seems to be moving in the direction of increasing the number of possible machine responses to environmental stimuli.

There exists a striking similarity between the use of human operating units in the *Walden Two* system and the use of physical equipment employed in contemporary system engineering. [. . .]

But what, specifically, is it that operating units are called upon to do? Briefly, they must sense, measure, compare, process, and regulate or handle (Folley and Van Cott, 1960).

Sensing refers to the job of detecting signals or information in the environment of the system. These signals may include radar returns, dial readings, and so on. The components involved may include such things as a photoelectric cell, a sound-pressure meter, and the human eye, ear, nose, skin or tongue. If the signals are enlarged or magnified by the system, we are in the presence of an *amplification* function. If some of the signals are suppressed or screened, we have a *filtering* function.

Measuring refers to the job of comparing information that has been sensed with a precalibrated standard or scale. It is possible to *store* measurements in a memory for use at some future time. Components used for this purpose include magnetized tape or disks, punched or marked cards, charged meshes of wire, mechanical relays, or the human brain.

Comparing consists of determining the difference between one measurement and another. Differences are called error signals or simply errors.

Processing consists of combining the available information with a number of different actions to produce some desired decision consequence.

Regulation or *handling* means acting upon a decision to produce some desired condition or result. Examples of this include: milling a cast to a specified tolerance, controlling the rate of flow of a liquid, and generating a message to another system or to men. The regulation function may be found associated with an actuating function and a power supply that starts and stops handling. It may also be found associated with a *monitoring* function that inspects the quality or quantity of an output.

When a system is conceptualized in these terms, an indispensable portion of its description consists of identifying the *program* it must execute. This is a set of commands given to the system for performing certain operations. When a commander or executive is available he may issue these commands as required. This, in effect, is 'real-time' programming. It is also possible, of course, to use some sort of memory to store and issue instructions to the system as they become necessary (Folley and Van Cott, 1960, p. 5).

But the concept of 'program' as used in this context can be quite deceptive. It seems to imply that when 'programmed', the system does only what it is told to do in the program, that is, that the actions it will take are listed in the program. But of course this is scarcely the case. The operating units of the system do what it is possible for them to do. What it is possible for them to do is dependent upon their own structural characteristics, the characteristics of their environment (including other units within the system), and the characteristics of their own internal states at the moment of action. One way of 'telling' a radar system to ignore random blips is to issue an instruction to the radar operator. You then have a 'programmed' operator. Another way of doing essentially the same thing is to substitute for the human operator a piece of equipment that will 'see' only nonrandom blips. The instruction to the piece of equipment does not exist in any usual sense of the term, yet the decision to use the equipment has the same kind of system effect as does the instruction. In one case, the command is contained within a 'program'; in the other it is not. [. . .]

In *Walden Two*, the problem of controlling the component operating units was accomplished through the behavioral engineering technique of psychological conditioning. As Frazier explains it, a code of conduct had been worked out that would presumably keep things running smoothly if everyone concerned behaved according to plan. It was recognized that to anticipate all future situations would be an impossible task. The planners, therefore, relied upon 'self-control' that permitted each individual to act essentially as a servomechanism obeying commands generated within the code of conduct.

The problem that contemporary system engineers have solved no better than the designers of *Walden Two* is that of how to build a mechanism for generating an ever appropriate code of conduct. Such a mechanism must be able to size up its environment, decide upon some universally acceptable values, and accomplish all this without doing violence to the structure of its operating units. Engineers understand very well what it means to overload an electrical circuit or to place an excessive strain upon a mechanical assembly. Where these operating units are human, the evidence of strain, load, or deterioration may not be quite so apparent.

Gardner Murphy (1958), whose primary concern is human beings, reminds us that most of our traditional utopias forget that men do not stay put. 'A utopia which would fit the men of today,' he tells us, 'would be insipid or become a straitjacket to the men of tomorrow' (p. 309). For one thing, the sheer specifications of these human equipments change. People produce people who produce people ad infinitum. But the people thus produced are by no means carbon copies of their predecessors. They vary in size, weight, memory, capacity, access time to memory, ability to manipulate the contents of memory, and in many other similar ways. Furthermore, they may be affected in unpredicted ways by new experiences or fresh sensations. As a human operating unit wears out, one searches in vain through the parts catalogue for an exact replacement.

The operating unit approach, it is clear, can indeed provide some solutions to the problem of system design for emergent situations. But a fundamental contradiction remains – the historical dilemma between freedom and control. To the extent that we increase predictability and performance reliability by selecting predictable and reliable components, to that extent we reduce the system's freedom and its capacity to deal with emergent situations effectively. In this sense, reliable components reduce overall system effectiveness. As we proceed in the other direction – that is, in the direction of building a system with self-sufficient operating units – we reduce the effectiveness of our control mechanism. This design problem poses the basic dilemma of freedom versus control. We shall keep exploring this dilemma throughout the remainder of our discussion. [. . .]

If one wishes to adhere to this engineering frame of reference, it is possible to think of human beings as materials with more or less specifiable performance characteristics. Assuming that you have an order to give, and that part of your circuit includes people, it becomes necessary to understand the amount of work that can be accomplished by these people components, the time necessary to accomplish the work, the reliability of performance, the maintenance schedule required, and so on.

The customary consequence of adhering to this frame of reference is to conclude that human components are exasperatingly unreliable, limited and inefficient. Furthermore, they are very difficult to control. The most obvious analogy to the physical control system involves the use of formal authority and its delegation as the energy or power source necessary to insure that the desired signals pass through the entire system. This, of course, is the basis for the insistence upon unquestioning obedience to orders traditionally found not only in military organizations but in all bureaucracies of both private industry and government organizations. Human groups unfortunately (or fortunately) have devised many mechanisms for disrupting systems that exercise control exclusively or even primarily through the use of authority.

What happens when authority control systems run amuck is an endless source of case history material for management development seminars. The case of the employees who do *everything* they are ordered to do by their supervisor – neither more nor less – is a classic. They ignore obvious emergent situations and engage in assigned repetitive tasks beyond reasonable termination points. The supervisor is gradually forced into behavior indistinguishable from that of a computer programmer giving instructions to a stupid but completely obedient machine. The case of the industrial work group ordered to use a new, unwanted piece of equipment is perennially effective slapstick comedy material; the ingenious steps taken by members of the group to prove the existence of unsuspected faults in the new equipment provide universally understandable material for comedy writers. The list of examples could be continued indefinitely. The point to be made is simply this: the idea of control results in highly unreliable performance when applied to human components of a system. [. . .]

The use of human operating units – a digression

Our immediate concern, let us remember, is the explication of the operating unit approach to system design, no matter *what* materials are used. We must take care to prevent this discussion from degenerating into a single-sided analysis of the complex characteristics of one type of system material: namely, human beings.

What we need is an inventory of the ways in which human behavior can be controlled, and a description of some instruments that will help us achieve control. If this provides us sufficient 'handles' on human materials so that we can think of them as one thinks of metal parts, electric power or chemical reactions, then we have succeeded in placing human materials on the same footing as any other materials and can proceed with our problems of system design. Once we have equated all possible materials, one simply checks the catalogue for the price, operating characteristics, and reliability of this material and plugs it in where indicated. For an engineer or industrial designer, these are precisely the terms upon which human beings must be considered. This is not, of course, to imply that engineers are cruel, heartless or inhuman. They are, as they would put it, 'simply trying to do a job'. It is, they would assert, 'inhuman' to insist that human beings perform duties that can be passed on to nonhuman materials. This frees human beings for golf, philosophy, music and business deals. [. . .]

There are, however, many disadvantages in the use of human operating units. They are somewhat fragile; they are subject to fatigue, obsolescence, disease and death; they are frequently stupid, unreliable, and limited in memory capacity. But beyond all this, they sometimes seek to design their own system circuitry. This, in a material, is unforgivable. Any system utilizing them must devise appropriate safeguards. [. . .]

A 'good' or 'effective' operating unit is one that has 'adjusted' to its environment. It accepts the environmental conditions postulated by its system designer as a 'given', and it does what its structure permits it to do. The central difficulty that arises lies in the definition of 'environment'. A 'bad' thermonuclear weapon would be one that exploded before some 'responsible' human being 'pressed the button', or because it simply 'felt' like exploding. Human beings generally don't want 'intelligent' thermo-nuclear weapons. But the man who presses the button is part of the environment of the weapon. The factors that lead to the button's being pressed are equally part of this environment. The social, economic, emotional, political or other issues that help determine whether the button will be pressed are all part of the bomb's environment. Do you design a bomb to be detonated with one finger, two fingers, or two hundred million fingers? This is all part of the system design problem when you design systems with the operating unit approach.

The safest procedure is to build a system with operating units resembling Mr Zero of Elmer L. Rice's (1922) *The Adding Machine*. Whether serving as a Roman galley slave, a serf or an American bookkeeper about to be displaced by an adding machine, Mr Zero is completely reliable, noninnovative and safe. The designer of his universe is undoubtedly a shrewd, cost-conscious engineer. He collects used souls in a sort of heavenly dry-dock, cleans and repairs them, and ships them out to occupy new bodies. For purposes of minimizing costs and maximizing efficiency within a predictable cosmos, this is obviously a highly intelligent solution. There is, of course, no requirement for Mr Zero to be intelligent; he remains eternally a Zero.

This is not to imply that Mr Zero is incapable of independent action. He can learn to speak, read, write, hold a job, raise a family, quarrel with his wife, and discuss politics. It is not necessary to program his daily activities; they will fall well within specified tolerances. His purpose in the scheme of things is simply to be himself. One might, of course, find it interesting to speculate about the long-range objectives of his designer, which are not specified – but that, as our new utopians might say, is another problem.

In any event, his designer seems to be faced with a constantly changing universe. He deals with this dynamic universe by using dependable operating units like Mr Zero. In doing so, he is confronted with the same issue that other operating unit system designers must resolve: How much self-determination should these operating units be allowed to possess? [. . .]

If a robot is allowed too much independent action, it may begin to assert the pre-eminence of its own goals over those of its designer. It is then a 'rebel' and its behavior is appropriately referred to as a 'revolt'.

But how 'intelligent' must an operating unit be before it is able to revolt? Or conversely, how 'stupid' must the designer insist that his operating unit be to insure reliable system performance? And, from the perspective of the operating unit, what are the necessary and sufficient conditions for effective rebellion? [. . .]

Decisions made by operating units acting either independently or as direct agents of a designer affect human populations directly through their impact upon the conditions of human existence. It is not only the human beings serving as operating units who are affected, but those outside the system as well. The critical point is not the location of people with respect to the system, but the nature of the decisions made and the actions taken which affect their destinies.

In this context, discussions about whether man should be adjusted to physical equipment or vice versa become gigantic *non sequiturs*. When the operating units are not simply tools but machines in varying states of operating independence, it is men who must adjust. Hannah Arendt (1958) has observed, 'Even the most primitive tool remains a servant unable to guide or replace the hand. Even the most primitive machine guides the body's labor and eventually replaces it altogether' (p. 129).

But this, of course, is a profound understatement. The replacement is much more than a simple substitution of machine for human labor. It is becoming increasingly more obvious that a surrender of decision-making prerogatives is involved. The values of human populations increasingly become excluded from the dialogue between operating units and their environments. Operating units requirements become both the short-run and long-range goals of human populations. The information necessary to understand operating unit characteristics becomes the content of educational programs; operating unit characteristics shape society's demand for natural resources, economic arrangements, philosophical orientations, and family life. This is the strength and the tragedy of human beings in search of systems within which they can assume their roles as operating units. [. . .]

Some social implications of the utopian renaissance

To the bona fide utopian, empiricism is not enough. He is not content with simply designing systems, organizations or societies that operate efficiently and effectively – he feels that they must act in ways he would assess as being 'good' rather than 'bad'. He has a more or less well-defined set of values at stake and is, to a considerable extent, a moralist as well as an engineer. Of course, it is quite possible to value efficiency or effectiveness above all other things, and this can, under some circumstances, lead to bizarre or even macabre consequences. For example, the characteristic American impatience with obvious inefficiency in other societies is a well-known phenomenon. Visions of cattle roaming the streets of Indian cities while human populations starve is a favorite illustration used by efficiency worshippers to demonstrate the tragic consequences of nonefficiency ideologies. [. . .]

The problem, of course, is not simply one of introducing greater degrees of specificity into the definition of various principles. We have seen how such specificity can result in procedure rigidity and lost games. If, however, we leave the path of specificity and follow one leading from low-level generality to high-level generality to still-higher-level generality, we ultimately arrive at the place called 'values'.

Now this is a region where many, if not most, scientists feel uncomfortable. It sounds and looks like something outside the science ballpark. If you insist upon going there, you are probably interested in things other than the science game.

What is the science game?

The obvious reply is to insist that science is a game whose objective is 'truth'. If you find truth, you win; if you fail to find truth, you lose. And for many people in our society – scientists and non-scientists alike – science is the game we should all be playing. We are told by serious thinkers that science is not merely a value prescribing the conduct of the scientist as he works alone, but that it is the overriding value for our entire Western society (see Bronowsky, 1959). If this is the case, a whole series of instrumental heuristics is indicated. They follow naturally and logically from the requirement to do those things which will help uncover truth. They include 'independence', 'dissent', and even 'freedom'. A truth-seeker must be independent – and society must protect his independence. He must be original – and society must protect his originality. He may wish to dissent – and society must provide him the opportunity to do so.

It would therefore seem that establishing the value of truth provides a means for achieving the historic American dream. It seems to invite the use of freedom of thought, speech and individual dignity. But this, unfortunately, is not the case. Indeed, it is possible to invoke the negative of each of the indicated instrumental heuristics and to show how necessary this negative is for achieving truth in some situations. [. . .]

Truth as a means to an end became a necessary antidote to esoteric representations of reality insisted upon by medicine men, soothsayers, pundits and politicians. The history of empiricism and scientific research is a history of debunked old-wives' tales. These tales served as instrumental heuristics for the ignorant, the superstitious, and representatives of special interests. But when truth alone becomes the end of human existence, one must not be surprised if humanity ultimately emerges as the loser.

The spawn of truth is efficiency. Efficiency as an instrumental heuristic leads to more rapid transportation, more automobiles, shoes, solid-state computers – and thermonuclear weapons.

Truth and efficiency are highly effective as instrumental heuristics. But as value heuristics they ignore the prejudices some of us have about the distinctive importance of human beings. There is nothing scientific or efficient about this prejudice; it simply exists. It says that the molecules that make up a human being are somehow more important than the molecules of a tree or a steel cabinet or a factory. This prejudice is something like the prejudice of ethnocentrism. We condemn ethnocentrism because it asserts the importance of one group of human beings over another group of human beings. Humanism simply asserts that humanity is more important than nonhumanity – and this is inconsistent with an orientation that values only truth and efficiency. Within a rigidly defined framework of these values, it is simply not true that the molecules of humanity have priority over other molecules.

Within the framework of systems, organizations and engineered societies, human beings become operating units. And now we must ask: what are these things called human beings in an operational sense? How do we deal with them in the context of our design specifications? [. . .]

The workaday new utopians seem to have implicitly turned Max Weber's Ethic on its head to read, 'Hard work is simply a temporarily unautomated task. It is a necessary evil until we get a piece of gear, or a computer large enough, or a program checked out well enough to do the job economically. Until then, you working stiffs can hang around – but, for the long run, we really don't either want you or need you.'

Depending upon one's religious orientation, this reversal may be viewed as either a good or bad thing in itself. Its potential implications for persons who continue to live in an economic situation whose traditional values are being overturned are, in any event, enormous. [. . .]

Here one may speculate regarding the successor to the Protestant Ethic. Will the unspoken creed, which once could be verbalized as 'I may not be a brain but I can always make a living with these hands; I am fundamentally the producer', be replaced by another, which when verbalized might say, 'All these hands (or all this mind) can do is what some machine hasn't yet gotten around to doing. The real producers in our society are the scientists, the engineers and maybe even the boss. I am not *really* a producer – I feel alienated from the productive process. I am the one who's asking the others for a free ride. I am the one who, in effect, is doing the exploiting – why not do it deliberately and systematically?'

Many segments of society can be characterized by what has been called the 'powerless' form of alienation – 'the expectancy or probability held by the individual that his own behavior cannot determine the occurrence of the outcomes, or reinforcements, he seeks' (Seeman, 1959, p. 784). The notion that those strange men who write equations on blackboards are the real arbiters of all our destinies is one that must be obliterated in any society that wishes to continue functioning in even an approximately democratic fashion.

Other segments are subject to the kind of alienation called 'isolation'. This results from assigning low reward value to goals or beliefs that are typically high-valued in a given society (Seeman,

1959, p. 789). Included among the groups affected are unquestionably some social scientists, some philosophers, and possibly some former bomber pilots. Funds for research on missile fuels are demonstrably more available than, say, funds for research in basic social theory, or philosophical theory, or manned bomber tactics. For some bomber pilots this may result in irrational and intemperate attacks upon the effectiveness of missiles. The rebellion of social scientists and philosophers against this imbalance in value structures can, and frequently does, take the form of avoiding professional involvement with some of the most centrally significant social issues in the contemporary world.

One implication of all this seems clear. In terms of sheer self-survival, it is necessary to expand the educational base of leaders and rank-and-file members of union and management organizations, military men, philosophers, social scientists and others through broad educational programs. Such programs should be addressed not only to the problem of making people more at ease with the concept of computers and computer programming, but also more fundamentally toward helping them become perceptive about the implications that contemporary large-scale system design has for each one of us. This should permit union leaders, social scientists, academicians, management, and government officials, as well as an informed public, to participate along with more hardware-oriented engineers in the design of large-scale systems at an early stage of formulation of these projects. This must be done to insure that the human implications of proposed automated systems are fully explored as fundamental design variables.

In turn, physical scientists and engineers must become increasingly more sensitive to the human purposes that improvements in automated technology will serve. They must broaden the educational base of their training so that they do indeed consider *all* significant variables in designing systems – rather than merely those that lend themselves to hardware implementation or formal modeling. [. . .]

References

ARENDT, H. (1958), *The Human Condition*, Doubleday.

BRONOWSKI, J. (1959), 'The values of science', in A. H. Maslow (ed.), *New Knowledge in Human Values*, Harper & Row, pp. 54–60.

FOLLEY, J. D., and VAN COTT, H. P. (1960), *Human Factors Methods for Systems Design*, American Institute of Research under Office of Naval Research, Contract no. Nonr–2700[00], pp. 4–5.

HEILBRONER, R. L. (1953), *The Wordly Philosophers*, Simon & Schuster.

MURPHY, G. (1958), *Human Potentialities*, Basic Books.

RICE, E. L. (1922), *The Adding Machine*, Samuel French.

SEEMAN, M. (1959), 'On the meaning of alienation', *American Sociological Review*, vol. 24.

SKINNER, B. F. (1948), *Walden Two*, Macmillan Co.

5 Alain Touraine

An Historical Theory in the Evolution of Industrial Skills

Excerpts from Alain Touraine, 'An historical theory in the evolution of industrial skills', in C. R. Walker (ed.), *Modern Technology and Civilization*, McGraw-Hill, 1962, pp. 425–37.

The evolution of skills: stages and direction

The most obvious fact in the evolution of skills is their massive downgrading in the factory. The worker specializing in a few repetitive and highly simplified jobs[1] replaces the craftsman wherever mass production[2] is installed. But does this important fact make intelligible the whole evolution of skills? Must we agree then with those who believe this development is a catastrophe and who see in the industrial history of the last half century the progressive disintegration of a time-honored system of work which rested on the quality of skill of the 'productive' worker? Assuredly no. We are not witnessing an organized system falling into chaos, but the transition from one system to another.

This concept of a transition repudiates optimistic theses as vigorously as pessimistic ones. And even more readily. It is false to assume that the growing complexity of machines is reflected in the skills of workers who operate them; a hasty visit, for example, to modern shops filled with transfer machines will supply convincing evidence on this point. The most refined form of the optimistic thesis, as defended by Ford and by admirers of the new methods of

1. The term used by M. Touraine is *l'ouvrier spécialisé*, the specialized worker; unfortunately this gives in English an impression quite the reverse of the French, implying as it does a worker with specialized skills. Since American usage seems to lack an exact equivalent, we have used in most cases in the pages that follow the term 'mass production worker'.

2. Here again there is no single English phrase that takes the place of the French term '*en grande série*' although in describing modern methods of mass production we speak of 'a series of operations'. The French '*en grande série*' has been translated in these pages sometimes 'mass production' sometimes 'progressive manufacture'.

work, cannot stand up before an elementary examination of the facts.

The common mistake of both trends of opinion, optimistic and pessimistic, is to consider the evolution of skills solely from the point of view of quantity, and to assume that the nature of the skill had not been modified. Representatives of both trends discuss the question whether there is more or less – or whether there *will be* more or less – skill required today or tomorrow than there was yesterday. But the most important fact is transformation in the worker's skill. The pessimism of certain observers derives perhaps from this fact that in the most modern factories they do not find the traditional types of skills. Such skills are often mythical in industry, and the observer is transferring to industry certain characteristics of the pre-industrial craftsmen.

This transformation in kind, or transition from one system to another, is not a continuous process; it does not proceed in a straight line, but by a series of contradictions. The old system of work, arranged around a task to be performed directly by the worker is not immediately changed into a system of indirect labor. This latter system begins to take form *only* after the jobs are broken down into their component parts. This notion of two systems of work, then, gives rise to the concept of three phases in the evolution of skills.

In our technical study of machine tools we separated their development into three phases, A, B and C,[3] and proposed this as a hypothesis, indispensable to understanding the facts as observed. These facts, almost all of which were relevant to phase B, could not be understood by a simple description of this phase, considered as a historical unity and self-defined. These phases led us to perceive a single process, not divergent and opposing ones, which constituted a new system of work, new insofar as it destroyed the old system and even by the very fact of destructive action. As a general view of industry helps us to put into perspective the frame-

3. By phase A, the author means the old system of work, characterized by skilled work or craftsmanship which required only universal or flexible machines (like lathes), not limited to the production of a single product; phase B is the period of transition, characterized by the development of mechanization, or the feeding of machines by unskilled workmen; phase C is the phase of automation, where direct productive work by human beings is eliminated.

work of our description, so the evolution of techniques and jobs is better understood by beginning at the central phase which is more easily observed in big industry. This phase has no unity of its own, no coherence, and no stability. It is simultaneously destructive and creative, and to the degree that it destroys the old multi-purpose machines and produces single-purpose specialized ones, it prepares for the emergence of the composite machine and evolves toward automation. Even as regards skill the dissolution into its component parts of 'productive' work is the necessary precondition to the mechanisation which liberates man from physical labor. This contradictory nature of phase B cannot be considered by itself; it is not the end of the evolutionary process, it is a link.

One cannot derive the idea of a three-phase evolution from the analysis of a single factory. For reasons which lie in the nature of the manufacturing process, complete mechanization comes only with phase C, except in the case of industries with continuous operations, such as oil refineries, gas, and production of electricity by steam or water. Through observations of a single manufacturing plant, therefore, we cannot investigate the concept of the three phases. We need not assume, however, that all branches of industry have followed the pattern of evolution in the same way. One industry has never come through phase A; another with favorable economic and exceptional technical conditions is able to pass from phase A directly to phase C. Many industries lacking sufficient volume and therefore steady production have not yet passed phase B or even phase A. But in all of these cases the proposed concept is valuable, for it allows us to *place* the factor or sector of industry which is being observed.

It is not necessary to assign these phases to successive historical epochs, to suggest for example, that for the French economy phase A belongs to the period of 1815 to 1880; phase B to that of 1880 to 1930; and phase C since 1930. Clearly, if, in a given epoch and for general reasons, no enterprise can belong to phase C, at a more advanced date in the same national economy even in the same industrial sector – enterprises can coexist which belong to different phases. In the Renault factory today are juxtaposed central electrical installations, or power plants, belonging to phase C, mechanical shops on the borderline between B and C, and a great number of shops in the classic B phase, as well as a certain number relevant to phase A.

One can only add that enterprises reaching a certain stage of evolution tend to impose a certain orientation on enterprises still in an earlier stage, so that it is possible to some degree to characterize each industrial sector, and even each national economy, according to the labels A, B and C. Thus the automobile industry is essentially in phase B, the production of electrical energy in phase C, the coal mines (in France) in phase A.

But all research concerned with the evolution of skills must study an enterprise, or a group of enterprises, in relation to economic conditions and techniques of production and not in the light of the state of the national economy in the world situation at the moment.

Technical and social aspects of work: the evolution of their relation to each other

The descriptive scheme used all along in this study would be without great interest if it did not introduce one of the principal problems of industrial sociology: that of the structure of work. By structure of work is meant the reciprocal relationship of its different aspects – technical, occupational, physiological, psychological, economic and also social, in its various meanings.

Among all these relationships, one seems particularly important: that between the technico-skill aspect and the economico-social aspect of industrial work. The rapid development of technology since the first, and above all since the second industrial revolution, as defined by G. Friedmann, places man more and more in an entirely new environment of life and particularly of work. The technical circumstances of civilization seem to impose themselves in all industrial countries as the 'facts of civilization', according to the celebrated phrase of M. Mauss, creating over and above differences in the social order (of which no serious observer neglects the importance) a common situation with certain specific problems.

Technical realities, as related to the conditions of economic and social life, depend upon the market, including the labor market, for example, but this dependence gives no answer to the problems. The dependence does explain the rhythm of technical progress, but it does not explain the social significance of modern production techniques or their role in social life, and especially their role as a factor in the behavior of the industrial work force![4]

Study of the evolution of vocational skills and of the passage from one system of work to another, clarifies this problem and so can furnish research principles capable of restating certain classic problems of industrial sociology.

The evolution of industrial work can be defined as the passage from a system of skills to a technical system of work. During phase A the top category of industrial workers, the craftsmen, possess a skill, and intervene directly and according to their particular and personal methods of work in production. However subject to an economic and social system he may be, the worker possesses *job autonomy*, a vocational stronghold, and in his demeanor and attitude to his work testifies by his independent actions to this aspect of his job. If the notion of pride in workmanship makes sense only in certain historic, well-defined, social conditions which permit relations between the worker and the user of the product,[5] nevertheless the craftsman, in regard to his work, takes an attitude largely independent of its social circumstances. This is true because the worker is directly and physically involved in that work. It is his cleverness, the rapidity of his reflexes, his visual, auditory and tactical sensibility that operate the machine or tool, and, quite as much as his technical knowledge, determine the quality of his workmanship. It is because his strength, his good sense, his rhythm of work, the rapidity of his reflexes are constantly and directly put into play, even in planning his job, that the task possesses for him a certain autonomy.

Consider now the last phase of the job evolution (C), and observe that the worker no longer actively intervenes in the manufacturing process. He superintends, he records, he controls. His job can no longer be defined as a certain relationship between man and materials, tools and machines, but rather by a certain role in the total production picture. In a system dominated by technology most aspects of skill are now absorbed into the social aspects. The rhythm and character of the work is no longer determined by the

4. The same problem can be posed apropos of some other technical categories: techniques of leisure, of communications, of transportation. But it is not necessary here to enlarge on an already vast subject.

5. We use here a remark of A. Haundicourt.

nature of the product manufactured, or the machine utilized, or by the character of human effort, but by the way in which the work is organized. Whether or not the worker is qualified for the job depends now on his capacity to integrate himself into the social group and to take responsibility. At this stage the nature of a worker's qualifications can no longer be determined by the technical conditions of work, but to begin with by the social circumstances in which he performs it. It is even possible that with comparable levels of technology, other factors such as the kind of labor force obtainable, the management of the enterprise, the attitude of the workers to management, etc. ... might result in quite different organizational hierarchies, administrative decisions, and working relationship. Education and promotion policies are also a factor. The worker under close supervision can be restricted to simple tasks which do not necessitate understanding technical problems; he can, on the other hand, work with more understanding by being associated with technical personnel and instructed and guided by them; he can perform his task mechanically, or exercise initiative and take the lead in innovation. These different possibilities are dependent on the psychology of management, supervision and workers, that is to say, on the state of human and industrial relations which, in turn, are social and organizational factors.

It is not a paradox to say that the new system of work, *precisely because of its technology, is entirely social and organizational.* For the workers, the work possesses a direction and value which depends entirely on social factors, a situation which is the opposite of that in which craftsmanship predominates. At this stage (C) an attitude which reflects simply the job as such no longer exists.

In place of the relative autonomy of a relationship that is limited to man as the possessor of certain occupational skills and to work as a situation where he exercises these skills, there is now substituted the relation between two totalities; on the one hand, the job, which mainly is social in its requirements; on the other hand, the worker, his social organizational role, and his personality all considered together. It would seem to us that this widening of perspective must lead, not only to an enlargement of psychotechnology,[6] but also perhaps to an overhauling of many of the

6. By this is meant the studies of industrial psychology which deal with aptitudes, vocational guidance, etc.

principles and methods of that branch of study, in the light of the relative unimportance of job skills in comparison with social elements in the organization of work.

What is true of phase C is also true of phase B, but the problem here is more complex.

During phase B while the values of skilled work are being in effect destroyed, the debris of the old system has not yet been eliminated, and a very large number of men are held down to work of an extremely simple, repetitive nature, often nothing more than machine tending, such as characterizes the big mechanized manufacturing industries, particularly textiles. But if the importance of monotonous over-specialized work is evident, one cannot conclude from this that the job itself is an autonomous factor in the work situation. On the contrary, psychologists of work, such as L. Walther, who consider work only from the aspect of the task itself, characteristically conclude that unconscious work is necessary. They recognize by this that the job no longer makes sense to those who do it, and on this plane cannot again be made worthwhile or humanized. This is another way of saying that whether or not work makes sense depends entirely on aspects other than the actual task, on social aspects, that is to say on the degree of social participation of various kinds by the worker. Unskilled work is thus in phase B for most men already entirely social in nature. Beyond official and purely formal designations, the job can actually have an entirely different value and meaning for those who perform it according to their social relations with those about them.[7]

Perhaps the foregoing remarks enable us to make precise the opposition which G. Friedmann insists upon between the *milieu*

7. This principle runs the risk of misinterpretation unless two remarks are added: (a) No hypothesis can be made *a priori* at this stage of the analysis on the importance of different social aspects of work. (b) It cannot be expected that the validity of the principle advanced here can be proved by showing that the trend toward the entirely social character of the job has been completed. Consequently, the observer must recognize in the behavior of groups of workers in socially different situations, common elements, insufficient by themselves, but constituting a relative check on the diverse ways that the social values of which we are speaking assert themselves. We do not think that it is possible to isolate attitudes to work that are not affected by social conditions which surround the job, but we also do not think that any society has developed a system of values in industrial work that is entirely unique.

naturel and the *milieu technique*. It is apparent that technological developments of all kinds place man in a newly conditioned psychosociological environment. But perhaps we should add that, although his environment in phase A is already to some extent affected by technology, man remains in relation to production a natural being, often the source of energy himself, and in any case an element in production which cannot be dissociated from the tools or machines that he utilizes. Phase B marks the complete disappearance of the natural environment, while with phase C there is permanently installed a system where work is completely determined by technology. The preceding remarks show that in speaking of a system entirely determined by technology, one is not stressing the importance of technological conditioning of work, but on the contrary, the disappearance of vocational conditioning and the return to a real unity in the work itself, now become entirely social.[8]

Social does not sufficiently clarify what is meant in regard to the problem of work because of the many different ways this word is used. One cannot draw any inferences in favor of the new factor or as to its particular value. It is necessary to analyze the relations which exist between different forms of social participation – human relations in the enterprise, level and type of consumption, participation in the social order, family life, etc. These are new and vast problems. We have indicated elsewhere the principles which must guide the analysis, that of the relativity of systems of value (Touraine, 1952).

From the principles that have been defined we can deduce a certain number of consequences which merit special study and which will only be indicated here.

1. The subordination of those aspects of the job concerned with skill to the social and organizational aspects, rules out of phases B and C the illusions of the technocrats. That in the course of the development of industry the role of the technician will be increased is incontestable, but output and productivity depend more and more on organizational social factors, the 'climate' of the enterprise, and above all on the attitude of the workers to their work.

8. In recalling here the expressions employed by G. Friedmann, we do not intend to suggest that he accepts our conclusions.

The relations between the technicians and the workers are an important element in this climate but its amelioration supposes the overcoming of all narrow managerial ideologies and in particular overcoming the present division between technicians and workers, an accomplishment which would actually contribute to technical efficiency. To consider a plant from a purely technical point of view is in opposition to different groups playing the social role which is now theirs and yet this role in a large measure governs the progress of productivity. Thus the evolution of technology condemns the technocratic spirit when it is invoked unduly.

2. More important, and more positive, are the repercussions of the suggested principles on vocational training. Beyond simple job training, vocational instruction strives to give to apprentices a real understanding, in a rational form, of the processes which will permit the worker to adapt to a wide variety of skilled work. But this clashes with the brutal reality of millions of unskilled or semi-skilled jobs which require no general vocational training. Some honest observers even ask themselves if the good intentions of the educator do not tend to aggregate the difficulties of subsequent adaptation by accentuating the opposition which exists between the aspiration for a true skill or craft, and the usual trivial job in industry. The nature of phase B and phase C suggests that this difficulty comes from opposing to the real character of work in these periods the mythical ideal of the craftsman of phase A.

Any vocational training which is to have value must be completed by social education, that is to say the preparation of the worker to be a social being and not simply a production worker. Such preparation must interest itself in every aspect of the worker's life, considered as a whole, and not only his work. Nor should it consider his leisure time activities solely as compensatory for his work.

The enlargement of vocational training into social training cannot be achieved solely by administrative measures; it supposes the participation of the workers in the life of the enterprise, which appears to us to be required by the technological and vocational evolution of industry beginning with phase B.

3. The enterprise considered as a social system has been studied in the classic works of American sociology, but in a perspective

which has in general been pragmatic. The sociologists too often describe the enterprise studied not in order to define the nature of the different groups or to understand the conflicts which develop among them, but to assure the best possible integration of the worker and the enterprise without modifying the more general characteristics of the latter. [. . .]

The problems of informal organization in shops and factories can be understood only in the framework of the three phases which we have outlined here, and which do not appear as a separate aspect of the problem of the evolution of skills. Phase A is characterized by an extensive unity of formal and informal organization. [. . .]

The advent of phase B in a social climate dominated by the technician accelerates the complete separation of formal and informal organization. But if in the formal organization man is considered simply as an element in the system of production, nevertheless an informal social organization develops spontaneously. American sociology has analyzed this remarkably well. And already in phase B during the evolution towards phase C, the need to consider the social factors that make for productivity brings a rapprochement of the two organizations, inasmuch as the role played by the social situation in work must be the new criterion of job qualifications which can no longer be understood in a narrow technical manner. [. . .]

Reference

TOURAINE, A. (1952), 'Ambiguité de la sociologie industrielle américaine', *Cahiers Internationaux de Sociologie*, vol. 12.

Part Two
The Current Condition

We are experiencing the difficulties caused by the existence of industrial-era jobs in an increasingly post-industrial world, which is evidenced in this set of Readings. The paper by Davis, Canter and Hoffman although quite early (1955), presents an important phenomenon that we believe still exists in many quarters today. This (the only available) survey of American industrial practice indicates that the most important consideration used in dividing work among operators is still the minimization of the time required to perform the operation. In a study of about the same period Mann and Williams show how jobs in a white-collar organization can become more like factory work with the introduction of automation.

From the world of machine systems design, the human engineer (applied experimental psychologist) confronts us with his implicit concept that men and machines are competitors and as such the machine qualities of men are those to be considered. Jordan, in his paper, makes a plea for complementarity of men and machines, calling for utilization of man's unique capabilities.

Finally, van Beinum raises issues of needed new trade union roles, which should evolve in response to a new orientation of workers to unions, employers and larger society, brought on by changes in society.

6 Louis E. Davis, Ralph R. Canter and John Hoffman

Current Job Design Criteria

L. E. Davis, R. R. Canter and J. Hoffman, 'Current job design criteria', *Journal of Industrial Engineering*, vol. 6, 1955, no. 2, pp. 5–11.

In an earlier article on job design (Davis and Canter, 1955), it was indicated that, in spite of all the research investigations of various aspects of jobs, such as job satisfaction, etc., so far there have been no principles formulated which can assist industry in organizing and assigning work to separate jobs. It was further asserted that designing jobs, i.e. determining what the work content of the various jobs should be, is an important phase of the manufacturing planning process. Also, job design was emphasized as probably being an important variable effecting productivity. A potentially valuable criterion was suggested for assessing the effectiveness of a given job design, mainly involving the extent to which the design of a job reduces total cost to produce rather than minimizes immediate or direct cost.

In general terms, the job design process can be divided into three activities: (a) the specification of the content of individual tasks, (b) the specification of the method of performing each task, and (c) the combination of individual tasks into specific jobs. The first and third activities determine the content of the job, while the second indicates how the job is to be performed. It is possible therefore to speak about the design of job content and the design of job methods.

Considerable detailed study has taken place and a large body of knowledge exists concerning the design of job methods, so much so that a specialized professional branch of industrial engineering called methods engineering has become devoted to it (Davis, 1953). On the other hand relatively little information has been available concerning the design of job content (Walker, 1954). For the purpose of our research program and to maintain some semantic agreement, we refer to the process of designing of job content as job design and that of the design of job methods as methods design.

Although sufficient data are lacking to make a conclusive statement, there appears to be a relationship between job content and productivity, quality, employee turnover, and other measures of effective work organization. Furthermore, at present there is not enough information in an integrated form to postulate a practical theory of job design.

Individuals undertaking the design of industrial jobs usually do so with certain criteria in mind, whether or not these are explicitly stated. There are strong indications at present that the apparent criterion of minimizing immediate costs implemented by the principles of minimizing skills, minimizing direct unit operation time, and maximizing specialization is not giving satisfactory results in terms of total costs of producing. As indicated previously, we suggest that job design principles should be based on the criterion of minimizing total costs, rather than of minimizing immediate or direct costs. The technical requirements for achieving production have been carefully studied and specified. However, many factors known to affect performance have never been fully evaluated as possible principles for the design of jobs, and of course, a unified theory of job design has never been developed.

The study reported in this paper was undertaken on the assumption that underlying principles for job assignment or job design (or whatever kind) do in fact exist and are in use. The purpose of the study was to bring them to light. We wanted to obtain information regarding the manner in which American industry designs jobs as to their content. It was proposed to carry out the purpose by investigating:

1. The decisions made in the process of designing jobs.

2. The precepts, principles, intuitions and other guides or referents used in the making of these decisions.

To investigate the decisions made and the referents used in job design, a list of general questions about the design process was developed. These formed the basis for a survey of current job design methods and criteria in American industry, carried out by means of interviews and mail questionnaires. The questions were:

1. Where does job design enter into the production planning procedure? Does this occur at any particular stage in the planning

procedure, such as before or after the production process is chosen, or before or after the individual operations making up the production process are chosen, or does job design take place at all stages of planning?

2. What are the factors considered in making a choice between various alternative methods available for performing required operations?

3. What criteria are used to specify the content of individual tasks and to combine these tasks into jobs? Are there any systematic methods for doing this?

4. Who in terms of position held in the company performs the job design functions?

5. How much control does the designer of jobs have over the content of various types of jobs?

6. Are there any methods for determining the effectiveness of job designs?

7. Is there any indication that job content affects productivity, employee turnover, or quality?

8. Are there any variations in job design methods, specific to different industries?

Detailed questions were developed from these general questions and used in the survey. The actual questions asked in the survey were of two types. First, questions pertaining to specific cases of job design and second, questions concerned with job design procedures in general. The interviews and questionnaires were divided into ten sections which dealt with the following subjects:

1. Identification of characteristics of the respondent companies.

2. Definition of terminology.

3. Approximate percentage of the total number of production workers in various major types of work.

4. Procedures employed and decisions made in setting up new operations or in revising existing operations.

5. Degree of standardization of individual tasks within the company.

6. General procedures employed in combining individual tasks into specific jobs.

7. Factors imposing restrictions on the assignment of tasks to individuals.

8. Policies used in dealing with problems concerning productivity, employee turnover, quality and employee transfers.

9. Persons performing the job design function within the company

10. Experience concerning the effect of job content on productivity

Method of investigation

The survey of job design practices as currently carried out in American industry was conducted using both personal interviews and mail questionnaires. The investigation was limited to industrial jobs of low or moderate skill requirements which included such typical industrial jobs as those in assembly, packing, inspection and fabrication. Clerical jobs and supervisory jobs such as those of managers and foremen were excluded from investigation.

Findings

The findings are based upon seven interviews with manufacturing firms and upon the analysis of the returns of 490 questionnaires sent to a selected sample of US industrial companies. The sample was limited to larger organizations with capital value being used as a gauge of company size. In all, a total of 12 per cent of the companies responded to the questionnaire. Twenty-four of the 490 completed the questionnaire and thirty-five indicated that for various reasons they could not participate. It may be inferred from this response that American industry is not concerned to any great extent with work organization or job design. Although the sample is quite small, and the industries diverse, the responses obtained are highly consistent. The findings are additionally significant if we further consider that the responses probably come from organizations having an interest in work organization or job design.

Interview findings

The findings in the interviews are reported separately from those in the questionnaire largely because the former are taken from non-directed responses to open-ended questions. In the interviews all of the companies were asked what factors they normally take into consideration in assigning tasks to workers and in combining the tasks to make specific jobs. All of the companies considered it very important to:

1. Break the job into the smallest components possible to reduce skill requirements.

2. Make the content of the job as repetitive as possible.

3. Minimize internal transportation and handling time.

4. Provide suitable working conditions.

5. Obtain greater specialization.

6. Stabilize production and reduce job shifts to a minimum.

7. Have engineering departments, whenever possible, take an active part in assigning tasks and jobs. (In all the companies the line foreman or supervisor was directly involved in carrying out activities.)

Questionnaire findings

The responding companies varied in numbers of employees from ninety-seven to 14,000. The majority of the production workers in fifteen of the twenty-four companies were machine operators or assembly workers. As indicated above, the questionnaire was divided into ten sections and posed questions pertaining to both specific cases of job design and job design procedures in general. The answers to the questions should provide us with an understanding of the decisions made in designing jobs and of the referents for these decisions.

The first question asked where job design enters into the manufacturing planning procedure. The interviews indicated that planning for manufacture is carried out in the following sequence of steps:

1. The overall manufacturing process is planned.
2. The process is subdivided into operations according to various criteria.
3. The operations are subdivided into elements.
4. The elements are organized into specific tasks.
5. The specific tasks are combined into individual jobs.

In all of the specific cases reported in interviews and questionnaires, the problems of work organization were centered around the planning of the individual operations making up the production process. Considerations as to the content of the tasks to be assigned to individual workers had some effect on the choice of methods for performing the operations. While it is entirely possible that the planning of an entire production process could be based on considerations of job content, it is probably satisfactory to generalize that the process of job design is centered around the phase of the manufacturing planning procedure concerned with planning of separate operations.

The second question asked what factors are considered in making a choice between various alternative methods available for performing required operations. Table 1 gives the factors ranked in order of importance, taking into account both number of mentions and weight of ratings assigned that were considered in choosing methods for performing twenty-four specific operations. While these factors pertain to specific operations and their order of importance may change with various situations, they provide an indication of the different kinds of factors that are considered.

Question three asked what criteria are used to specify the content of individual tasks and to combine these tasks into jobs. To answer this question we need to examine:

1. The considerations governing the division of operations between workers.
2. The criteria used to specify the content of tasks.
3. The criteria used to combine tasks into jobs.

Table 2 provides the considerations which governed the division of operations between workers. In addition, as expected, companies used both the parallel method of work assignment, i.e. assigning the same operation to a number of workers, and the sequential method whereby operations are divided in sequence among workers. The reason given as underlying the choice of specific methods for the division of operations are given in Table 3. In the cases reported, there seems to be no relation between the reasons given for the use of particular methods and the resulting methods used. In the majority of the cases several reasons were given to explain a choice made. Again, while the reasons apply to specific cases only, they do given an indication as to the basis for the division of operations between several employees.

Table 1 **Major considerations in choice of particular methods for performing operations** (based on 24 operations)

Major considerations ranked in order of weighted aggregate rating	Total number times mentioned order of importance from high to low					Weighted aggregate rating
	5	4	3	2	1	
Minimizing time required to perform operation	14	4	1	—	—	89
Obtaining highest quality possible	4	6	1	3	—	53
Minimizing skill requirements of operation	1	3	4	3	4	39
Utilization of equipment or tools presently on hand	1	4	2	—	—	27
Minimizing floor space requirements	2	2	1	1	—	23
Achieving specialization of skills	—	1	4	1	1	19
Minimizing learning time or training	—	—	4	—	1	13
Minimizing materials handling costs	1	—	—	2	1	10
Equalizing and developing full work load for workcrew members	—	1	1	1	—	9
Providing operator satisfaction	—	1	1	1	—	9
Minimizing equipment in tool costs	—	1	—	1	1	7
Controlling materials used in operation	—	—	1	2	—	7
Providing maximum production flexibility	—	1	1	—	—	7
Simplifying supervision of operation	—	—	—	—	3	3
Providing maximum safety in operation	—	—	—	1	1	3

An examination of the considerations governing the division of operations between workers and of the reasons underlying the choice of specific methods of division provide us with the criteria used for the specification of the content of tasks. From this we may infer that the following are the criteria used in industry to specify the content of individual tasks. The content of tasks is specified:

1. So as to achieve specialization of skills.
2. So as to minimize skill requirements.
3. So as to minimize learning time or operator training time.
4. So as to equalize and permit assignment of a full work load.

Louis E. Davis, Ralph R. Canter and John Hoffman 71

Table 2 Methods for dividing operations between two or more employees (based on 17 operations)

Methods for dividing operations	Per cent of instances used*
Each employee is assigned one particular element of the operation as a full-time job	5·9
Each employee is assigned a specific group of elements of the operation as a full-time job	41·1**
Employees assigned to the operation are allowed to divide the individual tasks in the operation among themselves informally	5·9
Each employee is assigned all the elements required to complete the entire operation	47·0***
Each employee is assigned a specific group of elements of the operation, but in cases of emergency or to provide themselves with training for promotion employees may voluntarily rotate or overlap in performance of assigned tasks	17·6****

   * In this and in following tables, percentages will total more than
      100 per cent because some respondents gave more than one response.
  ** In one case each employee was originally assigned a specific group of
      elements, but after receiving training was assigned all the elements
      required to complete the entire operation.
 *** In two cases operators are assigned groups of elements and permitted
      to rotate within limitations of job description as to equipment, etc.
**** In one case operation totalled among several employees to equalize
      good and bad jobs.

5. In a manner which provides operator satisfaction. (No specific criteria for job satisfaction were found in use.)

6. As dictated by considerations of layout of equipment or facilities.

To determine the criteria for job design there still remains the need to examine the criteria governing the combination of tasks into jobs. Table 4 reports the general policies in use. The three methods most frequently employed to combine tasks into specific jobs are:

1. Assign each employee a specific operation as a full-time job.

2. Assign each employee a specific group of elements of an operation as a full-time job.

3. Assign each employee one particular element of an operation as a full-time job.

Table 3 Reasons dictating choice of methods for dividing operations (based on 17 operations)

Reasons dictating choice	Percent of instances reason given for choice of methods in Table 2				
	a	b	c	d	e
Certain phases of the operation required higher skilled workers than other phases	5·9	11·8	—	—	5·9
Workers with different skills were required for certain phases of the operation	—	—	5·9	—	5·9
Operation was machine paced and was divided in such a manner as to provide maximum utilization of machines	—	11·8	—	—	—
Layout of equipment or facilities needed for the operation dictated this division of tasks	—	23·5	—	11·8	5·9
Task of each individual was made as specialized as was practical	5·9	5·9	—	11·8	5·9
Operation is such that certain groups of elements must be performed at one workplace	—	11·8	5·9	11·8	5·9
Operation was divided in the manner suggested by the workers	—	—	5·9	—	—
Operation was divided to permit workers to inspect their own work and correct if necessary	—	5·9	—	—	—
Operation was divided to equalize distribution of work load	—	5·9	—	5·9	5·9
Operation is not divided at present	—	—	—	5·9	5·9*
Permit rotation of good and bad jobs	—	—	—	5·9	—

* Permit flexibility of movement within job grades.

General comments indicated that the majority of companies believed in limiting the content of the individual jobs as much as possible. This means limiting the number of tasks within the jobs and limiting the variations permitted in tasks or jobs. This further indicates that specialization of work was a primary consideration. Another indication of this was obtained in the last section of the questionnaire which asked the respondents to report any indications they might hold concerning the relationship between job content and productivity. The pertinent comments made in this section are summarized as follows:

1. Tasks with too many elements of work reduce productivity.

2. Combining elements provides individual responsibility for those elements which usually improve quality and productivity.

Table 4 General policies used in combining tasks into jobs
(based on 24 companies)

Policies	Per cent of instances policies were used for job types indicated		
	All	Assembly	Machine operation
Assign each employee one particular element of an operation as a full-time job	8·3	16·9	8·3
Assign each employee one particular element of an operation and rotate employees at intervals to other elements of the operation	12·5	8·3	—
Assign each employee one particular element of an operation as a full-time job and encourage employees to rotate jobs informally if they wish	4·2	4·2	4·2
Assign each employee a specific group of elements of an operation as a full-time job	12·5	20·8	33·5
Assign each employee a specific operation as a full-time job	25·0	16·7	29·2*
Assign groups of employees to specific groups of elements or operations allowing the members of the groups to divide the individual tasks between themselves informally	—	4·2	4·2
Assign each employee as his job all of the operations required to complete a process or product	—	16·7	4·2

* In one instance – applies to toolsetters.

3. Productivity is improved by revising tooling to reduce the possibility of errors and to reduce fatigue.

4. The greater the number of tasks assigned to an individual, the longer the training time required, and the lower the output. In general productivity will remain low.

5. Experience has indicated that job content does not appreciably affect productivity.

6. Job content is not as important as employee attitude. Mental attitude is the most important consideration. '. . . We specify job content to fit our facilities – then sell it.'

7. Productivity was found to be higher when job content involved

horizontal assignments (all elements at approximately the same skill levels).

8. Best results have been obtained by combining relatively few tasks into jobs for average workers. Overspecialization has not proved effective. Workers who show high aptitude and desire for diversified work are transferred to jobs in repair, or special products departments.

9. Simpler jobs result in higher output and make the workers happier. The company believes in simplification and elimination of rotation for job satisfaction.

10. In general, the greater the degree of specialization, the higher the productivity. When specialization becomes so refined that the job becomes unbearably monotonous, productivity tends to decline; however, the monotony and decline in productivity are off-set to some extent by the ever-present challenge of the incentive system.

11. A change to an assembly line increases productivity.

In regard to systematic procedures for the design of jobs, i.e. specifying the content of tasks or combining tasks into jobs, none were reported in use in the companies surveyed.

Question four asked who, in terms of position held in the

Table 5 **Responsibility for job design** (based on 24 companies)

Responsibility of	Per cent of instances Specifies content of individual tasks			Combines separate tasks into specific jobs		
	Always	Sometimes	Never	Always	Sometimes	Never
Line foreman	25·0	66·7	—	25·0	58·3	16·7
Engineering department*	25·0	58·3	—	20·8	50·0	8·3
Personnel department	—	20·8	71·0	4·2	25·0	62·5
Plant superintendent	—	4·2	—	—	4·2	—
Department superintendent	4·2	—	—	4·2	—	—
Committee consisting of foreman, scheduling supt., tool room foreman and factory supt.	—	4·2	—	—	—	—
Production planning	—	4·2	—	—	—	4·2

* Including industrial engineering department.

company, performs the job design function. Table 5 provides this information. The findings show that the line foreman had a part in specifying the content of tasks in all instances, and in all but a few instances he also took part in combining individual tasks into jobs.

Question five asked, how much control does the designer of jobs have over the contents of various types of jobs. Tables 6 and 7 provide information concerning this. The respondents indicated that in general, training requirements controlled work assignment or restricted job design to the greatest degree. Where they existed, union agreements definitely imposed restrictions on work assignment. In addition, union agreements placed some restrictions on

Table 6 **Training requirements for industrial jobs requiring low or moderate skill** (based on 20 companies)

Amount of training time required	Per cent of instances with majority of production jobs in classification
Less than one month	25
Between one and three months	25
Between three and six months	20
Between six months and one year	25
Between one and two years	5

work that could be assigned to jobs in each established job classification.

Question six asked if there were any methods for determining the effectiveness of a job design. Attempts to determine what methods were used to evaluate the effectiveness of job designs proved so fruitless in the interviews that the question was not pursued in the questionnaire. In the interviews persons questioned about tests of effectiveness of job designs replied that all production jobs are kept under surveillance by engineering departments.

Question seven asked if there were any indications that job content has an effect on productivity, quality or employee turnover. The respondents were asked to describe the actions they had taken, or favored taking, to solve problems of low productivity, poor quality, high employee turnover, and excessive numbers of transfer requests. The remedies most frequently applied to problems of productivity were revision of methods, equipment, or

Table 7 Union agreements limiting job assignment
(based on 23 companies)

Type of limitation	Per cent of instances
Job assignments are limited by union agreements to the extent that jobs under jurisdiction of one union may not be performed by a member of another union	26·1
Union agreements place restrictions on the tasks that can be assigned to each specific job classification for	
(1) All the industrial classifications in the company	21·7
(2) Some of the industrial classifications in the company	4·4
Jobs are separated by union agreement into a class for men and a class for women	17·4
Union agreements require promotion by seniority	13·0
No union agreements restricting job assignment are in effect	56·6

product design, financial incentive programs, additional operator training, and employee indoctrination and educational programs. The remedies for problems of quality were revision in methods, equipment, or product design, disciplining of operators responsible for poor quality, additional training, statistical quality control programs, more inspection and more pressure on supervisors. The most frequent remedies applied to problems of turnover or transfers were improvement of working conditions, increased pay rates, and improved selection of personnel.

None of the companies reported considering alteration in job content as a possible remedy for any of these problems. A review of the literature indicates that in a number of instances benefits are being obtained by alterations in job content. In view of this, it would be worthwhile to speculate why no action of this kind had been considered by any of the responding organizations. It is possible that the participating companies had neither the degree of standardization of operations nor the degree of specialization of jobs necessary so that the effects of alterations in job content could be observed or measured.

Question eight asked if there were any variations in job design methods in different industries. The small response to the questionnaire precludes any industry-to-industry comparison. Thus no relationship between particular processes and products and job design practices can be given from the survey results.

Summary and interpretation of findings

In the survey reported here, we have been concerned with learning how American industrial concerns design jobs as to their content. Job design is the name we have given to the process of designing job content. The process is carried out by specifying the content of tasks and by combining individual tasks into specific jobs. To learn how job design was being carried out it was necessary to examine, in addition to the design process itself, the decisions made in the process of designing jobs and the precepts, principles and other guides or referents used in making these decisions. The findings of the survey may be briefly summarized as follows:

1. The job design process is centered around the phase of the manufacturing planning procedures concerned with the planning of separate operations.

2. In all instances the line foreman has a part in specifying the content of tasks and in all but a small number of instances he also takes part in combining individual tasks into jobs. The various engineering departments such as industrial, methods, tooling and standards engineering similarly take part in specifying the content of tasks, and in all but one instance also participate in combining tasks into jobs. Approximately 25 per cent of the time, the personnel department participates in these activities but in an advisory capacity only.

3. No systematic methods of job design can be said to exist.

4. No methods for evaluating the effectiveness of job designs can be said to exist. Determination of the effectiveness of a job design would actually consist of the application of two tests. The first test would involve checking the job design against the criteria originally used in designing to determine whether these have been satisfied. The second test would involve determining whether the desired end results, i.e. minimizing total costs of producing, has been achieved.

5. Overwhelmingly influencing the design of industrial jobs is the criterion of minimizing immediate cost of producing, i.e. immediate costs of performing the required operations. The usual indicator of achievement is minimum unit operation time. Designers of jobs see the criterion as being satisfied by the ap-

plication of the following principles or guides for specifying job content:

(a) The content of individual tasks is specified:
  (i) So as to achieve specialization of skills.
  (ii) So as to minimize skill requirements.
  (iii) So as to minimize learning time or operator training time.
  (iv) So as to equalize and permit the assignment of a full work load.
  (v) In a manner which provides operator satisfaction. (No specific criteria for job satisfaction were found in use.)
  (vi) As dictated by considerations of layout of equipment or facilities, and where they exist, of the union restrictions on work assignment.

(b) Individual tasks are combined into specific jobs so that:
  (i) Specialization of work is achieved whenever possible by limiting the number of tasks in a job and limiting the variations in tasks or jobs.
  (ii) The content of the job is as repetitive as possible.
  (iii) Training time is minimized.

6. As concerns the problems of achieving high productivity or high quality levels, and of minimizing employee turnover and transfers, the alteration of job content is never seen as a possible remedy for any of these problems. The literature indicates, however, that alteration of job content by means of job enlargement, etc., is used in a few scattered (numerically insignificant) instances (Walker, 1950; Tangerman, 1953).

Achieving or maintaining high levels of productivity or quality are considered by a number of companies to be primarily technical matters as indicated by their approach to solving these problems through the revision of work methods, equipment, and product design. Other companies indicate that the problems could be solved through greater control over the employees, using additional operator training, disciplining of operators, and more inspection of production. Some companies consider employee satisfaction to be the answer and seek to obtain it through incentive programs and employee indoctrination and education programs.

All companies having employee turnover and transfer problems believe them to be related to employee satisfaction. Two of the most frequently mentioned remedies, improved working conditions and increased pay rates, are aimed at increasing employee satisfaction. Another frequently used remedy, improved selection techniques, seeks to circumvent the problem of improving satisfaction by attempting to find employees who would be satisfied with what the company presently has to offer.

A review of the findings indicates that a great disparity exists between the ability to design effective job methods and to design job content. For the design of job methods an organized body of literature based upon experimentation and practice exists. For the design of job content no information or theories are as yet on hand and no systematic methods of job design exist. What criteria and principles the job designer does use are exceedingly narrow and directed to a very limited objective, although they do have the virtue of consistency. It is puzzling to attempt to explain why over the years so little has been done to evaluate the effectiveness of the methods of job design and of the criteria and principles upon which they rest in regard to the total cost of producing.

A question to be answered by future investigation is whether through the employment of these narrow criteria and presently used principles, the job designer obtains tasks and jobs that are organized in an effective manner in terms of minimizing the total cost of producing.

Conclusions

Based on the interview and questionnaire results, and from interpretations suggested by the results, we hypothesize the following:

1. Current job design practices are consistent with the principles of rationalization or scientific management. They minimize the dependence of the organization on the individual. At the same time they minimize the contribution of the individual to the work of the organization, i.e. its production process.

2. Current principles of job design reflect the mass production precepts of specialization of jobs and repetitiveness of work.

3. Job design practices minimize the effects of the individual's actions on the organization in regard to absenteeism, turnover, etc., by specifying jobs requiring short training time and having low

skill requirements. Current practices also minimize the effects of 'labor scarcity' whether due to high labor costs or unavailability of individuals or skills, and permit minimum hiring rates of pay.

4. Management designs jobs without systematic methods, without tested criteria, and without evaluating the effects of job designs on long-term productivity or costs. By adhering to the very narrow and limited criteria of minimizing immediate cost or maximizing immediate productivity, it designs jobs based entirely on the principles of specialization, repetitiveness, low skill content and minimum impact of the worker on the production process. Management then frequently spends large sums of money and prodigious efforts on many programs that attempt to: (a) counteract the effects of job designs; (b) provide satisfactions, necessarily outside the job, which the job cannot provide; and (c) build up the satisfaction and importance of the individual which the job has diminished.

In view of the disparity of goals, the question arises as to how effective such programs can be in making employees feel that they are a significant part of an organization. Subsumed in such programs, and rightly so, is the fact that identification with the organization and its work is needed for obtaining the high motivation necessary for achieving the goals of the organization. Therefore, in view of the consequences of job design practices, ostensibly undertaken to improve efficiency, and in view of the motivational needs for improving efficiency or performance, is management following a proper course in placing continued reliance and emphasis on the narrow criterion of immediate cost? In the long run it would appear that management is placing itself in the difficult position (which some are in already) of having to force improved achievement. Since motivation cannot be relied on, management depends upon technical improvements (usually costly) for improving performance.

5. It can be concluded that company policies and practices in job design are inconsistent with programs and policies in human relations and personnel administration. On the one hand, specific steps are taken to minimize the contribution of the individual, and on the other hand he is propagandized about his importance and value to the organization. Does this conflict in policies and

practices add to or minimize the problem of securing greater motivation?

6. Some questions that need to be raised are:

(a) From the point of view of the designer of jobs, i.e. the engineer, can the designer of jobs ever hope to predict the effectiveness of a job design in terms of minimizing total costs without an understanding and evaluation of all the variables operating?

(b) From the point of view of increasing motivation, can any human relations program or any other program undertaken to increase motivation and so productivity hope to succeed which does not begin with soundly conceived job designs based upon efficient criteria?

(c) From the point of view of minimizing total costs of producing, can the designer of jobs achieve this goal without integrating the motivational and technical requirements of the job?

References

DAVIS, L. E. (1953), 'Work methods, design and work simplification', in E. M. Mrak and G. F. Stewart (eds.), *Progress in Food Research*, vol. 4, Academic Press, p. 37.

DAVIS, L. E., and CANTER, R. R. (1955), 'Job design', *Journal of Industrial Engineering*, vol. 6, no. 1, p. 3.

TANGERMAN, E. J. (1953), 'Every man his own inspector, every foreman his own boss at Graflex', *American Machinist*, vol. 97, no. 3, p. 2.

WALKER, C. R. (1950), 'The problem of the repetitive job', *Harvard Business Review*, vol. 28, no. 3, p. 54.

WALKER, C. R. (1954), 'Work methods, working conditions and morale', in A. Kornhauser, R. Dubin and A. M. Ross (eds.), *Industrial Conflict*, McGraw-Hill, p. 315.

7 Floyd C. Mann and Lawrence K. Williams

Organizational Impact of White Collar Automation

Excerpts from F. C. Mann and L. K. Williams, 'Organizational impact of white collar automation', Proceedings of the Eleventh Annual Meeting, Industrial Relations Research Board, Chicago, 1958.

The working vocabulary of the office worker is slowly changing to include such works as programming, write-outs, bits, core memory, and drum storage. This new vocabulary has come to the office with the introduction of high-speed computers and accessory equipment. These complexes are now coming to be known in the literature as electronic data processing (EDP) systems. Computer systems [. . .] are being introduced into the office to compute and prepare customer bills, inventories, cost statements, premium notices, payrolls, and a host of other both simple and complicated tasks which have long provided the work base for the white collar worker.

In this paper we shall present some of the organization and social-psychological problems associated with these advanced automatic data processing systems. We will touch on [. . .] the effect of these new systems on the organization and its personnel. Our focus here (see Baldwin and Shultz, 1954) will be on changes relevant to industrial relations – changes in management philosophy, organizational structure, job content, and transitional problems. We will draw primarily on our own observations from an on-going, longitudinal study in a single firm over a period of years and on the research findings or observations of other investigators studying the impact of this new technology on the office. Our knowledge in this field is restricted in that our research has concentrated on the intra-organizational effects of these changes in a single firm. We have not examined certain broad economic and social consequences such as the effects of this white collar automation on the composition of the labor force, the 'unhired employee', leisure time activities, and other equally significant issues.

A number of empirical studies now provide us with a better basis for understanding the shape of things to come in this area. These include studies of large computer installations in insurance companies,[1] a study of an automatic airline ticket reservation system,[2] the use of EDP for maintaining inventory control in a shoe company (Wallace, 1956), and several studies of the introduction of IBM 650s in large and small insurance companies (Craig, 1955 and Jacobson, 1958). It is important to stress that the general impact on the organization is greatly dependent upon the degree of mechanization prior to change. This undoubtedly accounts for some of the marked differences in organizational change noted in these studies even where identical equipment is installed.

Technological changes which have been occurring in the past few years in the factory and the office are increasingly labeled 'automation'. While this general label is useful to connote simply 'more automatic',[3] most descriptions of these new automated processes have stressed the following basic characteristics: greater mechanization with more frequent use of automatic equipment and multiple, closed-loop feedback systems as controls. These technical and engineering characteristics in combination result in greater integration and centralization of control in systems of production and data processing.

Brief description of a change-over

A change-over to an electronic data processing system is different than a model conversion in an automobile plant, a turnaround in an oil refinery, or the starting up of a new plant. There can be no stock-piling in advance of suspending operations; there is little or no opportunity to make trial runs of new systems without the continual maintenance of the older system. Because continuity of office activities must be maintained and because the data of the old system can seldom be transferred directly to the new system, a change-over usually extends over a long period of time – from six months to three or four years. [. . .]

1. Studies of Automatic Technology (1955), and Canning (1957).
2. Studies of Automatic Technology (1958).
3. James Bright (1958a) feels that the 'common usage of automation to mean a significant advance in automaticity is a literal and appropriate application to the phenomena' with which he was concerned (p. 55).

A successful change-over to a complex EDP system necessitates a major reorganization of existing operations as well as the establishment of entirely new operations. There is a compounding of changes as the new equipment and its processes require large-scale structural and functional realignments in the organization. An organizational level may be added during the change-over, and functions are transferred across divisional lines as well as among sections and departments within the division at the vortex of the change. [. . .]

A change-over to EDP is thus a multiple-phase operation in which there is frequently a compounding of technological and organizational changes in an on-going system over an extended period of time.

Problems relevant to industrial relations
Management's conception of the change-over

Management's conception of the principal problems involved in a change-over determines the extent to which attention is focused solely on the equipment or on the entire system of which the equipment will become a part. When attention is focused on the equipment – 'the hardware approach' – management is primarily concerned with the selection of the correct machine or machines for a given operation. The problem is conceived to be one of sub-stitution of machines for existing operations. The potential to be realized by rethinking the division of labor and the resultant organizational structure in a broad way is ignored.

In the system approach, on the other hand, the introduction of electronic equipment is seen as an opportunity for re-evaluating organizational objectives and procedures and redesigning relevant sub-systems within the organization. This approach may result in not only a more efficient alignment and consolidation of functions in the immediate area of the change-over, but may also furnish the impetus for reconsideration of activities and procedures in other distant parts of the organization. Changes which could have been brought about without the introduction of an EDP system, but had been postponed for one reason or another, are incorporated into this broader conceptualization of the task. Thus, the change-over is seen as a complex parcel of organizational, administrative, human, *and* technical problems – not simply a technical problem of selection and installation of equipment within old organizational lines. The management which fails to realize that more than hardware is being changed also probably fails to understand the implications of such a change for its personnel policies and its people.

Elaboration of management philosophy

A change-over brings a number of revisions in management philosophy and its implementation. Existing policies must be re-examined, made explicit, occasionally changed; new policies must be developed; both old and new policies are given a thorough test as they are translated into action.

As functions, employees, and their supervisors are transferred from one major division to another, the extent to which common philosophies and policies exist is revealed. Contradictions and inconsistencies in the sharing of information, the joint planning of work, and the delegation of responsibility are the basis of some of the problems in this period for both supervisors and employees. The greater interdependence of divisions and their departments necessitates the consideration and resolution of these differences before the new operating system can be established.

A change-over forces further development and elaboration of management's personnel philosophy. That which was implicit becomes explicit; that which was ill-defined and ambiguous is clarified through discussions regarding operating problems; untested assumptions are evaluated against the hard criteria of employee support and rate of progress toward the conversion goal. [. . .]

Organizational structure

Transfer of functions, centralization of control, and greater interdependency of units are some of the interrelated structural modifications that accompany such a large-scale change.

The transfer of functions between major divisions and among departments within a division creates problems for both employees and supervisory personnel. In some cases the work force moves when functions are reassigned, in others only the functions are transferred. These kinds of changes result in the employees being faced with new supervision, new jobs, or both. Strains created by the usual reluctance of managers to relinquish responsibilities are also felt by the employees.

Centralization of control and decision-making follows greater integration in the system. Autonomy and flexibility are reduced. As supervisory tasks cease to exist, the supervisory level of work leader may be eliminated. The first line supervisor's area of freedom is also further restricted. Variations in work rate and work process within a work unit are reduced; most decisions must be made with the larger organizational system in mind. Many of these changes point toward a further loss of self-direction and the motivation which stems from this.

Increased integration also places a greater premium on the rapid transmission of information; communication cannot be left to chance but must be highly formalized. There is a need for a nerve center with complete understanding of the integrated system where normal operations can be coordinated and where breakdowns in some part of the system can be interpreted for all other parts.

Job content and structure

There are a number of similarities between the technological changes in the factory and the office as they affect the content and structure of jobs. The most routine jobs are eliminated, work pace is tied more closely to machines, promotional opportunities are reduced, and some shift work is introduced.

A few statistics from our research site provide some insight into the changing structure of the jobs and their content. Prior to the change, there were 140 jobs and approximately 450 positions in the central accounting area. It is estimated that 80 per cent of the jobs were either substantially changed or eliminated, and that this effected 90 per cent of the positions. Moreover, there was about 50 per cent reduction in the number of jobs.

While E D P installation eliminates the routine and more menial clerical jobs, a general up-grading of jobs is not a necessary consequence.[4] The net effect on the organization we studied was a change in average job grade from 8·0 to between 8·1 and 8·2, where the range is from 3 to 13. Tasks previously done by employees holding high job grades and by lower level supervisors and which

4. Bright (1958b) has compiled data from several *factory* sites which corroborate this point.

involved known criterion decisions also have been programmed.[5]

New jobs that are created tend to require either new skills or new combinations of skills previously used. While these jobs may be less routine and therefore more socially desirable, within the single organization there is the considerable problem that dislocated individuals may not be able to fill these new jobs. Retraining personnel having a restricted range of talent is not an adequate solution.

Job enlargement does not necessarily accompany a change-over. It did, however, in the situation we were studying. The work of the non-mechanized accounting groups responsible for the steps preparatory to machine processing was consolidated into a station arrangement with each member trained to handle five operations previously performed separately. The removal of many middle level decision-making jobs also means that there is even less opportunity for progression in the organization. This has long been true for the assembly line worker. The effect that such a promotion limit will have on the white collar worker is unknown as yet, but it will probably disturb his illusion of mobility.

The white collar worker has often thought of his regular, eight-hour, daylight working schedule as one of the rewards of his job. Now that management finds it economically desirable to run EDP systems on a two-shift basis, it becomes necessary for some white collar workers to accept shift work. The recruitment of these white collar shift workers presents new problems. One organization has now changed its hiring policy and employs married women almost exclusively on the evening shift.

Another characteristic of the new work conditions is the low tolerance for error. The highly rationalized system provides less opportunity for multiple checking than previously, and errors may not be caught until they reach either the central processing equipment or in some cases the customer. Specific allocations of work to a single position means that errors are almost always traceable to an individual. For the white collar worker, accustomed to the somewhat anonymous conditions of the typical office organization, this accountability is a new experience.

The specific allocation of work within a rationalized system also means that each job is of greater significance in the continuity of

5. The removal of such jobs has also been cited by Rush (1957).

the process. Absences, tardiness, and a high turnover rate take on added importance, and relevant policies are more rigorously enforced.

The new white collar worker also has problems of machine pacing. Operating on a fixed schedule, the system imposes very specific deadlines. While the office worker still has more freedom to leave his work place or to vary his production level than does the blue collar worker, very specific work quotas have been imposed. Feelings of loss of autonomy are reported by both the worker and his supervisor.

Transitional problems

Problems concerning temporary help, overtime, training, and allocation of the work force are encountered during the transition period. The change-over is a period of increasing work load for the organization. Paradoxically, the very system which is installed to eliminate jobs often necessitates a greater number of workers during the transition period. Added duties and the need for constant retraining result in a significant increase in required working hours. Both overtime and a temporary work force are needed. The recruitment of this temporary work force and its introduction into the organization presents important issues, especially where the workers are organized.

In our study as well as in Craig's (1955), supervisors complained persistently about training and overtime. The problem of overtime was heightened because of the large number of women employees who were restricted in the total amount of allowable overtime as well as the amount permissible in any one day. Excess in overtime appeared to result in lower productivity, and certainly in complaints about home life and leisure activities.

Training is a burden for all personnel during the change-over. In the two major divisions affected by the change-over in our study, there were 800 individuals who had to be retrained to some degree. Training for new jobs is often relatively abstract. The trainer can only describe what the new jobs will probably be like. Initially there is no opportunity for on-the-job training. In addition, many have to be trained for jobs that are not to be permanent assignments but instead are transition jobs, and some of the motivation for learning is thus lessened.

Because of the simultaneous operation of the new, transitional, and old systems, the efficient assignment and reassignment of the work force becomes an important problem. Care must be exercised that those assigned to the old or the transition jobs are not overlooked for eventual assignment to new jobs. Another problem exists if one has to replace an individual who has been operating at a new job for a year or more with a more qualified candidate who was essential to the maintenance of the old or transitional systems.

While these are problems of transition in terms of their origin, their effects will be felt in the organization for an extended time unless properly managed.

The major problem areas we have selected for presentation in this paper are not exhaustive of the problems confronting the organization or its personnel during a change-over to electronic data processing. The topics considered here have been included because they have received less attention.

It has of course been possible to indicate only the broad dimensions of these problems. These findings do indicate, however, something of what we have learned about the effects of these technological changes on the work world of the white collar worker. This is clearly an area where quantitative, longitudinal, multi-disciplinary research in a number of organizations is needed.

References

BALDWIN, G. B., and SHULTZ, G. (1954), 'Automation: a new dimension to old problems', *IRRA Proceedings*.

BRIGHT, J. (1958a), *Automation and Management*, Division of Research, Harvard Business School.

BRIGHT, J. (1958b), 'Does automation raise skill requirements?', *Harvard Business Review*, vol. 36, no. 4, pp. 85–98.

CANNING, R. G. (1957), *Installing Electronic Data Processing Systems*, Wiley.

CRAIG, N. F. (1955), *Administering a Conversion to Electronic Accounting*, Riverside Press.

JACOBSON, E. (1958), 'Employee attitudes toward the installation of an electronic computer in a medium sized insurance company', unpublished paper presented at the 13th Congress, International Association of Applied Psychology.

RUSH, C. H. (1957), 'Implications of electronic data processing for industrial relations research', *IRRA Proceedings*.

WALLACE, E. (1956), *Management Decisions and Automatic Data Processing*, unpublished doctoral dissertation, University of Chicago.

8 Nehemiah Jordan

Allocation of Functions Between Man and Machines in
Automated Systems

N. Jordan, 'Allocation of functions between man and machines in
automated systems', *Journal of Applied Psychology*, vol. 47, 1963,
pp. 161–5.

In a document entitled 'Factors affecting degree of automation in
test and checkout equipment' which, among other things, reviews
the problems of allocation of functions, Swain and Wohl (1961)
assert:

A rather stark conclusion emerges: *There is no adequate systematic
methodology in existence for allocating functions* (in this case, test and
checkout functions) *between man and machine.* This lack, in fact, is
probably the central problem in human factors engineering today. . . .
It is interesting to note that ten years of research and applications
experience have failed to bring us closer to our goal than did the
landmark article by Fitts in 1951 (p. 9).

These two competent and experienced observers summarize ten
years of hard and intensive labor as having basically failed. This
is a serious problem. Why this failure?

We can attempt to seek a possible answer to the question by
seeking a similar case in other fields of scientific endeavor and
seeing what can be learned from it. And another case is easy to find;
it is in fact a classical case. In their book *The Evolution of Physics*,
Einstein and Infeld (1942) spend some time discussing the
problems which beset pre-relativity physics in which they focus
upon the concept of 'ether'. They point out that ether played a
central role in physical thinking for over a century after having first
been introduced as a necessary medium for propagating electro-
magnetic waves. But during all this time all attempts to build and
expand upon this concept led to difficulties and contradictions. A
century of research on ether turned out to be sterile in that no
significant advance was made during that time. They conclude:
'After such bad experiences, this is the moment to forget ether

completely and try never to mention its name' (p. 184). And they do not mention the concept anymore in the book. The facts underlying the concept were not rejected, however, and it was by focusing upon the *facts* while rejecting the *concept* that Einstein could solve the problems which bedeviled the physics of his day.

The lesson to be learned from this momentous episode is that when a scientific discipline finds itself in a dead end, despite hard and diligent work, the dead end should probably not be attributed to a lack of knowledge of facts, but to the use of faulty concepts which do not enable the discipline to order the facts properly. The failure of human factor engineering to advance in the area of allocation of functions seems to be such a situation. Hence, in order to find an answer to the question 'Why this failure?' it may be fruitful to examine the conceptual underpinnings of our contemporary attempts of allocating functions between men and machines. And this brings us back to the landmark article by Fitts (1951) mentioned earlier.

This article gave rise to what is now informally called the 'Fitts list'. This is a two-column list, one column headed by the word 'man' and the other by the word 'machine'. It *compares* the functions for which man is superior to machines to the functions for which the machine is superior to man. Theoretically, this leads to an elegant solution to the allocation of functions. Given a complex man–machine system, identify the functions of the system and then, based on such a list which was expected to be refined with time and experience, choose machines for the functions they are best suited for and men for the functions they are best suited for. This is a clean engineering approach and it is not surprising that great hopes were placed upon it, in *1951*. The only gimmick is that it did not and does not work.

The facts to be found in all the existing versions of the Fitts list are all correct, just as the facts underlying the concept ether were all correct. Hence the inutility of these lists must be attributed to what we are told to do with these facts, to the instruction to compare man to the machine and choose the one who fits a function best. I question the *comparability* of men and machines. If men and machines are not comparable, then it is not surprising that we get nowhere when we try to compare them. Just as the concept of ether led to inutility, perhaps the concept of man–machine comparability does the same. Let us explore somewhat the background to the concept *comparability*.

The literature on the place of a man in man–machine systems converges to two posthumous articles by Craik (1947a; 1947b). These articles are recognized by almost all as being the basis upon which much that followed is built. Craik argues that in order to best be able to plan, design and operate a complex system, man functions and machine functions should be described in the same concepts, and, by the very nature of the case, these concepts have to be engineering terms. In other words, Craik recommends that we describe human functions in mathematical terms *comparable* to the terms used in describing mechanical functions.

In fairness to Craik's memory, it must be stressed that these two papers, published after his death, were notes for a discussion and probably not meant for publication. Hence he should not be blamed for failing to recognize the simple fact that anytime we can reduce a human function to a mathematical formula we can generally build a machine that can do it more efficiently than a man. In other words, to the extent that man becomes comparable to a machine we do not really need him any more since he can be replaced by a machine. This necessary consequence was actually reached but not recognized in a later paper, also a fundamental and significant paper in human factor engineering literature. Birmingham and Taylor (1954) in their paper, 'A design philosophy for man–machine control systems', write: 'Speaking mathematically, he (man) is best when doing least' (p. 1752). The conclusion is inescapable – design the man out of the system. If he does best when he does least, the least he can do is zero. But then the conclusion is also ridiculous. Birmingham and Taylor found themselves in the same paradoxical situation which Hume found himself some 200 years earlier where his logic showed him that he could not know anything while at the same time he knew he knew a lot.

This contradiction, so concisely formulated by Birmingham and Taylor yet not recognized by them or, it seems, by their readers, should have served as a warning that something was wrong with the conceptualization underlying the thinking in this area. But it did not.

Now we can see why the Fitts lists have been impotent. To the extent that we compare, numerically, human functions to machine functions we must reach the conclusion that wherever possible the machine should do the job. This may help to explain a curious aspect in designers' behavior which has annoyed some: an annoyance expressed trenchantly by a human factors engineer over a glass of beer thus: 'Those designers, they act as if they get a brownie point every time they eliminate a man.'

Let us return to the Fitts lists. They vary all over the place in length and in detail. But if we try to abstract the underlying commonalities in all of them we find that they really make one point and only one point. Men are flexible but cannot be depended upon to perform in a consistent manner, whereas machines can be depended upon to perform consistently but they have no flexibility whatsoever. This can be summarized simply and seemingly tritely by saying that men are good at doing that which machines are not good at doing and machines are good at doing that which men are not good at doing. Men and machines are not comparable, they are *complementary*. Gentlemen, I suggest that complementary is probably the correct concept to use in discussing the allocation of tasks to men and to machines. Rather than compare men and machines as to which is better for getting a task done, let us think about how we complement men by machines and vice versa to get a task done.

As soon as we start to think this way we find that we have to start thinking differently. The term 'allocation of tasks to men and machine' becomes meaningless. Rather we are forced to think about a task that can be done by men *and* machines. The concept 'task' ceases to be the smallest unit of analysis for designing man–machine systems though still remaining the basic unit in terms of which the analysis makes sense. The task now consists of actions, or better still activities, which have to be shared by men and machines. There is nothing strange about this. In industrial chemistry the molecule is the fundamental unit for many purposes and it does not disturb anybody that some of these molecules consist of hundreds, if not thousands of atoms. The analysis of man–machine systems should therefore consist of specifications of tasks and activities necessary to accomplish the tasks. Man and machine should complement each other in getting these activities done in order to accomplish the task.

It is possible that with a shift to emphasizing man–machine

comparability new formats for system analysis and design will have to be developed, and these formats may pose a problem. I am convinced, however, that as soon as we begin thinking in proper units this problem will be solved with relative ease. Regardless of whether this is so, one can now already specify several general principles that may serve as basic guidelines for complementing men and machines.

Machines serve man in two ways: as tools and as production machines. A tool extends man's ability, both sensory and motor; production machines replace man in doing a job. The principle underlying the complementarity of tools is as follows: man functions best under conditions of optimum difficulty. If the job is too easy he gets bored, if it is too hard he gets fatigued. While it is generally silly to use machines to make a job more difficult, although this may be exactly what is called for in some control situations, tools have, since their inception as eoliths, served to make a difficult job easier and an impossible job possible. Hence tools should be used to bring the perceptual and motor requirements of a task to the optimum levels for human performance. We have had a lot of experience with tools and they present few, if any, problems.

The problem is more complex with machines that do a job in place of man. Here we can return with benefit to the commonalities underlying the Fitts lists. To the extent that the task environment is predictable and *a priori* controllable, and to the extent that activities necessary for the task are iterative and demand consistent performance, a production machine is preferable to man. To the extent, however, that the environment is not predictable, or if predictable not controllable *a priori*, then man, aided by the proper tools, is required. It is in coping with contingencies that man is irreplaceable by machines. This is the essential meaning of human flexibility.

Production machines pose a problem rarely posed by tools, since they replace men in doing a job. They are not perfect and tend to break down. When they break down they do not do the job. One must always then take into account the criticality of the job for the system. If the job is critical, the system should so be designed that man can serve as a manual backup to the machine. Although he will then not do it as well as the machine, he still can do it well enough to pass muster. This is another aspect of human flexibility – the ability for graceful degradation. Machines can either do the job as specified or they botch up; man degrades gracefully. This is another example of complementarity.

Planning for feasible manual backup is a difficult job in the contemporary complex systems that we are constructing. It has generally been neglected. In most simple systems explicit planning is not necessary since man's flexibility is generally adequate enough to improvise when the relatively simple machines break down. But this changes with growing system complexity.

It is here that 'automation' should be mentioned. Some of you may have been bothered by the fact that automation is in the title of this paper but has, as yet, still to be introduced. The reason is rather simple. Although automation represents a significant technological breakthrough which has generated many specific problems, the allocation of tasks to men and machines being one of them, conceptually, an automated machine is just another machine, albeit radically different in its efficiency and performance characteristics. The problems that were generally latent or not too critical in the older, simpler man–machine systems became both manifest and critical, however, with its introduction. One of the most critical areas is manual backup.

We customarily design automated systems by allocating to man those functions which were either difficult or too expensive to mechanize, and the rest to machines. As many articles in the literature indicate, we have looked upon man as a *link* in the system and have consequently given him only the information and means to do the job assigned to him as a link. When the system breaks down a man in a link position is as helpless as any other machine component in the system. We have tended to design out his ability to take over as a manual backup to the system. At the same time the jobs performed by the machine have become more and more important and the necessity for a manual backup consequently greater. How to design a complex automated system to facilitate its being backed up manually is a neglected area. One thing seems certain. It will most probably call for 'degradation' in design, that is, systematically introducing features which would not have been necessary were no manual backup needed. This is an important area for future human factors engineering research.

Another area of complementarity which is gaining in significance as the systems are getting more and more complex is that of responsibility. Assuming we lick the problems of reliability, we can depend upon the machines to do those activities assigned to them consistently well, but we never can assign them any responsibility for getting the task done; responsibility can be assigned to men only. For every task, or for every activity entailed by the task, there must be a man who has assigned responsibility to see that the job be done as efficiently as warranted. This necessitates two things: the specification of clear-cut responsibilities for *every* man in the system and supplying the men with means which will enable them to exercise effective control over those system tasks and activities for which they are responsible. You may think that this is obvious – yes it is. But it is surprising how rare, and then how in-effective, our planning and design in this area are. Experience to date with automated systems shows that the responsibilities of the individuals involved are generally nebulous so that when some-thing unexpected occurs people often do not know who is to do what. Even to the extent that these responsibilities are clarified with time and experience, the system hardware often makes it difficult for men to assume these responsibilities, the means for man to exercise control over the areas of his responsibility being inadequate or lacking.

The complementarity of men and machines is probably much more profound and subtle than these aspects which I have just highlighted. Many other aspects will undoubtedly be identified, elaborated and ordered to the extent that we start thinking about how one complements the other. In other words, to the extent that we start *humanizing* human factors engineering. It is not surprising that the ten years of lack of progress pointed to by Swain and Wohl (1961) were accompanied by the conceptual definition of treating man as a machine component. Man is not a machine, at least not a machine like the machines men make. And this brings me to the last point I would like to make in this paper.

When we plan to use a machine we always take the physical environment of the machine into account; that is, its power supply, its maintenance requirements, the physical setting in which it has to operate, etc. We have also taken the physical environment of man into account, to a greater or lesser extent; that is, illumination and ventilation of the working area, noise level, physical difficulties, hours of labor, coffee breaks, etc. But a fundamental difference between men and machines is that men also have a psychological environment for which an adequate physical environment is a necessary condition but is ultimately secondary in importance. This is the truth embedded in the adage: man does not live by bread alone. The psychological environment is subsumed under one word: motivation. The problems of human motivation are at present eschewed by human factors engineering.

You can lead a horse to water but cannot make him drink. In this respect a man is very similar to a horse. Unless the human operator is motivated, he will not function as a complement to machines, and the motivation to function as a complement must be embedded *within the task itself*. Unless a task represents a challenge to the human operator, he will *not* use his flexibility or his judgement, he will *not* learn nor will he assume responsibility, nor will he serve efficiently as a manual backup. By designing man–machine systems for man to do *least*, we also eliminate all challenge from the job. We must clarify to ourselves what it is that makes a job a challenge to man and build in those challenges in every task, activity and responsibility we assign to the human operator. Otherwise man will not complement the machines but will begin to function like a machine.

And here too men differ significantly from machines. When a man is forced to function like a machine he realizes that he is being used inefficiently and he experiences it as being used stupidly. Men cannot tolerate such stupidity. Overtly or covertly men resist and rebel against it. Nothing could be more inefficient and self-defeating in the long run than the construction of man–machine systems which cause the human components in the system to rebel against the system.

Herein lies the main future challenge to human factors engineering.

References

BIRMINGHAM, H. P., and TAYLOR, F. V. (1954), 'A design philosophy for man–machine control systems', *Proc. IRE*, vol. 42, pp. 1748–58.
CRAIK, K. J. W. (1947a), 'Theory of the human operator in control systems: 1. The operator as an engineering system', *British Journal of Psychology*, vol. 38, pp. 56–61.

CRAIK, K. J. W. (1947b), 'Theory of the human operator in control systems: 2. Man as an element in a control system', *British Journal of Psychology*, vol. 38, pp. 142–8.

EINSTEIN, A., and INFELD, L. (1942), *The Evolution of Physics*, Simon & Schuster.

FITTS, P. M. (ed.) (1951), *Human Engineering for an Effective Air Navigation and Traffic Control System*, National Research Council.

SWAIN, A. D., and WOHL, J. G. (1961), *Factors Affecting Degree of Automation in Test and Checkout Equipment*, Dunlap & Associates.

9 Hans J. J. van Beinum

The Relation Between the Role of the Trade Union in
Modern Society and the Attitudes of Workers

Excerpts from H. van Beinum, *The Morale of the Dublin Busmen*,
Tavistock Institute of Human Relations, 1966, ch. 7, pp. 79–87.

In the last fifty years large changes have occurred in society
which have affected the role of the trade union.

Industrialization has been one of the contributive factors
towards increasing wealth throughout society. An important
development here has been the change from a production centred
economy to a consumer economy.

As a result of the rise in the economic position of the workers
and of the changes in their environment, workers have developed a
different mentality. The 'need structure' of the workers has
changed and, with that, their basic outlook. The new mentality is
characterized by a decreasing feeling of a collectively shared fate,
and an increasing focus on individually and situationally determined problems. Class consciousness is changing into self
consciousness. We can speak of the 'privatization' of the worker, by
which we mean the tendency to evaluate the affairs of the world in
terms of his own needs, rather than in terms of the needs of the
traditional social group of which he is a part. One of the reasons
for the 'privatization' of the worker is that he finds it difficult to feel
emotionally involved about affairs which gradually become part
of normal living conditions.

A major characteristic of change in modern society is its
development into a pluralistic power structure in which industry,
government and the large economic and political organizations
become more and more interwoven, and in which the economic
power of the state is taking over much of the economic autonomy
of the individual employer. Instead of the nineteenth-century
dichotomy of working class and upper class, we now see a more
complex stucture of occupational, power, owner, interest and
status groups which are in continuous interaction with one

another. We have experienced the enormous developments in technology, the intermingling of state and society, the rise of a new middle class of white collar workers and the emergence of what is known as the tertiary sector (administrative services in government and private industry, banking insurance, etc.). Society has become more differentiated, social mobility has increased and dynamic factors have become more and more predominant.

A particularly important aspect of modern society for the traditional role of the trade union is the fact that the state accepts increasing responsibility for conditions of full employment and for economic and social security. The various social changes of the last fifty years had a profound effect on the background ideology of the trade union movement, yet the ideology of the class struggle has not really been replaced by a new ideology of the welfare state. There are certain trends, however, which focus more and more on the development and the growth of the total individual. We see such tendencies in the search for social conditions in the various areas of society which will enable the development of the whole personality. We see among younger generations a process of individualization with an increasing focus on personal problems. If ideologies with regard to the organization of society would, parallel to these developments, undergo a *personalization* themselves they would, in a more natural way, meet the developing needs of our time.

Trade union roles

Generally speaking, we can distinguish two trade union functions:

1. External with regard to society at large, concerning industry, and the workers in general.
2. Internal with regard to its own members.

With regard to the first function, the increasing social interdependency of our society has a profound effect. As the various activities in the different areas become more and more interconnected with each other, activities in the economic, social, political, judicial and cultural sectors develop into a process which cannot be disentangled. In this way the trade union becomes, via its socio-economic role, involved in problems of productivity, co-partnership, work classification, consumer interest, and leisure time activities.

With this development the trade union replaces its methods of direct action with a system of indirect negotiation with state and semi-state bodies. Together with employer organizations and government, the trade union shares the responsibility for socio-economic policy, and this new role is becoming gradually institutionalized.

There is a change from craft unions to unions covering large industrial sectors, with the result that the trade union is less able to focus specifically on the interest of a particular category of workers and is more inclined to guard the balance between various socio-economic groups.

In individual industries there is a growing involvement on the part of the union in the various social aspects of company policy. An example of this is the unions' orientation and participation in such fields as work classification, function analysis, and merit rating.

The protection of workers and the improvement of their wages was, and still is, the traditional role of the unions. Originating in a direct concern for the material impoverishment of workers, their wages have been one of the most important concerns of the union. Gradually this role has been recognized and accepted by public opinion, employers, the government, and industry, and is, more and more, being carried out on the national level, with government and employers' representatives in the form of longer term socio-economic planning.

With regard to the second function, that concerning their own members, we see, however, that the union is playing a decreasing role. A worker's need for assistance when he is sick or without work, and the social security when he is too old to work, used to be a second function of the trade union. In many countries, however, these needs are now cared for by the state in the form of accident coverage, health services, unemployment payments, old age pensions, etc. This means that important parts of the internal function of a trade union towards its members are being taken over by other bodies and organizations which again affect the relationship of the trade union to its members. Gradually the most important specific function of the trade union with regard to its own members has become individual service, that is to say, advice and support in case of personal conflict in the work situation.

The above picture, of the changes in society, in the environment of the trade union, and in the roles of the trade unions, shows that in modern society the mentality of the workers has changed towards an increased focusing on more personal and situationally determined problems, with a weakening of their collective aspirations. The trade unions, however, have developed in an opposite direction. The internal functions focused on the individual members have decreased and the external functions with regard to total society, industry and workers in general have increased. These processes of individualization of the needs of workers and collectivization of trade union functions, developing as they do in opposite directions, form the background against which the present relationship between members and their trade union must be understood.

The above description is, of course, one of tendencies and trends, and will differ in its actual form in different countries and cultures. However, the consistencies in the findings of various studies done in Western Europe and America are such that we can accept it in its general characteristics. It is the neglected area of work organization on the shop floor where the individualization of the needs of the workers manifest themselves and which is the new area of opportunity for the trade union. The extent to which the trade unions are able to recognize these situationally determined needs, and moreover, the way in which they are able to relate themselves to them will determine the relationship between the modern trade union and its members and, thereby, the overall functioning of the trade union organization.

This discrepancy between the needs felt by the workers and the perceived role of the trade union leads to organizational apathy which expresses itself in low attendances at union meetings, high turnover of members and wild unauthorized strikes, lack of control and inability to communicate. The resulting organizational apathy is reinforced by the fact that the increasing complexity of processes in society reduces the readily perceivable effects of participation. The development of trade unions as complex organizations with centralization of power and growing internal differentiation makes it increasingly difficult for the individual member to perceive participation as being meaningful. The overall result is a vicious circle which, for that matter, is equally valid for the modern big industrial organization as it is for the modern trade union, and which goes as follows:

1. Increasing complexity, bureaucratization and centralization of administration mean that psychological needs are increasingly less satisfied through participation.

2. As a result more members develop apathy towards the organization.

3. This further increases centralization in decision making and in the leadership system.

4. Which in turn further reduces participation and so gives rise to even less psychological satisfaction, so that even further apathy of members results.

Whether the trade union can maintain its character as a democratic social system will be determined by the extent to which trade union leadership is able and prepared to break through this vicious circle. This means that the trade union has to what extent it can, in addition to the roles it plays at present, enlarge in an appropriate way its internal function with regard to its own members. The modern trade union organization is in interaction with a complex environment in various ways. The only possible way for it to deal with the increasing complexity of this environment is by increasing its internal variety and differentiation.

We have sketched the typical characteristics of the shop floor. It is an organization of men and their tasks, it has the characteristics of a socio-technical system, it centers around the designs of jobs which should be based on a complementary relationship between a worker and his task. Therefore, the concern of management for the effective functioning of the enterprise and the concern of the trade union for the situationally determined needs of the workers, makes the optimization of the human system on the shop floor a primary and shared objective of both parties. This is the basis of industrial relations on the shop floor and distinguishes it from other levels and other areas of industrial relations.

We can recognize at least three different levels of industrial relations:

1. The national level where the union participates with govern-

ment and employer organizations in long term planning and development.

2. The industrial and company level where management and the union are involved in direct negotiations concerning the conditions of employment of specific categories of workers.

3. The shop floor level where the management–union relationship is concerned with the local working conditions of specific workers in a specific work situation, and moreover with the relationship between workers and their tasks.

Each of these levels places both management and the trade union in a relationship of inter-dependency. Each of these levels will have its own characteristics and will have its own way for the appropriate handling of the interdependencies and have its own specific requirements in terms of internal organizational competence.

In this study of the Dublin City Services we are concerned with the third level, i.e. the interaction processes between the unions and the shop floor, the daily work environment of their members. It is in this relationship that the earlier mentioned discrepancy is experienced, and it is in this area that the unions are faced with their greatest challenge.

The question of how the contact and communication between members and union officials can be improved, i.e. how the discrepancy between the needs and expectations of the workers and union policy and activities can be reduced, can be formulated for the situation in the Dublin City Services as: 'How can the role of the garage representatives and the branch committee be defined and structured in such a way that it will facilitate the matching of the needs, demands and expectations of the busmen with the present and future potential of the union organization?' It will be clear that this will not be met by just providing the technical organizational facilities for communication. What is required is a definition of the role of the union representatives not only in terms of being a function of the activities of the trade union on a company and national level, but also and primarily as a function of the concern of the trade union with the worker in his specific relationship with his task and his daily work environment. This means that the union has to decide to what extent it is concerned with the relationship between a worker and his task and his work situation, other than in terms of the more general financial conditions of employment.

Industrial relations on the shop floor are typical in two ways:

1. They deal with a matter which is, or more accurately should be, mainly of a non-conflict nature.
2. It is a relationship which is relatively independent.

Out of these properties follows the type of conditions necessary in order to make industrial relations on this level effective.

The fact that the major matter to be dealt with, i.e. the optimization of the human resources, the social system, is mainly one of non-conflict, requires that it should be dealt with in a specific way. It demands its own strategy and it has its own approaches. The fact that the shared area of concern in this field of industrial relations is characterized by being a dilemma and not a conflict, makes the way it should be handled one of problem-solving and not one of bargaining.

In a 'bargaining' situation in the strictest sense of the word, the goals of one party are in basic conflict with those of the other party, and the gain of one party is a loss to the other. A dilemma, however, is the type of situation whereby both parties have a common concern, a problem, which permits solutions which benefit both parties, or at least when the gains of one party do not result in equal sacrifices by the other. The task of the parties, in this case management and trade union on shop floor level, is to *discover* the highest pay-off possibilities. Usually the various alternatives and solutions are not known to the two parties before they start dealing with a matter, and the maximum results are available only by means of joint problem solving. This means being involved in a continuous process of identifying the problem, of searching for alternative solutions and their consequences and of selecting a course of action. However, this process can develop only if there is continuous and appropriate contact and communication between shop floor management and trade union representatives, the shop stewards.

The types of conditions necessary for an effective functioning of this process are of various kinds and include such matters as organizational structure, as well as common values and the opportunity to develop a high level of mutual trust and social skills and to learn about this process through repeated experience of it.

As a first list we propose the following set of requirements:

1. There must be regular meetings between the two parties as a matter of common practice.

2. The functions of both lower and middle management and the shop steward should be defined in such a way as to make it possible for them to play this role.

On the management side, in addition to their primary area of responsibility, which should be stated explicitly to be concerned with the managing of a social as well as a technical system, this function should also explicitly include the handling of the relationship with the shop stewards. On the trade union side, it means that the shop steward, in addition to being a representative, is also concerned with the human system and the way it is related to the technology. Furthermore he should be responsible in the first instance for all dealings with shop floor management.

One of the conditions for this is a sufficiently large area of responsibility and level of authority on both sides. So very often we see that the situationally determined problems of the shop floor, if tackled at all in the area of industrial relations, are being dealt with not on shop floor level, but by management and trade union officials higher up in their respective organizations. This means it is handled by people on both sides who have neither sufficient knowledge of the local factors involved nor the right frame of reference. The result is that it becomes more an object of bargaining and conflict resolution than one which can be dealt with in terms of joint problem solving. The type of competence for dealing with industrial relations on a company level is usually not the same as the type of competence required for handling industrial relations on shop floor level.

3. Shop floor management and shop stewards need the support of their higher echelons. The concern with the development of human resources and the optimization of the human system must be possible within the framework of the policy and the values of the enterprise, and of the objectives of the trade union. Industrial relations on shop floor level cannot function properly unless the objectives of the enterprise and of the trade unions and the

governing set of values in each of these organizations include a direct concern for the content of the relationship between a worker and his task and for the way the human system is related to the effective functioning of the total system.

On the management side, it means searching for answers to such complicated matters as how to develop a total cost criterion. This should include, in addition to the direct cost of production, the relevant long-term implications in money, time, growth and psychological and social cost. How can we determine how total economic cost is to be measured in terms of economic, engineering, organizational, social, psychological and human resources cost criteria?

4. A particularly difficult aspect is the fact that industrial relations on the shop floor are relatively independent. They can develop only if they have the independence to function in accordance with the specific property of the particular shop floor in question and its requirements, and that means being in accordance with the specific interrelationship between workers, local management, shop stewards and with the socio-technical system of each particular workplace.

On the other hand, however, industrial relations on this level cannot be fully independent, but will also have a relationship of dependency with the way management and trade unions are involved with each other on company and national levels. It is not clear, though, what the exact nature of this dependency relationship is or should be. We suspect that it is much more complex than simply assuming that the objectives of one level are subordinate to the objectives of the other level, or that the functioning of one level is fully dependent on the effective functioning of another level. We do think, however, that there will be some systematic way by which the various relationships are related to each other in a hierarchical manner. We also think that it will be necessary to understand the role of the time factor and the way in which short, medium and long term objectives and relationships operate. There are indications that recent developments in system theory will help us to understand the properties of these complicated relationships with their dimensions in time and space.

At this stage we believe we could make a significant advance if we could distinguish between the national, company and shop floor levels of industrial relations and could identify and develop the type of competence which is required for each level.

5. It will be clear that good functioning of industrial relations on the shop floor will also require certain skills of management and shop stewards and an understanding of the socio-technical problems they will be dealing with. These skills and the ability to understand the nature of a work organization will have to be included in the criteria used for the selection and promotion of shop floor management. On the trade union side, there is the special problem of how these types of criteria can be developed and used in a system based on elections. [. . .]

These various conditions (1–5 above) together make up an over-all prerequisite which underlies the whole system of industrial relations on the shop floor: in order to be able to carry out joint problem solving both management and shop stewards should have, or should continuously search for, a positive and relatively close relationship with the worker. [. . .]

By developing industrial relations on the shop floor in their logical relationship with work organization, a major contribution can be made towards uncovering a large area of unknown and untapped human resources, or, put another way, towards reducing the wastage going on today, of creativity, of learning ability and of potential productivity. [. . .]

Part Three
Recent Theoretical Trends

This selection of Readings represents the state of thinking
among social scientists in the two most recent trends in job
design: job content and role content. Unfortunately, a paper
reporting the present theories, concepts and assumptions of the
job rationalization movement is unavailable. An exhaustive
search of the literature failed to provide a paper that dealt with
other than techniques for how to simplify ('improve') or
fractionate jobs.

Starting from different bases and concepts, Herzberg, Turner
and Lawrence, and Hackman and Lawler each contributes to the
conceptualization of enriched or enlarged jobs. The primary
emphasis in all three papers is on the individual worker in
relationship to his product – in short, *his* 'job content'.

Davis comments on the increasingly recognized sterility of
the historical job satisfaction concept in advancing the field
of design. He discusses the encouraging progress in the study of
job content, or the nature of the task itself. He also introduces
the recent moves toward recognition of the joint operation of
social systems and technical systems in the design of work, or
role content.

The final two selections by Emery and Bucklow illustrate the
importance, mentioned by Davis, of including the social
environment in any consideration of the technical work
system.

The papers indicate that we are in the midst of an evolution,
with discontinuities, in the development of man-made or
designed jobs. Each development reflects the culture, including
technology, of this era. The discontinuities reflect the very large
changes under way in the social environment.

10 Frederick Herzberg

One More Time: How do you Motivate Employees?

Excerpt from F. Herzberg, 'One more time: how do you motivate employees?', *Harvard Business Review*, vol. 46, 1968, pp. 53–62.

The theory was first drawn from an examination of events in the lives of engineers and accountants. At least sixteen other investigations, using a wide variety of populations (including some in the Communist countries), have since been completed, making the original research one of the most replicated studies in the field of job attitudes.

The findings of these studies, along with corroboration from many other investigations using different procedures, suggest that the factors involved in producing job satisfaction, and motivation, are separate and distinct from the factors that lead to job dissatisfaction. Since separate factors need to be considered, depending on whether job satisfaction or job dissatisfaction is being examined, it follows that these two feelings are not opposites of each other. The opposite of job satisfaction is not job dissatisfaction but, rather, *no* job satisfaction, and, similarly, the opposite of job dissatisfaction is not job satisfaction, but *no* job dissatisfaction.

Stating the concept presents a problem in semantics, for we normally think of satisfaction and dissatisfaction as opposites, i.e. what is not satisfying must be dissatisfying, and vice versa. But when it comes to understanding the behavior of people in their jobs, more than a play on words is involved.

Two different needs of man are involved here. One set of needs can be thought of as stemming from his animal nature – the built-in drive to avoid pain from the environment, plus all the learned drives which become conditioned to the basic biological needs. For example, hunger, a basic biological drive, makes it necessary to earn money, and then money becomes a specific drive. The other set of needs relates to that unique human characteristic, the ability to achieve and, through achievement, to experience psychological growth. The stimuli for the growth needs are tasks that induce growth; in the industrial setting, they are the *job content*. Contrariwise, the stimuli inducing pain-avoidance behavior are found in the *job environment*.

The growth or *motivator* factors that are intrinsic to the job are: achievement, recognition for achievement, the work itself, responsibility, and growth or advancement. The dissatisfaction–avoidance or *hygiene* factors that are extrinsic to the job include: company policy and administration, supervision, interpersonal relationships, working conditions, salary, status, and security.

A composite of the factors that are involved in causing job satisfaction and job dissatisfaction, drawn from samples of 1685 employees, is shown in Figure 1. The results indicate that motivators were the primary cause of satisfaction, and hygiene factors the primary cause of unhappiness on the job. The employees, studied in twelve different investigations, included lower-level supervisors, professional women, agricultural administrators, men about to retire from management positions, hospital maintenance personnel, manufacturing supervisors, nurses, food handlers, military officers, engineers, scientists, housekeepers, teachers, technicians, female assemblers, accountants, Finnish foremen, and Hungarian engineers.

They were asked what job events had occurred in their work that had led to extreme satisfaction or extreme dissatisfaction on their part. Their responses are broken down in Figure 1 into percentages of total 'positive' job events and of total 'negative' job events. (The figures total more than 100 per cent on both the 'hygiene' and 'motivators' sides because often at least two factors can be attributed to a single event; advancement, for instance, often accompanies assumption of responsibility.)

To illustrate, a typical response involving achievement that had a negative effect for the employee was, 'I was unhappy because I didn't do the job successfully.' A typical response in the small number of positive job events in the Company Policy and Administration grouping was, 'I was happy because the company reorganized the section so that I didn't report any longer to the guy I didn't get along with.'

As the lower right-hand part of the figure shows, of all the factors contributing to job satisfaction, 81 per cent were moti-

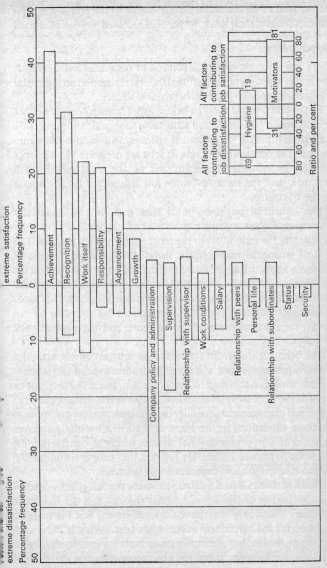

Figure 1 Factors affecting job attitudes, as reported in twelve investigations

vators. And of all the factors contributing to the employees' dissatisfaction over their work, 69 per cent involved hygiene elements.

Eternal triangle

There are three general philosophies of personnel management. The first is based on organizational theory, the second on industrial engineering, and the third on behavioral science.

The organizational theorist believes that human needs are either so irrational or so varied and adjustable to specific situations that the major function of personnel management is to be as pragmatic as the occasion demands. If jobs are organized in a proper manner, he reasons, the result will be the most efficient job structure, and the most favorable job attitudes will follow as a matter of course.

The industrial engineer holds that man is mechanistically oriented and economically motivated and his needs are best met by attuning the individual to the most efficient work process. The goal of personnel management therefore should be to concoct the most appropriate incentive system and to design the specific working conditions in a way that facilitates the most efficient use of the human machine. By structuring jobs in a manner that leads to the most efficient operation, the engineer believes that he can obtain the optimal organization of work and the proper work attitudes.

The behavioral scientist focuses on group sentiments, attitudes of individual employees, and the organization's social and psychological climate. According to his persuasion, he emphasizes one or more of the various hygiene and motivator needs. His approach to personnel management generally emphasizes some form of human relations education, in the hope of instilling healthy employee attitudes and an organizational climate which he considers to be felicitous to human values. He believes that proper attitudes will lead to efficient job and organizational structure.

There is always a lively debate as to the overall effectiveness of the approaches of the organizational theorist and the industrial engineer. Manifestly they have achieved much. But the nagging question for the behavioral scientist has been: What is the cost in human problems that eventually cause more expense to the organization – for instance, turnover, absenteeism, errors, violation of safety rules, strikes, restriction of output, higher wages, and greater fringe benefits? On the other hand, the behavioral scientist is hard put to document much manifest improvement in personnel management, using his approach.

The three philosophies can be depicted as a triangle, as is done in Figure 2, with each persuasion claiming the apex angle. The motivation–hygiene theory claims the same angle as industrial engineering, but for opposite goals. Rather than rationalizing the work to increase efficiency, the theory suggests that work be *enriched* to bring about effective utilization of personnel. Such a systematic attempt to motivate employees by manipulating the motivator factors is just beginning.

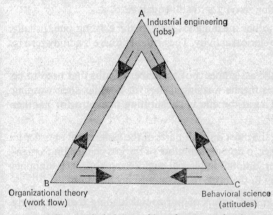

Figure 2 'Triangle' of philosophies of personnel management

The term *job enrichment* describes this embryonic movement. An older term, job enlargement, should be avoided because it is associated with past failures stemming from a misunderstanding of the problem. Job enrichment provides the opportunity for the employee's psychological growth, while job enlargement merely makes a job structurally bigger. Since scientific job enrichment is very new, this article only suggests the principles and practical steps that have recently emerged from several successful experiments in industry.

Job loading

In attempting to enrich an employee's job, management often succeeds in reducing the man's personal contribution, rather than giving him an opportunity for growth in his accustomed job. Such an endeavor, which I shall call horizontal job loading (as opposed to vertical loading, or providing motivator factors), has been the problem of earlier job enlargement programs. This activity merely enlarges the meaninglessness of the job. Some examples of this approach, and their effect, are:

1. Challenging the employee by increasing the amount of production expected of him. If he tightens 10,000 bolts a day, see if he can tighten 20,000 bolts a a day. The arithmetic involved shows that multiplying zero by zero still equals zero.

2. Adding another meaningless task to the existing one, usually some routine clerical activity. The arithmetic here is adding zero to zero.

3. Rotating the assignments of a number of jobs that need to be enriched. This means washing dishes for a while, then washing silverware. The arithmetic is substituting one zero for another zero.

4. Removing the most difficult parts of the assignment in order to free the worker to accomplish more of the less challenging assignments. This traditional industrial engineering approach amounts to subtraction in the hope of accomplishing addition.

These are common forms of horizontal loading that frequently come up in preliminary brainstorming sessions on job enrichment. The principles of vertical loading have not all been worked out as yet, and they remain rather general, but I have furnished seven useful starting points for consideration in Table 1.

A successful application

An example from a highly successful job enrichment experiment can illustrate the distinction between horizontal and vertical loading of a job. The subjects of this study were the stockholder correspondents employed by a very large corporation. Seemingly, the task required of these carefully selected and highly trained correspondents was quite complex and challenging. But almost all

Table 1 Principles of vertical job loading

Principle	Motivators involved
A. Removing some controls while retaining accountability	Responsibility and personal achievement
B. Increasing the accountability of individuals for own work	Responsibility and recognition
C. Giving a person a complete natural unit of work (module, division, area, and so on)	Responsibility, achievement, and recognition
D. Granting additional authority to an employee in his activity; job freedom	Responsibility, achievement, and recognition
E. Making periodic reports directly available to the worker himself rather than to the supervisor	Internal recognition
F. Introducing new and more difficult tasks not previously handled	Growth and learning
G. Assigning individuals specific or specialized tasks, enabling them to become experts	Responsibility, growth, and advancement

indexes of performance and job attitudes were low, and exit interviewing confirmed that the challenge of the job existed merely as words.

A job enrichment project was initiated in the form of an experiment with one group, designated as an achieving unit, having its job enriched by the principles described in Table 1. A control group continued to do its job in the traditional way. (There were also two 'uncommitted' groups of correspondents formed to measure the so-called Hawthorne Effect – that is, to gauge whether productivity and attitudes toward the job changed artificially merely because employees sensed that the company was paying more attention to them in doing something different or novel. The results for these groups were substantially the same as for the control group, and for the sake of simplicity I do not deal with them in this summary.) No changes in hygiene were introduced for either group other than those that would have been made anyway, such as normal pay increases.

The changes for the achieving unit were introduced in the first two months, averaging one per week of the seven motivators listed in Table 1. At the end of six months the members of the achieving unit were found to be outperforming their counterparts in the control group, and in addition indicated a marked increase in their liking for their jobs. Other results showed that the achieving group had lower absenteeism and, subsequently, a much higher rate of promotion.

Figure 3 illustrates the changes in performance, measured in February and March, before the study period began, and at the end of each month of the study period. The shareholder service index represents quality of letters, including accuracy of information, and speed of response to stockholders' letters of inquiry. The index of a current month was averaged into the average of the two prior months, which means that improvement was harder to obtain if the indexes of the previous months were low.

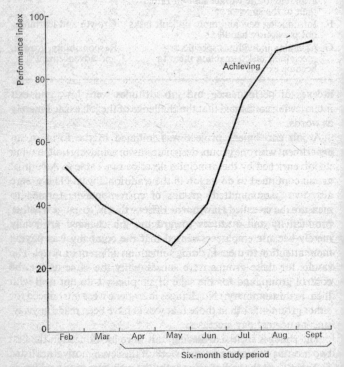

Figure 3 Shareholder service index in company experiment (three-month cumulative average)

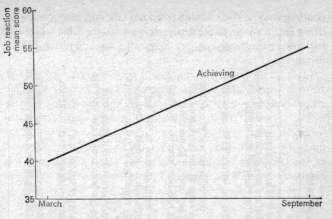

Figure 4 Changes in attitudes toward tasks in company experiment (changes in mean score over six-month period)

The 'achievers' were performing less well before the six-month period started, and their performance service index continued to decline after the introduction of the motivators, evidently because of uncertainty over their newly granted responsibilities. In the third month, however, performance improved, and soon the members of this group had reached a high level of accomplishment.

Figure 4 shows the two groups' attitudes toward their job, measured at the end of March, just before the first motivator was introduced, and again at the end of September. The correspondents were asked sixteen questions, all involving motivation. A typical one was, 'As you see it, how many opportunities do you feel that you have in your job for making worthwhile contributions?' The answers were scaled from 1 to 5, with 80 as the maximum possible score. The achievers became much more positive about their job, while the attitude of the control unit remained about the same (the drop is not statistically significant).

How was the job of these correspondents restructured? Table 2 lists the suggestions made that were deemed to be horizontal loading, and the actual vertical loading changes that were incorporated in the job of the achieving unit. The capital letters under 'Principle' after 'Vertical loading' refer to the corresponding letters in Table 1. [. . .]

Table 2 Enlargement vs. enrichment of correspondents' tasks in company experiment

Horizontal loading suggestions (rejected)	Vertical loading suggestions (adopted)	Principle
Firm quotas could be set for letters to be answered each day, using a rate which would be hard to reach.	Subject matter experts were appointed within each unit for other members of the unit to consult with before seeking supervisory help. (The supervisor had been answering all specialized and difficult questions.)	G
The women could type the letters themselves, as well as compose them, or take on any other clerical functions.	Correspondents signed their own names on letters. (The supervisor had been signing all letters.)	B
All difficult or complex inquiries could be channeled to a few women so that the remainder could achieve high rates of output. These jobs could be exchanged from time to time.	The work of the more experienced correspondents was proof-read less frequently by supervisors and was done at the correspondents' desks, dropping verification from 100 per cent to 10 per cent. (Previously, all correspondents' letters had been checked by the supervisor.)	A
The women could be rotated through units handling different customers, and then sent back to their own units.	Production was discussed, but only in terms such as 'a full day's work is expected.' As time went on, this was no longer mentioned. (Before, the group had been constantly reminded of the number of letters that needed to be answered.)	D
	Outgoing mail went directly to the mailroom without going over supervisors' desks. (The letters had always been routed through the supervisors.)	A
	Correspondents were encouraged to answer letters in a more personalized way. (Reliance on the form-letter approach had been standard practice.)	C
	Each correspondent was held personally responsible for the quality and accuracy of letters. (This responsibility had been the province of supervisor and the verifier.)	B, E

Steps to job enrichment

Now that the motivator idea has been described in practice, here are the steps that managers should take in instituting the principle with their employees:

1. Select jobs in which (a) the investment in industrial engineering does not make changes too costly, (b) attitudes are poor, (c) hygiene is becoming very costly, and (d) motivation will make a difference in performance.

2. Approach those jobs with the conviction that they can be changed. Years of tradition have led managers to believe that the content of the jobs is sacrosanct and the only scope of action that they have is in ways of stimulating people.

3. Brainstorm a list of changes that may enrich the jobs, without concern for their practicality.

4. Screen the list to eliminate suggestions that involve hygiene, rather than actual motivation.

5. Screen the list for generalities, such as 'give them more responsibility', that are rarely followed in practice. This might seem obvious; but the motivator words have never left industry; the substance has just been rationalized and organized out. Words like 'responsibility', 'growth', 'achievement', and 'challenge', for example, have been elevated to the lyrics of the patriotic anthem for all organizations. It is the old problem typified by the pledge of allegiance to the flag being more important than contributions to the country – of following the form, rather than the substance.

6. Screen the list to eliminate any *horizontal* loading suggestions.

7. Avoid direct participation by the employees whose jobs are to be enriched. Ideas they have expressed previously certainly constitute a valuable source for recommended changes, but their direct involvement contaminates the process with human relations *hygiene* and, more specifically, gives them only a *sense* of making a contribution. The job is to be changed, and it is the content that will produce the motivation, not attitudes about being involved or the challenge inherent in setting up a job. That process will be over shortly, and it is what the employees will be doing from then on

that will determine their motivation. A sense of participation will result only in short-term movement.

8. In the initial attempts at job enrichment, set up a controlled experiment. At least two equivalent groups should be chosen, one an experimental unit in which the motivators are systematically introduced over a period of time, and the other one a control group in which no changes are made. For both groups, hygiene should be allowed to follow its natural course for the duration of the experiment. Pre- and post-installation tests of performance and job attitudes are necessary to evaluate the effectiveness of the job enrichment program. The attitude test must be limited to motivator items in order to divorce the employee's view of the job he is given from all the surrounding hygiene feelings that he might have.

9. Be prepared for a drop in performance in the experimental group the first few weeks. The changeover to a new job may lead to a temporary reduction in efficiency.

10. Expect your first-line supervisors to experience some anxiety and hostility over the changes you are making. The anxiety comes from their fear that the changes will result in poorer performance for their unit. Hostility will arise when the employees start assuming what the supervisors regard as their own responsibility for performance. The supervisor without checking duties to perform may then be left with little to do.

After a successful experiment, however, the supervisor usually discovers the supervisory and managerial functions he has neglected, or which were never his because all his time was given over to checking the work of his subordinates. For example, in the R & D division of one large chemical company I know of, the supervisors of the laboratory assistants were theoretically responsible for their training and evaluation. These functions, however, had come to be performed in a routine, unsubstantial fashion. After the job enrichment program, during which the supervisors were not merely passive observers of the assistants' performance, the supervisors actually were devoting their time to reviewing performance and administering thorough training.

What has been called an employee-centered style of supervision will come about not through education of supervisors, but by changing the jobs that they do.

Concluding note

Job enrichment will not be a one-time proposition, but a continuous management function. The initial changes, however, should last for a very long period of time. There are a number of reasons for this:

1. The changes should bring the job up to the level of challenge commensurate with the skill that was hired.

2. Those who have still more ability eventually will be able to demonstrate it better and win promotion to higher-level jobs.

3. The very nature of motivators, as opposed to hygiene factors, is that they have a much longer-term effect on employees' attitudes. Perhaps the job will have to be enriched again, but this will not occur as frequently as the need for hygiene.

Not all jobs can be enriched, nor do all jobs need to be enriched. If only a small percentage of the time and money that is now devoted to hygiene, however, were given to job enrichment efforts, the return in human satisfaction and economic gain would be one of the largest dividends that industry and society have ever reaped through their efforts at better personnel management.

The argument for job enrichment can be summed up quite simply: If you have someone on a job, use him. If you can't use him on the job, get rid of him, either via automation or by selecting someone with lesser ability. If you can't use him and you can't get rid of him, you will have a motivation problem.

11 Arthur N. Turner and Paul R. Lawrence

Industrial Jobs and the Worker

Excerpts from A. N. Turner and P. R. Lawrence, *Industrial Jobs and the Worker*, Harvard University Press, 1965, Foreword, by C. R. Walker, and chapter 6, pp. v–vii, and pp. 109–30.

Foreword

The problem addressed by the authors can be expressed very simply and sharply. 'Our purpose,' they write, 'was to develop and implement a method of measuring job attributes that would help predict workers' response to their jobs across a wide range of differing technologies.' [. . .]

The authors did develop a *method* of *measuring* job attributes, calling it a 'Requisite Task Attributes Index', RTA for short.* They *implemented* their measuring method in a varied sample of industrial jobs drawn from eleven industries. They *predicted workers' response*, both subjective and behavioral, across *differing technologies*. [. . .]

Another short passage from the first chapter is even more useful in underscoring the book's aim, and the authors' basic hypotheses. '. . . this research started with the concept that every industrial job contained certain technologically determined task attributes which would influence workers' response. By "task attributes" we meant such characteristics of the job as the amount of variety, autonomy, responsibility, and interaction with others built into its design.' [. . .]

The words 'workers' response' can be usefully expanded. Evidence from this and other recent research shows that 'response' is a spectrum stretching from mild satisfaction to enthusiastic involvement in one's work; and negatively from mild dissatisfaction to obsessive dislike, behaviorally expressed in absenteeism, turnover, sabotage, or the strike. A better understanding of 'response' and its social implications as used in this

* A description of this measure is included in the selection by Hackman and Lawler (Reading 12) in this volume [Ed.].

research report emerges when one considers the nature of the job attributes considered, 'autonomy, responsibility, interaction with others', etc. Notice that the authors are here stating their initial assumption that these socially significant aspects of human work are in considerable degree 'technologically determined' and also that they have been built into the job design. The phrase 'built into' suggests that somebody has built them in. Indeed the book contains many practical hints for the architects of new industrial jobs in the future, as well as for the redesign of existing jobs which are causing work problems.

Implicit in these brief introductory sentences are the major hypotheses which the authors set out to test. There were two of them. In each the sums of the attributes of each job studied, and expressed in the R T A Index, were taken as independent variables. On the other hand, the workers' responses, measured mainly, though not wholly, by an index of high or low attendance at work, and by subjective expressions of satisfaction, were the dependent variables.

In greatly oversimplified form then, the two major hypotheses were these: That job satisfaction will be high on high R T A Index jobs, i.e. jobs that are high on autonomy, responsibility, interaction opportunities, etc., whereas satisfaction will be low on low R T A Index jobs. That there will be high attendance (low absenteeism) when R T A Index scores are high, and low attendance on low R T A jobs.

Generally speaking, these two major hypotheses were validated, a certain ambiguity, however, appearing in the 'satisfaction' finding. The ambiguity fortunately led the authors into a wholly new research path which yielded useful and unexpected results. Before turning to those results it is important to ask: What about the other factors and features of work life, supervision, the union, wages, personality traits, and other topics which previous research had tended to highlight? Did they have no effect, or did Turner and Lawrence ignore them? They had their effects, of course, and they were fully considered by the investigators as 'supplementary variables'. In fact the precise way in which each of them did or did not have substantial bearing on the other detailed findings presented is an incisive and satisfactory section of the book. The most important and definitive finding, however, is that for the total population studied – no matter what the effect of intervening variables in influencing response variables in individual cases – technologically job-determined attributes dominated worker response. This was true whether that response was positive or negative. [. . .]

As mentioned above, in analyzing the data validating one of their major hypotheses, the authors were puzzled by an ambiguity, which fortunately led to the discovery that they had neglected an important 'supplementary variable', subcultural influence. When their hypotheses were applied to two cultural subgroups in their total population, their findings were modified in a fashion to open up several useful and challenging questions. The two subcultural groups were workers in rural or town surroundings, and workers in urban or city environments. The authors called the subgroups, for short, 'Town' and 'City'. [. . .]

Chapter 6: summary and conclusions

The purpose of this chapter is to summarize the major findings of this study and their implications, as we see them, both for those responsible for the design and administration of industrial work and for researchers who wish to explore further the impact of task attributes on workers' attitude and behavior. There is a danger of reading too much into a study of this kind; at the same time our findings do have some important implications which deserve to be stated.

Summary of findings

The essential findings of the study can be stated very briefly. When attendance records were gathered and questionnaires administered to 470 male blue collar workers across a wide range of technological settings, the results, briefly stated in outline form, were as follows:

1. Perceived task attribute scores were positively related to requisite task attribute scores and to job satisfaction scores for the total population, (a) more strongly for the Town subpopulation; (b) than for the City subpopulation.

2. Requisite task attribute scores were positively related to available attendance records for the total population, (a) especially in the case of certain separate attributes (motor variety, required

interaction, autonomy, learning time, responsibility); (b) because of the strong relationship between task attributes and attendance records for the Town subpopulation; and (c) for the City subpopulation, there was no significant relationship.

3. Requisite task attribute scores were *not* significantly related to job satisfaction scores for the total population. (a) Certain separate attributes (optional interaction off-the-job, learning time, and time span of discretion) *were* positively related to job satisfaction measures; (b) for the Town subpopulation there was a *positive* relationship between job satisfaction and task attribute scores (especially object variety, required interaction, optional interaction off-the-job, learning time, ambiguity of remedial action, and cycle time); and (c) for the City subpopulation there was a negative relationship between job satisfaction and task attribute scores (especially motor variety and required interaction).

4. 'Situational factors', some of which might be considered as alternate attitudinal measures of response to task attributes, did not in general alter the above relationship between task attributes and response, although the following findings were noted: (a) company satisfaction and union satisfaction were positively related to task attributes for Town workers and negatively related to task attributes for City workers; union satisfaction was negatively related to interaction and responsibility for the total population; (b) foreman satisfaction was negatively related to task attributes, especially for City workers, and to variety for the total population; and (c) pay was negatively related to attendance, and Town workers in the lowest pay quartile tended to have low job satisfaction; pay had a curvilinear relationship to task attributes (low on medium jobs, high on high and low jobs).

5. Individual background factors did not in general alter the above relationships between task attributes and response, although the following findings were noted: (a) age was positively related to job satisfaction for Town (and all) workers, to task attributes for City (and all) workers, and negatively to pay for City workers; (b) seniority was positively related to job satisfaction for Town workers, to task attributes for all workers, to pay for Town workers, and negatively to pay for City workers; (c) education was

negatively related to job satisfaction for City workers, positively to task attributes for Town and City workers, and positively to pay for Town (and all) workers; and (d) F-scale scores were positively related to job satisfaction for City (and all) workers and to pay for Town workers.

The above outline summarizes the major findings of this study. Each of these findings implies further research steps that could be taken as well as possible actions by management. What follows is a discussion of the implications of the various findings that appear most important or interesting to us. [. . .]

Implications for practice

What are the action implications of this study for the management of industrial work? There are always two dangers in evaluating the practical impact of a study of this kind: the findings may be taken too literally; on the other hand, the findings may not be taken seriously enough. In order to avoid these dangers, perhaps the most useful question for a manager to ask is not 'What does this study tell me I should do?' but 'What can I learn from this study that will help me in deciding for myself what ought to be done?' We believe that the procedures and findings of this study can indeed help a manager predict some of the human consequences of alternative courses of action, and in this sense help him in deciding what policies to pursue.

The difficulty of specifying the action implications of a study of this kind is that our findings are based upon the response of workers with various predispositions to a wide range of situations, whereas intelligent action by management necessitates knowledge and understanding in depth of the concrete details of one particular situation. From the point of view of increasing knowledge of organizational behavior in general, it helps to discover that among 470 workers on forty-seven jobs in eleven organizations the response to various task attributes was as we have described it. But to guide policy and action, the need is to know how a particular group of workers, with their own needs and predispositions, will respond to the specific variations in *job design* and *supervisory behavior*,* for example, that are feasible under circumstances peculiar to that situation.

* Italics added [Ed.].

Our findings cannot answer that question. However, our findings can provide, we believe, more useful ways than existed previously of asking such questions and of attempting to find answers for them. Therefore, our format for discussing the implications of this research will *illustrate* how it could be used in raising and trying to answer questions under certain specified conditions. Since we have been concerned with a *range* of task attributes from 'simple' to 'complex', and with two different patterns of response (Town and City 'predispositions'), we have organized the following discussion under four polar or prototypical sets of circumstances, depending upon whether the technology tends to establish 'simple' or 'complex' task attributes, and whether the social system or subculture tends to establish a 'Town' or a 'City' pattern of response. Of course these four sets of circumstances are hypothetical; they are, in a sense, four 'ideal types', selected only to help illustrate how under different kinds of actual circumstances the approach and findings of this study might be utilized. Inevitably also the discussion will bring out how much we do *not* know about questions raised by this approach. Therefore, although what follows is organized around implications for the practitioner, we will simultaneously be repeating some implications for the researcher. ... To us this overlap between action and research implications is inevitable, since our main research interest in this area is to increase that kind of knowledge which can usefully be applied to the questions which the practitioner should raise.

General relevance of attribute scores

Before taking up the questions raised by this study for managements in each of the four 'prototypical' situations just referred to, it is important to re-emphasize the practical consequences for any management of the strong relationships in our total population between requisite and perceived task attributes, and between perceived task attributes and job satisfaction. These findings imply that the task attribute rating scales used in this study, or at least the general way of thinking about job characteristics which these scales represent, should be useful to managers and engineers responsible for the design of new jobs or for the redesign of existing jobs. In particular, these procedures should be practically useful whenever a management wants to experiment with new approaches to job design in which human response to the intrinsic nature of the work is more carefully taken into account. Not only how the job scores on these various attributes but also how workers *perceive* the particular attributes will be highly relevant in predicting worker response to any projected change in job design. During the course of this research, we came into contact with several managers and industrial engineers who were actively experimenting with various ways of 'enlarging' the job. We hope that this study not only will encourage such efforts in a general way, but also will provide specific procedures for studying the impact of the relevant job characteristics. Only through continued work of this kind within interested organizations can the usefulness of these procedures be proved and, more importantly, improved.

Town setting and simple technology

When the technology establishes inherently low scoring task attributes, the Town type of predisposition to work will tend to produce an unfavorable response to the job. What can management do about this situation?

One approach to the problem would be to attempt to alter the predisposition, for example, through a hiring policy which selects only workers who do not share the prevailing, more involved attitude toward the characteristics of the work they are asked to perform. There are many obvious difficulties in such a policy. It would take a long time to implement through normal turnover. If a technological change in the direction of more task complexity should occur, the success of such a policy would have most undesirable consequences. And it would result in a working population that might well become more resistant to technological change of any kind; disinvolvement in the task itself probably is associated, over time, with disaffection with wider organizational goals. In short, even if it were possible to change from a Town to a City type of predisposition – which is not at all clear – to do so would contradict a value shared by many managements that workers' experience on the job should be more rather than less meaningful and involving for them.

Nevertheless, for certain jobs, where no change in the direction of greater potential interest seems likely or possible, it will presumably be advisable to try to select those workers who do not object to, or who prefer, simple, less demanding work. In part this will be accomplished by a natural selection process, especially where there is considerable voluntary mobility between jobs. In any case, management needs to be aware of the unintended consequences that may result from any selection policy favoring workers whose values and behavior are noticeably different from the prevailing norms of a particular subcultural setting.

Another approach would be to attempt to compensate for lack of interest in the job by increasing pay and other extrinsic rewards. In the long run this does not seem likely to succeed in Town settings. Such a policy incurs the risk of arousing attitudes of felt injustice, especially if Town values are prevalent, when work which asks more of the individual, e.g. medium R T A jobs, receives lower pay than work which requires a lower personal investment or opportunity to contribute. Furthermore, such a policy implies that management assumes that workers perceive the task primarily in terms of cost rather than as potentially rewarding for its own sake. A worker with a strong Town predisposition is likely to be insulted by such an assumption. In certain cases it is, of course, necessary to utilize extrinsic rewards in order to induce the performance of inherently unpleasant work. But it appears to us that paying more for intrinsically less rewarding work should only be undertaken as a conscious choice, after weighing the possible long-run consequences against the immediate necessity.

A more promising solution to the problem of simple task attributes in Town settings is to experiment with modifications in the attributes themselves, and in formal role requirements, in order to structure a situation at work which engages more of the potential interest in the task that is characteristic of the Town worker's attitude. More frequently than is usually realized, it is possible in new job designs to increase requisite autonomy and responsibility beyond the levels traditionally assumed by modern work methods study. In the case of existing technologies and jobs, it is also possible to increase variety, for example, by encouraging job rotation. And even within highly automated technologies, many steps can be taken to increase perceived autonomy and responsibility, for example, through encouraging worker decision making on many aspects of quality control, scheduling, etc., as well as on issues not directly related to task attributes such as hours of work and rest pauses.

In short, this study strongly implies that management faced with Town predispositions and the kind of modern technology usually associated with simple, undemanding work, should recognize that even if the technology requires some low scoring attributes, often other requisite and associated attributes can be changed. We suggest that management experiment, in these cases, with a more discriminating and selective form of job enlargement. Often a careful investigation of a particular situation may show that the particular attributes which are contributing most strongly to workers' dissatisfaction can be considerably 'enlarged' without any significant change in the basic technology.

Some of the disappointing results from 'job enlargement' to date seem to have been the result of a too indiscriminate application of the concept. For example, a technology that permits little variation or choice in pace of working (e.g. a mechanized assembly line) does *not* necessarily prevent considerable enlargement of autonomy and responsibility in regard to quality or even methods. Sometimes a failure to think separately about the different task attributes has led management to install, without adequate consultation with the workers themselves, dramatic enlargement of some attributes only at the expense of unpopular changes in other attributes that were equally as or more important to the workers involved. The same change that greatly increases variety and responsibility may produce large and very unwelcome decreases in interaction and autonomy. For example, a group of fifteen workers on a rotary conveyor are given individual work stations surrounded by high banks of parts, and each is assigned to assemble the total product according to a carefully predetermined method and sequence. This tendency to overemphasize variety and to underemphasize autonomy and optional interaction seems to have characterized several unsuccessful examples of job enlargement that have come to our attention. The worker may perceive his task as a whole, but management, in designing changes, needs to consider separately the different attributes which compose the total task. The task rating procedures of this study are designed for this purpose, and can be improved as they are further used in this way.

Town setting and complex technology

What important questions are raised for management when the technology requires or permits high scoring task attributes and the predominant worker predisposition is for a favorable response to relatively complex work? In this case, presumably the demands of the technology and the predispositions of the work force are 'in line' with each other, and the problem is to preserve and capitalize on the inherently satisfying and productive relationship. It is important to remember that in this situation, more clearly than in any other, *intrinsic* rewards are important. The underlying predisposition implies perceiving the job itself as a potentially rewarding and involving experience; it is important (and also comparatively easy, thanks to the technology) for management also to think of the worker's task in this way, to recognize the value of what the worker can contribute. While this point may seem obvious, all too often management, by misapplying work simplification and standardization to situations of this kind, frustrates not only the logic of the given technology, but the predispositions of the work force as well. The conceptual approach to task attributes we have presented can help management identify this type of situation and thus avoid this kind of mistake.

In addition, of course, management may have the problem of preserving existing task complexity when faced with the necessity for technological change. Some needed changes in process or product may inevitably threaten to decrease some of the high scoring task attributes to which workers are responding favorably. If so, the most important thing to remember may be the importance, to these workers, of perceived autonomy. More clearly than in other situations, undesirable consequences of technological change can be avoided to the extent that these workers actively participate in recognizing the need for change and in planning its impact. They are likely, it would seem, to have both the predisposition and the ability to devise ways of adapting to needed change while preserving existing levels of commitment to the importance of the work itself and of total organizational goals.

City setting and simple technology

The favorable response both of Town workers to complex tasks and of City workers to simple tasks can be interpreted as alternate expressions of the same underlying human tendency to value highly a sense of control and predictability in the environment. To a Town predisposition high perceived responsibility and autonomy imply a sense of predictability and control, whereas to a City predisposition high required interaction and motor variety threaten it. City workers apparently adapt to relatively low scoring task attributes as part of a total work environment which they have learned to expect.

The City type of response to low scoring task attributes underlies the importance of external rewards, and of a feeling of equity in regard to personnel policies as a whole. There is more chance here than in other situations for management to preserve an existing favorable level of morale by means of what Herzberg has called 'hygienic factors': security, fair treatment, expeditious handling of grievances, high 'consideration' in supervisory behavior, and so forth. A high degree of job involvement is not available and apparently of less importance as a means of encouraging a favorable response. Both management and the worker may have learned to be satisfied with 'a fair day's work for a fair day's pay'.

Many managers may well feel, however, that this state of affairs is not entirely satisfactory, in fact that it raises some very serious questions for the long run. As was suggested in an earlier chapter, it may be a kind of adaptation that leads over time to strong feelings of frustration at having become so comfortably adapted to a situation in which the work itself is comparatively meaningless to the individual. There may be a danger of creating a working population that is essentially unconcerned with the larger purposes of the organization and that is exceptionally resistant to future needs for change. Managers with these concerns will want, in spite of a presently 'favorable' response, to experiment with selective changes in task attributes to determine the extent to which a need to contribute more constructively to the immediate job can be stimulated among workers whose previous experience has taught them not to expect to become very personally involved in the work itself.

If the technology requires task complexity, but the work force is characterized by what we have called 'City predisposition', the major question for management is whether such a predisposition is permanent or subject to change over time. The use of the word 'predisposition' in this study unfortunately may have a more fundamental and unchanging implication than is warranted. The fact is that on the basis of the present research we do not know how amenable to change the City pattern of response may be. Further research on this subject is needed, especially clinical studies of various groups of City workers *over time*, influenced by different kinds of management practices and supervisory behavior.

Pending further evidence, our tendency is to think of the two patterns of response *not* as though they represented basically different sets of needs, but as alternative ways of attempting to satisfy much the same kinds of underlying needs. We assume that to a large extent workers are or can be *trained* to prefer one of these alternatives to the other, trained by their past and continuing interaction with their total environment, including management and supervision. It is emphatically not a useful assumption to label all 'City' workers as incapable of learning a more positive response to task complexity. Such an assumption is dangerously likely to become a self-fulfilling prophecy, since workers are not likely to learn to pay more attention to the intrinsic rewards in the work itself if management believes them incapable of doing so.

In considering the susceptibility to change of City response patterns we should reiterate our belief that these are essentially group or social system phenomena. This suggests that efforts to change the City-type response to complex work, for example, may only succeed if perceived as congruent and not threatening to a wider set of social values and norms in the particular group involved. It is difficult if not impossible to make any general statements about how this might be done, except by means of a sensitive understanding of the total human and social content of the particular situation. One very definite statement *can* be made: this kind of change in predisposition will *not* come about simply by telling individual workers that they ought to have a different attitude toward the job, nor can it be effectively forced by external pressure.

In order to stimulate a higher level of job interest and involvement, and consequently a more favorable response to complex work, it is first necessary to assume that the workers involved are capable of such a response. For management and supervisory behavior based on this assumption to be successful requires in addition a high level of ability to understand the complexities of a given human and social situation, and great skill in relating effectively to it.

Especially in relationship to the 'City' response, it is important to appreciate the danger of reaching too many hasty conclusions based on the data of this study before additional research has been conducted to test and refine the present findings. However, even with the present limited data, it appears that certain experimental actions might well be taken, especially when there exist methods of investigating the consequences of what is done. For example, the fact that satisfaction appeared to be higher for City as well as for Town workers on jobs with high scores on time span of discretion should be noted. This is another attribute in which changes can be made without necessarily changing the basic technology. It appears to us that many workers in City as well as Town settings are willing and anxious to take a much higher degree of interest in quality questions than is usually assumed by present job-design procedures. In certain situations there may be an opportunity purposefully to increase time span of discretion beyond the existing level, while holding other variables relatively constant, and then to discover whether this increase in responsibility is associated with a more favorable response to the job.

It is important to remember that the negative relationship between task characteristics and job satisfaction for City workers was only significant, in a statistical sense, for two of our separate task attributes, motor variety and required interaction. This seems to confirm the utility of Baldamus' concept of 'Traction' in explaining favorable response to relatively repetitive work. The finding suggests that when the nature of the technology requires low scoring task attributes, it is important for the job design and supervisory procedures to avoid interruptions (dis-tractions) if workers are to continue to feel pleasurably pulled along by the rhythm inherent in the activity.

This also serves as a reminder that just because the various task attributes were very closely associated with one another in this study, this does not have to be the case. Many jobs *could* be designed, for example, so as to combine relatively high perceived responsibility and autonomy with low motor variety and infrequent interrupts of the 'working mood'. According to our findings, such a combination might result in a favorable response from workers with *both* kinds of predisposition. It would seem that performing even simple work smoothly and well can be inherently satisfying, especially when there are opportunities for workers to contribute directly to improvements in methods and to solving the design problems associated with product or model changes. It would be a mistake to generalize with confidence about how workers with various predispositions will respond to such combinations of task attributes, but some imaginative experimentation of this kind by management in a particular location might well uncover ways of stimulating a more positive response to work formerly regarded as irritatingly monotonous.

Before closing, let us emphasize that the preceding discussion has presented some *illustrations* of how the findings and approaches of this study could be utilized in certain prototypical situations. In practice, predispositions are not wholly 'Town' or 'City', and usually the work is not clearly 'simple' or 'complex'. Nevertheless, we hope to have suggested some practical approaches to structuring more positive responses to work under any particular combination of predispositions and task attributes.

Primarily this research argues for greater flexibility, experimentation, and open-mindedness concerning technology and human response to work. Both critics and defenders of modern technology have overgeneralized its human impact because they lacked a practical way to study the specific job characteristics that were relevant. The administration of changing technological settings and the study of the relationships between technology and organizational behavior can both be improved by continued detailed attention to those concrete task attributes that have proved relevant to workers' response.

Finally, this need is clearly becoming increasingly acute with the increasing rate of technological change. Automation apparently has varying effects on the nature of work; sometimes greater task complexity results when a process is automated, and sometimes the work becomes much less demanding and less complex. And the effects of automation on different task attributes may well be in opposite directions – less interaction but more responsibility, for example. Furthermore, whether or not automation exists or is feasible, any technological change may eventually render obsolete associations that are culturally attached to different kinds of work. Often the job label stays the same after a radical change in the nature of the work experience. We need to keep our ideas about work in touch with the reality that is experienced on the job. We need to increase our ability to understand and take into account how human beings do in fact respond to different concrete characteristics of work. Only in this way will we increase our ability to cope realistically with what Mayo called 'the seamy side' of technological progress.

12 J. Richard Hackman and Edward E. Lawler III

Conditions Under Which Jobs Will Facilitate Internal Motivation: A Conceptual Framework

Excerpts from J. R. Hackman and E. E. Lawler III, 'Employee reactions to job characteristics', *Journal of Applied Psychology*, vol. 55, 1971, pp. 259–65.

Researchers and managers alike are increasingly attending to the way jobs are designed as an important factor in determining the motivation, satisfaction, and performance of employees at work. This is not to say that jobs previously have been seen as irrelevant to organizational administration. On the contrary, earlier in this century when scientific management was in its prime, considerable research effort was expended to find ways that jobs could be simplified, specialized, standardized, and routinized. At the same time, industrial psychologists were developing rather complex and sophisticated procedures for describing and analyzing jobs in terms of their simplest components, as a means of evaluating the skill levels required for different jobs. The results of job analyses have been used to establish fair rates of pay, for training purposes, and in personnel selection (see, for example, Ghiselli and Brown, 1955; Lytle, 1946; Stigers and Reed, 1944). The general expectation of the scientific management approach was that by simplifying jobs, work could be carried out more efficiently; less-skilled employees would be required; the control of management over production would be increased; and, ultimately, organizational profits would be enhanced.

In recent years, numerous scholars have documented a number of unintended and unfortunate consequences of the trend toward work simplification (for example, Argyris, 1964; Blauner, 1964; Davis, 1957; Friedmann, 1961; Guest, 1955; Herzberg, Mausner and Snyderman, 1959; Walker, 1950; Walker and Guest, 1952). In brief, it has been shown that simple, routine nonchallenging jobs often lead to high employee dissatisfaction, to increased absenteeism and turnover, and to substantial difficulties in effectively managing employees who work on simplified jobs.[1] The expected increases in profitability from work simplification have not materialized as had been hoped, and the reasons apparently have very much to do with the human problems encountered when jobs are standardized and simplified.

Partially in response to the above findings, a number of researchers began experimentally enlarging various jobs to determine whether or not worker productivity and satisfaction would increase if jobs were designed so as to be more generally meaningful and challenging to employees. By and large, those job enlargement experiments which have been reported in the literature have been considered successful (see, for example, Biggane and Stewart, 1963; Conant and Kilbridge, 1965; Davis and Valfer, 1965; Ford, 1969; Kilbridge, 1960; Pelissier, 1965). With few exceptions, however, job enlargement experiments have been case studies and often have lacked appropriate experimental controls. Hulin and Blood (1968) review the research literature on job enlargement in some detail and are especially attentive to possible difficulties in procedure and methodology which may cast doubt on the generality or the validity of the findings reported.

Perhaps equally as disturbing as the uneven level of methodological rigor which has characterized job enlargement studies is the almost total absence of any systematic conceptual or theoretical basis for the studies which have been done. As a result, after dozens of experiments, little cumulative knowledge has been gained regarding the effects and effectiveness of job redesign. Job enlargement experiments, for example, have typically involved a number of simultaneous changes – such as in the amount of variety in the work, the amount of responsibility required, the degree to which working with others is an important part of the enlarged job, etc. Very little is known about which of these (or of other) aspects of the redesigned job are in fact responsible for observed behavioral and attitudinal changes. Further, the generality of job enlargement effects is largely unknown (e.g., whether they are effective only for certain types of workers or whether they are relevant only to certain kinds of jobs). More case studies are not likely to contribute very much to the development of answers to crucial

1. These observations have not, however, gone unchallenged. See, for example, Kilbridge (1961) and MacKinney, Wernimont and Galitz (1962).

questions such as these. Instead, what appears to be needed are conceptual frameworks which generate testable propositions about how job characteristics affect employees under various circumstances, and empirical research which is designed explicitly to test these propositions. This article proposes one way of conceptualizing the impact of job characteristics on individual work behavior and attitudes. [. . .]

Previous theory and research

Some progress toward the development of theory relevant to job design has been made in recent years. The well-known two-factor theory of Herzberg (Herzberg, Mausner and Snyderman, 1959; Herzberg, 1966), for example, can be used to derive general propositions regarding conditions on the job which will be motivating and satisfying to employees. In particular, the theory suggests that a job should enhance employee motivation to the extent that it provides opportunities for (a) achievement, (b) recognition, (c) responsibility, (d) advancement, and (e) growth in competence. These principles have given rise to a series of generally successful job enlargement experiments in the American Telephone and Telegraph Company (summarized by Ford, 1969).

Unfortunately, a number of researchers have been unable to provide empirical support for some of the major tenets of the theory from which the principles used in the AT&T studies were derived (e.g., Dunnette, Campbell and Hakel, 1967; Hinton, 1968; King, 1970), and the general conceptual status of the theory must presently be considered uncertain. Further, the theory has not yet been elaborated to specify how characteristics of workers interact with the presence or absence of the five motivating conditions in determining worker performance and satisfaction. Finally, the theory in its present form does not specify how the presence or absence of the motivating conditions can be measured for existing jobs. This makes it very difficult to test the theory and to generate unambiguous predictions from it about the effects of specific changes which may be contemplated for existing jobs.

The problem of measuring job characteristics has been explicitly and carefully dealt with by Turner and Lawrence (1965). These authors developed operational measures of six 'requisite task attributes' which, on the basis of a review of existing literature and an *a priori* conceptual framework, were predicted to be positively related to worker satisfaction and attendance. The six attributes are: (a) variety, (b) autonomy, (c) required interaction, (d) optional interaction, (e) knowledge and skill required, and (f) responsibility. [. . .]

Examination of the relationships among the six requisite task attributes for forty-seven jobs revealed that the attributes were very closely related to one another. Therefore, Turner and Lawrence developed a summary measure called the Requisite Task Attribute Index (RTA Index) by formulating a linear combination of the six separately measured attributes. This summary index was then used in ascertaining the relationships between the attributes of the jobs and worker job satisfaction and attendance.

The authors' expectation that employees working on jobs which were high on the RTA Index would have higher job satisfaction and lower absenteeism was not fully supported. Instead, it appeared that the predicted relationship between the RTA Index and employee reactions held only for workers from factories located in small towns. [. . .]

Blood and Hulin (1967) and Hulin and Blood (1968) provide additional data on the importance of subcultural factors in determining worker responses to the makeup of their jobs. These authors hypothesize that an important moderating factor is alienation from the traditional work norms which characterize the middle class. When employees hold traditional values regarding the value of work and achievement in work settings (as would be expected of the employees in small town factories in the Turner and Lawrence study), more complex jobs should be responded to positively. When employees are alienated from these norms (as might be expected of urban workers), more complex jobs should be responded to negatively. Blood and Hulin (1967) provide data supporting this general proposition and propose a three-dimensional response surface (Hulin and Blood, 1968) which specifies the expected interrelationships among worker alienation, job level, and satisfaction with work. [. . .]

Both Turner and Lawrence (1965) and Hulin and Blood (1968) choose to deal with individual differences on a subcultural or sociological level (i.e. in terms of differences between town and city workers or in terms of the alienation of city workers from middle-class work norms).

An alternative strategy would be to attempt to conceptualize and measure the relevant individual differences directly at the individual level of analysis. The town–city conceptualization assumes a substantial homogeneity of worker characteristics and response tendencies for employees within the two cultural settings. To the extent that there are substantial individual differences among town workers and among city workers, an attempt to measure relevant individual differences directly at the individual level would seem to have considerable merit. The difficulty in implementing this alternative approach, of course, is that it requires prior specification on a conceptual level of what specific differences among people are responsible for the results reported by Turner and Lawrence (1965) and Blood and Hulin (1967), i.e. what it is about people that moderates the way they react to their jobs. In the following paragraphs, we will propose such a conceptualization, and derive from it a number of predictions about the effects of job characteristics on employee satisfaction and motivation.

Jobs and individuals: a conceptual framework

The present conceptualization of the interaction between job characteristics and individual differences is based primarily on the expectancy theory of motivation, as formulated by Lewin (1938) and Tolman (1959), and as applied to work settings by Vroom (1964), Porter and Lawler (1968), and others. In particular, five propositions based on expectancy theory are suggested below, which address the specific problem of how employee motivation can be enhanced through the design of jobs.

1. To the extent that an individual believes that he can obtain an outcome he values by engaging in some particular behavior or class of behaviors, the likelihood that he will actually engage in that behavior is enhanced. Relevant valued outcomes can be both intrinsic (e.g. feelings of accomplishment or of personal worth) and extrinsic (e.g. material goods); the only requirement is that the outcomes be valued by the individual. When an individual anticipates obtaining some valued outcome as a result of a con-

templated action or course of action, that outcome may be termed an incentive for engaging in the action.

2. Outcomes are valued by individuals to the extent that they satisfy the physiological or psychological needs of the individual, or to the extent that they lead to other outcomes which satisfy such needs or are expected by the individual to do so. Such need satisfaction need not, of course, be in the objective best interest of the individual. People frequently strive for satisfying states of affairs which are quite inconsistent with their long-term well-being (Locke, 1969). Nevertheless, if an outcome is not somehow linked to satisfaction, it will not continue to be valued and therefore cannot continue to serve as an incentive.

3. Thus, to the extent that conditions at work can be arranged so that employees can satisfy their own needs best by working effectively toward organizational goals, employees will in fact tend to work hard toward the achievement of these goals (McGregor, 1960).

4. Most lower level needs (e.g. physical well-being, security) can be, and often are, reasonably well satisfied for individuals in contemporary society on a continuing basis and, therefore, will not serve as motivational incentives except under unusual circumstances. This is not the case, however, for certain higher order needs (e.g. needs for personal growth and development or for feelings of worthwhile accomplishment). A person may experience higher order need satisfaction on a continuing basis without the strength of desire for additional satisfaction of these needs diminishing. Indeed, it may be that additional satisfaction of higher order needs actually increases their strength (Alderfer, 1969). This is an important possibility since it suggests that the opportunity for the development of continuing (and possibly even increasing) motivation is much more a reality when higher order needs are engaged than is the case for more easily satisfied lower order needs. There is, of course, a major cost associated with any motivational approach in which higher order needs are central: not all employees can or will respond to opportunities for the satisfaction of higher order needs, and thus motivational approaches based on these needs cannot be applied indiscriminantly. Maslow (1943, 1954) and Alderfer (1969, 1971) discuss in much

more complete detail the nature of higher order needs and their motivational implications.

5. Individuals who are capable of higher order need satisfaction will in fact experience such satisfaction when they learn that they have, as a result of their own efforts, accomplished something that they personally believe is worthwhile or meaningful (see Argyris, 1964; Lewin, Dembo, Festinger and Sears, 1944). Specifically, individuals who desire higher order need satisfactions should be most likely to obtain them when they work effectively on meaningful jobs which provide feedback on the adequacy of their personal work activities. To establish conditions for internal work motivation, then, it appears that a job must: (a) allow workers to feel personally responsible for an identifiable and meaningful portion of the work, (b) provide work outcomes which are intrinsically meaningful or otherwise experienced as worthwhile, and (c) provide feedback about performance effectiveness. The harder and better an individual works on such a job, the more opportunities he will have to experience higher order need satisfactions and the more incentive there can be for continued effective performance. Higher order need satisfactions, therefore, are seen both as (a) a result of, rather than a determinant of, effective performance (Lawler and Porter, 1967), and (b) an incentive for continued efforts to perform effectively.[2]

The five propositions outlined above lead to the conclusion that it may be possible under specifiable conditions simultaneously to achieve high employee satisfaction and high employee effort toward organizational goals. Specifically, the long-term congruence of high satisfaction and high effort is seen as depending upon (a) the existence of employee desires for higher order need satisfaction and (b) conditions on the job such that working hard and effectively toward organizational goals will bring about satisfaction of these needs.

2. It should be noted that only higher order satisfactions are predicted to be increased by effective work on a job with the characteristics outlined above; other satisfactions, e.g. pay satisfaction, satisfaction with supervision, may not be affected.

•

Characteristics of motivating jobs

The three general job characteristics identified above as central in developing a congruence between individual need satisfaction and organizational goal achievement must be describable in more measurable terms if the validity of the conceptualization proposed here is to be tested. In the following paragraphs, therefore, each of the three general characteristics are examined in somewhat more detail. In addition, it will be proposed that four of the requisite task attributes proposed by Turner and Lawrence (1965) are likely to be useful as measures of the three general job characteristics.

1. The job must allow a worker to feel personally responsible for a meaningful portion of his work. What is accomplished must be through the individual's own efforts. He must realize that the work he does is his own. And he must believe that he personally is responsible for whatever successes and failures occur as a result of his work. Only if what is accomplished is seen as one's own can an individual experience a feeling of personal success and a gain in self-esteem. This does not mean, of course, that feelings of personal responsibility for work outcomes cannot occur in team projects; all that is required is for team members to feel that their own efforts are important in accomplishing the task at hand.

The autonomy dimension, as specified by Turner and Lawrence (1965), would seem to tap the degree to which workers feel personal responsibility for their work. In jobs high on measured autonomy, workers will tend to feel that they own the outcomes of their work; in jobs low on autonomy, a worker may more often feel that successes and failures on the job are more often due to the good work, or to the incompetence, of other workers or of his supervisor.[3]

2. The job must provide outcomes which are intrinsically meaningful or otherwise experienced as worthwhile to the individual. If a

3. Having high autonomy on the job does not, of course, necessarily imply that one will have major control over the work outcomes achieved. There may be a number of factors in the work environment which affect the nature of work outcomes, over which the worker has little meaningful control. For example, a football quarterback has high autonomy in selection plays but only a moderate level of personal control over the outcomes obtained from execution of the plays. Thus, work autonomy is probably best viewed as a necessary but not sufficient condition for feeling personal responsibility for work outcomes.

worker feels that the results of his efforts are not very important, it is unlikely that he will feel especially good if he works effectively. Instead, he must achieve something that he personally feels is worthwhile and important if he is to be able to experience positive feelings about himself as a result of his efforts. It clearly is not possible to indicate for people in general what kinds of job characteristics will be likely to provide outcomes seen as meaningful and worthwhile; people differ too much in the kinds of things they value for any statement of such generality to be made. It is possible, however, to provide some such specifications for individuals who have high desires, for higher order need satisfaction and, of course, these are the individuals to whom the present conceptualization is intended to apply.

There are at least two ways that work can come to be experienced as meaningful for employees with relatively high desires for higher order need satisfaction. The first is for the job to be a sufficiently whole piece of work that the worker can perceive that he has produced or accomplished something of consequence. In terms of a Turner and Lawrence task attribute, this would be expected to be the case when a job is high on task identity. According to Turner and Lawrence (1965, p. 157), jobs high on task identity are characterized by (a) a very clear cycle of perceived closure – the job provides a distinct sense of the beginning and ending of a transformation process, (b) high visibility of the transformation to the worker, (c) high visibility of the transformation in the finished product, and (d) a transformation of considerable magnitude. For a worker who has high needs for developing and using his competence, a job with such characteristics generally would be expected to be experienced as highly meaningful and worthwhile.

In addition, the experienced meaningfulness of work may be enhanced when a job provides a worker with the opportunity to accomplish something by using skills and abilities which he personally values. For example, a strongly motivated duffer feels good when he hits a solid tee shot, even though the broader significance of this event is doubtful. His golfing skills are on the line when he steps to the tee; those skills are important to him; he performs well – and that, in itself, is enough.

Jobs high on the Turner and Lawrence (1965) dimension of

variety would be expected to provide opportunities for workers to experience this kind of meaningfulness on the job, since high variety jobs typically tap a number of different skills which may be important to the employee. Thus, working on high variety jobs may become personally meaningful to some employees through a process very analogous to that which makes golf meaningful to the duffer. It should be noted, however, that only variety which does in fact challenge the worker will be expected to be experienced as meaningful to workers with desires for higher order need satisfaction; screwing many different sizes of nuts on many different colors of bolts, if this could be considered variety, would not be expected to be experienced as meaningful.[4]

To summarize, it may be that jobs can come to be experienced as meaningful to employees to the extent that they involve doing a whole piece of work of some significance, i.e. have high task identity, and, at the same time, to the extent that they give employees the chance to use their valued skills and abilities, i.e. to be challenged, in doing the work. In many cases the latter condition may be met on jobs which have high variety.

3. The job must provide feedback about what is accomplished. Even if the two general conditions discussed above are met, an employee cannot experience higher order need satisfaction when he performs effectively unless he obtains some kind of feedback about how he is doing. Such feedback may come from doing the task itself, e.g. when a telephone operator successfully completes a long distance person-to-person call, but performance feedback also may come from some other person – an esteemed co-worker, a supervisor, etc. The crucial condition is that feedback be present in a form that is believable to the worker, so that a realistic basis exists for the satisfaction, or frustration, of higher order needs.

It should be emphasized that, for all of the job characteristics discussed above, it is not their objective state which affects em-

4. It is also possible, of course, for a job to have too much variety. Activation theory (e.g. Scott, 1966) suggests that when variety is too high, employees may experience a general state of muscular and mental hypertension which can greatly handicap performance effectiveness. In addition, Hall and Lawler (1970) found that among research scientists, high job variety can be associated with low job satisfaction, apparently because jobs with high variety also tended to be low in task identity and feedback.

ployee attitudes and behavior, but rather how they are experienced by the employees. Regardless of the amount of feedback (or variety, or autonomy, or task identity) a worker really has in his work, it is how much *he perceives that he has* which will affect his reactions to the job. Objective job characteristics are important because they do affect the perceptions and experiences of employees. But there are often substantial differences between objective job characteristics and how they are perceived by employees, and it is dangerous to assume that simply because the objective characteristics of a job have been measured, or changed, that the way that job is experienced by employees has been dealt with as well.

In summary, then, it has been argued that the characteristics of jobs can establish conditions which will enhance the intrinsic motivation of workers who desire higher order need satisfaction. In particular, it has been suggested, in terms of a subset of the Turner and Lawrence (1965) dimensions, that such individuals will be able to obtain meaningful personal satisfaction when they perform well on jobs which they experience as high on variety, autonomy, task identity and feedback. Further, the harder and better an individual performs on a job which is perceived as high on these dimensions, the more satisfaction he is likely to feel. [. . .]

References

ALDERFER, C. P. (1969), 'An empirical test of a new theory of human needs', *Organizational Behavior and Human Performance*, vol. 4, pp. 142–75.

ALDERFER, C. P. (1971), *Human Needs in Organizational Settings*, Free Press.

ARGYRIS, C. (1964), *Integrating the Individual and the Organization*, Wiley.

BIGGANE, J. F., and STEWART, P. A. (1963), *Job Enlargement: A Case Study*, Research Series no. 25, State University of Iowa, Bureau of Labor and Management.

BLAUNER, R. (1964), *Alienation and Freedom*, University of Chicago Press.

BLOOD, M. R., and HULIN, C. L. (1967), 'Alienation, environmental characteristics and worker responses', *Journal of Applied Psychology*, vol. 51, pp. 284–90.

CONANT, E. H., and KILBRIDGE, M. D. (1965), 'An interdisciplinary analysis of job enlargement: technology, costs and behavioral implications', *Industrial and Labor Relations Review*, vol. 3, pp. 377–95.

DAVIS, L. E. (1957), 'Job design and productivity: a new approach', *Personnel*, vol. 33, pp. 418–29.

DAVIS, L. E., and VALFER, E. S. (1965), 'Intervening responses to changes in supervisor job designs', *Occupational Psychology*, vol. 39, pp. 171–89.

DUNNETTE, M. D., CAMPBELL, J. P., and HAKEL, M. D. (1967), 'Factors contributing to job satisfaction and job dissatisfaction in six occupational groups', *Organizational Behavior and Human Performance*, vol. 2, pp. 143–74.

FORD, R. N. (1969), *Motivation Through the Work Itself*, American Management Association.

FRIEDMANN, G. (1961), *The Anatomy of Work*, Free Press.

GHISELLI, E. E., and BROWN, C. W. (1955), *Personal and Industrial Psychology*, McGraw-Hill.

GUEST, R. H. (1955), 'Men and machines: an assembly-line worker looks at his job', *Personnel*, vol. 31, pp. 3–10.

HALL, D. T., and LAWLER, E. E. (1970), 'Job design and job pressure as facilitators of professional–organization integration', *Administrative Science Quarterly*, vol. 15, pp. 271–81.

HERZBERG, F. (1966), *Work and the Nature of Man*, Harcourt, Brace & World.

HERZBERG, F., MAUSNER, B., and SNYDERMAN, B. (1959), *The Motivation to Work*, Wiley.

HINTON, B. L. (1968), 'An empirical investigation of the Herzberg methodology and two-factor theory', *Organizational Behavior and Human Performance*, vol. 3, pp. 286–309.

HULIN, C. L., and BLOOD, M. R. (1968), 'Job enlargement, individual differences, and worker responses', *Psychological Bulletin*, vol. 69, pp. 41–55.

KILBRIDGE, M. D. (1960), 'Reduced costs through job enlargement: a case', *Journal of Business of the University of Chicago*, vol. 33, pp. 357–62.

KILBRIDGE, M. D. (1961), 'Turnover, absence and transfer rates as indicators of employee dissatisfaction with repetitive work', *Industrial and Labor Relations Review*, vol. 15, pp. 21–32.

KING, N. A. (1970), 'A clarification and evaluation of the two-factor theory of job satisfaction', *Psychological Bulletin*, vol. 74, pp. 18–31.

LAWLER, E. E., and PORTER, L. W. (1967), 'Antecedent attitudes of effective managerial performance', *Organizational Behavior and Human Performance*, vol. 2, pp. 122–42.

LEWIN, K. (1938), *The Conceptual Representation of the Measurement of Psychological Forces*, Duke University Press.

LEWIN, K., DEMBO, T., FESTINGER, L., and SEARS, P. (1944), 'Level of aspiration', in J. McV. Hunt (ed.), *Personality and the Behavior Disorders*, Ronald Press.

LOCKE, E. A. (1969), 'What is job satisfaction?', *Organizational Behavior and Human Performance*, vol. 4, pp. 309–36.

LYTLE, C. W. (1946), *Job Evaluation Methods*, Ronald Press.

MACKINNEY, A. C., WERNIMONT, P. F., and GALITZ, W. O. (1962), 'Has specialization reduced job satisfaction?', *Personnel*, vol. 39, pp. 8–17.

MASLOW, A. H. (1943), 'A theory of human motivation', *Psychological Review*, vol. 50, pp. 370–96.

MASLOW, A. H. (1954), *Motivation and Personality*, Harper.

MCGREGOR, D. (1960), *The Human Side of Enterprise*, McGraw-Hill.

PELISSIER, R. F. (1965), 'Successful experience with job design', *Personnel Administration*, vol. 28, pp. 12–16.

PORTER, L. W., and LAWLER, E. E. (1968), *Managerial Attitudes and Performance*, Irwin.

SCOTT, W. E. (1966), 'Activation theory and task design', *Organizational Behavior and Human Performance*, vol. 1, pp. 3–30.

STIGERS, M. F., and REED, E. G. (1944), *The Theory and Practice of Job Rating*, McGraw-Hill.

TOLMAN, E. C. (1959), 'Principles of purposive behavior', in S. Koch (ed.), *Psychology: A Study of a Science*, McGraw-Hill, vol. 2.

TURNER, A. N., and LAWRENCE, P. R. (1965), *Industrial Jobs and the Worker*, Harvard University Graduate School of Business Administration.

VROOM, V. H. (1964), *Work and Motivation*, Wiley.

WALKER, C. R. (1950), 'The problem of the repetitive job', *Harvard Business Review*, vol. 28, pp. 54–8.

WALKER, C. R., and GUEST, R. H. (1952), *The Man on the Assembly Line*, Harvard University Press.

13 Louis E. Davis

Job Satisfaction Research: The Post-Industrial View

Excerpts from L. E. Davis, 'Job satisfaction research: the post-industrial view', *Industrial Relations*, vol. 10, 1971, pp. 176–93.

'The study of man at work is exposed to dangerous errors if it does not rest on the study of work itself, on the principles of the unity of its several aspects, and their reciprocal relationship.'[1]

Research into job satisfaction has been a focal point of studies on organizational behavior for over forty years. It has proved a fruitful area of study, and application of research results on job satisfaction has materially affected management practices. However, it is the thesis of this paper that our methods of inquiry into job satisfaction must now be substantially altered. This contention is based on the observation that we are in transition from an industrial era to a post-industrial era. This evolving post-industrial period is ushering in new cultural values and new designs of work organizations, and these changes require coordinate changes in the basic premises of job satisfaction research.

The cultural matrix of the industrial era required organizations to be structured in a certain way with jobs designed to fit that structure. Moreover, the cultural factors that molded organizations and jobs also molded research into these matters along certain lines. That is, the researcher's process of asking questions about job satisfaction depended on the tacit assumptions of the industrial value system.

The coming phase, that of the post-industrial era, will also shape organizational structures and designs for jobs, but these will be markedly different from those of the industrial era. We are beginning, in some industries and some nations, to see quite clearly the new cultural outline. Thus, the kinds of questions that researchers ask about job satisfaction – including the factors they

1. Touraine (1955).

take to be given and the assumptions which constrain their results – will spring from the value system of the post-industrial era.

The concept of job satisfaction, as conventionally drawn, is attacked here because it is almost exclusively concerned with adaptation to jobs that, in the post-industrial context, begin to seem fundamentally unsuited for man. The study of job satisfaction has come to be the study of the minimal gratifications possible under deprived conditions. This has occurred, in part at least, because the opportunities for providing greater satisfaction to organizational members while at the same time meeting organizational objectives are not well understood.

To elaborate, we are witnessing a split between two approaches to the study of job satisfaction. In the first approach, a small concentration of researchers and managers are examining and, in action research undertakings, are changing the structure and content of jobs along post-industrial lines, and thereby materially influencing the motivation and satisfaction of job-holders. In the other approach, researchers who cling to the industrial era model continue to examine all aspects of the work situation but the work itself, while searching for economic, community, group, and personality variables that correlate with measures of job satisfaction. The two sets of endeavors simply exist in different worlds, i.e. they stem from substantially different sets of views, values and concepts.

In the following sections, we will first describe the relationship between present job satisfaction studies and the cultural values of the industrial era. We will then examine the implications of the changing nature of job design in the post-industrial era for job satisfaction research in the future.

The industrial era

Historically, concern with job satisfaction began when the central conditions of modern industrial organization appeared, about 175 years ago. Industrialism gave rise to, and was most strikingly characterized by, that social innovation called the factory system, under which men were collected, assigned to work (usually at simple, repetitive jobs), and then closely controlled by supervision and by the flow of the work process. The technology of the industrial era was 'deterministic'. Where it persists today (largely in manufacturing), 'deterministic' technology continues to support, and be supported by, the factory system or scientific management. Industrial era technology assumed that cause and effect relationships were known, and that all actions or tasks could be specified to obtain desired results. In this context, the building blocks of an organization were taken to be the individual and his tasks. The interdependencies among tasks and among individuals were controlled by strict hierarchical arrangements, systems of payment, and scheduling. When these regulating devices proved inadequate, management tried to reduce variance by tighter task definitions and control of the work rate through pacing (as on assembly lines), or by exercising social control over the individual through external supervision, fractionation of tasks, and increasingly more complex incentive or piece-rate wage payments.

Values

A number of values and beliefs were particularly crucial to the nature of organizations and jobs in the industrial era. First, there is the deeply held belief that the individual can be viewed and treated as an operating unit (a phenomenon fully and insightfully described by Boguslaw, 1955, ch. 5). As operating units, individuals may be adjusted and changed by training and incentives to suit the needs of the organization. That individuals may have needs is of secondary concern and, at best, simply a constraint.

A second crucial value concerns the reliability of individuals, including the much-discussed concept of responsibility. The societal view that most individuals are unreliable fostered the development of the concept of men as spare parts, and therefore members of organizations were (and are) assigned work in such a manner that they can be treated as interchangeable. That is, as individuals are believed to have only narrow capabilities and limited utility to organizations, they are given narrowly defined tasks and responsibilities. By contrast, in those segments of our society where individuals organize their own work – notably in the professions and some of the crafts – we find the contrasting 'requisite-repertoire-of-skills' concept applied. This latter concept postulates that a wide range of capabilities must be available if individuals are to adapt to the changing or evolving requirements of their work situation. Nevertheless, most of our industrial training schemes are based on the spare parts concept.

Three other industrial-era values are relevant here as well. The first is that labor is a commodity to be sold by the individual and purchased by the organization. This stands in contrast to the emerging reality that individuals are organizational members, who may, over time, have changing contributions to make and other needs to satisfy. A second value is that of materialism in its narrow sense, under which the end of achieving higher material comfort justifies the means required to achieve it. Lastly, reflecting the values of the industrial era, many managers view the typical job as a disjointed increment, an isolated event in the life of the individual. This noncareerism syndrome explains how jobs (except those for managers themselves) get to be what they are – fragmentary, unintegrated and asystemic.

Organization design

When we examine the industrial era's approach to organization, 'scientific management' – which in reality is the machine theory of organization – we find some deeply disturbing omissions. No clear objectives concerning roles for men as men are visible, although objectives are clearly defined for men as machines.[2] When man is considered only as a link in a system, design rules do not exist for allocating appropriate tasks to man. Nor are there design rules for constructing task configurations to make complete and meaningful jobs. Consideration is not given to the unit-of-analysis concept, which is concerned with determining appropriate boundaries of systems containing men, machines, materials, and information needed to pursue specific goals or outcomes in an operating system.

The characteristic organizational structure that we see today can be explained in terms of this theory of organization. The superstructure of the organization is designed to coordinate the elements in which work is done, join them together, counter variances arising within the elements and within the social links created by workers, and adjust the system to variances in either the input or in the output requirements. In such organizations, planning, coordinating and controlling exist within the super-

2. Charles Perrow (1970) gives us an insight into the strength of industrial culture by reporting an instance in which animals were rejected, partly on compassionate grounds, as appropriate performers of single-purpose, machine-element tasks. Lamentably, the organization found these same jobs acceptable for its personnel to perform.

structure; the performance of activities (most of which are 'programmable') occurs at the worker level.

If we turn to how technology is translated into requirements for job designs, we see widespread acceptance of the notion of the 'technological imperative', put forth by most engineers and managers. That a substantial part of the technical design of production systems involves social system design is little understood or appreciated. Thus some rather frightful assumptions, supported by our industrial era values, are made about man and are built into machines and processes as system and operational requirements. To a large extent, psychological and social requirements of the work system are considered only as boundary conditions of the technical system. Attempts are then made to reduce these to boundary constants by contractual specifications which define how man must relate to the requirements of the technological system.

Job satisfaction research in the industrial era

The preceding section attempted to outline the implicit and explicit values underlying industrialism and the machine theory of organization, and to show how these were manifested in the design of jobs within the industrial framework. A large portion of past and present research into job satisfaction is based on this industrial-era value system. Either explicitly, or by tacit assumption, it shares the values and beliefs of its environmental context.

Technology as a given

Job satisfaction studies have been and are still undertaken almost exclusively by psychologists and sociologists. Fully acknowledging the difficulty of conducting research on such a complex and multivariate problem, we must still contend that most of these studies have a singular defect – a defect that makes the results difficult to interpret and, in some instances, dangerous to apply: almost universally the studies take technology as a given.[3]

Technology includes the combination of skills, equipment,

3. Although it is not directly related to job satisfaction, the comparative analysis of organizations whose conceptual framework has been sketched out by Perrow is a notable exception in the sociological field. Perrow's analysis concerns itself explicitly with technological differences and their impact on roles in organizations. Similarly, much of the work of William F.

facilities, tools, and relevant technical knowledge needed to bring about desired transformations in materials, information, or people. But technology often differs significantly from one transformation process to another, and these differences materially affect the entire work situation and the relationship obtaining within it. Consider for a moment the different images that are evoked by the phrases 'educational technology', 'production-line technology', and 'computer technology'. It is clear that technology largely determines what the work is about and what demands are placed on the individual and the organization.

Nevertheless, in the psychological and sociological studies of job satisfaction, only the variables not influenced by technology are typically examined.[4] Further, in job satisfaction studies characteristic of the industrial era there is an unfortunate propensity for treating job satisfaction either as an isolated variable or as an end state in itself. When technology is a given, the use of correlational and factor-analytic research methods ignores the interaction between social and technical systems and thus tells us little about cause and effect relationships.

In sum, the most striking feature of most past and present research on job satisfaction is its failure to study the job itself. One must question how, if the nature of the relevant technology is omitted, the research results can be understood or effectively used. Some of the effects of this omission are illustrated in the following paragraphs.

Job enlargement controversy

Psychologists concerned with work content – again, consistently taking technology as a given – have been led off in the direction of

---

Whyte, while not focusing directly on job satisfaction, does examine the responses of organization members to the technology of the immediate work place.

4. Most recently, industrial psychologists have been embroiled in a frequently vicious conflict over whether the two-factor theory of job satisfaction by Herzberg (1966), or the traditional unidimensional theory in Ewen, Hulin, Smith and Locke (1966), Graen (1966), Hulin and Smith (1967), Graen and Hulin (1968) explains satisfaction–dissatisfaction. The imbroglio may represent a subconscious playing of games to avoid fundamental considerations of technology and values in determining job content. Herzberg's two-factor theory fortunately raises these issues.

examining relationships between repetitive work and monotony, monotony and satisfaction, task length or job size and satisfaction. The recent tempest in a teapot over job enlargement illustrates the dangers inherent in using such research. No sooner was it proposed that 'larger' jobs, i.e. more of the same dehumanizing tasks in a job, lead to higher satisfaction than the spurious battle over this fiction was on (MacKinney *et al*,. 1962, Kilbridge, 1960). The nonpsychologists* purportedly recommending enlargement (Argyris, 1957; Argyris, 1964; Davis, 1957a; Davis, 1957b; Davis and Werling, 1960; Guest, 1957) were in fact misinterpreted, for they were largely recommending the addition of different tasks – those leading to closure, self-regulation and autonomy and resulting in fundamentally different relationships of the jobholder to the work process. (This process is now referred to as 'vertical enlargement' or 'job enrichment' by Herzberg.) Most of the latter recommendations inferentially raised value questions related to the roles of men *as men* and, consequently, questions about the allocation of tasks between men and machines. Nowhere in this tempest was it recognized by the psychologists that tasks, in addition to meeting the demands of the technical system, also had to satisfy the needs of human systems.[5]

Extrinsic factors

Another body of research differing in purpose and outlook comprises the studies on extrinsic or job-context factors affecting job satisfaction and motivation, including working conditions, pay, supervisory relationships, community, and industry type. Related to this research is that focusing on leadership and managerial style. These studies focus on conditions and factors surrounding jobs and use factor-analytic and correlational methods to identify attitudes of job-holders in existing work situations. This work is represented in studies by Hulin and Smith (1967), Graen and Hulin (1968), Hulin and Blood (1968), Blood and Hulin (1967), Ewen *et al*. (1966), Smith (1963), and Dunnette *et al*. (1967) and – with important modifications – Herzberg and his associates (1959).

* i.e., those social scientists outside the area of classical industrial psychology [Ed.].

5. Neither did they recognize the concept of complementarity which Jordan (1963) finally stated as a systems concept for task allocation in joint man–machine systems.

In terms of methodology, these studies are meticulously executed – with one crucial exception that makes interpretation of results virtually impossible for those who have any concern for the relationships between job content and motivation and satisfaction. In contrast to the careful sampling, control, data collection and analysis exercised with respect to job attitudes, absolutely no control over or identification of the content of jobs held by [or the work experience of]* the subjects in these studies is undertaken. Completely disregarded are the variables concerned with job boundaries, activities performed, regulation and control of system variations, control of input and output, and access to information within and across job boundaries, all of which have a strong bearing on the satisfaction responses that a job-holder would make. These job content variables clearly are not constant from job to job. The omission of their identification and measurement in the face of their differential effects makes it impossible to interpret such findings as Hulin's (1969) that community characteristics are predictors of job satisfaction.**

Given fractionated, dehumanized jobs, the responses of job-holders are to some extent related to individual differences – to their particular acceptance of and adaptation to, a working life of this quality. Predicting the satisfaction of job-holders in such a working environment is complicated by their state of alienation, which in turn appears to be related to their social environments, i.e. rural, simple *vs* urban, or cosmopolitan (Blood and Hulin, 1967; Hulin and Blood, 1968). These relationships constitute an argument for considering work systems in a social-ecological framework. But almost all of the studies readily accept the requirements seemingly imposed by technology – single-purpose fractionated tasks calling for machine-element responses (Dubin, 1965, ch. 1). That the relationship with the technological system could be otherwise configured has apparently been treated as an off-limits consideration. Fortunately, this notion is now being laid to rest by the growing incursion of sophisticated technology that itself

* Ed. insert.
** Turner and Lawrence (1965) (Reading 11) are less liable to this criticism in that they systematically classify job content while assessing home location of the subjects; but they do not consider individual work history or experience [Ed.].

performs such tasks and calls for higher order interactions between man and the technical system.

The post-industrial era

The evolution of technology has been widely studied and described in recent years, as scholars and other social observers have become aware that the new technology is ushering in a new system of social and organizational values. Two trends are particularly relevant in this regard. The first is the continuing substitution of mechanical and electrical energy sources for human energy in the performance of work. The second is the absorption by machines of tasks or activities which are programmable (limited by the particular skills required for the performance of individual tasks). It is not the specific manual or decision-making skills that are relevant here, but whether the sequence in which the activities must be performed can be identified and written down in such a manner as to produce the desired outcome. Future human interventions will largely be of the 'nonprogrammable' variety. That is, people will be called on to provide adaptive responses in situations where there are many exceptions, or where a high degree of variability exists (making programming infeasible), or where people provide linkages between programmable segments. Such jobs will require skills, contents, and organizational structures quite different from those presently before us.

Values

The values of a society and its institutions slowly evolve in response to social and physical conditions and to the conceptions the society holds of its environment. It is the emergence of some new values and the change in relative importance of others that leads to the recognition that we are witnessing the evolution of a new epoch, the post-industrial era. Perhaps the best way of stating the changes in emphasis is to present two tables of Trist's (1970; 1967, p. 34) (Tables 1 and 2).

Our social environment is one of continuous irreversible change proceeding at an accelerating rate. Its salient characteristic is that of a turbulent field (Emery and Trist, 1965). As Trist (1970) indicates:

This turbulence arises from the increased complexity and size of the

Table 1 Occupational structure and education

Aspect	Salient in 1935	Salient in 1965 (and 1970)
Composition of work force	Blue collar	White collar
Educational level	Not completing high school	Completing high school
Work/learning ratio	Work force	Learning force
Type of career	Single	Serial

Table 2 Changes in emphasis of social patterns in the transition to post-industrialism

Type	From	Towards
Cultural values	Achievement	Self-actualization
	Self-control	Self-expression
	Independence	Interdependence
	Endurance of distress	Capacity for joy
Organizational philosophies	Mechanistic forms	Organic forms
	Competitive relations	Collaborative relations
	Separate objectives	Linked objectives
	Own resources regarded as owned absolutely	Own resources regarded also as society's resources
Ecological strategies	Responsive to crisis	Anticipative of crisis
	Specific measures	Comprehensive measures
	Requiring consent	Requiring participation
	Short planning horizon	Long planning horizon
	Damping conflict	Confronting conflict
	Detailed central control	Generalized central control
	Small local government units	Enlarged local government units
	Standardized administration	Innovative administration
	Separate services	Coordinated services

total environment, together with increased interdependence of the parts and the unpredictable connections which arise between them as a result of the accelerating but uneven change rate. This turbulence grossly increases the area of relevant uncertainty for individuals and organizations alike. It raises far-reaching problems concerning the limits of human adaptation. Forms of adaptation, both personal and organizational, developed to meet a simpler type of environment no longer suffice to meet the higher levels of complexity now coming into existence (p. 6).

In response to these environmental conditions, we see growing acceptance of the values of adaptability and composite capability – in Ashby's terms, the possession by individuals of a requisite variety of responses to meet a variety of external demands, or in Emery's terms, a society in which individuals exhibit redundancy of functions rather than being themselves treated as redundant or spare parts.

Developed technology appears to provide limitlessly for material needs and to banish the fear of scarcity. By eroding the bases for the Protestant work ethic this capability of technology reinforces the evolving values of self-actualization and self-expression. Further, advanced technology removes man's conventional work role and requires of him self-directed decision making to counter unexpected variations, which also supports the value of self-actualization.

Trist's review of occupational structure and education reflects yet another impact of the new technology. Stimulated by the emergent reorganization of society and industry, the view is evolving that the job is an event or stage in an integrated, life-long career – that not only doctors and lawyers but hospital workers, clerks and machinists are engaged in work that can be viewed as a step on a career ladder. (Some may say this is history turning full circle.) On the part of both managers and workers, new questions are being raised about the opportunities that jobs provide for learning and self-development, and about the career opportunities provided by organizations. The emerging value of careers is reinforced by those of self-actualization, self-expression and interdependence. Together, these values are forming a comprehensive set that will markedly alter the nature of jobs and organizations.

Socio-technical systems

An ecological focus is evolving that provides useful insights for the theory and practice of structuring organizations and determining job content. This focus is a response to changes in the technological and social environment and in cultural values. It led to the development of a conceptual and theoretical framework known as socio-technical systems (see Emery and Trist, 1960), and its utility for the post-industrial era lies in its comprehensive view of the interactions among society, its organizations, and the members within them. At the societal level, it takes as central the requirement for organizations and individuals to respond to an environment exhibiting a high rate of change – an environment in which relative uncertainty is high and previous values are being re-examined. At the institutional level, the socio-technical approach takes organizations to be purposive, relating to their surrounding social and technological environments and interacting with them across permeable boundaries. It takes technology as a relevant variable interacting with social and personal variables to *jointly* shape the system for accomplishing the purposes of an organization. At the individual level it takes the organization's members to be purposive, whole human beings reflecting and shaping the values of society, interacting with technology and seeking to satisfy their own and the organization's needs. Socio-technical systems applications lend strong support to the prospect of developing a work-world humane in its objectives and satisfying in its consequences to both the individual and the organization. A number of recent developments, both theoretical and empirical, indicate that we can design satisfying, economically efficient jobs which meet these value requirements.

The Norwegian experience

The evolution of socio-technical systems concepts has taken place over the last fifteen years in the course of attempts here and in England to overcome the deficiencies of existing work situations. Furthermore, within the last four years Norway has made a national commitment to changing values about man at work through a series of experiments with job and organization design, under tripartite support from the Confederation of Employers, the Confederation of Trade Unions, and the Norwegian government. In these experiments, socio-technical systems theory has been applied with the active participation of both management and labor, and the results have been held up for national examination by the representatives of all interested parties, leading in late 1969 to acceptance of the objectives and modes of organizing as national policy (Thorsrud and Emery, 1969). As might be expected, given the present rapid spread of ideas and its similar values, Sweden is under pressure to undertake a similar form of development.

Socio-technical systems theory is concerned with any organizational setting in which men combine their efforts in cooperative activity with technology toward the achievement of a goal. The theory provides us with two essential concepts basic to the study of man at work. The first is that of open systems and the second is that of correlated but independent social and technological systems operating under joint causation.

Open systems. The concept of open systems focuses our attention on the relationship between the individual or work group and the external environment. The organizational unit is viewed as operating within and interacting with its environment. It receives inputs, alters them, and exports outputs to that environment. We see that we cannot understand an organizational unit without understanding its environment, that the unit is not independent of its environment, and that there is a mutual permeation of the unit and its environment. We are provided with a theoretical basis for considering spontaneous restructuring of organizational units, growth, self-regulation, and the achievement of a 'steady state' at levels permitting work to be done even though there may be disturbances in the environment.

Joint optimization. Socio-technical systems theory conceives of the working world as consisting of independent technological systems and social systems operating under joint causation. This leads to the central concept of joint optimization, which states that when achievement of an objective depends on independent but correlated systems, such as a technological and social system, it is impossible to optimize for overall performance without seeking to optimize these correlative systems jointly. Among a number of concepts that derive from these propositions, the concept of boundary control is of great importance for the design of jobs and of organizational units. Raised are questions of tasks and relationships to be included within the boundary of a job or organizational unit for self-regulation and control of functioning and of functions to be performed by higher levels that will maintain the boundary of a stable organizational unit.

Job satisfaction research in the post-industrial era

In the preceding section, some of the emergent values of the post-industrial era were sketched out in terms of socio-technical systems theory and the concepts underlying it. The emerging post-industrial value system is stimulating new modes of organizing work and structuring jobs and, correspondingly, it is giving rise to a body of research into job satisfaction that asks new questions and depends on new premises. Here, we attempt to collect a set of references to research that forms part of this new and growing stream.[6]

The work itself

Within this group are those who recognize the relationship of motivation and satisfaction to the intrinsic, substantive contents of jobs. The recent work of Lawler (1969), Herzberg (1968), Paul *et al.* (1969), the continuing work [of] the Institute of Social Research at the University of Michigan, and that of Meyers (1964; 1968) represent significant contributions.

The studies of the organizational behavior group at the Harvard Graduate School of Business Administration provide insights into the technological and environmental conditions of the emerging post-industrial era. Turner and Lawrence (1965) examined the impact of technologically determined variations on responses of workers living under differing social and cultural influences. Lawrence and Lorsch (1967) studied the impact on organization design and social relationships of accelerating rates of market and technological change.

6. Some of the researchers who have been grouped together here may express surprise that they are being thus clustered. Their relationship is not necessarily one of direct contact and explicit agreement, but rather of unity within the conceptual framework we postulate as being characteristic of the post-industrial 'nouvelle vague'.

Individual v. *organization*

Within this cluster of studies are significant developments that directly confront the issue of values relating to man and organization. In England (Emery, 1968) and Scandinavia (Thorsrud and Emery, 1969, and Herbst, 1962) one stream of these developments has been referred to as democratization of the workplace. In the US, the values issue is strongly reflected in the work of Argyris (1964), Davis (1971), Herzberg (1966), and Likert (1967). Another development focuses on the interactions between technology and social organization in shaping the roles of men. In this context, using the socio-technical systems framework, jobs and organizations are being designed that are motivating and satisfying to men and groups and suitable to the organization and its technology. This line of development is reflected in the research of the Tavistock Institute of Human Relations, London (Emery and Trist, 1960; 1965, Trist *et al.*, 1963 and Miller and Rice, 1967), of the Institute of Work Research, Oslo, Norway (Thorsrud and Emery, 1969, Engelstad, 1970), and DaBis (1971, p. 4; 1966). A good deal of this work was stimulated by the early endeavors of Walker and his associates (see Walker and Guest, 1952).

Related to the work of these researchers, there has been a somewhat fragmented series of industrial and business applications directed at enhancing the motivation and satisfaction of employees by changing the content of their jobs and extending their responsibilities and authority. Some of these developments in job enlargement and job enrichment are described by Ford (1969) and Foulkes (1969).

Thus, the researchers who reflect post-industrial changes are concerned with the impact of changing technology, social environment, and personal values, and the enormous loss in human resources potential (see Gooding, 1970a, 1970b) stemming from continued application of organization concepts increasingly unsuited to the present era. They see that the sum of the technological and social forces operating on organizations and their members leaves management with no option but to provide satisfying, meaningful work (Davis, 1971, p. 4).

Job design

Depending on the type of industry, state of technology, and characteristics of the environment, an extensive number of propositions for the design of jobs along post-industrial lines can be derived. A number of these have been tested in the socio-technical studies referred to earlier and are still in the process of evolution and testing in studies currently underway.

A summary report of the English and US socio-technical field studies has been published by Davis (1966). In general, successful job-design outcomes, as measured by various objective criteria, seem to depend on finding an accommodation between the demands of the organization and the technology on the one hand, and the needs and desires of its members on the other, so that the needs of both are jointly maximized. The studies lend support to the general model of responsible autonomous job behavior as the key facet of individual–organization–technological relationships in productive organizations. *Responsible* behavior as defined here implies (a) acceptance of responsibility by the individual or group for the cycle of activities required to complete the product or service, (b) acceptance of responsibility for the rate, quantity and quality of output, and (c) recognition of the interdependence of the individual or group on others for completion of a cycle of activities. Similarly, *autonomous* behavior encompasses (a) self-regulation of work content and structure within the job (where the job is an assigment having inputs, facilities and outputs), (b) self-evaluation of performance, (c) self-adjustment in response to work system variability, and (d) participation in the setting of job goals or objectives. Lastly, the studies provide a partial demonstration of the positive effects of responsible autonomous job behavior on objective organizational performances as well as on the attitudes, perceptions and satisfactions of members of the organization.

Future job satisfaction studies

Recognizing the emerging value trends of the post-industrial era and their implications for organization and job design, what will, or at least what should, be the shape of future job satisfaction studies? It seems clear that it will be unprofitable to continue static examinations of variations in employee attitudes under deprived work conditions. Instead, meaningful future research in this area will focus on broad, dynamic dimensions of the ongoing process of designing and redesigning the socio-technical system in line with these new values.

Given this focus, it seems unlikely that job satisfaction will be studied as a distinct phenomenon. Rather, it will tend to focus on the higher systems level and will thus raise new issues about relationships between the individual and his group, requirements for self-sufficiency or autonomy, and the compatibility between these requirements and their associated regulatory or control systems. This new focus will blur the distinction we currently make between organization and job satisfaction. Moreover, the determinants of satisfaction for all job-holders will come to be viewed more like those presently associated with scientists, engineers, teachers and other professionals working in large complex organizations.

Future dimensions of job satisfaction

To be somewhat more explicit, an extrapolation of the post-industrial trends discussed earlier suggests that the social and technological environments of organizations will hasten the widespread use of various forms of self-sufficient, autonomous work groups. Their primary role, in relation to their transformation technologies, will be that of regulator and controller (or absorber) of systems variances. In organizations where these work groups exist, strict control of members' behavior to achieve organizational objectives is neither particularly useful nor necessary. But at the same time, the organization must ensure that the goals of its units are relevant to those of the organization as a whole and that the organization remains adaptive to the environment. Thus, to a large extent, job satisfaction issues will be centered around the forms and means of goal setting, multiple goal satisfaction (institutional, social, personal), individual and organizational adaptability, self-sufficient operational autonomy, and feedback and rewards. For each of these issues a number of variables will probably be studied in relation to job satisfaction in specific instances and, in addition, as aids in the design of jobs, careers and organizations.

Some of the variables revolving around careers and organizational adaptability may be concerned with the learning content of jobs, role access to learning, degree and form of self-regulation, control and feedback in operations. Centering around technology are likely to be such variables as man–machine complementarity, access to process variables, congruence of social and technical systems boundaries, scope of process variance regulation authority, and requisite variety of response capabilities, and their accessibility. At the institutional level, variables likely to be studied are participation in goal setting, access to the institution's environment, feedback and rewards, access to total cost data, and permeability of internal boundaries.[7]

New methods of job satisfaction research

As the focus of future job satisfaction research shifts toward these new dimensions, the methods by which it is undertaken will also shift – in fact, they will be forced to undergo rather dramatic revision. Specifically, researchers will need an in-depth understanding of both the technology used in the transformation process and its related social system. Required, also, will be a relatively complete understanding of the organization's environment.

Understanding both the technology and the environment of the organization requires painstaking analysis in order to determine the variations generated, the means for controlling these variances, the responses called for on the part of the social system, and the apparent structural requirements for its operation. Such information is usually held only by organization members who are expert in the technology, and the researcher must therefore work closely with these people. [. . .]

Conclusions

Evolving technology indicates that we have to prepare people to be adaptable, to hold a number of job sequences in a lifetime, and to be committed to their work situation. In organized work situations, current practices are inimical to achieving such needs. As a nation, we need what Vickers (1968) calls a new 'appreciation' of the world of work if we are going to prepare for future changes. We need to examine the compatibility between the emerging

7. For interrelated issues of future study requirements of job design, see Davis (1957a, p. 305).

post-industrial values of our culture and the values of organizations; the autonomy of the individual and control by the organization; the compatibility between demands of the work system and the responses men feel equipped to give; the conflict between demands of jobs and man's needs; the extent to which the technology imposes a rigidity on job content and structure; the requirements, if any, of modern organizational planning and control that impose detail specification and restriction on jobs rather than the specification of minimal critical tasks appropriate to the goals of the organization; and the consequences for our society of considering jobs as isolated events rather than stages in a career. Lastly, we must face the consequences of achieving compatibility between man as worker and man as citizen.

Our present national concern with technology has concentrated largely on its impact on skills and on types and number of jobs, and not on the need to evolve new job designs to fit emergent technological configurations. As a consequence, we may miss opportunities provided by the evolution of sophisticated technology to design jobs and organizations that are suited to both men and machines (see Davis, 1962).

A prior condition of future job satisfaction is the development of organizations and jobs that reflect the needs and environmental trends of the post-industrial era. When such organizations and jobs exist it is likely that job satisfaction research issues will cluster around goal development, multiple goal achievement, and short- and long-term adaptability. Not likely to be seen again are studies of jobs which are created according to mechanistic rules and whose viability is dependent on systems of coercion. Future studies of job satisfaction will be integral with job design.

Future job satisfaction research methods will reflect the realities of studying living organizations characterized by constant large and small changes, by the reality of the impact of both the environment and changes within the organization on its members, and by their adaptations to this reality. At the same time there are crucial research issues of bias, replicability, and post-hoc theory to be guarded against. No longer will the cozy notion hold that organization members are objects waiting to be researched, who in the name of science can be manipulated, so that we can learn something about them. We now recognize that we have to learn through developments which are in the interests of the researched with those of the researcher following.

References

ARGYRIS, C. (1957), *Personality and Organization*, Harper.

ARGYRIS, C. (1964), *Integrating the Individual and the Occupation*, Wiley.

BOGUSLAW, R. (1955), *The New Utopians*, Prentice-Hall.

BLOOD, M. R., and HULIN, C. L. (1967), 'Alienation, environmental characteristics and worker responses', *Journal of Applied Psychology*, vol. 51, June, pp. 284–90.

DAVIS, L. E. (1957a), 'Toward a theory of job design', *Journal of Industrial Engineering*, vol. 8, June, pp. 305–9.

DAVIS, L. E. (1957b), 'Job design and productivity: a new approach', *Personnel*, vol. 33, March, pp. 418–30.

DAVIS, L. E. (1962), 'The effects of automation on job design', *Industrial Relations*, vol. 2, October, pp. 53–71.

DAVIS, L. E. (1966), 'The design of jobs', *Industrial Relations*, vol. 6, October, pp. 21–45.

DAVIS, L. E. (1971), 'The coming crisis for production management: technology and organization', *International Journal of Production Research*, vol. 9, no. 4.

DAVIS, L. E., and WERLING, R. (1960), 'Job design factors', *Occupational Psychology*, vol. 34, April, pp. 108–32.

DUBIN, R. (1965), 'Supervision and productivity: empirical findings and theoretical considerations', in R. Dubin, G. C. Homans, F. C. Mann and D. C. Miller, *Leadership and Productivity*, Chandler.

DUNNETTE, M. D., CAMPBELL, J. P., and HAKEL, M. D. (1967), 'Factors contributing to job satisfaction and job dissatisfaction in six occupational groups', *Journal of Organizational Behavior and Human Performance*, vol. 2, pp. 143–74.

EMERY, F. E. (1968), 'Democratization of the work place', *Manpower and Applied Psychology*, vol. 1, pp. 118–29.

EMERY, F. E., and TRIST, E. L. (1960), 'Socio-technical systems', in C. W. Churchman and M. Verhulst (eds.), *Management Science, Models and Techniques*, Pergamon, vol. 2.

EMERY, F. E., and TRIST, E. L. (1965), 'The causal texture of organizational environments', *Human Relations*, vol. 18, February, pp. 21–32.

ENGELSTAD, P. H. (1970), *Technology and Social Relationships in the Workplace*, Tanum Press, Oslo.

EWEN, R. B., HULIN, C. L., SMITH, P. C., and LOCKE, E. A. (1966), 'An empirical test of the Herzberg two-factor theory', *Journal of Applied Psychology*, vol. 50, December, pp. 544–50.

FORD, R. N. (1969), *Motivation Through the Work Itself*, American Management Association.

FOULKES, F. K. (1969), *Creating More Meaningful Work*, American Management Association.

GOODING, J. (1970a), 'Blue-collar blues on the assembly line', *Fortune*, July.

GOODING, J. (1970b), 'It pays to wake up the blue collar worker', *Fortune*, September, pp. 133–5.

GRAEN, G. B. (1966), 'An addendum to an empirical test of the Herzberg two-factor theory', *Journal of Applied Psychology*, vol. 50, December, pp. 551–5.

GRAEN, G. B., and HULIN, C. L. (1968), 'An addendum to an empirical investigation of two implications of the two-factor theory of job satisfaction', *Journal of Applied Psychology*, vol. 52, August, pp. 341–2.

GUEST, R. H. (1957), 'Job enlargement – a revolution in job design', *Personnel Administration*, vol. 20, January, pp. 9–16.

HERBST, P. G. (1962), *Autonomous Group Functioning*, Tavistock.

HERZBERG, F. (1966), *Work and the Nature of Man*, World.

HERZBERG, F. (1968), 'One more time: how do you motivate employees?', *Harvard Business Review*, vol. 46, January, pp. 53–62; see Reading 10 above.

HERZBERG, F., MAUSNER, B., and SNYDERMAN, B. B. (1959), *The Motivation of Work*, Wiley.

HULIN, C. L. (1969), 'Sources of variation in job and life satisfaction: the role of community and job-related variables', *Journal of Applied Psychology*, vol. 53, August, pp. 279–91.

HULIN, C. L., and BLOOD, M. R. (1968), 'Job enlargement, individual differences and worker responses', *Psychological Bulletin*, vol. 69, February, pp. 41–55.

HULIN, C. L., and SMITH, P. C. (1967), 'An empirical investigation of two implications of the two-factor theory of job satisfaction', *Journal of Applied Psychology*, vol. 51, October, pp. 396–402.

JORDAN, N. (1963), 'Allocation of functions', *Journal of Applied Psychology*, vol. 47, June, pp. 161–5.

KILBRIDGE, M. D. (1960), 'Do workers prefer larger jobs?', *Personnel*, vol. 37, September/October, pp. 45–8.

LAWLER, E. E. (1969), 'Job design and employee motivation', *Personnel Psychology*, vol. 22, Winter, pp. 426–35.

LAWRENCE, P. R., and LORSCH, J. W. (1967), *Organization and Environment*, Harvard Business School.

LIKERT, R. (1967), *The Human Organization: Its Management and Value*, McGraw-Hill.

MACKINNEY, A. C., WERNIMONT, P. F., and GALITZ, W. O. (1962), 'Has specialization reduced job satisfaction?', *Personnel*, vol. 39, January/February, pp. 8–17.

MEYERS, M. S. (1964), 'Who are your motivated workers?', *Harvard Business Review*, vol. 42, January, pp. 73–88.

MEYERS, M. S. (1968), 'Every employee a manager', *California Management Review*, vol. 10, Spring, pp. 9–20.

MILLER, E. J., and RICE, A. K. (1967), *Systems of Organization*, Tavistock.

PAUL, W. J., ROBERTSON, K. B., and HERZBERG, F. (1969), 'Job enrichment pays off', *Harvard Business Review*, vol. 47, March, pp. 61–78.

PERROW, C. (1970), *Organizational Analysis: A Sociological View*, Wadsworth.

SMITH, P. C. (1963), 'The Cornell studies of job satisfaction', unpublished, Cornell University.

THORSRUD, E., and EMERY, F. E. (1969), *Mot en Ny Bedriftsorganisasjon*, Tanum Press, Oslo.

TOURAINE, A. (1955), *'L'evolution du travail ouvrier aux usines Renault'*, Centre National de la Recherche Scientifique, Paris.

TRIST, E. L. (1967), 'The relation of welfare and development in the transition to post-industrialism', *Proceedings of the International Seminar on Welfare and Development*, Canadian Centre for Community Studies.

TRIST, E. L. (1970), 'Urban North America: the challenge of the next thirty years', *Journal of the Town Planning Institute of Canada*, vol. 10, pp. 4–20.

TRIST, E. L., HIGGIN, G. W., MURRAY, H., and POLLOCK, A. B. (1963), *Organizational Choice*, Tavistock.

TURNER, A. N., and LAWRENCE, P. R. (1965), *Industrial Jobs and the Worker*, Harvard Business School.

VICKERS, SIR G. (1968), *Value Systems and Social Process*, Basic Books.

WALKER, C. R., and GUEST, R. H. (1952), *Man on the Assembly Line*, Harvard University Press.

14 Fred E. Emery

Characteristics of Socio-Technical Systems

Excerpts from F. E. Emery, *Characteristics of Socio-Technical Systems*,
Tavistock Institute of Human Relations Document no. 527, 1959.

The individual and the task

Individuals are brought into an enterprise to perform at least those
tasks dictated by the technological requirements. In the first
instance it is necessary that the tasks and persons are so matched
that it is physically possible for the persons to perform them and
keep on performing them. This matching process may involve job
analysis, selection, training and job re-design. Insofar as this
process is concerned only with what is physically possible, it
refers to what the task requires of the individual, not what the
individual requires of the task. However, as soon as an enterprise
goes beyond mere possibilities to the problem of making it likely
that employees will in fact perform their tasks, then the enterprise
must take some account of the psychological properties of its
employees and make some modifications in its structure that go
beyond those dictated by technological requirements alone. As
mentioned earlier, the dependence of an enterprise upon persons
to operate its technology constitutes one of its inescapable
dilemmas. Within an ongoing enterprise it is frequently possible
for a 'hard-headed' leadership to deny the reality of the problem,
but it is extremely doubtful if any institution, industrial or otherwise, can persist without making some actual accommodations to
the fact that whole men are employed, not just the psychological
bits that fit the technological requirements:

The whole individual raises new problems for the organisation, partly
because of the needs of his own personality, partly because he brings
with him a set of established habits as well, perhaps, as commitments
to special groups outside of the organisation (Selznick, 1948, p. 26).

If individuals are to be expected to perform certain tasks, then one or more of the following general psychological conditions must exist:

1. Performance of the task itself satisfies some psychological needs of the individual.

2. Performance of the task is not in itself satisfying but it is an unavoidable prerequisite to
(a) achieving other psychological satisfactions, i.e. it has means characteristics,
(b) avoiding other more unpleasant conditions.

3. Performance is induced by demands perceived to arise from the task itself, i.e. it arises from 'task orientation'.

Only the first and last conditions refer to satisfactions that are intrinsic to the task. Consideration of these may reveal some of the ways in which tasks may be modified further to meet the psychological requirements of the workers and thus bring their activities more closely into line with the overall purposes of the enterprise. The second condition presents the typical situation of extrinsic rewards and punishments (incentives) with its usual inherent dilemmas. In particular it may be noted that if this is the dominant way of relating a worker to his task, then:

1. A considerable part of the efforts of the enterprise must be devoted to a system of constraints that will prevent an individual achieving 'unearned' rewards or avoiding 'earned' penalties.

2. Whatever the attempts of the enterprise to meet the other psychological requirements of the individual (e.g. for satisfying interpersonal relations and for a meaningful relation to his larger society), they will be in part negated by the unsatisfactory nature of the task relation. Nor does this solution of attaching incentives to the task performance necessarily mean that tasks can therefore be designed solely to meet technological requirements. The need for a close control of the effort–reward relation exerts pressure toward greater and greater breakdown and isolation of tasks into measurable units of individual performance. Many observers have expressed their belief that this process frequently goes beyond what is technologically required (see Trist and Bamforth, 1951, Warner and Low, 1947, Gouldner, 1955 and Bell, 1956).

It may well be that for all its drawbacks this is the only method of relating the worker to his task that is generally practicable in modern industry, but, before assuming this, it is desirable to consider some of the alternative possibilities.

There has been something of a tendency in both specialist and general writings on industry to evade the unpleasant side of this problem by assuming that work, at the operative level, is, or readily could be, a source of immediate psychological satisfaction. The reported evidence, over a wide range of industrial and commercial occupations, makes it very doubtful whether this is the case. More general evidence, particularly that gained from the clinical study of man, makes it very doubtful whether it could readily become so.

The sort of work that is demanded of most operatives yields little opportunity for libidinal satisfaction. It is only a favoured few who are engaged in creative work or are otherwise able to work according to their inclinations and impulses. [. . .]

Within this general condition of *alienation* one does observe a great diversity of specific satisfactions that are enjoyed by workers. Some of these appear to have their source in the framework of rewards and punishments with which the performance of the task is surrounded; some appear to arise from a process of socialization that makes work 'a neurotic necessity , . . an attempt to make oneself feel valuable even though there is no particular need for one's working' (Chisholm, 1946, p. 31); and some appear to be relative satisfactions – accepting the necessity to work, individuals can and do distinguish between tasks in terms of the demands they make. The first of these sources is extraneous to the task performance and reflects the requirements that individuals have of the social system of the enterprise. For this reason they are rightly considered in that context rather than the present one. Unfortunately there has been very little study of the 'neurotic' satisfactions.

Pedersen-Krag (1951) has suggested that one can expect to find neurotic roots for deep personal satisfactions with an alienated task, i.e. 'a job that demands that the worker, day in and day out, whether he is inclined or not, shall be at a certain place doing a certain task for a specified number of hours' (p. 441). In a series of instances she illustrates the thesis that in certain cases an individual's defence mechanisms may be such that they are re-inforced by 'the excessive demands for libidinal output and aggressive relations' of his particular job.

An examination of the conditions leading to these idiosyncratic satisfactions leads Pedersen-Krag to suggest that the 'normal' reaction will be different: 'The first effect of work will be exclusion from reality to the extent to which the job is incomprehensible, repetitive, non-demanding and performed under circumstances which isolate the worker socially' (p. 448).

This may, even for well-adjusted people, provide a temporary haven from social and domestic care (p. 449) but will in general tend to act with 'the excessive demands' to create hostility and fatigue. [. . .]

Thus, consideration of the exceptional cases who find satisfaction in alienated work throws light upon the general phenomenon of fatigue. There are also grounds for believing that this line of thought can throw light on the phenomenon of an habitual working mood which Baldamus has described as 'dull contentment'. This 'dull contentment' is a sort of borderline satisfaction, apparently quite distinct from the elation experienced in pleasurable activities or the quieter satisfaction of an engaging task, but so prevalent in industry as to warrant some consideration. Baldamus, in reviewing his own work and that of Ryan and Bartley and Chute, notes that they are in agreement regarding this dull contentment as the opposite of fatigue (weariness) in that it denotes a willed resignation to alienated labour and as being subject to spontaneous reversals so that fatigue becomes the dominant subjective reaction. This spontaneous reversal suggests that the psychological conditions found to be persistently dominant in Pedersen-Krag's cases are present, although not persistently dominant, in the normal person engaged in alienated labour. The normal worker tends to achieve this state of dull contentment by a process of narrowing down his psychological field to the task at hand, putting out of mind any alternative attractions and thus suppressing certain of his impulses and tendencies. This is the usual process of 'settling in' and is associated, in group labour, with the spontaneous cessation of chatting and the achievement of a smooth flow of work. Continued denial of one's impulses toward other activities can be expected to lead to unconscious resentment which, as in Pedersen-Krag's cases, may reinforce the use of the task as an aggressive outlet or, more normally, may be directed against oneself and built up to the point where they paralyse the will to work. [. . .]

The third source of specific satisfactions – relative satisfactions – raises an entirely different set of considerations, and directs attention to the specific features of tasks that form a basis for comparison. Consideration of the specific work realities associated with workers' task preferences reveals two major factors. On the one hand is a preference for tasks that induce strong forces within the individual to complete or continue them, and on the other hand a preference for tasks over which the individual has considerable personal control. These factors contribute to the development of what has been described above as 'task orientation' – that is, a state of affairs in which the individual's interest is aroused, engaged and directed by the character of the task.

While it is difficult to see how there could be, in modern industry, any substantial increase in the proportion of creative or otherwise libidinally satisfying tasks (although there is a consistent trend toward the reduction of working hours and a corresponding increase in the proportion of time that may be devoted to libidinal satisfaction), it is possible to conceive of a considerable reduction in the degree of alienation associated with work. This, if it can be done by creating the conditions for task orientation, need not necessarily negate the technological requirements of an enterprise, nor seriously modify its primary task or purpose. It should be noted that these modifications are still modifications of 'relative satisfactions'. It is not suggested that they could make work so satisfying as to eliminate the distinction between work and leisure, i.e. to restore the ancient distinction of work and rest (see Curle, 1949). None of the modifications discussed here is likely to lessen the pressure toward shorter working hours. It is this conception of a satisfying task relation that appears to be implicit in Rice's general proposition that: 'the effective performance of a primary task can provide an important source of satisfaction for those engaged upon it' (1958, p. 33).

Both the possibilities and the limitations of such changes should become clearer from a discussion of the conditions under which task orientation will tend to emerge and the effects such an orientation is likely to have. The two primary conditions for 'task orientation' to emerge seem to be those that underlie workers' task preferences, namely that:

1. The individual should have control over the materials and processes of the task.

2. The structural characteristics of the task be such as to induce forces on the individual toward aiding its completion or continuation.

Both of these aspects have tended to be ignored by experimental psychologists because of their assumption that an individual will only be motivated to work when impelled by his own internal forces, i.e. conditions (1) and (2) above. The present distinction arises from recent efforts to understand those instances in which 'there is activity growing out of interest in the task itself, in the problems and challenges it offers. The task guides the person, steers his action, becomes the centre of concern' (Asch, 1957, p. 303). This distinction does not imply that personal motivations are absent but asks 'whether the ego can lend itself to a task or whether it remains the centre of reference' (Asch, 1957, p. 304).

In the absence of control over his task, an individual will find himself split between a concern for the task and a constant 'looking over the shoulder' at the alien source of control.[1] [. . .]

The degree of control possessed by the individual will depend not only upon the nature of the task or the authority that is delegated to him, but also upon the knowledge and skill he brings to the task. Thus, the knowledge that a skilled man brings to a job enables him to make choices between alternative modes and rates of operation that are not obvious to an unskilled man. As pointed out by Jaques (1956), these aspects refer to the *discretionary content* of a task, 'of all those elements in which choice of how to do a job was left to the person doing it . . . having to choose the best feeds and speeds for an improvised job on a machine; having to decide whether the finish on a piece of work would satisfy some particular customer; . . . having to plan and organize one's work in order to get it done within a prescribed time' (p. 34). Degree of control is also dependent upon the extent to which an individual is free from intervention in the form of inspection or supervisory check-up

1. Such as external control by the supervisor [Ed.].

(what Jaques, 1956, has termed *the time span of responsibility*).

The second set of conditions affecting task orientation are structural characteristics of the tasks. Within the mass of experimental work on learning, it has been amply proven that degree of structure of a task has considerable psychological influence. Thus, if the task is too complicated for an individual he will display vicarious trial and error activity provided he is motivated to try to learn. If the task is so simple in structure as to appear 'structureless', learning will again only occur if rewarded or punished in a strictly scheduled fashion and will take the form of blind conditioning. Between these limits there is a recognized range of meaningfully structured material in which the individual learns by varying degrees of insight and, significantly, learns without extrinsic reward or punishment.

From the point of view of performance as distinct from learning, the effect of structure has been less studied. It has, however, been demonstrated that:

1. There can be psychological forces toward performance of a task other than those arising from pre-existent needs within the person (see Asch, 1957, p. 308–310, Hente and Aull, 1953, and Lewis, 1944). 'To the extent that the individual grasps the task and his function, he places himself within the demands of the system: the needs of the task become *the environment of requirements* to which he subordinates his actions' (Asch, 1957, p. 175).

2. Repetitive performance of a task more quickly leads to satiation, the smaller and simpler is the task (see Lewin's review of these experiments, 1951, p. 283–4). Visual attention has been found to be similarly influenced by the pattern of changes in the perceptual field (Dember and Earl, 1957). The most general statement of the relation between structure of a task and activity has come from Peak (1958):

The condition of maximum duration of activity is to be expected, therefore, at some distance between parts which is great enough to prevent immediate onset of decrement and yet small enough to provide relatively high probability of continuing transmission of activation from one part of the structure to another (p. 831).

This principle of optimum structure does not, however, indicate the particular structural forms most conducive to maintaining performance (though this problem receives some attention from Katz, 1949, and Wertheimer, 1945). Within the field of industrial work Baldamus (1951) has done much to bring together the available data. He postulates several different forms of 'traction' and sources of resistance that commonly arise in modern industrial work. He distinguishes the different types of traction 'according to the external objective cause which tends to bind successive cycles into a continuous flow of activity' (p. 48), e.g. fine traction, process traction, batch traction (see Smith and Lem, 1955) and object traction (corresponding to the oft observed tendency to complete a whole object). The sources of resistance are located primarily in those things that break the continuity of work, e.g. poor tools and materials, brief work cycles. Tasks do vary with respect to these structured features and, on the available evidence, it seems that such variations make it more or less easy for a worker to become absorbed in his task.

Where the definition of the work role and the nature of the task permit the development of task-orientation, the following differences tend to emerge between behaviour in these conditions and that in conditions of 'ego-orientation'.[2]

1. ... task-orientation frees one for seeing and understanding situations in their own terms. In contrast, focusing on the self may interfere with giving oneself to the task, it may restrict or narrow the outlook by introducing directions alien to the task and deprive the person of freedom to abandon pre-determined paths and follow in new directions.

2. The attitude of intrinsic interest may produce a more serene relation to the task.

3. Whether a person can command a sustained interest in a given direction may depend on the nature of his relation to it: if the interests of the ego are no longer served by a given activity the ground for its pursuit will vanish ... we would expect the dynamics of task-oriented interests to be different, that the activity itself would provide a force for its continuation and proper completion. In general we would expect a task-oriented person to be more steady and reliable.

4. ... the important possibility must be considered that the ego may simply not be able to furnish the forces for dealing with certain situations no matter how strong the ego forces may be.

  2. Instrumental work; or work done as a means to an end outside the work setting [Ed.].

Unfortunately, a great many industrial tasks lack the structural characteristics required for task orientation and the demand for close coordination makes intolerable the discontinuity and variation that would arise from delegating responsibility for the task to the individual.

There is much greater scope in the development of group responsibility for group tasks. If the individual's tasks are genuinely interdependent with the group task, then it is possible for the individual to be meaningfully related to his personal activity through this group task (see Deutsch, 1949a, b, and Horwitz, 1954). A group task with its greater size and complexity is more likely to provide structural conditions conducive to goal setting and striving. If it has a measure of autonomy and a wide sharing of the skills needed for its task, a group is also able to provide a degree of continuity in performance that is unlikely to be achieved by individuals under the control of a supervisor.

Such work groups also have the effect of countering one of the undesirable by-products of the alienation of the individual from his productive activity – his estrangement from his fellow-workers. If a worker dislikes his personal task he is little likely to be interested in maintaining the relations with others that arise from interdependence of their tasks. Attempts by others to get his help or offer theirs are likely to be regarded by him as attempts to manipulate him for alien ends. If, on the other hand, a worker finds that his participation in the group gives meaning to his activity, it is likely that his task-mediated relations will become satisfying. Offers or requests for help will tend to be referred to the shared goals and norms and not to be interpreted as condescension or manipulation.

In many cases, the needs for coordination may be met effectively by embedding work-roles into a primary work group with its corresponding group task (see Trist, 1953, paras. 69–73). By allowing an appropriate degree of self-government to such groups, the first level supervisory requirements are re-centered on relating the task performances of such groups to each other and to the various service groups. The supervisor himself would be less concerned with wielding sanctions under these conditions. When the internal sanctions of the group are inadequate, the matter would normally concern a higher level of management. The supervisory role would, however, require a higher level of conceptual skill. The groups to be supervised are more complex than the individual role and the extent of their activities over space and time makes it more difficult to oversee them directly and hence necessary to attempt some conceptual representation of what is going on. Effective supervision would entail planning further ahead so that the groups receive sufficient support and servicing to keep them functioning. The orientation of the first level supervisory role would then be more clearly toward the overall task of co-ordination (and thus similar to the orientation of higher level management) and less preoccupied with creating and maintaining the individual task relation that is otherwise a prerequisite of his coordinating function (see NIIP, 1951, pp. 27–30). As a general proposition, it is suggested that the *primary task of the supervisor is to manage the immediate boundary conditions of the worker – task relation, and thus effectively relate them to the larger organizational structures.*[3] If he gets involved directly in this relation, his primary task is likely to suffer.

While this comparison helps to reveal the nature of the supervisory requirements, it should be clear that an enterprise is not completely free to choose between the isolated and group organization of tasks: 'The degree to which a work group is capable of responsible autonomy is a function of the extent to which its work task is itself autonomous, in the sense of being an independent and self-completing whole' (Wilson and Trist, 1951, para. 22).

The definition of group powers, and hence the delegation of responsibility, is easier to achieve when 'tasks performed by individuals and groups can be performed within definable physical boundaries'. Those responsible for the task can then 'own' their 'territory', 'they can easily identify what is theirs and who belongs in it. They can raise questions about the right of others, not engaged on the task, to be there' (Rice, 1958, p. 35).

There are always certain additional limits implicit in the kinds of persons in the group, the ability of the group effectively to exercise control over the task and its ability to take responsibility.

These conditions are not always present. Merely dictating that such-and-such operatives shall constitute a group would not, in

3. Italics added [Ed.].

the absence of these conditions, make any significant difference to the supervisory requirements. [. . .]

Work relationship structures and occupational roles

Assuming that a technological system creates demands, Trist and Bamforth (1951) have postulated that these are met, in the first instance, by 'bringing into existence a *work relationship structure*' (p. 9). This structure is related to a set of *tasks and task-inter-dependencies* that together with what is done by the machines and apparatus constitute the cycle of *component operations* required by the productive process under its particular conditions of mechanization, spatio-temporal scale, immediate environment, etc. For a longwall coal mining technology Trist and Bamforth (1951) showed that analysis of these last three sets of conditions (dimensions of technological systems) revealed much of what the technological system required for task performances of different kinds and intensities and for task coordination. They also indicated a need for further concepts that would describe the task requirements in ways which would link up with the experience of the person doing it (see their discussion of the role of the filler) and describe the task interdependencies in ways which would allow them to be compared directly with corresponding patterns of social work relations. A key part was attributed to the concept of *occupational role* in that it serves to identify the point at which the individual is located within the work relationship structure and where he stands in relation to the production process: 'Occupational roles express the relationship between a production process and the social organization of the group. In one direction they are related to tasks which are related to each other; in the other to people who are also related to each other' (p. 14).

The role concept does not in itself explain how an individual will experience his tasks, nor does it meet the need for concepts to explain the various forms of interdependence that exist between tasks and between workers.

Regarding the first mentioned deficiency, the concept of role does, however, structure this problem so that one would theoretically expect a task to be experienced not in isolation but in the context of carrying a role which simultaneously generates experience of dependence, subordination, selfworth, trust, isolation, etc. Thus, although an individual may find his immediate task distasteful (and this is probably the most typical situation at operative level in modern industry), he may gain some compensatory satisfaction from those other aspects of his role that concern his relations to fellow workers, supervisors and the enterprise. (See Sharp, 1954, pp. 231–5, who gives some evidence that a very distasteful task may be tolerated because 'the boss is a good type'.) [. . .]

Thus, although it is analytically necessary to distinguish the components of a role, it is likely that they are normally experienced by the role encumbents as parts of a *gestalt*. This conclusion corresponds broadly to Katz's summary formulation of his 'laws of mental work': 'the duration and degree of reliability of the process of work on a set piece of material are conditioned by the nature of the whole task into which this fits as a part' (1949, p. 175).

Workers' own perceptions appear to be such that they have difficulty in thinking about any part of their role without referring it to the rest of the role (see Wyatt and Marriott, 1956, p. 4). [. . .]

The concept of occupational role suggests, secondly, that at the next level of analysis task interdependencies need to be coordinated primarily to role relationships rather than to inter-personal relations, i.e. to the social relations that are formed to cope with demands of the task rather than to those that arise directly between the workers as persons.

This distinction corresponds to that made by Jennings (1947) between '*socio-group*' and '*psycho-group*'. The socio-group is based on the feelings of individuals towards each other as group members contributing more or less usefully to the group tasks: the psycho-group consists of persons who have chosen each other because of individual preference. Jennings found a tendency for socio-group members to subjugate their psycho-group preferences, while within the socio-group, even to the point of choosing others whom they personally dislike.

Gross (1956) has aptly described the underlying processes as those of *symbiosis* and *consensus* respectively. This distinction draws attention to a further distinction between formally defined symbiotic role structure, informal symbiotic relations and informal consensual relations. In the informal symbiotic relations, the individuals remain orientated to the institutional goals but in the consensual relations individuals are (according to our use of the terms) orientated toward personal goals that are not adequately catered for, or may even be threatened by, the formal organizational goals. These primary groups on a consensual basis will be functional to the extent that they save the organization the trouble of catering for these personal feelings and interests and prevent more extreme individual solutions of absenteeism and accidents (in military organization these groups appear to lessen the chances of desertion and self-wounding). They will be dysfunctional if they can only pursue their interests at the expense of organizational goals for, in this case, they will be more able to resist organizational pressures than they would as isolated individuals (Collins *et al.*, 1946, Roy, 1952, 1954, and Dalton, 1948).

The distinction between formal and informal symbiotic relations arises in the operation of almost any organization because of the difficulty and undesirability of formally specifying the structure so as to account for all contingencies. It is undesirable to 'overstructure' the role system because of the rigidity and lack of responsibility this engenders. Contingencies, by their very nature, cannot be planned so that they occur when a particular class of persons is present and able to deal with them; if everyone is made formally responsible then, in practice, no one is responsible. The inadequacies of formal role definition are likely to become more obvious the more detailed and precise the division of labour. Analysing several organizations (industrial and military), Gross (1953) found that the narrowing and multiplication of roles had got to the point where important task interdependencies had been lost sight of. The gap had been filled by the formation of informal groups (where ecological factors permitted). These informal groups reflected the formally unrecognized interdependencies and functioned to provide the individual with an assurance of support for his task performance that he otherwise was without. 'Isolates' were found to be particularly vulnerable in the inadequacies of the formal role structure. (See Blau, 1954 and Hughes, 1946, for evidence of similar informal groups.)

Responsive to the same factors, the formal and informal

symbiotic ties may be regarded as two aspects of the role structure. 'Informality' does not imply the lack of tradition or sanctions but simply that the traditions are carried by the peers and not explicitly recognized by the management.

From what has been mentioned above, it is clear that there is an acute practical problem in trying to 'map' the task structure with a formal role structure. '*Over-structuring*' or '*under-structuring*' can result in difficulties; reliance on informal 'mapping', while it may be immediately effective, reduces the area of control of the enterprise leadership and hence makes it more difficult for them to direct the development of the enterprise to meet wider challenges (quite apart from the fact that such informal groups are more likely to be subverted by personal interests, i.e. shift toward a consensual basis). The considerable body of evidence about working groups suggests that formal recognition of group responsibility may close the gap between the definition of roles and the wide range of task interdependencies that have to be accounted for. A difficulty remains, however, in detecting within the total task structure a genuine basis for such groups.

A distinctive contribution to the practical problem of 'mapping' has been made in the recognition that there may be, and frequently are, groupings of tasks within the productive process that have 'whole' characteristics and that a qualitatively different relation of tasks and roles can emerge when there is a set of *connected roles* grouped around such a whole task. Clearly, this allows for a closer coordination of role and task interdependencies than where these are mediated only by the overall tasks. Among other properties these 'role-sets' (see Merton, 1957) show greater autonomy and are less dependent upon external supervision and coordination (see Trist and Bamforth, 1951, on the longwall ripping team, and Rice, 1958, on the reorganized weaving teams). It is also suggested that this enables an individual to experience through his group membership the satisfaction of completing a whole task which is denied to him in his individual tasks (Wilson and Trist, 1951, para. 38; for experimental evidence of this effect see Horwitz, 1954, and Asch, 1957).

A group consisting of the smallest number that can perform a 'whole' task and can satisfy the social and psychological needs of its members is, alike from the point of view of task performance and of those

performing it, the most satisfactory and efficient group (Rice, 1958, p. 36).

It will be noted that the recognition of this phenomenon has been bound up with the assumption that it operates through the psychological identification of the individual with the other persons in the group rather than through the role definition of an individual's task as part of the whole task. Thus Rice (1958) discusses the optimum size of the group in terms of clinical experience (p. 37) and Wilson and Trist (1951) express surprise when they find this phenomenon in a group of nineteen: 'We had thought that a group of nineteen might be rather large, but experience of relations on the face has considerably reassured us on this point' (Wilson and Trist, 1951, para. 46).

In a later mining study, this phenomenon was observed in a primary work group of over forty members. This question of group size is but one further facet of the general problem that has plagued attempts to analyse the relation between task structures and work relationship structures (see Trist and Murray, 1958).

Briefly, *this problem has been that of reconciling personal obligations and role obligations*. It has been frequently observed that men work better when the relations on the job are friendly, and yet there are some facts to suggest that this is only part of the story – that men will carry out their jobs regardless of personal feelings, if their roles are well enough related to each other. If this were all of the story, the scope for 'mapping' by groups would be limited and the procedures for selecting and establishing such groups would be different to those otherwise suggested.

The assumption that 'friendliness' is the critical factor has been at the centre of [the] semi-ideological 'human relations' movement. [. . .]

This argument has been elaborated with the demonstration that the amount of interaction tends to be positively related to the degree of friendliness (see Homans, 1951) and by distinguishing between two phenomena that tended to be read into the concept of 'friendship', i.e. 'willingness to help' and 'awareness of the needs of others'. [. . .]

If friendship is a suspect source of 'will to help', is there no other way in which interpersonal relations can be ordered for quite large primary work groups so that such a 'will to help' is

created? It is suggested that what is required are relations in which men see their task performances as mutually supporting. Awareness of such mutually supportive relations is not equivalent to, or dependent upon, friendships and would tend to be disrupted by interpersonal hostility or intensive friendships. Several important facts point to the significance of 'mutual support' in productive relations:

1. An individual may not be willing to accept his task in the absence of support even though he could perform it (Marshall, 1947, and Hughes, 1946).

2. If he sees support as coming, at least in part, from the group with whom his task makes him interdependent, then he will tend to value the group, to accept the group task as in part his own and, as a corollary, wish to be a person of significance for the group and to have his task performance accepted as a significant contribution to the group task.

There is little doubt that some friendliness will tend to develop under these circumstances but (a) it will be constrained by the task requirements, and (b) it remains essentially a by-product of group formation, not in itself crucial for enhanced performance. From this latter viewpoint, it is clear that friendship might be expected to occur with high performance even though it is not causally related to the latter, and one would expect to find it constrained, e.g. to on-the-job relations. Lafitte (1958) in his study of six factories found that only a third of the workers had any sort of mutual personal contact with each other off the job and only 1 per cent had close friends.

What appears to be required is that support be built into the organization of the roles, if the task performance demands it: that with interdependent tasks the roles be so defined as to enhance mutual support and the tasks be so organized or rewarded as to facilitate identification of part-tasks with the whole. [. . .]

Not only does the concept of role serve to structure [the] problem, but, in relating social and psychological phenomena, [it] helps to delimit the area within which psychological explanations can be regarded as alone adequate. Along with the tendency in social science to treat technological factors in a light-

hearted and arbitrary fashion, there has been a tendency to give psychological explanations of phenomena that one might well suspect of needing sociological explanation (or explanation in terms of the objective demands of the work situation). This 'psychologizing' has taken both the extreme form of interpreting collective behaviour as if it were individual clinical behaviour and the less obvious form of assuming that the answers to the key problems of socio-technical systems lie within the sphere of small face-to-face group behaviour (see Wilensky's, 1957, discussion of these biases).

The appropriate level for analysis of the social system and the roles is that of sociology. Within this sociological setting the concept of role retains its function of bridging the gap between the individual and the social structure by being coordinated to the concept of 'psychological power-field', i.e. of being such that it has the power of inducing force-fields in the life space of an individual. [. . .]

The appropriate area for the employment of psychological concepts will be that which is concerned with the way in which the individual copes with these forces, particularly as they confront him in his occupational role (see Trist and Bamforth, 1951, and Jaques, 1951). Precisely because the psychological problems centre around roles, there will be similarities in what different individuals experience and hence a tendency for phenomena to emerge that require concepts of collective psychology as well as individual psychology. [. . .]

Higher mechanization and the problems of alienation

Under conditions of higher mechanization, it may be easier to engage an operative's interests and loyalties in the mission of the enterprise. If the trends remarked on earlier are predominant, then enterprises with advanced technologies are more likely consciously to relate themselves to their markets on a long-term basis, to seek distinctive competence and to cultivate an elite leadership with a high degree of solidarity. A relatively smaller work force, fewer levels of authority and a smaller proportion of wage-earners should make it easier to communicate and establish a shared, articulate set of goals of behavioural norms.

Alienation from one's activity remains a more complex

problem. It may be relevant for a smaller proportion of the work roles as the operative roles decline in numbers relative to maintenance and other skilled supporting activities. Maintenance work normally allows the worker greater control over his activities and, in restoring machinery and apparatus to working order, is high in 'object traction' (see Walker, 1957, on the general satisfaction of maintenance men with their roles). The other supporting roles in an advanced technology are likely to include a high proportion of decision-making and scientific roles.

It is more difficult to specify the trends in the operative roles. From the few case studies that deal with the psychological aspects of automation it is not possible to separate out with any certainty what is general from what is transient or peculiar to the particular enterprise. The following statement of trends is, therefore, to be regarded as suggestive of matters worth further attention.

1. Change in task requirements (*operative skills*) from lower order gross motor skills to perceptual and conceptual skills. The current developments in the technology of physical forming industries will tend to cluster at the lower end with fewer tasks requiring conceptual skill.

2. A substantial increase in the cycle time with a consequent increase in the rate of repetition of each unit operation. Loss of traction due to this (see Baldamus, 1951) may be offset by increase in the range of tasks allotted to roles. With the unevenness of mechanization that is characteristic of the lower stages of development, three main types of operative roles emerge, each with its own features:

(a) A considerable increase in job pressure (and physical fatigue) in those anachronous tasks in which substantial physical energy must be expended to complete the work of the machines (e.g. Walker, 1957, pp. 33–4, 86–7, on the jobs of piercer and plugger[4]). The physical nature of these tasks tends to preclude an enlargement to offset the shorter cycle time of the unit operation to which it is associated.

(b) Increased pressure for persistent surveillance in those jobs

4. Walker (1957) is the primary reference for the following discussion. Walker's study of the Lorain Tube Mills is the most important study we yet have of the effects of automation in a given enterprise over a considerable period of time.

where the physical labour is eliminated but no self-correcting controls built into the machines. The strain of attending to the perceptual task will vary with the structural features of what is being attended to, and hence no general inference is at present feasible (see Dember and Earl, 1957).

(c) No one-to-one relation between speed of production and the pressure on jobs requiring conceptual skills. These jobs usually entail watching for the odd occasions on which a self-regulating process tends to move out of control.

3. In the first type of job the increase in rate of production may be such as to turn any element of 'line-traction' into a pressure, i.e. the worker no longer feels more or less unconsciously drawn into the tempo of the task, but must consciously strive to keep up with it (Walker, pp. 86–7). Under these circumstances the 'resistances' and 'interruptions' become more salient and one could expect a 'narrowing' of the psychological field with a consequent lessening of any element of 'whole traction' that may exist (Walker, p. 200), i.e. the worker becomes so involved in surmounting the obstacles of his immediate task that he has not time to care about the contribution he is making to the overall task.

In the second type of job the monitor-corrector is so tied to his job of watching that he also will tend to have less concern with the overall task (less 'object traction'), but there may be some remaining line traction (e.g. the evidence of the nine-stand and bar inserter operators, pp. 90, 104 and 203).

In the third type of job there would tend to be a considerable degree of traction. However, the outstanding difference between these jobs is not encompassed by notions of work traction and resistance. These notions seem appropriate to the continuous expenditure of effort but not to the maintenance of a 'set to respond'. With the type (a) jobs, one gets the impression that the operator has little influence on the overall production process. If he fails to keep up with the push of the preceding machines, the effects tend to be confined to loss of production. With types (b) and (c) jobs, failure may lead to serious accidents (Walker, 1957, pp. 32 and 33), and hence they have to sense the requirements of tasks preceding and following their own (p. 172). In the latter jobs the actual range of responsibilities tends to be extended to cover coordination of more phases and sometimes technical super-

vision of others. Thus on the Lorain Mill, the mandrel mill operator has a type (c) job and he carries the responsibilities of a charge-hand over the reheating furnace and sizer-reducer; on the Assel Mill (reported by P.E.P., 1957) it is a type (b) job and the operator is more or less confined to it. Jobs demanding conceptual or perceptual skills tend to be more concerned with keeping the system in operation, rather than with producing as such, and with damage avoidance and quality control. These are matters that are normally the concern of management. [. . .]

Thus, technological changes toward greater automaticity promise no automatic solution of the human problems of industry. The problems of alienation may become even more acute in certain transitional work roles, while offering better conditions in the more advanced work roles. The gravest danger probably lies in trying to carry over into the new situation the role structures of the old. This appears to have happened in the Tube Mills studied by Walker (1957) and P.E.P. (1957). In both cases the evidence suggests an attenuation of work team relations: more isolated roles occur and, while there is heightened dependence, there is less interdependence. One suspects that the social system as well as the technology needs to be thought through afresh with each major change.

References

ASCH, S. E. (1957), *Social Psychology*, Prentice-Hall.

BALDAMUS, W. (1951), 'Incentives and work analysis', *University of Birmingham Studies in economy and society*, Monog. A.1.

BALDAMUS, W. (1958), 'Types of work and motivation', *British Journal of Sociology*, vol. 2, pp. 44–58.

BARTLEY, S. H., and CHUTE, E. (1947), *Fatigue and Impairment in Man*, McGraw-Hill.

BELL, D. (1956), *Work and Its Discontents*, Beacon Press.

BLAU, P. (1954), 'Patterns of interaction among a group of officials in a government agency', *Human Relations*, vol. 7, pp. 337–48.

CHISHOLM, G. B. (1946), 'The re-establishment of peacetime society: the responsibility of psychiatry', *Psychiatry*, vol. 9, pp. 3–11.

COLLINS, D., DALTON, M., and ROY, D. M. (1946), 'Restriction of output and social cleavage in industry', *Applied Anthropology*, vol. 5, no. 3, pp. 1–14.

CURLE, A. (1948), 'Transitional communities and social reconnection: a follow-up study of the civil resettlement of British P.o.W.'s, Part I', *Human Relations*, vol. 1, pp. 42–68.

CURLE, A. (1949), 'Incentives to work: an anthropological appraisal', *Human Relations*, vol. 2, pp. 41–8.

DALTON, M. (1948), 'The industrial "rate-buster": a characterization', *Applied Anthropology*, vol. 7, no. 1, pp. 5–18.

DEMBER, W. N., and EARL, R. W. (1957), 'Analysis of exploratory, manipulatory and curiosity behaviors', *Psychological Review*, vol. 64, pp. 91–6.

DEUTSCH, M. (1949a), 'A theory of co-operation and competition', *Human Relations*, vol. 2, pp. 129–52.

DEUTSCH, M. (1949b), 'An experimental study of the effects of co-operation and competition upon group processes', *Human Relations*, vol. 2, pp. 199–231.

GOULDNER, A. W. (1955), 'Metaphysical pathos and the theory of bureaucracy', *American Political Science Review*, vol. 49, pp. 496–507.

GROSS, E. (1953), 'Some functional consequences of primary controls in formal work organizations', *American Sociological Review*, vol. 18, pp. 368–73.

GROSS, E. (1956), 'Symbiosis and consensus as integrative factors in small groups', *American Sociological Review*, vol. 21, pp. 174–9.

HENTE, M., and AULL, G. (1953), 'Factors decisive for resumption of interrupted activities: the question reopened', *Psychological Review*, vol. 60, pp. 81–8.

HOMANS, G. (1951), *The Human Group*, Routledge & Kegan Paul.

HORWITZ, M. (1954), 'The recall of interrupted group tasks: an experimental study of individual motivation in relation to group goals', *Human Relations*, vol. 11, pp. 3–38.

HUGHES, E. C. (1946), 'The knitting of racial groups in industry', *American Sociological Review*, vol. 11, pp. 512–19.

JAQUES, E. (1951), *The Changing Culture of a Factory*, Tavistock.

JAQUES, E. (1956), *The Measurement of Responsibility*, Tavistock.

JENNINGS, H. H. (1947), 'Leadership and sociometric choice', *Sociometry*, vol. 10, pp. 32–49.

KATZ, D. (1949), 'Gestalt laws of mental work', *British Journal of Psychology*, vol. 39, pp. 175–83.

LAFITTE, P. (1958), *Social Structure and Personality in the Factory*, Routledge & Kegan Paul.

LEWIN, K. (1951), *Field Theory in Social Science*, Harper.

LEWIS, H. B. (1944), 'An experimental study of the role of the ego in work: 1. the role of the ego in co-operative work', *Journal of Experimental Psychology*, vol. 34, pp. 113–26.

MARSHALL, S. L. A. (1947), *Men Under Fire*, Morrow.

MERTON, R. K. (1957), 'The role-set: problems in sociological theory', *British Journal of Sociology*, vol. 8, pp. 106–20.

N.I.I.P. (1951), *The Foreman*, Staples Press.

PEAK, H. (1958), 'Psychological structure and psychological activity', *Psychological Review*, vol. 65, pp. 325–47.

PEDERSEN-KRAG, G. (1951), 'A psychoanalytic approach to mass production', *Psychoanalytic Quarterly*, vol. 20, pp. 434–51.

P.E.P. (1957), *Three Case Studies in Automation*, Political and Economic Planning.

RICE, A. K. (1958), *Productivity and Social Organisation: The Ahmedabad Experiment*, Tavistock.

ROY, D. (1952), 'Quota restriction and goldbricking in a machine shop', *American Journal of Sociology*, vol. 57, pp. 427–42.

ROY, D. (1954), 'Efficiency and "the fix": informal intergroup relations in a piecework machine shop', *American Journal of Sociology*, vol. 60, pp. 255–66.

RYAN, T. A. (1947), *Work and Effort*, Ronald Press.

SELZNICK, P. (1948), 'Foundations of the theory of organization', *American Sociological Review*, vol. 13, pp. 25–35.

SHARP, G. B. (1954), 'The place of work in social life', in O. A. Oeser and S. B. Hammond (eds.), *Social Structure and Personality in a City*, Routledge & Kegan Paul, ch. 17, pp. 223–37.

SMITH, P. C., and LEM, C. (1955), 'Positive aspects of motivation in repetitive work: effects of lot size upon spacing of voluntary work stoppages', *Journal of Applied Psychology*, vol. 39, pp. 330–33.

TRIST, E. L. (1953), 'Some observations on the machine face as a socio-technical system', *T.I.H.R.*, doc. 341.

TRIST, E. L., and BAMFORTH, K. W. (1951), 'Some social and psychological consequences of the Longwall method of coal-getting', *Human Relations*, vol. 4, pp. 3–38.

TRIST, E. L., and MURRAY, H. (1958), 'Work organization at the coal face: a comparative study of mining systems', *T.I.H.R.*, doc. 506.

WALKER, C. R. (1957), *Toward the Automatic Factory*, Yale University Press.

WARNER, W. L., and LOW, J. O. (1947), *The Social System of the Modern Factory*, Yale University Press.

WERTHEIMER, M. (1945), *Productive Thinking*, Harper; new edn, Tavistock, 1961.

WILENSKY, H. L. (1957), 'Human relations in the workplace: an appraisal of some recent research', in C. M. Arensberg *et al.* (eds.), *Research in Industrial Human Relations*, Harper, ch. 3.

WILSON, A. T. M., and TRIST, E. L. (1951), 'The Bolsover system of continuous mining', *T.I.H.R.*, doc. 290.

WYATT, S., and MARRIOTT, R. (1956), 'A study of attitudes to factory work', *M.R.C.*, *Special Report Series No. 292*, HMSO.

15 Maxine Bucklow

A New Role for the Work Group

Excerpts from M. Bucklow, 'A new role for the work group', *Administrative Science Quarterly*, vol. 11, 1966, pp. 59–78.

This article discusses the role assigned to the work group to bring about desired changes in employee motivation, and suggests that the role proposed by the Tavistock Institute of Human Relations in London has been more successful than earlier approaches which derived largely from the Hawthorne studies (Roethlisberger and Dickson, 1949). The Hawthorne work directed attention to the existence of small informal face-to-face groups within larger work groups. Members of the informal groups shared in a variety of activities and beliefs common to the group, which were a source of satisfaction, strength and security, and provided a buffer against the demands of the larger world of department and factory. Elton Mayo (1933, 1946, 1947) extrapolated from these studies to a general social theory centered on the assumption of a basic human need to be gregarious. His influence was largely responsible for the widely held belief that employees were motivated by membership in small primary groups.

The influence of Lewin

This interest in small groups was greatly reinforced in the immediate post-war years by the research associated with Kurt Lewin. He defined the group as a dynamic system of interaction between at least two people, and group life as involving a continuous process of adaptation of individuals to one another and to their mutual needs and problems. In this process a structure emerged, which became more stable and organized as the group continued to function. Lewin initiated an era of rigorous laboratory studies into the dynamics of group functioning, designed to reveal fundamental laws of group life. Although much was learned about communication networks, leadership, group cohesion, norms,

and so on, empirical results were often conflicting and progress toward basic laws disappointing.

Participation in group decision making

Lewin's influence on industrial practice came largely from the three field studies he directed with children's play groups, housewives, and young-girl pajama machinists at the Harwood Manufacturing Company. The results suggested that involvement in group decision and democratic methods of leadership increased output and member satisfaction. This evidence gave rise to a long period of uncritical adherence to participation and democratic management as means of increasing employee motivation (see Lewin, 1948, and Lewin, Lippitt and White, 1939).

In industry, research did not reproduce results as marked as those of the original Lewin studies, and in general democratic practices were more successful in achieving satisfaction than efficiency. Research workers such as Maier, Likert and McGregor realized that their techniques had to be linked to the organizational framework. Likert (1961) used overlapping group families and linking-pin functions to tie his participation groups to all levels of the organization. Similarly, Maier's new look at organization envisaged participation in problem-solving conferences at all levels through overlapping membership (Maier and Hayes, 1962). Katz (1964) and Argyris (1964) criticized these proposals because they only softened organizational impact, and made no basic change in the distribution of rewards, and of power and authority. It would also be difficult for the rank-and-file worker to take part in such proposals.

The results achieved at Harwood were consistently interpreted in terms of the motivating power of involvement in group decision making, irrespective of the kind of decision or the extent of participation. Maier (1952) saw unanimous group decision as the critical motivating device. He considered the type of problems involved as unimportant, and restricted decisions largely to human relations problems. He has more recently been concerned to demonstrate that the quality of decisions need not be lowered by the use of group methods (Maier, 1963). Likert (1961) saw the central role of the face-to-face work group almost through Mayo's eyes. The group motivated members through their need for ap-

proval and support and maintained a sense of personal worth. For Likert an important device in building effective groups of this kind was group participation in a limited area of decisions, although decisions did not have to be unanimous. This approach of Likert's is widely held by managers and researchers at the present time. [. . .]

Involvement in T-groups

Lewin's second major influence was in the development of the training laboratory by those working at the National Training Laboratory at Bethel from 1947 onwards. New psychological knowledge about groups was used to facilitate group and individual learning, largely through the development of the T-group. [. . .]

Bennis (1963) pointed to the shift in emphasis from personal change to organizational development among those anxious to demonstrate impact by the laboratory. In 1957 and 1958, a new training program for staff and action leaders was conducted at Bethel, and special programs were developed and used in firms. [. . .]

Their long-term program was directed at changing individual cognitive maps through the instrumented T-group, which involved virtual self-direction by participants. This modification was intended to strengthen motivation to transfer learning from the laboratory. For this reason the program was also tied to the organization through the use in laboratories of members from diagonal slices of levels and horizontal units, and superior–subordinate pairs. Special problem-solving groups were also set up within the organization to diagnose needs, clarify goals and plan for organizational change.

Shepard's (1960) evaluation showed that this long-term program had no greater impact than the typical short laboratory. Personal change was widespread through many levels and groups, but this had little impact on organizational practices. As Blake and his associates (1964) were more concerned with organizational than individual development, their latest program excluded the T-group and used a more structured seminar approach. This was built around the managerial grid, a device to help participants assess their managerial styles and attitudes, using concepts from Blake's integrated theory of management. The program was tied to the

organization through problem-solving groups, which used simulated organizational problems and later real problems of increasingly more critical and long-term significance. An evaluation within a firm showed that managers could learn these new styles and apply them with some effectiveness for the organization.

The evidence suggests that the use of T-group training in industry leads to increased self-knowledge, but that other approaches are needed if organizational development is desired. Blake's ambitious program concentrated on changing managerial behavior and tying the learning process to the organization by considering organizational needs and problems. He failed to consider the limitations imposed by technology and organization structure, and to see that basic changes in these might be necessary.

Argyris (1964) has been the only T-group exponent to understand these limitations and to suggest ways to overcome them. He recommends that laboratory training should be used only with management groups, as behavior at the top is considerably influenced by skill in interpersonal relationships. Behavior at lower levels is determined largely by technology and control systems, and can be changed only by new thinking about job design, controls and the authority system.

The concept of group autonomy

It is difficult to accept the concept of the motivating power of the primary work group in the face of research results. Herbert Thelen (1954) drew attention to the limitations imposed by technology on the use of T-groups, and suggested the development of small, autonomous work groups. This would involve responsibility for the organization of work, goal setting and training. This proposal was neglected by the T-group adherents, but taken up by Argyris in *Personality and Organization* in 1957. At the time there were few studies on such groups. George Strauss reported a study in which a group of girls in a paint room was given control over the speed of the conveyor, which resulted in marked increases in output and satisfaction. More recently Non-Linear Systems Inc. in California, carried the implementation of McGregor's Theory Y down to the level of the rank-and-file worker. The assembly line was abolished and workers re-organized into small, self-paced groups of seven members responsible for building com-

plete instruments. The result was an increase of 30 per cent in productivity. Motivation was believed to come partly from gregariousness, but largely from the opportunity to use skills, learn and teach, and to take responsibility (see Strauss, 1955, and Kuriloff, 1963).

In 1954, Katz cautioned against 'the glorification of the primary group as a source of work satisfaction', and suggested the importance of group autonomy. This led to the well-known study by Morse and Reimer (1956) in which autonomous groups were compared with hierarchically controlled ones. The autonomy of these groups, however, was largely restricted to decisions about work assignments, length of recess, lunch periods, and so on. It was in no way comparable to the self-direction envisaged by Thelen and Argyris. Workers tried to expand the scope of their decisions, but management refused to delegate more authority, and 'the curve of worker decisions soon reached a peak and began to decline'. Morse and Reimer concluded that 'the granting of "safe" areas of decision making and the withholding of "hot" ones is not likely to work for long' (see Wilensky, 1957, p. 42; and Morse and Reimer, 1956, p. 129).

Disappointment with small groups and employee participation focused attention on the concepts of power and control and on power equalization (Strauss, 1963; Leavitt, 1964; Leavitt and Bass, 1964; and Bass, 1965). Michigan studies of organizational control structures suggested that there was no basis for management's fears that the granting of more control to groups at the bottom would lessen their own authority. Organizational efficiency was found to be related to increased control at all levels, and control was not considered undesirable by low-level workers, when it was a source of involvement for them (Smith and Tannenbaum, 1963; Tannenbaum, 1962). Research into communication networks by Guetzkow and Simon (1955), by Trow (1954), and by Mulder (1959) has made it doubtful that group performance is related to the degree of centrality in networks, but decision centrality, freedom to exert power, responsibility for the completion of one's task, and position autonomy have been found important.

Research at IBM has shown that engineer control of work standards from outside the department was not thought to be legitimate by employees, and correlated negatively with output and satisfaction (Sirota, 1963, and Klein, 1963). Leavitt (1964) points out that despite general agreement that power equalization is a key step in organizational change, there is no movement for its achievement at present. In America the problems of the nature and degree of control to be given to employees, including the rank-and-file-worker, are little understood, and recent significant English research has either been overlooked or misinterpreted by research workers (Bass, 1965).

The influence of Bion

W. R. Bion (1961, 1955), a psychoanalyst of the Melanie Klein school at the Tavistock Clinic in London, used his wartime experiences with group selection methods and small therapy groups to make an important reformulation of psychoanalytic concepts to explain group as well as individual behavior. He thought that the emotional life of the group could best be understood by the use of psychotic mechanisms, particularly regression. He proposed the concept of work as necessary to keep the group related to reality and to the external environment, in much the same way as the ego functioned to maintain personality and its links with reality.

He assumed a basic capacity for cooperation within the group to achieve its task. He further assumed that the group functioned always at two levels, at the conscious level toward its work task and at the unconscious level toward satisfaction of powerful emotional drives. [. . .]

Autonomous work groups

In their early studies in coal mining, the Tavistock workers used his assumptions as a guide to the nature of the work group. These related to size, whole task, a basic capacity for cooperation to achieve the primary task, and satisfactions deriving from its effective accomplishment. Their first comparison of the earliest hand methods with those of the conventional longwall production system focused attention on the responsible autonomy of the multiskilled individual miner, and on the organization of the small underground work group. Responsibility for the work and for supervision rested with the men themselves, requiring a high level of interdependence between members, rotation of roles and tasks, and sharing in a common paynote. This work organization was productive and did not place undue stress on the men and suggested that industrial production systems were essentially sociotechnical systems, in which the social and technical aspects could be causes of stress (Trist and Bamforth, 1951).

Rice (1958) developed the first detailed formulation of the Tavistock's view of the work group in his research in an Indian textile mill. He began with more detailed assumptions about the way in which groups should be organized as to size, skills, status, roles, member control of tasks, opportunity to complete a whole task, and the location of tasks within definite physical boundaries. These were used to develop a theoretical work group organization for an experimental reorganization of the automatic weaving department, in which there had been problems of output and damage following the introduction of automatic looms.

The workers' acceptance of the idea of internally led small groups and their determination to make the new system work, were felt to be some indication of its goodness of fit. After many difficulties and setbacks, quality and quantity were established at higher levels than before the reorganization, so that Rice felt that assumptions about task organization had some validity. Similar reorganization into small internally structured groups was later introduced into a non-automatic shed with similar results. Recent evidence from India indicated that the increase in efficiency and decrease in damage had been maintained in both sheds, and that the group system had been extended (Rice, 1963).

Autonomous groups in coal mining

Rice's Indian study was limited by subjectivity and language difficulties. These were not problems, however, in the Tavistock's rigorous research into problems arising from mechanization in the British coal industry, a study undertaken at the request of the National Coal Board. Comparative studies were made of different stages of technological development, from the early hand methods through the longwall, to more advanced mechanization. The introduction of the longwall had replaced the many different short coal faces throughout the seam with a continuous longwall of coal up to 200 yards long. In its early stage there were no machines and the face was still worked by pairs of men. Later, however, a moving mechanical conveyor belt was introduced to take the coal away from the face. This transformed the whole underground operation. The belt moved along the whole face, so that it had to be treated as a single unit requiring forty to fifty men.

The operation underground was now rather like a small factory, and managers and engineers drew on factory practice to organize the production of coal under these new conditions. The whole coal-getting cycle was broken down into a standard series of operations, each requiring a minimum of skill, and the cycle was finished every twenty-four hours instead of each shift as before. Men were no longer multi-skilled but spent their lives in one job and on one shift. Instead of one rate of payment, there were now five different ones, which brought new differences in pay and status among the men. To keep the cycle running smoothly close co-operation was needed between the various categories of workers and between the shifts. Responsibility for this now rested with management, not with the men. The men did little to help, so great strains were placed on the managers.

There were many problems in this production system. Coal output was below standard and shifts rarely finished their part of the cycle, as the men tended to do only those tasks for which they were paid. Absence rates were high and men were leaving the industry. There was friction between the shifts and many miners that the factory type of work organization was not well suited to the demands of the longwall situation, judged either by output or by the men's reactions. It went against all the long-standing traditions of British coal mining by eliminating the complete self-supervising miner, taking responsibility for the allocation, co-ordination, and supervision of the cycle away from the work team, and destroying the small interdependent group.

The research team devised a new composite work organization for the longwall. This was based on their theoretical assumptions, and on changes already introduced by miners dissatisfied with the conventional longwall. In the composite organization, a small group of men shared a common paynote and carried out all the production operations in each shift. It was successfully tried out in short faces where six to eight men were responsible for the planning of the total cycle in one shift. There was, however, some doubt that the composite would work with much larger coal faces where forty to fifty men would be needed to produce coal.

In a face where the conventional system was in use, management, miners and the union agreed to try the new system. Forty men worked out a new shift pattern, reorganized production operations, and agreed to share equally in a paynote. The men also accepted responsibility for a wider range of jobs, and jobs were rotated. Responsibility for the whole cycle rested largely with the men, and management provided supporting services rather than direct supervision.

A careful comparison was made over one year of a conventional and a composite work organization under very similar underground conditions. The composite work organization rated better in measures of output, turnover, absence, accidents and stress illnesses. This was important confirmation that the composite, which relied on the characteristics of traditional methods, was a more satisfactory form of work organization. Its strength lay in altering the basis of the task and shift systems, so that miners were again multiskilled, and had responsibility for the cycle. It was later found that with still higher levels of mechanization, the work organization that best fitted the new technology again had much in common with the earlier unmechanized system.

A new role for the work group

In the most recent reporting of their work, Trist and his colleagues have reformulated their theoretical position (Trist, Higgin, Murray and Pollock, 1963). The concept that integrates the technological, economic and socio-psychological aspects of a production system is the primary task: the work it has to perform. Work is the key transaction which relates an operating group to its environment and allows it to maintain a steady state. The concept of organizational choice is introduced so as to direct attention to the existence of a range of possible production systems. The task of management is to choose that which best fits the technical and the human requirements.

Major theoretical importance is now given to the concept of responsible autonomy. The organization of small autonomous work groups has been demonstrated in mining and textile situations. Success with composite longwall groups of forty men would widen the practical implications of the concept.

Responsible autonomy is seen as crucial for the satisfactory design of production systems. It gives the work group a central role in the production system, not the peripheral supporting role envisaged by Mayo and Likert, and has successfully motivated rank-and-file workers to greater cooperative effort than other methods. It also makes more basic changes in the distribution of control and power, by transferring some of the traditional authority of management for the control and coordination of jobs, i.e. the part appropriate to the primary group's task, to the men who actually perform the task. Trist criticizes the proposals of McGregor and Likert to achieve these ends, for failing to understand the difficulties involved, particularly the initial anxiety at relaxing traditional management controls over the primary group.

This real transferring of power and control to the group for the operation of the primary task has other advantages. The coal study supports other evidence that increasing control at lower levels does not decrease control at higher levels nor adversely affect efficiency. As Trist suggests, it exerts an upwards pressure in the managing system which affects all roles, so that all levels have more, rather than less, opportunity to carry out their managerial roles in a broader way. Trist now believes that the transfer of some control to autonomous work groups is the only means of overcoming the split at the bottom of the executive system at Glacier Metal Co.

Emery has recently reassessed the Tavistock work at Glacier, and criticizes the early concern with the working through of problems and with the formal aspects of industrial democracy, without making any basic change in the role of the rank-and-file worker. He now sees the development of autonomous work groups as 'the democratization of the work place' and suggests that industrial democracy, while making decisions more democratic, has not altered the content of a worker's relation to his job (Emery, 1963).

Herbst (1962) who made the first detailed day-to-day study of the interactions of a composite group of miners, criticized the Morse and Reimer study for changing only the locus of decision making and not the activities about which decisions were made. He suggested that joint participation in the task may be a necessary prerequisite for joint decision making to be maintained.

It has been argued that the Tavistock concept of the autonomous work group goes far towards solving some of the problems of worker motivation, participation and power equalization, with which American researchers are preoccupied. The Tavistock concept also provides a new role for the work group different from that advocated by Mayo, Lewin and Likert. The re-organized groups at Non-Linear Systems, which were virtually autonomous, give further support to the Tavistock concept. King's re-organizations and retraining of women in a Norwegian clothing factory can also be cited as supporting evidence. They were given responsibility for control over their work and work organization, and the result was an increase in output and satisfaction and a broadening of the functions of the unit manager (King, 1964).

Implications

The success of autonomous work groups where other group techniques have failed highlights the failure of research workers and managers to make basic changes in organizational structure, and in the nature and the organization of work. This failure has its roots in unquestioned acceptance of the methods and assumptions of scientific management and the traditional management theorists.

Louis Davis's survey of management practices and assumptions about job design showed the strong influence of scientific management. Adverse effects of greatly reduced job content were thought to be adequately controlled by selection, training, incentives and working conditions (Davis, Canter and Hoffman, 1955). Miles (1964) demonstrated that long exposure to the ideas of democratic management had not changed managers' perceptions and attitudes; these were closer to those of Taylor than to McGregor's Theory Y.

Taylor (1947) and the early management theorists believed that their proposals would eliminate the problems of restriction of output, lack of cooperation, apathy and worker–management conflict. The persistence of these problems over the years led to a succession of new approaches. Human relations and group techniques were part of this pattern, and had only limited success.

There is very little awareness that new thinking about structure and the design of work is a necessary condition for the elimination of apathy, restriction of output and similar problems. For this reason the Tavistock research and the transformation of Non-Linear Systems are of major significance. They both involve basic organizational changes and suggest that the motivation of rank-and-file workers can be achieved by increasing job content and giving men control of their work environment. Louis Davis (1957) has worked toward a new theory of job design which avoids the limitations of scientific management. He has successfully re-designed assembly-line jobs so that the individual carries out a whole task and is responsible for control of quality. The assumptions on which he enlarges individual jobs are similar to those of the Tavistock group. [. . .]

Conclusion

It has been argued that the Tavistock concept of the autonomous work group has more explanatory power than those concepts deriving from traditional group-dynamic thinking. Their coal and textile studies could well supplement the classical studies of Mayo and Lewin as the mainsprings of thinking and action.

References

ARGYRIS, C. (1964), *Integrating the Individual and the Organization*, Wiley.

BASS, B. M. (1965), *Organizational Psychology*, Allyn Bacon.

BENNIS, W. G. (1963), 'A new role for the behavioral sciences: effecting organizational change', *Administrative Science Quarterly*, vol. 8, pp. 125–65.

BION, W. R. (1955), 'Group dynamics: a review', in M. Klein, P. Heimann and R. E. Money-Kyrle (eds.), *New Dimensions in Psycho-Analysis*, Tavistock.

BION, W. R. (1961), *Experiences in Groups and Other Papers*, Tavistock.

BLAKE, R. R., and MOUTON, J. S. (1964), *The Managerial Grid*, Gulf Publishing Co.

BLAKE, R. R., MOUTON, J. S., BARNES, L. R., and GREINER, L. E. (1964), 'Breakthrough in organizational development', *Harvard Business Review*, vol. 42, pp. 133–55.

DAVIS, L. E. (1957), 'Job design and productivity: a new approach', *Personnel*, vol. 33, pp. 418–30.

DAVIS, L. E., CANTER, R. R., and HOFFMAN, J. F. (1955), 'Current job design criteria', *Journal of Industrial Engineering*, vol. 61.

EMERY, F. E. (1963), 'Technology and social organization', *Scientific Business*, vol. 1, pp. 132–6.

GUETZKOW, H., and SIMON, H. A. (1955), 'The impact of certain communication nets upon organization and performance in task-oriented groups', *Management Science*, vol. 1, pp. 233–50.

HERBST, P. G. (1962), *Autonomous Group Functioning*, Tavistock.

KATZ, D. (1954), 'Satisfactions and deprivations in industrial life', in A. Kornhauser, R. Dubin and A. Ross (eds.), *Industrial Conflict*, McGraw-Hill.

KATZ, D. (1964), 'The motivational basis of organization behavior', *Behavioral Science*, vol. 9, pp. 131–46.

KING, D. (1964), *Training Within the Organization*, Tavistock.

KLEIN, S. M. (1963), 'Two systems of management', *Proceedings of the Sixteenth Annual Meeting of the Industrial Relations Research Association*, publication no. 32.

KURILOFF, A. H. (1963), 'An experiment in management – putting Theory Y to the test', *Personnel*, vol. 40, pp. 8–17.

LEAVITT, H. J. (1964), 'Applied organizational change in industry: structural, technical and human approaches', in W. W. Cooper *et al.* (eds.), *New Perspectives in Organization Research*, Wiley.

LEAVITT, H. J., and BASS, B. M. (1964), 'Organizational psychology', in P. R. Farnsworth, O. McNemar and Q. McNemar (eds.), *Annual Review of Psychology: Volume 15*, Palo Alto, California.

LEWIN, K. (1948), *Resolving Social Conflict*, Harper.

LEWIN, K., LIPPITT, R., and WHITE, R. K. (1939), 'Patterns of aggressive behavior in experimentally created social climates', *Journal of Social Psychology*, vol. 10, pp. 271–99.

LIKERT, P. (1961), *New Patterns of Management*, McGraw-Hill.

MAIER, N. R. F. (1952), *Principles of Human Relations*, Wiley.

MAIER, N. R. F. (1963), *Problem-Solving Discussions and Conferences*, McGraw-Hill.

MAIER, N. R. F., and HAYES, J. J. (1962), *Creative Management*, Wiley.

MAYO, E. (1933), *The Human Problems of an Industrial Civilization*, Macmillan.

MAYO, E. (1946), *The Social Problems of an Industrial Civilization*, Harvard University Press.

MAYO, E. (1947, *The Political Problems of an Industrial Civilization*, Harvard University Press.

MILES, R. E. (1964), 'Conflicting elements in managerial ideologies', *Industrial Relations*, vol. 4, pp. 77–91.

MORSE, N., and REIMER, E. (1956), 'Experimental change of a major organizational variable', *Journal of Abnormal and Social Psychology*, vol. 52, pp. 120–29.

MULDER, M. (1959), 'Power and satisfaction in task-oriented groups', *ACTA Psychologica*, vol. 16, pp. 178–225.

RICE, A. K. (1958), *Productivity and Social Organization: The Ahmedabad Experiment*, Tavistock.

RICE, A. K. (1963), *The Enterprise and its Environment*, Tavistock.

ROETHLISBERGER, F. J., and DICKSON, W. J. (1939), *Management and the Worker*, Harvard University Press.

SHEPARD, H. A. (1960), 'An action research model', in *An Action Research Program for Organization Improvement*, Foundation for Research on Human Behavior.

SIROTA, D. (1963), 'A study of work measurement', *Proceedings of the Sixteenth Annual Meeting of the Industrial Relations Research Association*, publication no. 32.

SMITH, C. G., and TANNENBAUM, A. S. (1963), 'Organizational control structure: a comparative analysis', *Human Relations*, vol. 16, pp. 299–317.

STRAUSS, G. (1955), 'An experiment in worker control over pacing', in W. F. Whyte (ed.), *Money and Motivation*, Harper.

STRAUSS, G. (1963), 'Some notes on power equalization', in H. J. Leavitt (ed.), *The Social Science of Organizations*, Prentice-Hall.

TANNENBAUM, A. S. (1962), 'Control in organization, individual adjustment and organizational performance', *Administrative Science Quarterly*, vol. 7, pp. 236–57.

TAYLOR, F. W. (1947), *Scientific Management*, Harper & Row.

THELEN, H. (1954), *The Dynamics of Groups at Work*, University of Chicago Press.

TRIST, E. L., and BAMFORTH, K. W. (1951), 'Some social and psychological consequences of the longwall method of coal getting', *Human Relations*, vol. 4, pp. 3–38.

TRIST, E. L., HIGGIN, G. W., MURRAY, H., and POLLOCK, A. B. (1963), *Organizational Choice*, Tavistock.

TROW, D. B. (1954), 'Autonomy and job satisfaction in task-oriented groups', *Journal of Abnormal and Social Psychology*, vol. 54, pp. 204–9.

WILENSKY, H. L. (1957), 'Human relations in the work place: an appraisal of some recent research', in C. M. Arensberg *et al.* (eds.), *Research in Industrial Human Relations*, Harper.

Part Four
Job Design Cost Criteria

The traditional measure of success in job rationalization has been the minimization of time taken to perform specific operations. That this criterion was insufficient in the measure of an effective job design is evidenced by the sustained growth of the job design field, which now encompasses enrichment in both job and role content. As we will see in Parts Five and Six, minimized operation time has been subsumed under the criterion of quantity, and other major criteria have been added.

Among these emerging criteria have been the dimension of quality (usually improved by job enlargement), and satisfaction.[1] Davis (Reading 13) has described the place of satisfaction originally as a measure of the fit between existing jobs and job occupants. Job enlargement (or a new class of jobs), as we have seen, has grown out of this concern for satisfaction and toward a concern for motivation. It has been assumed that the absence of satisfaction or morale has costly effects on the organization's ledger sheet, but this cost has not been made explicit. Satisfaction has traditionally been isolated as a criterion based simply on trust in this assumption rather than on the actual costs.[2]

The senior editor of this volume has long decried the absence of suitable comprehensive cost measures for making

1. Other criteria in increasing use today are more direct measures of worker behavior around cooperation and coordination with others in joint decision making, as well as such measures as absence and turnover.

2. Other criteria such as improved 'profitability' have been recently introduced, but usually rely on cost ratios involving nothing more than reduced scrap rates and absenteeism divided by increased quantity. Satisfaction enters this equation as a factor improving scrap rate and absence data.

design decisions in the process of designing jobs. The first paper (Reading 16) is a short excerpt from an early paper (1957) in which he introduces a proposal for such a criterion: total economic cost.

The Reading (17) by Likert continues the plea in a more detailed proposal for a human resources accounting system.

Scoville (Reading 18) indicates that economists have overlooked the issue of job content and therefore have not considered the cost effects of the variety of feasible constellations of tasks and duties in job designs. He presents a theoretical cost analysis program in the form of a model of jobs and training.

Although appeals for better cost criteria for the design of jobs have been made for longer than a decade, the content of this section reveals the serious underdevelopment of theory and practice on this central requirement. Two recent empirical studies in human resources accounting are footnoted by the editors in Reading 17. This appears to be the state of the art. We may expect a continued low rate of diffusion into practice of the proposals made by the job and role content schools of job design until criteria and feedback are adopted that reflect post-industrial conditions.

16 Louis E. Davis

Toward a Theory of Job Design

Excerpts from L. E. Davis, 'Toward a theory of job design', *Journal of Industrial Engineering*, vol. 8, 1957, no. 5, pp. 19–23.

Those who create, design or establish jobs (exclusive of tradition-determined jobs) are guided almost entirely by the following few criteria:

1. Economic considerations or hypotheses.
2. Process considerations.
3. Time or space considerations.
4. Kinds of skills available and numbers of people available.
5. Tools and equipment required.
6. Union–management agreements.
7. Custom or tradition.

By relying on these narrow criteria we have designed jobs which have a host of disturbing secondary effects in terms of dissatisfaction, monotony, resistance and obstruction. In addition, designs of jobs have frequently failed to yield predicted results. Such failures to achieve anticipated results frequently have been laid to the 'contrariness of human nature'. This may be taken as another way of stating that, given the current state of knowledge, the effects of job designs cannot be estimated. In view of the engineering, economic, psychological and social consequences of job designs, the inability to predict the effectiveness of a particular design raises two fundamental questions:

1. What factors should guide the design of jobs?
2. What criteria should be used to evaluate the effectiveness of job designs? [. . .]

The area of job design is complex and multi-dimensional, involving organizational, technical and personal dimensions. Job design may be conceived as the organization of the content of a job to satisfy the technical–organizational requirements of the work to be accomplished and the human requirements of the person performing the work. [. . .]

Considering job design as creation and specification of job content, then it must be viewed as a design problem which raises the needs to:

1. Identify boundaries and evaluate boundary conditions.
2. Identify factors operating and determine the effect of each.
3. Determine methods of estimating and controlling the factors operating.
4. Develop systematic design methods.
5. Develop methods of predicting consequences of design.
6. Develop methods of feed-back to evaluate predictions and to make adjustments in design.
7. Develop criteria for evaluation (total economic cost measure). [. . .]

Development of the criterion:
the total economic cost measurement

A good many of the difficulties, the inconsistencies of results and the opinions held concerning the design of jobs can be traced to the lack of a fundamental or true criterion. Before much progress can be made beyond the current status, an adequate criterion and sub-criteria will need to be developed. The lack of a criterion has led to job designs based upon the satisfaction of apparent economic criteria. The term 'apparent' is used because total costs are seldom considered, for there are little data available to provide yardsticks for total cost analysis of a given job design. This is indicated by the results obtained in a survey of job design practices in American industry (see Davis, Canter and Hoffman, 1955, p. 5). In this survey it was found that the design of industrial jobs is overwhelmingly influenced by the criterion of minimizing immediate cost of producing, that is, immediate cost of performing required operations. The usual indicator of achievement is taken to be minimum unit operation time. Designers of jobs see the criterion as being satisfied by the application of principles or guides that have been previously indicated. The acceptance of immediate costs or lowest apparent unit costs explains many current practices in job design as well as the inconsistencies in policy and programming that exist between the technical and the personnel sides of an organization.

We need to develop a total economic cost criterion which is concerned with the total cost of achieving productivity, and therefore includes relevant long-term changes in the form of money, time, growth, and psychological, social and cultural stress costs. One of the serious research problems that confronts us is to determine how total economic cost is to be measured in terms of economic, engineering, organizational, social, psychological, physiological, resource and human resource cost criteria. [. . .]

[What] must be pursued is concerned with criteria formulation. Needed is a determination of the means of establishing a minimum economic cost or maximum economic productivity criterion. Of concern here are such criteria as absenteeism, quality, productivity, turnover, and hidden costs such as organizational flexibility, employee grievances, etc. In addition there will need to be developed measures of the effectiveness of job designs. Such measures will be concerned with or account for criteria related to job conditions, job content, job methods, organizational structure, social organization, communication and feed-back, company–community relations, physical and physiological factors, attitudinal and motivational factors.

Reference

DAVIS, L. E., CANTER, R. R., and HOFFMAN, J. F. (1955), 'Current job design criteria', *Journal of Industrial Engineering*, vol. 6, no. 2, March.

17 Rensis Likert

Human Asset Accounting

Excerpts from R. Likert, *The Human Organization: Its Management and Value*, McGraw-Hill, 1967, chapter 9, pp. 146–55.

Evidence was presented for the necessity of including estimates of the current value of the human organization and of customer goodwill in all financial reports of a firm.

The absence of these estimates for each profit center and for the entire corporation is not due to a lack of interest on the part of the accounting profession (Hermanson, 1964). Cultural lag and the usual gaps in communication among the relevant sciences are the culprits. To create human asset accounting and to make reasonably accurate estimates of its two dimensions – the current value of the human organization and customer goodwill – require close cooperation between accountants and social scientists highly competent in the measurement of the causal and intervening variables.

Such cooperation is now starting.[1] It will require from five to ten years and many million dollars' worth of work to collect the data and to make the computations required before human asset accounting can become fully operational. Sophisticated measurement and accounting procedures should emerge from this work, enabling firms to incorporate in their financial reports reasonably accurate estimates of the current value of the human assets of an enterprise. These procedures will enable a firm not only to know the current value of these resources, but also what changes or trends are occurring from time to time in the magnitudes of these assets. In addition, it will be possible to prepare these estimates for each profit center of the firm and, where appropriate and useful, for any smaller unit within a firm.

Computing a firm's original investment in its human organization is a much simpler problem than estimating the current value

1. For recent empirical work in this area, see the following studies: Pyle (1970a, 1970b, 1970c) and Alexander (1971). [Ed.]

of that investment. This is true for the company as a whole and for such units as profit centers, departments and other sub-units. There are several alternative methods for obtaining estimates of the original investment in the human side of an enterprise.

One way is to base these estimates on start-up costs. The problem in many ways is comparable to estimating a firm's current investment in machinery which it has built itself and continues to use for a period of time. The actual cost of building a machine can readily be computed. The human start-up costs of a new plant, unit, or department can be computed similarly, although the task of doing so is more complex and difficult. These start-up costs should include what it has cost to hire and train the personnel and to develop them into a coordinated organization operating in a reasonably satisfactory manner.

Start-up costs can be computed for various kinds of operations and for various-sized units. As these human investment costs become available for the widely different kinds of operations performed by a particular enterprise, they can be used as a basis for estimating the magnitude of the investment a firm has in its human organization – for the entire corporation or for any of its units.

A second way of estimating the magnitude of the investment in the human organization is to obtain data on the costs of hiring and training personnel for each of the many different kinds of positions in the company. The sum of these costs for every person in the firm usually will be substantial. It underestimates, however, the true investment in the human side of the enterprise, since it does not reflect the additional investment made during the period when the members of the firm were establishing effective cooperative working relationships with one another. These cooperative working relationships might appropriately be called the synergistic component. To establish them takes an appreciable period of time and involves substantial costs.

This approach will require a tremendous amount of work if it is done for every kind of position and every member of the organization. The cost and effort of making these estimates can be reduced substantially by probability sampling. Efficient designs will yield estimates closely approximating those which would be obtained were all the jobs and all the positions examined. [. . .]

Human asset accounting

Human assets refer both to the value of the productive capacity of a firm's human organization and to the value of its customer goodwill.

The productive capability of its human organization can be illustrated by thinking of two firms in the same business. Both are of the same size and have identical equipment and technology. One, however, produces more and earns more than the other, because its personnel is superior to the other's with regard to such variables as the following:

1. Level of intelligence and aptitudes.

2. Level of training.

3. Level of performance goals and motivation to achieve organizational success.

4. Quality of leadership.

5. Capacity to use differences for purposes of innovation and improvement, rather than allowing differences to develop into bitter, irreconcilable, interpersonal conflict.

6. Quality of communication upward, downward and laterally.

7. Quality of decision making.

8. Capacity to achieve cooperative teamwork versus competitive striving for personal success at the expense of the organization.

9. Quality of the control processes of the organization and the levels of felt responsibility which exist.

10. Capacity to achieve effective coordination.

11. Capacity to use experience and measurements to guide decisions, improve operations, and introduce innovations.

The difference in the economic value of the human organizations of these two firms would be reflected by the differences between them in present and future earnings, attributable to the differences in their human organizations. Similarly, differences in the value of customer goodwill would be reflected in the differences between them in the ease and costs of making sales, i.e. in the difference in the motivation among customers to buy the product of one firm, rather than that of the other.

Human asset accounting refers to activity devoted to attaching dollar estimates to the value of a firm's human organization and its customer goodwill. If able, well-trained personnel leave the firm, the human organization is worth less; if they join it, the firm's human assets are increased. If bickering, distrust and irreconcilable conflict become greater, the human enterprise is worth less; if the capacity to use differences constructively and engage in cooperative teamwork improves, the human organization is a more valuable asset.

Since estimates of the current value of a firm's human organization are both necessary and difficult to obtain, it is highly desirable to use several alternate approaches in developing methods for making these estimates. The results from one approach can serve as a check on those obtained from the others. The initial estimates from any procedure, of course, are likely to have relatively large errors of estimate. As the methodology improves, two important developments will occur. The size of the errors will decrease, and the accuracy of estimating the magnitude of these errors will increase. The accuracy of human asset accounting will increase correspondingly.

The essential first step in developing procedures for applying human asset accounting to a firm's human organization is to undertake periodic measurements of the key causal and intervening variables. These measurements must be available over several years' time to provide the data for the needed computations. The data required for the initial computations should be collected at quite frequent intervals, quarterly or even more often.

The optimum frequency for the measurements will vary with the kind of work involved. The more nearly the work involves the total man, such as research and development (R and D) tasks, the shorter should be the intervals between successive measurements, for the time lag between changes in the causal, intervening and end-result variables is much less for such work than for work which is machine-paced. [. . .]

The measurements of the causal and intervening variables should be obtained for the corporation as a whole and for each profit center or unit in the company for which productivity, costs, waste and earnings can be computed. After these measurements have been made over a sufficient period of time for relatively stable relationships to develop or for the sequence of relationships to complete their full cycle, the necessary data will be available to relate the causal and intervening measurements to the earnings record. By using appropriate statistical procedures, relationships can be computed among the causal, intervening, and such end-result variables as costs and earnings. The resulting mathematical relationships will enable one to estimate the productive and earnings capability of any profit center, or smaller unit, based upon its present scores on the causal and intervening variables. These estimates of probable subsequent productivity, costs and earnings will reveal the earning power of the human organization *at the time* the causal and intervening variables were measured, even though the level of estimated subsequent earnings may not be achieved until much later. These estimates of probable subsequent productivity, costs and earnings provide the basis for attaching to any profit center, unit, or total corporation a statement of the present value of its human organization.

Corporations which have a number of relatively comparable units, such as chain stores, will have a distinct advantage in using the method just suggested. The data from several comparable units will yield more reliable estimates by providing far more observations upon which to base calculations. Moreover, differences among the units can be used as well as changes for any particular unit over time. Based on these differences, computations can be made of the relation of earnings to each pattern of causal and intervening variables using, of course, optimum time intervals. By capitalizing the greater earnings of the better units, estimates of the present value of the human organization can be obtained.

It is probable that after sufficient research has been done and sufficient data and experience obtained, it will be feasible to do human asset accounting in much the same way that standard costs are now used to estimate the manufacturing costs of new products. Another use of standard estimates is the MTM (Methods–Time Measurement) process of setting a standard time for the performance of a particular task. Experience has shown that standard estimates can be used successfully in accounting and in industrial engineering. A comparable process should be equally successful in human asset accounting.

Present earnings may yield incorrect estimate

Many corporations at present are making estimates of the current value of the human organization and of customer goodwill. This is done whenever a new firm or division is acquired. Every year there are a substantial number of acquisitions. In each instance, an appropriate value has to be placed on the acquired firm. The purchase price generally is substantially larger than the current value of the physical and financial assets and reflects allowances for both customer and employee goodwill. Both the firm which is acquired and the corporation acquiring it make these estimates in arriving at a fair price. An important factor in arriving at these estimates usually is the current and recent earnings of the acquired firm. This approach has to be used cautiously, however, since it contains a source of error which at times can be sizable. If the acquired firm has been using the approach to cost reduction based on personnel limitations, tightened budgets and tighter standards and is at a point of high earnings but decreasing value of the human organization, then an estimate of the value of the human assets based on current earnings is likely to be appreciably inflated.

Estimating the value of customer goodwill

Customer goodwill, like the value of the human organization, is an asset of substantial magnitude in most companies. The sizable costs in opening new markets or marketing new products demonstrate the magnitude of the current value of this asset in most companies.

This asset can vary appreciably from time to time, depending upon the behavior of the firm's management (a causal variable), the resulting motivation and behavior of the firm's personnel (intervening variables), and the corresponding price and quality of product and service provided to customers (end-result variables).

Cash income can be increased for a period of time by selling shoddy products and rendering poor service while charging the usual prices. This income should not be reported and treated as earnings in financial statements, however, since it is actually achieved by cashing in on the firm's customer loyalty. It represents a liquidation, often at a fraction of its value, of customer goodwill. Such 'earnings' are as spurious and misleading as those derived from liquidating part of the firm's investment in its human organization. [. . .]

Imbalance in fiscal management

In considering the desirability and expense of undertaking the work required for human asset accounting, it should be recognized that the present practice of treating, with great precision, a fraction of the firm's assets and completely ignoring assets of roughly the same or greater magnitude represents a serious imbalance. A firm's financial reports would be much more useful and appreciably more accurate if approximately the same level of accuracy were maintained in dealing with *all* of the firm's assets. The equity of the shareholders would be protected far better than at present if there were more balance in the accounting effort.

It is perfectly feasible for a company to establish a balanced effort in their accounting activities without an appreciable increase in their total accounting costs. This can be done by placing all accounting on a sample basis and using sample designs which yield estimates of acceptable accuracy. There would be a substantial reduction in the costs of the usual physical asset and financial asset accounting, and this saving could be used for human asset accounting, i.e. for obtaining estimates of the current value of the human organization and of customer goodwill. [. . .]

References

ALEXANDER, M. O. (1971), 'Investments in people', *Canadian Chartered Accountant*, July, pp. 33–45.

HERMANSON, R. H. (1964), 'Accounting for human assets', *Bureau of Business and Economic Research*, occasional paper no. 14, Michigan State University.

PYLE, W. C. (1970a), 'Accounting system for human resources', *Innovation*, no. 10, pp. 46–55.

PYLE, W. C. (1970b), 'Monitoring human resources – "on line"', *Michigan Business Review*, July, pp. 19–32.

PYLE, W. C. (1970c), 'Human resource accounting', *Financial Analysts Journal*, September–October, pp. 69–78.

18 James G. Scoville

A Theory of Jobs and Training

J. G. Scoville, 'A theory of jobs and training', *Industrial Relations*, vol. 9, 1969, pp. 36–53.

Concern with the kinds of work performed is not new among economists, although it has never occupied a central position in economic thinking. With rare exceptions, economics has chosen the easy road of homogeneous factors: jobs and machines – the specific forms which labor and capital take – drop out of most models. Analytical concern with the nature and consequence of work has been left largely to other social scientists, particularly sociologists and psychologists. The lack of an appropriate economic theory of jobs limits the analysis of human capital and training, whose costs and benefits must be integral parts of the theory of job content.

In the economic literature on work, one must start with Adam Smith for more than perfunctory reasons of tradition. A good deal of the analysis in *The Wealth of Nations* is based upon the relationship between job specialization and labor productivity. Put very simply, the particular 'art' – the industry-specific technology involved – determines the extent to which division of labor *can* be pursued; given the technology, the size of product markets determines how far it *will* be pursued. Thus job design is determinate in Smith's model, and so (presumably) is job-related training.

In the classical approach to determination of job content, as central to Marx as it was to Smith, the nature of jobs is rooted in the technology of production. A new train of thought is found however, among more recent writers, such as Lancaster (1966) and Mandelbrot (1962). These form a neoclassical school in which the emphasis shifts to the question of choice by individuals among pre-existing occupations.[1] The task of this essay is to fuse

1. The essence of this school of thought is phrased succinctly: 'an individual chooses that occupation for which the present value of his expected income stream is a maximum.' Benewitz and Zucker (1968).

the two theoretical approaches, that is, to incorporate both the supply of job types and the choices which are made regarding them by workers and managements. On the one hand, technology presents a range of job options; on the other are ranged managements' and workers' preferences among those options. As a natural part of the model, a new approach is taken to the nature of work-related training. In place of the Beckerian dichotomy between 'general' and 'specific' training, the relevance of training to internal and external labor markets is embodied in managements' costs and workers' benefits (see Becker, 1964, pp. 7–28).

Flexibility of job options

That a number of job options – bundles of specific jobs – do indeed exist to carry through a quantity of work is central to the arguments that will follow. It is held here that the apparent fixed relationship between means of production and specific jobs, which impresses itself upon observers of work in highly capitalized industries, is either illusory or a short-run phenomenon, and that, in fact, for the accomplishment of many kinds of work there is a choice among technologies (Bhalla, 1965).[2] Given the work to be done and the basic technology, the recent literature on job design suggests that different constellations of tasks and duties incorporated in varying bundles of jobs are feasible. Tasks and duties can be reshuffled among jobs in several ways – by altering the 'horizontal' time and function sequence involved, by incorporating or deleting 'vertical' (supervisory and quality control) functions, by inclusion or separation of maintenance, repair and supply functions, or combinations of these adjustments. Moreover, that which appears fixed at a point in time may be quite variable in the face of options presented by continual technological advance (Piore, 1968).

Employer preferences on job content

Adam Smith laid down the principle that gross labor productivity is a direct function of the degree of subdivision of work. Jumping over a great deal of history, the Scientific Management movement

2. On heavy industry, a number of the UN *Studies in the Economics of Industry* have been utilized in the ILO's *Human Resources for Industrial Development* Studies and Reports, n.s. 71, 1967.

marks the high point of practical application of Smith's law. These engineers, of whom F. W. Taylor is the best-known writer, observed that all work could be broken into microscopic functions, which were then directly assessable in terms of the optimal time required to perform each one. Scientifically arranged rest and leisure were part of the total work package.

In fact, there is very little reason to suppose that net labor productivity continues to rise as job specialization proceeds further and further. The uncritical acceptance and application of that viewpoint, however, accounts for a counter-movement which was seeded in the twenties and thirties and bloomed in the fifties. The apostles of job enlargement found in reality that the division of labor had frequently overshot the mark – that productivity would rise if jobs were broadened. The examples they brought forward – changing assembly jobs from line work to bench work, rotation of equally narrow tasks among members of a work group, or increasing the number of functions in a line job – established that division of labor must have some optimal point.

Costs and job design

If one looks at job subdivision in the framework of the entire production process, focusing attention more broadly than just on measures of output per manhour for specific work functions, it is possible to identify the kinds of costs which depend on the breadth of jobs. The content of jobs affects output and the costliness of labor inputs in a variety of ways.

Declining costs as jobs are narrowed

Efficiency and productivity. The rate at which the worker can turn out product depends inversely on the breadth of his job. Within some broad limits, this tendency taken alone remains true, although at some point, the tedium and goallessness of the work may have psychological effects (frustration and conflict) which impede the flow of output.

Training costs. In general, the broader the job, the longer is the required period of training. If one considers the case where training takes place within the firm, the following major costs of training a worker to the job can be identified:

1. Costs of supervision – either by taking a trained worker off his

job, leading to foregone production, or any losses of output suffered by a general relaxation of supervision elsewhere due to attention given to the learner.

2. Foregone production as compared with use of a fully qualified worker.

3. Increased materials wastage, and possible increased wear and tear on the machine.

As the length of the training period – the time elapsed while a new worker performs worse than one with training – is shortened by narrowing the range of duties to be covered in training, all of these costs are reduced.[3] Of course, if 'fully qualified' workers are abundantly available, then newly hired workers reach full productivity in a very short period. In such a case (clearly rather hypothetical over the long run), the training cost aspect of choice and job content would vanish.[4]

Increasing costs as jobs are narrowed

Work quality and quality control. One of the discoveries of the job enlargement school centered on the relationship between job content and quality. When workers were made responsible for a greater number of tasks than usually associated with assembly line jobs, the proportion of work rejected generally fell.[5] There are several reasons for this, although the 'psychological' argument – that increased interest content to work leads to better motivated, more accurate work – has tended to dominate the literature. Prominent among the other reasons are those based on the amount of the supervisory planning and control function designed into the job. As jobs are further and further broken down, particularly when the micro-jobs are part of a long assembly line, one loses the ability to exploit the reservoir of self-direction and self-control which each worker possesses, while the individual's responsibility for quality become less enforceable.[6]

3. For some evidence, see National Industrial Conference Board (1967).
4. A summary discussion of employer adjustments and the costs involved is found in Doeringer and Piore (1965).
5. See, for example, the study of A. R. N. Marks, cited in Guest (1957).
6. For a survey of a number of studies indicating the 'positive effects on total performance of job and organization designs which lead to responsible autonomous job behavior', see Davis (1966).

Supervision. Closely related to the question of quality control are the unit costs of supervision and management. When jobs are very narrow, supervision becomes external to them. Exceedingly narrow jobs may lead to a need for increased direct supervision when any change is to be made in plant procedures, equipment, or product mix.[7]

Work force stability. There appears to be evidence that narrower jobs are related to work force characteristics which generate higher unit costs. Absenteeism and levels of labor turnover seem to have been reduced by various experiments in job enlargement.[8]

Cost effects which are less clear

There are several other effects of job design which must be mentioned, but for which no general rule can be formulated.

Capital costs. As jobs are further subdivided, what happens to capital–output ratios and the period of production? Experience gives us very little guidance on this question. The level of goods-in-process per worker (and hence inventory costs) should be affected by the choice (for example between bench and line jobs). The period of time required for a unit of product to appear can also be altered by the design of work.

Flexibility. Clearly narrow jobs and narrowly experienced workers reduce the size of internal labor pools which can be drawn on to fill a job which is temporarily open due to illness or other cause of absence. At the extreme, this could produce inabilities to fill the job in the short run, hence increasing costs.[9] On the other side of

7. Joan Woodward's (1958) findings are not inconsistent with this argument, as technical complexity of production is not synonymous with the breadth of jobs in an industry or firm. Moreover, broad and narrow jobs under highly different technologies cannot be meaningfully compared in terms of the present argument.

8. Davis (1966, p. 35) gives the example of coal miners whose absence rate fell roughly 60 per cent under new job design. Another experiment reported two pages later seems to have found the reverse. See also, Hulin (1968).

9. This point, particularly regarding increased training costs, is made by Biggane and Stewart (1963). This study provides an excellent introduction to the case literature of job enlargement. For economists, it is of greater value than the more conventional social-psychological studies.

the coin, however, it is possible that narrowly specialized jobs may be easier (and less costly) to fill in the long run from the general labor market.

Industrial relations and control of the work place. Costs and benefits in this regard are difficult to quantify, but it is clear that the kinds of jobs in an enterprise will affect the operation of its industrial relations system. The various substantive rules on pay methods, job and promotion rights of workers, layoffs, etc., will be affected by the content of jobs. Moreover, the balance of power between the actors in the system (hence management's sense of control over the work place) will be involved. It is clear that, in the good old days, narrow job division made individual workers much more dispensable and replaceable, giving management extensive control of the actions at the work place, as Alfred Marshall once noted.

A summary model: employers

The factors affecting unit costs discussed above can now be presented in summary form. Such an overall survey will emphasize the fact that the co-existence of these effects poses questions of choice of job content in the light of varying production costs. The problem becomes the choice of an *optimal* bundle of jobs with which to accomplish a certain quantity of work.

In order to be able to reduce the problem to one of minimizing costs for a fixed level of output (Q^0), consider a department of a firm producing a certain commodity. The work of the department is to get the commodity from one stage of completion to another, or to produce a part of the final commodity. Thus the price and output of the total commodity can be taken as fixed; the duty of the department manager is to minimize unit costs in this stage of processing. To further simplify, assume that the wage rate is fixed by the market *and* is invariate with respect to the nature and content of the job.

The factors entering employers' decisions are thus listed, with the probable signs of their derivatives. In the expressions below, n is number of workers, j is the breadth of 'the' job.[10]

10. We leave aside the problem of what such an index job breadth would look like. This point is touched on in the author's report to the Office of Manpower Research, US Department of Labor.

(1) Smith's Law: Q^0/n (average *gross* labor
 productivity) $= p(j)$ $p'(j) \le 0$

(2) (definition) $= Q^0 s q_n$ where Q_N is *net* output
 per worker [see (9) below]

(3) (training costs for a worker per unit of
 time measured by lost production[11] $C_{t_1} = t_1(j), t_1'(j) \ge 0$

(4) (training time for a worker) $C_{2} = t_2(j), t_2'(j) \ge 0$

(5) (turnover effect expressed as
 Expected Time of Worker Retention) $E_w = e(j), e'(j) \ge 0$

(6) (supervisory costs) $C_s = s(n,j), \partial s/\partial n \ge 0, \partial s/\partial j \le 0$

(7) (capital costs per unit of
 output) $C_k = K(n,j), \partial K/\partial_N = ?, \partial K/\partial j = ?$

(8) (wastage and quality control
 costs per unit of output) $C_w = W(j), W'(j) \le 0.$

Hence, from the above set of effects, it appears that the output
net of training costs per worker per unit of time can be expressed as

(9) $q_n = [p(j)e(j) - t_1(j)t_2(j)]/e(j)$

and we may reformulate (2) above as

(10) $n = Q^0 e(j)/[p(j)e(j) - t_1(j)t_2(j)].$

Total costs of production in this department are the sum of
capital, supervisory, wastage and labor costs (the latter defined to
include training costs):

(11) $C = Q^0 K(n,j) + Q^0 S(n,j) + Q^0 W(j) + \bar{w}n,$

where $\bar{w}$ is the market wage rate.

Writing the wage bill as $\bar{w} Q^0/q_n$, then unit costs can be expressed
as:

(12) $c = K(n,j) + S(n,j) + W(j) + \bar{w}/q_n.$

This equation can be differentiated and set equal to zero in the
traditional manner, but it may be more fruitful to look at the problem graphically. After all, if we were to prove that the resulting
equation system is truly a minimum cost solution, we would have
to establish that $\partial^2 c/\partial j^2 > 0$, etc. In the light of our uncertainty
about – and the lack of data on – the second derivatives of most of
the functions above, it will be just as well to go ahead and make the

11. It is recognized that, in reality, such costs will be large at the outset of
training and approach zero. Here they are averaged over the training time.

assumptions underlying the well-behaved curves below without spending more time differentiating equations.

The employers' model in graphic form

In Figure 1 are shown all the cost curves associated with a constant output and variations in the breadth of job, taking account of any effects on the number of workers required which stem from changing job content. The *levels* of the curves are of less importance than their shapes, which are based upon the following assumptions:

1. Supervisory costs fall as the supervisory function is incorporated with production work by job enlargement.

2. Materials, wastage and quality control costs are high for very broad jobs (as Adam Smith would have it), declining with increased specialization, but are also high in very narrow jobs, as workers become less motivated and/or penalized for their errors.

3. Capital costs per worker rise on the assumption that capital–labor ratios fall more slowly than the length of the period of production rises: direct capital cost decreases (if any) are more than offset by increases in inventory cost of goods in process.

4. Turnover effects are important for narrow jobs, while training

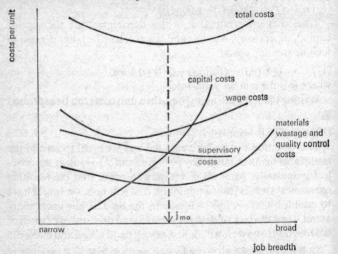

Figure 1

costs do not fall to zero. As jobs are broadened, improvements in employee retention have a limit, while training costs continue to go up. Thus net labor productivity, q_n, will be low for narrow jobs, rise to a maximum, and then decline. When divided into a fixed wage rate, the wage cost curve will be as shown.

Given the arguments (1) through (4), it is likely that the per-unit total cost curve will look roughly like that shown, with j_{mo} being the optimal job breadth from management's point of view.

Worker preferences and job breadth

As was the case from management's point of view, varying the content of jobs affects worker well-being in a number of ways, some detrimental, others beneficial.

The role of productivity. The increase in output per worker which tends to accompany job specialization affects workers in two ways. In the first case, it is obvious that advances in productivity unmatched by increases in output affect the level of employment by reducing the number of men required. Workers and their organizations are thus concerned, not only with direct redesign of currently existing jobs, but with the development of new products and processes. From the Philadelphia Cordwainers on, workers have sought to restrict the impact of deskilled job specialization (Barnett, 1926).

Secondly, it affects wages in the long run, though the relationship between the breadth of jobs and wage levels is fairly complicated.

Almost any theory of wages (except cost-of-production-of-labor versions) would lead one to expect increased productivity to be reflected in the wage rates of labor services in the long run. Thus, if productivity per man is increased by division of labor, wages should go up.[12]

Insofar as narrowing a job reduces the investment in training which a worker makes, the problem becomes further confused. If, as seems likely, the return on human capital investments far exceeds that on any alternative investment which a worker is able to make, then workers may wish to retain this investment option as a

12. Such an effect may explain part of the wage differentials discussed in Richard A. Lester (1967).

means of obtaining higher income. In such a case, the impact of productivity may be offset by reduced investment in human capital.

Possible unemployment. As suggested above, productivity increases may reduce the likelihood of finding employment. To protect their jobs, and to augment the probability of being employed in the future, workers may take a variety of actions.[13] They may seek to strengthen the product market and hence the level of demand for their work, for example, through promotional campaigns (advertising of products by labor organizations, union labels, etc.) or through monopolistic collusion with employers. They may seek to reduce labor supply through exclusionary policies. And they may seek to level off peaks and valleys of work through redistribution of overtime – or to spread available work across the labor force, as the printing and garment trades do on occasion. (Note that extreme task specialization would make it harder to implement such redistributive policies.)

In any case, the broader the scope of the work which is controlled by a group of workers, or their union, and the broader their training and jobs, the better situated they are when confronted by economic and technological changes. For example, broadly trained workers in complex jobs can be adapted to new functions, or (as with the glass bottle blowers) they may control the earlier process so thoroughly that they are able to control the introduction of new technology and assure that – even if the new technology cannot be defeated – the work which remains falls into their hands.

A number of minor factors which could bear upon the optimal choice of job content from the worker's vantage point have been neglected at this stage. Among them are the relationships among job content, wage costs, prices, and product demand, and the amount of transfer costs associated with moving from one employer, or assignment, to another in a broad content job. Also left aside have been any connections between job breadth and finished product quality which might have an independent effect on price and demand levels for the finished goods. All these are likely to be of some long-run significance.

13. This range of concerns is treated in more detail (giving numerous references) by Barbash (1968).

Effects upon training costs borne by workers. The breadth and content of jobs is directly related to the length of training. There is thus an element of cost involved in choosing broader jobs and longer training times. From the worker's point of view, considering either a typical apprenticeship program or employment under an incentive system, the training costs are the amount by which his wage falls short of alternatives available during the training period plus any actual out-of-pocket costs involved.[14] We shall deal with the distribution of such costs between workers and employers later; for the time being let us simply assume that worker-borne training costs rise with broadening jobs.

Psychic costs of narrow jobs. Psychological and sociological investigators have long dwelt on the dissatisfactions that come from finely divided jobs. The tedium, lack of responsibility or independence, and absence of clear purpose to the work associated with extreme division of labor impose psychic costs upon individual workers.[15] In determining workers' preferences, we therefore postulate the existence of costs directly related to degree of specialization.[16]

A static model of worker preferences

Returning to the simple framework developed at the end of the previous section, let us draw together the influences on worker choice of job breadth in a basic 'job control' model. There follows a listing of the principal functional relationships discussed above, with indications of the probable signs of some of their derivatives.

(13) (productivity-wage nexus) $w = f(j)$

$$f'(j) < 0 \text{ (at least for some range of } j)$$

(14) (employment probabilities for a 'closed group') $P_e = g(j)$ $\qquad g'(j) > 0$

(15) (expected earnings of a worker) $E(Y = w \cdot P_e = f(j)g(j)$

(16) (training costs borne by workers)

---

14. The reader should consult Mincer (1962) for examples and a general theoretical treatment.

15. A lengthy exploration of this literature is to be found in Vroom (1964).

16. For examples of the dimensions along which this can be measured, see Conant and Kilbridge (1965).

$$T_w = \sum_{t=1}^{T_t} t_w(j)t_t(j),$$

where $t_w(j)$ is the cost per time period and $t_t(j)$ is the length of that period, both as functions of j, the breadth of jobs.

(17) (the 'disutility of labor' as affected by tedium, worker irritation and loss of psychic income is also a function of job specialization, lumped together as psychic costs.)

$$\omega = \omega(j) \quad \omega'(j) < 0.$$

In such a case, workers' maximand will be shown below, with T_w being workers' time-horizon length and r, their rate of time preference.

(18) Net Benefit $=$

$$\sum_{t=1}^{T_w} [P_e \cdot w/(1+r)^t] - \sum_{t=1}^{t_t(j)} [t_w(j)t_t(j)/(1+r)]^t - \sum_{t=1}^{T_w} [\omega(j)/(1+r)^t],$$

which can be differentiated at the reader's leisure.

The workers' model in graphic form

The formal result looks both meaningful economically and solvable as a function of only one variable, j, but let us retreat to a graphical analysis comparable to that given for managements' preferences. The principal influences on economic benefits are shown in Figure 2 below, where the wage-productivity and employment probabilities curves are 'multiplied' to produce the discounted expected earnings curve.

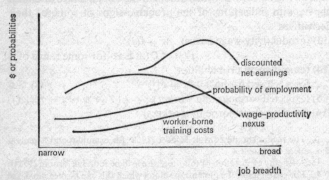

Figure 2

From Figure 2, a curve of net economic benefits can be obtained (by subtraction of the training-cost curve from the probable discounted earnings curve) which should have the shape shown in Figure 3. In the latter diagram, benefits are compared with the psychic costs to show the optimal division of labor from the worker's point of view, j_{wo}.[17]

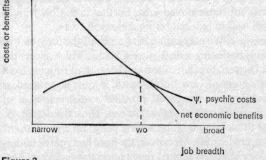

Figure 3

The relationship of job and training breadth

In order to make clear the relationships and ideas proposed, the discussion above has been stated primarily in terms of job breadth. Obviously, this is only part of the story – workers and managers are equally concerned with the breadth of training which goes along (but is not identical) with the breadth of the job. Thus, when we try to bring together the preferences of workers and managers in a single model, it is necessary to introduce training breadth as an explicit variable.

As far as workers are concerned, broader, 'excess' training has many of the same characteristics of broader jobs. The Beckerian distinction between general and specific training is replaced by a continuum describing the value of training to the worker. The narrowest relevance of training is to the man's current job; the broadest involves the whole economy. In any case, the influences upon employment and promotion probabilities, future earnings and training costs are similar to those discussed earlier. Training

17. Some evidence supporting the behavioral assumptions of the model will be found in Chapter 3 of the author's report to the Office of Manpower Research.

beyond the needs of the job may even affect the psychic costs borne by the worker.

Managements also have a substantial concern with the training breadth of their workers, above and beyond the demands of the job itself. The impacts on costs and productivity are analogous to those for job breadth alone. Moreover, 'excess' training influences the promotability of workers and hence the ability of the firm to obtain workers for more skilled jobs. Further, a flexibly trained workforce will lead to reduced hiring and layoff costs.

A graphic summary. We may summarize much of the foregoing in graphical form, beginning with Figure 4 below, which shows the relationships between breadth of job and breadth of training from the employer's point of view. Job breadth, it must be recalled, is viewed as defining the narrowest possible *equilibrium* level of training which would suffice, optimal or not. Thus, the dotted 45° line shows all those minimal job-training pairs; no combinations below that line are feasible. Moreover, the hard facts of the underlying technology impose a limited range upon the variations possible in job breadth compatible with performing a certain quantity of work. These possibilities are indicated by the solid line *TT*, within which range choices must be made.

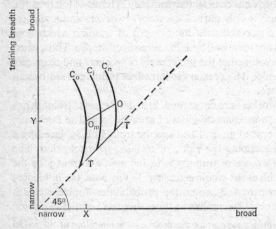

Figure 4

From the arguments in foregoing sections, it would seem that employers' iso-cost curves can be drawn, predicated upon a given distribution of training costs: $c_o, \ldots c_i, \ldots c_n$, as shown in Figure 4.[18] These lines indicate that unit costs of production remain the same for varying combinations of job breadth and training. They are given their particular shape to incorporate the expected returns to training outlined earlier. Given a certain job breadth, as employees become more broadly trained the firm takes advantage of any economies of supervision and advantage of flexibility and moves to lower unit cost curves. At some point, however, increasing training costs should cause the iso-cost curves to bend backward as shown. As should be obvious, the arguments about the particular shape of the curves are less important than the conceptual apparatus involved.

In order to put out the fixed level of work underlying the iso-cost curves, the firm would choose the minimum cost feasible solution, namely the point on iso-cost curve C_o labelled O_M, corresponding in this case to the minimum job breadth X and a training breadth of Y. The line $O_M O$ shows the set of similar combinations reflecting the 'second-best' optima for other, broader jobs.

Workers' benefits. Workers' preferences can be analyzed in the same fashion, as shown in Figure 5. Given the same technologically-fixed range of possible job breadths, we can draw a series of iso-benefit curves, $b_o \ldots b_i, \ldots b_n$. These iso-benefit curves reflect all the considerations of worker benefits and costs discussed above. They are drawn on the assumption that, for a given job breadth, workers move to higher levels of net economic and psychological benefit through the accumulation of training in excess of that required by the job. Beyond a certain level of excess training, though, the advantages of improved employment and earning probabilities are more than offset by increases in training costs borne by the worker.

In Figure 5, we can easily see that within the limits imposed, the very best that a worker could do would be to attain point O_L. The

18. Included are hiring costs for higher job classifications. The optimal 'excess training' for a lower-rung job on a ladder depends, in part, upon how the costs of producing a higher-level worker in this fashion compare with the costs of obtaining him in some other fashion.

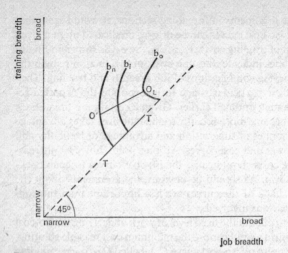

Figure 5

worker's reaction curve, if forced to accept a narrower job, would be described by the line $O_L O'$.[19]

The determination of job and training breadth

It is now time to bring together the preferences of workers and managers sketched out in the preceding pages. In Figure 6, a set of 'well-behaved' iso-cost and iso-benefit curves are shown for a single job of possible breadth range TT. The dependence of both sets of curves on the costs and benefits of the job above and below this one, and the distance along the $45°$ line which separates them from TT are assumed to be incorporated in the iso-cost and iso-

19. A number of subsidiary points should be raised at this juncture. (1) Cannot the iso-cost and the iso-benefit curves depart from the pleasing monotonic nature depicted? (2) What is the impact of the tightness of external labor markets upon the curves? (3) What is the role of workers' organizations in structuring and controlling workers' preferences? (4) What happens when wages are allowed to vary? (5) How can internal labor market operations and the location of ports of entry be explained? (6) More narrowly, how do these curves for one job depend upon and affect those for jobs above and below it? These questions are explored in some detail in the author's report for the Office of Manpower Research 30 September, 1969.

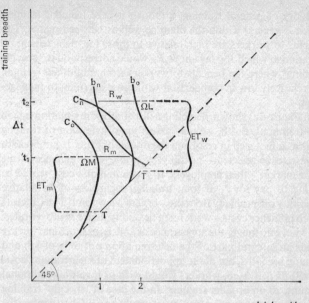

Figure 6

benefit curves shown. Moreover, the initial assumption is made that employers bear all the costs of training; hence the workers' iso-benefit curves look slightly different than in Figure 5. They are now drawn asymptotic to total irrelevancy of the excess training from a benefit standpoint.

Under the conditions shown, management would minimize costs at the point Ω_M – choosing a narrow job breadth j_1 and a narrow level of training t_1 of which ET_M reflects the desired amount of 'excess training'. Workers, on the other hand, would prefer to arrive at the point Ω_L (or above it) on their highest possible net benefit curve. They seek in this case a broad job (j_2) with broad training (t_2 or more), of which ET_w is training beyond the needs of the job itself. The locus of alternative points which are the best that can be done by workers and managers at non-optimal job breadth are shown by R_w and R_M respectively.

The situation shown in Figure 6 roughly corresponds to Becker's category of general training, although it here includes training which is general within the plant as well as between plants. The benefits to workers are high relative to those for management. A situation in which R_M lay above R_w would correspond to 'specific training' where the benefits to workers from additional training are relatively low in comparison with those accruing to management.

In Figure 6 as shown, depicting a disequilibrium situation on job and training breadth, we may assess the distribution of training costs as a first step in resolving the disequilibrium. If job breadth j_1 were to be selected – possibly by employer dominance in the labor market – then employers, to reach minimal cost, would be willing to pay for t_1 of total training, regardless of its relative generality or specificity from the workers' viewpoint. Thus, factors which influence costs – work force flexibility, labor turnover rates, etc. – have no longer the appearance of a 'deus ex machina' but are rather an integral part of the determination not only of job and training breadths, but of the apportionment of their training costs as well. If j_1 is fixed, workers would wish to invest an additional amount, Δt, in broader training. In the case of 'specific' training where R_M lies above R_w, employers would be willing to assume the entire cost of training. Thus, in this situation, our conclusion agrees with that of Becker, while for general training under our definition, we have come a bit closer to identifying the share of the cost that employers will be willing to pay.

The means by which equilibrium is reached in Figure 6 proceed through the redistribution of training costs. For every possible combination of workers' and managers' shares of these costs, an optimal job breadth-training breadth pair exists, derived as in Figures 4 and 5. Each job, training and cost distribution determines a level of workers' net benefits and managers' unit costs, as shown in Figure 7. The points Y and Z for the particular job reflect influences of general conditions in the rest of the economy: Y is workers' minimum acceptable benefit; Z, the maximum cost which managements can bear or pass on. If the curves do not intersect – Y to the right of Z – then the job will not exist unless a third party shares the costs. In the case shown, the equilibrium distribution of costs would fall as X per cent for management. The reader may explore with this apparatus the impacts on the shape

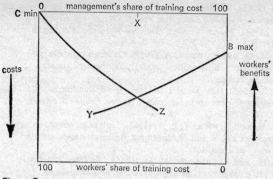

Figure 7

and level of these curves (hence, on distributions of training costs, etc.) arising from imperfections in the product market or from organization of workers.

Conclusion

The model of jobs and training here developed yields a solution in which job design, total amounts of training, and the apportionment of training costs between workers and employers are determined. Turnover rates, wages and costs of production – among other variables – would appear in a more complete specification of the model. For simplicity and brevity, however, attention has been focused on the first three items, in the context of a single idealized job.

The value of the model may best be seen by contrasting it to Becker's dichotomous treatment of the training cost problem. The distinction between internal and external marginal products (which makes little sense anyway until job design is determined) is no longer the cornerstone of the theory. Instead, the preferences of workers and the cost concerns of managements are brought together with the available technology to yield a more comprehensive and realistic picture, less fettered by neoclassical preconceptions about labor markets.

References

BARNETT, G. E. (1926), *Chapters on Machinery and Labor*, Harvard University Press.

BARBASH, J. (1968), 'Union interests in apprenticeship and other training forms', *Journal of Human Resources*, vol. 3, Winter, pp. 63–85.

BECKER, G. (1964), *Human Capital*, National Bureau of Economic Research.

BENEWITZ, M. C., and ZUCKER, A. (1968), 'Human capital and occupational choice – a theoretical model', *Southern Economic Journal*, vol. 34, January.

BHALLA, A. S. (1965), 'Choosing techniques: handpounding *v.* maching-milling of rice: an Indian case', *Oxford Economic Papers*, March, pp. 147–57.

BIGGANE, J. F., and STEWART, P. A. (1963), 'Job enlargement: a case study', Bureau of Labor and Management Research Series, no. 25, *State University of Iowa*, July.

CONANT, E. H., and KILBRIDGE, M. D. (1965), 'An interdisciplinary analysis of job enlargement: technology, costs, and behavioral implications', *Industrial and Labor Relations Review*, vol. 18, April, p. 389.

DAVIS, L. E. (1966), 'The design of jobs', *Industrial Relations*, vol. 6, October, pp. 21–45.

DOERINGER, P. B., and PIORE, M. J. (1965), 'Labor market adjustment and internal training', *Proceedings of the Industrial Relations Research Association*, pp. 250–63.

GUEST, R. H. (1957), 'Job enlargement: a revolution in job design', *Personnel Administration*, vol. 20, pp. 12–13.

HULIN, C. L. (1968), 'Effects of changes in job satisfaction levels on employee turnover', *Journal of Applied Psychology*, vol. 52, pp. 122–6.

LANCASTER, K. J. (1966), 'A new approach to consumer theory', *Journal of Political Economy*, vol. 74, April, pp. 132–57.

LESTER, R. A. (1967), 'Pay differentials by size of establishment', *Industrial Relations*, vol. 7, October.

MANDELBROT, B. (1962), 'Paretion distributions and income maximization', *Quarterly Journal of Economics*, vol. 76, February, pp. 57–85.

MINCER, J. (1962), 'On the job training: costs, returns, and implications', *Journal of Political Economy*, vol. 70, October.

National Industrial Conference Board (1967), *The Conference Board Record*, NICB, January, pp. 33–42.

PIORE, M. J. (1968), 'The impact of the labor market upon the design and selection of productive techniques within the manufacturing plant', *Quarterly Journal of Economics*, vol. 82, November, pp. 602–20.

VROOM, V. H. (1964), *Work and Motivation*, Wiley, pp. 126–50.

WOODWARD, J. (1958), 'Management and technology', *Problems of Progress in Industry*, no. 3.

Part Five
Job-Centered Studies

Three separate strategies for the design of job content are presented in these empirical studies. In Reading 19, Paul, Robertson and Herzberg present the results of a series of separate experiments testing Herzberg's concepts of job enrichment.

Although job enrichment is one of the useful approaches to satisfying most of the criteria of effective job designs, it has the present limitation, shared by other job-centered approaches, of not seeking to connect the job to the larger work system. This may impede the usefulness of the job-centered approach in sophisticated technology systems.

In Reading 20, Biggane and Stewart report on an early, but excellent, case study of job enlargement.

Finally, Hackman and Lawler (Reading 21) test the conceptual framework presented earlier in Reading 12. Here, they present data suggesting that not only do jobs require study and modification, as indicated by job enlargement (more variety of duties), and job enrichment (more autonomy and responsibility), but also that the need structure of the job occupant should be taken into account. Hackman and Lawler also present evidence that there are a number of separable (and measurable) job attributes that interact in the service of improved performance and satisfactions.

19 William J. Paul, Jr, Keith B. Robertson and Frederick Herzberg

Job Enrichment Pays Off

Excerpts from W. J. Paul, Jr., K. B. Robertson and F. Herzberg, 'Job enrichment pays off', *Harvard Business Review*, vol. 47, 1969, pp. 61–78.

In his pioneering article, 'One more time: how do you motivate employees?' Frederick Herzberg put forward some principles of scientific-job enrichment and reported a successful application of them involving the stockholder correspondents employed by a large corporation. According to him, job enrichment seeks to improve both task efficiency and human satisfaction by means of building into people's jobs, quite specifically, greater scope for personal achievement and its recognition, more challenging and responsible work, and more opportunity for individual advancement and growth. It is concerned only incidentally with matters such as pay and working conditions, organizational structure, communications, and training, important and necessary though these may be in their own right.

But like a lot of pioneering work, Herzberg's study raised more questions than it answered. Some seemed to us to merit further consideration, particularly those in regard to the (a) generality of the findings, (b) feasibility of making changes, and (c) consequences to be expected. Consider:

1. *Generality.* Can similarly positive results be obtained elsewhere with other people doing different jobs? [. . .]

2. *Feasibility.* Are there not situations where the operational risk is so high that it would be foolhardy to attempt to pass responsibility and scope for achievement down the line? [. . .] Do all employees welcome having their jobs enriched, or are there not some who prefer things to be left as they are? [. . .] Is not the best route to motivational change through participation?

3. *Consequences.* In view of so many possible difficulties in the way, are the gains to be expected from job enrichment significant or

only marginal? Do they relate primarily to job satisfaction or to performance? What are the consequences for supervision if jobs are loaded with new tasks taken from above, i.e. does one man's enrichment become another's impoverishment? [. . .]

There are undoubtedly more questions that could be raised and investigated. But these seem particularly important from a corporate point of view if job enrichment is to take place on a widespread basis, as part of management practice rather than as a research activity. Accordingly, the purpose of this article is to probe into the complexities of job enrichment in an attempt to shed light on these questions and to determine how the concept may be most effectively applied in furthering the attainment of corporate business objectives.

In order to do this, we shall report in Part I on five studies carried out in Imperial Chemical Industries Limited and other British companies. [. . .] In Part II, the main conclusions emerging from the studies will be presented in the form of answers to the questions raised at the beginning of this article.

Each study was initiated in response to a particular problem posed by management, and the conclusions drawn from any one can be only tentative. Among them, however, they cover not only widely different business areas and company functions, but also many types and levels of jobs. Collectively, they provide material which adds to our understanding of both theory and practice.

Part I: the job enrichment studies

As in all studies on job satisfaction and performance, the need to measure results introduced certain constraints which do not exist in normal managerial situations. Consequently, three main features were common to the studies we are reporting in this discussion.

First, the 'hygiene' was held constant. This means that no deliberate changes were made as part of the investigation, in matters such as pay, security, or working conditions. The studies were specifically trying to measure the extent of those gains which could be attributed solely to change in job content.

Second, recognition of the normal hygiene changes led to the need to have an 'experimental group' for whom the specific changes in job content were made, and a 'control group' whose job content remained the same.

Third, the studies had to be kept confidential to avoid the well-known tendency of people to behave in an artificial way when they know they are the subject of a controlled study. Naturally, there was no secret about the changes themselves, only about the fact that performance was being measured.

All studies set out to measure job satisfaction and performance for both the experimental and control groups over a trial period following the implementation of the changes. The trial period itself generally lasted a year and was never less than six months. The performance measures always were specific to the group concerned and were determined by local management of the subject company. To measure job satisfaction, we relied throughout on a job reaction survey which measures the degree of people's satisfaction with the motivators in their job as they themselves perceive them.

Laboratory technicians

Managers in an industrial research department were concerned about the morale of laboratory technicians, or 'experimental officers' (EOs). This group's job was to implement experimental programs devised by scientists. [. . .]

The average age of the experimental officers was increasing. A quarter of them had reached their salary maximums, and fewer now had the chance to move out of the department. Their normal promotion route into plant management had become blocked as manufacturing processes grew more complex and more highly qualified people filled the available jobs. [. . .] They felt their technical ability and experience was being wasted by the scientists' refusal to delegate anything but routine work. [. . .]

Changes and experimental design. Here is the specific program of action devised and implemented for the experimental officers.
Technical: EOs were encouraged to write the final report, or 'minute', on any research project for which they had been responsible. Such minutes carried the author's name and were issued along with those of the scientists. [. . .]

EOs were involved in planning projects and experiments, and were given more chance to assist in work planning and target setting.

They were given time, on request, to follow up their own ideas, even if these went beyond the planned framework of research. Written reports had to be submitted on all such work.

Financial: EOs were authorized to requisition materials and equipment, to request analysis, and to order services such as maintenance, all on their own signature.

Managerial: Senior EOs were made responsible for devising and implementing a training program for their junior staff.

Senior EOs were involved in interviewing candidates for laboratory assistant jobs, and they also acted as first assessor in any staff assessment of their own laboratory assistants.

These changes drew on all the motivators. Each one gave important chances for achievement; together, they were designed to make the work more challenging. Recognition of achievement came in the authorship of reports. Authority to order supplies and services was a responsibility applying to all the EOs involved. The new managerial responsibilities reserved to senior EOs opened up room for advancement within the job, while the technical changes, particularly the opportunity for self-initiated work, gave scope for professional growth.

Some forty EOs in all were involved in the study. Two sections of the department acted as experimental groups (N = 15) and two as control groups (N = 29). [. . .]

Research work is notoriously difficult to measure, but as the aim was to encourage more scientific contribution from EOs, this was what had to be judged in as objective a way as possible. All EOs were asked to write monthly progress reports of work done. Those written by experimental and control group EOs were assessed by a panel of three managers, not members of the department, who were familiar with the research work concerned. [. . .]

The other main measure was to use the same system to assess research minutes written by the EOs. These were compared against an equivalent sample of minutes written by scientists over the same period, which were submitted to the panel for assessment, again without identification.

Motivational results. Both experimental and control groups improved their monthly report scores at about the same rate during the first five months. There is no doubt that with practice all were getting better at report writing, and it may be that the mere fact of being asked to write monthly reports itself acted as a motivator for both groups.

Once the changes had been fully implemented in the experimental groups, however, performance began to diverge. Although the reports of the control groups continued to improve for a time, they were far outpaced by those of the experimental groups. With some fluctuations, this performance differential was maintained throughout the rest of the trial period. [. . .]

During the twelve months of the trial period, a total of thirty-four research minutes were written by EOs, all from the experimental groups, compared with two from the department as a whole during the previous twelve-month period. [. . .]

It is one thing for laboratory technicians to write research minutes, but whether the minutes they write are any good or not is a different matter. [. . .] All EO scores except three fell within the range of scores obtained by the scientists; the three exceptions were written by one man. Three of the EOs' minutes, one in fact written by a laboratory assistant with guidance from an EO, were judged to be as good as the best of the scientists' minutes. [. . .]

Three staff assessments on EOs were carried out – at the beginning, middle and end of the trial period. Each followed the normal company procedure. The only group which showed a consistent improvement was one of the experimental groups.

The job reaction survey was given both before and after the trial period. In the initial survey, experimental and control group EOs could not be specifically identified, and so an exact comparison of the before and after scores of each group cannot be made. The overall mean score attained by all EOs in the department was no higher at the end of the trial period than it had been at the beginning. Although managers believed there had been a positive change in job satisfaction, that is not a conclusion which can be supported with data.

Sales representatives

The company concerned had long enjoyed a healthy share of the domestic market in one particular product range, but its position was threatened by competition. [. . .] The critical factor in the situation appeared to be sales representatives' effort. [. . .]

Their mean score in the job reaction survey, like that of other groups of salesmen, was higher than most employees of equivalent seniority, which suggested that they enjoyed considerable job satisfaction.

The problem in this case, therefore, was that for the vital business objective of regaining the initiative in an important market, sustained extra effort was needed from a group of people already comparatively well treated and reasonably satisfied with their jobs. Here, job enrichment would stand or fall by the sales figures achieved.

Changes and experimental design. Here is the specific program of action devised and implemented for the sales representatives.

Technical: Sales representatives were no longer obliged to write reports on every customer call. They were asked simply to pass on information when they thought it appropriate or request action as they thought it was required.

Responsibility for determining calling frequencies was put wholly with the representatives themselves, who kept the only records for purposes such as staff reviews.

The technical service department agreed to provide service 'on demand' from the representatives; nominated technicians regarded such calls as their first priority. Communication was by direct contact, paperwork being cleared after the event.

Financial: In cases of customer complaint about product performance, representatives were authorized to make immediate settlements of up to $250 if they were satisfied that consequential liability would not be prejudiced.

If faulty material had been delivered or if the customer was holding material for which he had no further use, the representative now had complete authority, with no upper limit in sales value, to decide how best to deal with the matter. He could buy back unwanted stock even if it was no longer on the company's selling range.

Representatives were given a discretionary range of about 10 per cent on the prices of most produces, especially those considered to be critical from the point of view of market potential. The lower limit given was often below any price previously quoted by the company. All quotations other than at list price had to be reported by the representative.

The theme of all the changes was to build the sales representative's job so that it became more complete in its own right. Instead of always having to refer back to headquarters, the representative now had the authority to make decisions on his own – he was someone the customer could really do business with. Every change implied a greater responsibility; together they gave the freedom and challenge necessary for self-development. [. . .]

The experimental group (N = 15) was selected to be representative of the sales force as a whole in age range, experience and ability. [. . .] The rest of the sales force (N = 23) acted as the control group.

Motivational results. During the trial period the experimental group increased its sales by almost 19 per cent over the same period of the previous year, a gain of over $300,000 in sales value. The control group's sales in the meantime declined by 5 per cent. The equivalent change for both groups the previous year had been a decline of 3 per cent. The difference in performance between the two groups is statistically significant at the 0·01 level of confidence. [. . .]

In view of the greater negotiating authority granted to the experimental group representatives, it is important to check whether their substantial increase in turnover was achieved at the expense of profit. As all quotations other than at list price were reported by the representatives, it was possible to analyze the gross margin achieved by both groups. The analysis showed without doubt that the gross margin of the experimental group's sales was proportionally as high, if not higher, than that of the control group's sales. [. . .]

Over the trial period the control group's mean score in the job reaction survey remained static. In contrast, the experimental group's score rose by 11 per cent.

Design engineers

The engineering director of one of the divisions of I C I wanted to see whether the job of design engineer might lend itself to motivational change. His design department faced an increasing work load as more design work for the division's plants was being done internally. The situation was exacerbated by difficulties in recruiting qualified design engineers. People at all levels in the department were being overloaded and development work was suffering.

Changes and experimental design. Here is the specific program of action devised and implemented for the design engineers.

Technical: Experienced engineers were given a completely independent role in running their projects; the less experienced technical men were given as much independence as possible. Occasions on which reference to supervision remained obligatory were reduced to an absolute minimum. The aim was that each engineer should judge for himself when and to what extent he should seek advice.

Group managers sponsored occasional investigatory jobs, and engineers were encouraged to become departmental experts in particular fields. They were expected to follow up completed projects as they thought appropriate.

When authority to allocate work to outside consultants was given, the engineers were to have the responsibility for making the choice of consultants.

Financial: Within a sanctioned project with a budget already agreed on, all arbitrary limits on engineers' authority to spend money were removed. They themselves had to ensure that each 'physical intent' was adequately defined and that an appropriate sum was allocated for it in the project budget. That done, no financial ceiling limited their authority to place orders.

Managerial: Engineers were involved in the selection and placing of designers (drawing office staff). They manned selection panels, and a recruit would only be allocated to a particular engineer if the latter agreed to accept him.

Experienced engineers were asked to make the initial salary recommendations for all their junior staff members.

Engineers were allowed to authorize overtime, cash advances, and traveling expenses for staff.

Motivational results. In summary fashion, these are the deductions that can be drawn from this study:

1. Senior managers saw a change in both the amount and the kind of consultation between experimental group design engineers and

heir immediate supervisors. The supervisors' routine involvement in projects was much reduced, and they were able to give more emphasis in their work to technical development. Some engineers still needed frequent guidance; others operated independently with confidence. The point is that not all were restricted or the benefit of some; those who could were allowed to find their own feet.

2. The encouragement of specialist expertise among design engineers was a long-term proposition, but progress was made during the trial period.

3. The removal of any financial ceiling on engineers' authority to place orders within an approved project with an agreed budget proved entirely effective. Whereas before the design engineers had to seek approval from as many as three higher levels of management for any expenditure over $5,000 – a time-consuming process for all concerned – now they could, and did, place orders for as much as $500,000 worth of equipment on their own authority.

4. There is no evidence of any poor decision having been taken as a result of the new arrangements. In fact, at the end of the trial period, none of the senior managers concerned wanted to revert to the old system.

5. The changes involving the engineers in supervisory roles were thought by the senior managers to be at least as important as the other changes, possibly more so in the long term.

6. There was no doubt about the design engineers' greater involvement in the selection process, which they fully accepted and appreciated. Significantly, they began to show a greater feel for the constraints involved in selection.

7. The responsibility for overtime and travel claims was fully effective and taken in people's stride. There was no adverse effect from a budgetary control point of view.

8. The involvement of design engineers in making salary recommendations for their staff was considered by the senior managers to have been a major improvement. If anything, engineers tended to be 'tighter' in their salary recommendations than more senior management. There was general agreement that the effectiveness of this change would increase over time.

9. Senior managers felt that none of the changes of its own accord had had an overriding effect, nor had all problems been solved. But there was no doubt that the cumulative effect of the changes had been significant and that the direction of solutions to some important problems had been indicated.

The changes may have been effective, but in this particular study the important question was whether they had a significant impact on job satisfaction. Some of the motivators introduced into the experimental groups had been in operation in the control group for some time; others – because of the specialist nature of the control group's work – were not as important to it as to the experimental groups. The control group had scored high in the initial job reaction survey, while the experimental groups had both achieved very low scores. If the experimental groups' scores did not improve, doubt would inevitably be cast on the relationship between job content and job satisfaction. As it turned out, comparison results of the before and after job reaction surveys revealed that the mean scores of the two experimental groups had increased by 21 per cent and 16 per cent, while those of the control group and all other design engineers in the department had remained static.

Factory supervisors

The final two studies, one in ICI and one in another British company, concerned factory supervisors: production foremen on shift work fabricating nonferrous metals, and engineering foremen on day work providing maintenance services. As the two studies seem to be complementary, they are considered jointly.

In both cases management was concerned about the degree to which the traditional role of the foreman had been eroded in recent years. The increasing complexity of organizational structures, plant and equipment, and industrial relations had left the foreman isolated. Decisions in the areas of planning, technical control, and discipline – originally in his province – were now passed up the line or turned over to a specialist staff. Many managers believed that as a consequence small problems too often escalated unnecessarily, managers were being overloaded, and day-to-day relationships between the foreman and his men had been weakened.

Changes and experimental design. Here is the specific program of action devised and implemented for the production and engineering foremen.

Technical: Foremen were involved more in planning. Production foremen were authorized to modify schedules for loading and sequencing; engineering foremen were consulted more about organizational developments, given more responsibility for preventive maintenance, and encouraged to comment on design.

All were assigned projects on specific problems such as quality control, and could draw on the necessary resources for their implementation.

Other changes included giving foremen more 'on the spot' responsibility, official deputizing for engineers, the writing of monthly reports, and more recognition of foremen's achievement of plans.

Financial: Engineering foremen were given complete control of certain 'on cost' budgets. Production foremen were encouraged to make all decisions on nonstandard payments.

Managerial: Production foremen were given the authority to hire labor against agreed manning targets. They interviewed candidates for jobs and made the decision on their selection.

All the foremen were given complete disciplinary authority, except for dismissal. They decided what disciplinary action to take, consulted the personnel department if they thought it necessary, conducted the interviews, and kept the records.

All were given formal responsibility for the assessment, training and development of their subordinates, and in some cases for the appointment of their own deputies. On the production side, a newly appointed training officer acted as a resource person for the foremen. Engineering foremen were involved more in the application of a job appraisement scheme and in joint consultation and negotiation with union officials.

The objective of integrating the foreman more fully into the managerial team dictated that responsibility should be the motivator chiefly concerned in these changes. Control of his own labor force, backed up by more technical and financial responsibility, was designed to give the foreman more opportunities for achievement and personal growth in the job. The main issue in these studies was whether foremen would prove themselves capable of carrying the increased responsibility. Thus, in monitoring the effectiveness of the changes, the aim was primarily to detect any instability or shortcomings in performance.

Motivational results. In summary fashion, these are the deductions that can be drawn from this study:

1. In six months the production foremen recruited nearly 100 men, and were judged by the personnel officer to be 'hiring a better caliber of man at an improved rate'. Their immediate supervisors were categorical in their approval and noted that the foremen were taking special care to 'design their own shifts'. Recruitment interviews were said to have improved the foremen's ability to handle encounters with existing staff and shop stewards.

2. Training was handled equally successfully by the production foremen. For each job it was specified that there should be a certain number of men trained to take over in an emergency. During the trial period, the margin by which the target number was missed was reduced from 94 to 55; the number of operators unable to do another's job fell by 12 per cent, and the number of assistants unable to do the job of the man they assisted fell by 37 per cent. No comparable improvement was achieved in the control group.

3. It became clear from both studies that foremen were fully capable of carrying disciplinary responsibility. An analysis of all cases arising during the trial year showed that there had been a reduction in the number of 'repeat offenses' among employees with poor disciplinary records and a substantial reduction in short-term work stoppages. The analysis concluded that foremen were not prone to take one kind of action rather than another, they had developed a purposeful approach to such problems, and there had been no adverse union reaction.

4. About 50 per cent of the engineering foremen's monthly reports during the trial year referred to consultation and negotiation with union officials – this on a site not noted for its harmonious industrial relations. Topics included demarcation, special payments, and the easing of bans imposed on 'call outs'. The incidence of such reports was spread evenly throughout the experimental group; their frequency increased during the trial period as the

foremen became more confident of their abilities. All such matters appear to have been handled capably.

5. From both studies came evidence, confirming what has long been demonstrated in training courses, that special investigatory projects give foremen much needed opportunity to contribute their experience and expertise to the solution of long-standing technical and organizational problems. In only three cases where financial evaluation was possible, the estimated annual savings totaled more than $125,000.

6. Regarding the engineering foremen's control of budgets, in some cases the aim was to meet the target exactly; in others it was to reduce costs as much as possible. Both aims were achieved by the foremen at least as well as they had been by the managers. There is no evidence that plant efficiency or work effectiveness suffered in any way as a result of cost savings achieved by the foremen.

7. In the case of the engineering foremen, the experimental group's staff assessments at the end of the trial year were markedly better than those of the control groups. Despite the attempt made in the initial selection of experimental and control groups to achieve as good a balance as possible in ability and experience, there can be little doubt that the experimental group did in any case contain some more able men. But no one anticipated that such a large difference would show itself at the end of the trial period. As evidence of development, 45 per cent of the experimental group's assessments referred to significant improvements in performance during the year, and 36 per cent made particular mention of how effectively the foreman had dealt with increased responsibility received during the year. These assessments were written by managers who were not party to the study.

8. In the production foremen's study, superintendents reported that the new conditions were 'separating the wheat from the chaff'; some of those who had previously been thought to be among the best of the foremen had not lived up to their reputations in a situation which placed little value on compliance, while others had improved enormously.

9. The production foremen's job reaction survey scores showed no particular improvement over the trial period. In the case of the engineering foremen, the experimental group's mean score showed

a 12 per cent increase, while the control group's had only risen by 3 per cent.

Part II: the main conclusions

What has been described in the first part of this article is the consistent application of theory in an area where custom and practice are normally only challenged by individual hunch or intuition. As we have seen, each study posed a separate problem concerning a different group of employees; the only common element among them was the conceptual framework brought to bear on the problem, enabling a specific program of action to be devised and implemented. Much was learned in the process, by ourselves and managers alike.

Now in Part II, the main conclusions which emerged from the job enrichment studies are presented in the form of answers to the questions raised at the beginning of this article.

Generality of findings

Can similarly positive results be obtained elsewhere with other people doing different jobs?

Yes. The studies reflect a diversity of type and level of job in several company functions in more than one industry. From the evidence now available, it is clear that results are not dependent on any particular set of circumstances at the place of study. Our investigation has highlighted one important aspect of the process of management and has shown that disciplined attention to it brings results. The findings are relevant wherever people are being managed. [. . .]

Feasibility of change

Are there not situations where the operational risk is so high that it would be foolhardy to attempt to pass responsibility and scope for achievement down the line?

Probably there are, but we have not encountered one. The risks attached to some of the changes in the sales representatives' study seemed frightening at the time. Few managers who have not tried it can accept with equanimity the thought of their subordinates placing orders for $500,000 worth of equipment on their own authority, even within a sanctioned project. [. . .]

Theory provides an explanation for the remarkable absence of disaster experienced in practice. Bad hygiene, such as oppressive supervision and ineffectual control systems, constrains and limits performance, and may even lead to sabotage. Administrative procedures that guard against hypothetical errors and imaginary irresponsibility breed the very carelessness and apathy which result in inefficiency. With too many controls, responsibility becomes so divided that it gets lost. Hygiene improvements at best list the constraints.

The motivators, on the other hand, make it possible for the individual to advance the base line of his performance. The road is open for improvement, while present standards remain available as a reference point and guide. When a man is given the chance to achieve more, he may not take that chance, but he has no reason to achieve less. The message of both theory and practice is that people respond cautiously to new responsibility; they feel their way and seek advice. When responsibility is put squarely with the person doing a job, he is the one who wants and needs feedback in order to do his job. His use of the motivators, not our use of hygiene, is what really controls performance standards. [. . .]

Do all employees welcome having their jobs enriched, or are there not some who prefer things to be left as they are?

Individual reaction to job enrichment is as difficult to forecast in terms of attitudes as it is in terms of performance. Those already genuinely interested in their work develop real enthusiasm. Not all people welcome having their jobs enriched, certainly, but so long as the changes are opportunities rather than demands, there is no reason to fear an adverse reaction. If someone prefers things the way they are, he merely keeps them the way they are, by continuing to refer matters to his supervisor, for example. Again, there is nothing lost. [. . .]

Is not the best route to motivational change through participation?

Yes and no. We have to define our terms. So far as the process of job enrichment itself is concerned, experimental constraints in the studies dictated that there could be no participation by jobholders themselves in deciding what changes were to be made in their jobs. The changes nevertheless seemed to be effective. On the other hand, when people were invited to participate – not in any of the reported studies – results were disappointing. In one case, for example, a group of personnel specialists suggested fewer than thirty fairly minor changes in their jobs, whereas their managers had compiled a list of over 100 much more substantial possibilities.

It seems that employees themselves are not in a good position to test out the validity of the boundaries of their jobs. So long as the aim is not to measure experimentally the effects of job enrichment alone, there is undoubtedly benefit in the sharing of ideas. Our experience merely suggests that it would be unwise to pin too many hopes to it – or the wrong hopes. [. . .]

Participation is indeed the best route to motivational change, but only when it is participation in the act of management, no matter at what level it takes place. And the test of the genuineness of that participation is simple – it must be left to the subordinate to be the prime mover in consultation on those topics where he carries personal responsibility. For the manager as for the subordinate, the right to be consulted must be earned by competence in giving help. Therein lies the only authority worth having.

Expected consequences

In view of so many possible difficulties in the way, are the gains to be expected from job enrichment significant or only marginal?

We believe the gains are significant, but the evidence must speak for itself. In all, 100 people were in the experimental groups in the studies described. A conservative reckoning of the financial benefit achieved, arrived at by halving all estimated annual gains or savings, would be over $200,000 per year. Cost was measurable in a few days of managers' time at each place.

Do the gains relate primarily to job satisfaction or to performance?

Contrary to expectation, the gains, initially at least, seem to relate primarily to performance. [. . .]

When direct measurement of job satisfaction was possible, the most significant gains seemed to come when the trial period was longest. There is every reason to think that in the long term attitudes catch up with performance and that job enrichment initiates a steady and prolonged improvement in both.

What are the consequences for supervision if jobs are loaded with new tasks taken from above, i.e. does one man's enrichment become another's impoverishment?

The more subordinates' jobs are enriched, the more superfluous does supervision, in its old sense, become. [. . .]

The enrichment of lower-level jobs seems to set up a chain reaction resulting in the enrichment of supervisors' jobs as well. Fears that the supervisor may somehow miss out are based on the premise that there is a finite pool of responsibility in the organization which is shared among its members. In practice new higher-order responsibilities are born. [. . .]

The main consequence is that management becomes a service, its purpose to enable, encourage, assist and reinforce achievement by employees.

20 James F. Biggane and Paul A. Stewart

Job Enlargement: A Case Study

Excerpts from J. F. Biggane and P. A. Stewart, 'Job enlargement:
a case study', Bureau of Labor and Management, College of Business
Administration, *State University of Iowa Research Series* no. 25, July,
1963.

Preparing for job enlargement

The Maytag Company's experience with job enlargement has been
a very specific thing, starting at a known point in time and involving explicit jobs. Nevertheless, certain programs and activities
which preceded our initial work with job enlargement appear to
us, in retrospect, to have been most significant in building support
for our efforts with job enlargement. This is not to imply that these
particular activities are prerequisites to successful experience with
job enlargement. We do, however, consider them as having been
important and will comment on them at this point.

Attitude surveys

Shortly after the close of the Second World War and after the most
pressing steps of return to domestic manufacture had gotten
underway, the Maytag Company collaborated with a leading
educational institution to carry out an intensive and comprehensive survey of attitudes of personnel in the operating division of
the company. The survey was carefully planned and designed, and
involved all factory employees and supervision. A full-time study
director from the university directed all aspects of the survey, and
at no time was the confidence of the employee violated. The local
union endorsed this program and was provided the same findings
and reports from the university as were supplied to the company.

It was the purpose of the survey to find out on a scientifically
designed basis, without bias and in an entirely objective manner,
how people (as individuals and in work groups, and in both supervisory and non-supervisory positions) felt about their work, their
associates, their supervisors, and the company. Attitudes were
sought concerning specific items such as wages, incentive work, and

working conditions, and about less tangible items such as interests, opportunities, security and company-union relationships. [. . .]

Work simplification

Work simplification at the Maytag Company was another post-Second World War activity. The program was initiated under the general direction of the Industrial Engineering Department. [. . .]

It is our opinion that this plan, which has been in effect for the past fifteen years, has established a relationship between employees and the company which is open and collaborative. Under such a condition most employees would not be surprised at new ideas or changes, since, as a result of this plan – and in most cases as a result of actual participation – they recognize the company's interest in (and desire for) improvement of any kind. It was felt, and results appear to indicate, that the introduction of job enlargement would be substantially enhanced by this employee–company mutual involvement in the work simplification program. It would be improper to leave the impression that the work simplification program, in itself, made possible what we deem to be a successful experience with job enlargement. More accurately, we believe that it was, and continues to be, of genuine value.

Methods–time measurement

Methods–Time Measurement, known as MTM, is a system of predetermined time values which analyzes any manual operation into the basic motions required to perform the operation, and assigns a time value to each motion which is determined by the nature of the motion and the conditions under which it is performed. The Maytag Company had employed time study as the basis for establishing labor standards prior to the introduction of MTM as a device for performing this work, and still does employ time study where appropriate. [. . .]

This background of experience and training has established a non-controversial atmosphere with respect to labor standards, and has removed from the enlarged job setup one element which could otherwise have been the basis for question or doubt. The evidence of the contribution made in recent years, particularly with respect to job enlargement, has been the continuing decline in the number of grievances filed by the union related to labor standards and, further, the fact that most of such grievances are related to principle rather than the use of M T M itself.

Working foremen

In the sense in which the Maytag Company employs the title 'working foremen' – it means exactly what it says. Such a person is one who leads others in the performance of their work, or one who may (and does from time to time) perform manual work similar to (or the same as) that performed by those for whom he is responsible, for purposes of teaching correct methods of doing work. He is the first level of supervision, directly above the production worker. He is basically a leader who carries out the instructions of his superior, the salaried foreman, and who, by his job knowledge and ability as a natural leader, is qualified to function in this capacity. He may be a member of the bargaining unit if he so desires; he is an hourly-rated employee; he is paid a premium as a working foreman; he is subject to all the terms of the labor agreement; and he is the logical and natural link between management and worker. [. . .]

As a result of establishing and implementing the working foreman classification, it was possible to provide direct, constant and on-the-scene direction of the work on each job enlargement installation. This included pre-installation tryout, de-bugging, training and follow-up. The earlier experiences uncovered some faulty situations in this relationship; however, based upon such experience, it has been possible to refine and improve later installations of enlarged jobs.

It will be noted that running through these comments there is an underlying concern with close and effective communication with workers. The product of the survey, work simplification, M T M and the initiation of the working foreman classification, have all been supportive to improved communications. There is much room for improvement; however, we believe that without such programs the task of installing successfully the new job designs for job enlargement would have been more difficult.

Job enlargement experience

With the above programs in effect to help attain understanding and communication among workers, line supervisors and management staffs, we were in a good position to proceed with the installation of job enlargement.

During the past three years, we have installed a total of fifteen job enlargement projects which were formerly conveyor-paced group assemblies. Another seven are now in various stages of completion, others are planned. Approximately 110 employees have worked on these job enlargements, of whom over eighty have had experience on both this type of work design and on paced conveyorized assembly lines. This provides a sufficient sample to draw reasonably valid conclusions concerning employee acceptance of job enlargement, as well as the attainment of various manufacturing objectives.

There are several important results that have been characteristic of those installations:

1. Quality has improved.

2. Labor costs are lower.

3. A large majority of operators came to prefer job enlargement in a relatively short time.

4. Problems inherent in paced groups have been largely eliminated. For example, realignment of each operator's job content is no longer necessary whenever production levels change, resulting in less training, higher productivity, fewer changes in production standards, reduction in grievances, etc.

5. Equipment and installation costs have been recovered by tangible savings in an average of about two years.

6. Space requirements for enlarged jobs, of the type included in this report, are comparable to that required for powered conveyor-line assembly [. . .]

Case: top cover for programmed automatic washer

This example illustrates the application of job enlargement to a top cover assembly involving forty-six component parts, some of which are large shapes, and require extensive testing of the electrical circuit. The design of the top cover is substantially different than for other models being assembled on paced conveyors, and the volume is low.

With the introduction of the 'push-button' automatic washer, which resulted in major design changes in the top cover assembly as compared to previous washing machine models, there were several choices in designing the assembly system. We could have made major changes in the existing top cover assembly line, integrating this substantially different model with other more common models, but resulting in greater complexities in scheduling and assembly; a separate paced-conveyor assembly system could have been utilized; or job enlargement could be applied.

It was concluded that many of the advantages of previous job enlargement installations could be attained here, particularly in quality and costs. However, we had not had experience with enlarged jobs having such large components, such a variety of parts, or where the operator's work content of about nine minutes (equivalent to the cycle time of about twenty-five line operators) was so great. Each presented unique problems.

Original method. The top cover is composed of forty-six component parts and the completed assembly measures twenty-five inches by twenty-seven inches in size and includes the control panel with its instruments and wiring. Previously the control panel was assembled by a group of operators as the panel passed by them on a continuously moving conveyor. The panel was then transferred to another similar moving conveyor on which another group of operators assembled the top cover, incorporating the control panel. The cycle time for each group was approximately 0·50 minutes, and the groups earned approximately 135 per cent of the labor standard on incentive. No inspection of their work was performed at this point; their work was checked by the Inspection Department later after the top cover had been assembled to the complete washing machine on another assembly line. Necessary correction was then done by a repairman who was not a member of the group.

Job enlargement method. Because of the low volume, material handling of the large parts was designed around the use of portable racks to store and transport the parts and completed assemblies, rather than installing an elaborate and costly mechanized handling system. The work station was designed so that all assembly and testing was done at one bench, with the racks located within arm's reach of the operator, and tools were suspended from overhead. [. . .]

The operator tested the finished assembly by connecting the unit to a test panel and going through a systematic procedure of checking the electrical circuit. If a defect was detected, the operator made the necessary repairs.

Results. With each operator having responsibility for a complete assembly, including testing, the quality is considerably better than experienced with less complicated models assembled on the paced line. Also, adjustments to correct defects are now made before the unit is assembled to the washer, eliminating extra handling of an assembled machine and simplifying repairs.

Costs that would have resulted had the existing assembly line been used, or a new paced line installed, were saved. These include imbalance of work among operators, cost of change-over of materials, reassignment of operators for the various models, and so forth.

In addition, the benefits of reduced problems of operator turnover, improved housekeeping, assimilation of new operators, and ease of changing production levels . . . were present in this application.

Installation plan. We found that the cycle time of nine minutes presented training problems that we had not anticipated. This was our first introduction and installation of job enlargement in this plant. Training techniques had not been adequately refined before the installation was made, nor had the operators been properly prepared psychologically for the change from their previous jobs, normally having highly repetitive cycles of less than 0·5 minutes, to one requiring a nine-minute work cycle. Consequently, one of the very few grievances on job enlargement was entered against the standard for this installation. Needless to say, immediate modifications in training procedures, and preparation of operators for long-cycle jobs, were initiated. In later installations, these problems have not occurred, and the longer-cycle operations have not been a particular problem or deterrent to job enlargement.

Employee reaction. Initially, we needed twelve operators for this application, six on each of two shifts, who were obtained through our job-bidding procedure. Some of the common reasons the operators gave for bidding on the job were: 'I'm tired of the line and want a change', 'This job is a higher labor grade and I feel I can earn more money', and 'I just thought I'd like a bench job'.

Because the operators each chose to go on this new job, when they could have stayed on their previous job, it can be assumed that their attitude toward job enlargement was favorable. However, as indicated earlier, some of them found the nine-minute cycle took longer to learn than they had expected and their performance was low, resulting in a grievance contending that the labor standard was improper. For the average assembly operator, about two weeks is required to achieve satisfactory incentive performance on this nine-minute job, as compared with about three days for an operator in a paced-line group where the cycle time is about 0·50 minutes. During the grievance, some of the operators became discouraged and bid to other jobs. After the labor standard was proven to be proper, the remaining operators increased their performance to very satisfactory levels. They stayed on the job, and came to like it. [. . .]

Advantages and limitations

Having discussed the background leading up to our firm's experience with job enlargement, and having described a specific example of job enlargement, it now seems appropriate to discuss the principal advantages and limitations of job enlargement as we see them.

Advantages

Job satisfaction and responsibility. With the enlarged job design, the operator is able to identify his work as a significant segment or part of the total operation. The content of his work evidences to him a concrete, complete unit which has meaning and, therefore, he derives from his work the sense of completeness and satisfaction that goes with such a job. It is accomplishment of something of value and significance.

Improvement of quality. As can be seen from the case described earlier in this paper, the operator on the enlarged job checks his own work. This has two basic benefits. First, he is able to find out, as a part of his job, whether or not the job is done correctly. This is a matter of pride of workmanship and is well illustrated by the impromptu comments of one employee working on an enlarged job:

Question: How do you like working with this unit assembly?

Answer: I like it very much. I'm happy here.

Question: What do you like about this job?

Answer: Well, I'll tell you, one of the things I like is the time goes so fast; before you know it, it is noon-time. Sometimes I even forget to take a break; whereas, on the assembly line I used to watch for the time when my reliefman was due. Here, I have all these parts to put together, and I have to think all the time or I get into trouble and have to do my work again. You see, after I get this all assembled, I check my assembly by pushing each of these eight buttons. Each button lights certain lights, as the chart shows, and every time I push the eight buttons and all of them have checked good, I get a thrill and great satisfaction. I put my number on the finished assembly and put it in the rack. All of these units in the rack are mine, and I'm proud of them, and if I should get one back tomorrow, I'd worry about it. You know, it is like you are creating something – maybe like painting a picture, or maybe like painting a house – you get the paint, work hard and put it on and, when it is finished, you step back and enjoy looking at the work you have done.

Question: How does this job compare with working on the assembly line?

Answer: Over there, I used to beat my brains out all day, and when the day was over I felt like I didn't do anything. Somebody may see all those machines, but I never did – and the time went so slowly and I was always more tired out at the end of the day; at least I thought so. Many times I have thought that a factory wasn't a good place for a woman to work but, on this job, I feel differently.

The second benefit is a reduction in inspection expense. Speaking about this particular job, our Quality Control Manager said, 'The quality of workmanship from these assembly stations has been excellent. We conduct no after-inspection of the units (other than on the finished machine) and experience a very low rate of rejection; whereas on the assembly of other top covers (conducted on a continuous line and group assembly basis), we have an inspector in the group to assure quality. Without an inspector in the group, the main assembly line would be stopped because of rejections.'

Stability of production (incentive labor) standards. The fact that the work design of an enlarged job is not modified to accommodate increases or decreases in production requirements, but rather that such production schedule changes are met by increasing or decreasing the number of work stations or operations, is a distinct advantage in that no change in the production (incentive labor) standard is necessary. The individual job method itself does not change. The number of people doing the same job does change. The changed production requirements are met by simply adding or decreasing operator (job enlargement) stations.

Flexibility of production rates. This advantage is closely related to the factor of stability noted above. When a change in production level is made upward, an additional operation (or operators) are placed at the formerly idle work stations; or an additional shift may be added. Those employees formerly assigned to the job continue without any drop in productivity, such as would be expected if a line were rebalanced for labor purposes. The new operators know, by observation, what the experienced operators are doing, and so there is no question about the job possibilities or expectations and they, therefore, tend to come up to standard promptly. In other words, this knowledge smoothes and accelerates the learning experience. If the production change is downward, an operator or operators are removed (or work hours reduced), and nothing else is changed. Obviously, there is no effect upon the productivity of those who remain on the enlarged job.

Material handling. Good job design of a practical job enlargement work station tends to reduce the amount of general material handling, since all the work for the enlarged job is performed at one work station and the intermediate handling from specialized operation to specialized operation is eliminated. This advantage exists only within certain physical limitations, taking into account the bulk, weight and character of components and the finished unit of work.

Uninhibited pace. The employee on an enlarged job is largely free from the effect of other operators upon his pace and productive potential, such as exists when several persons are working in a group and are interdependent, or when paced by a conveyor or similar working arrangement. The employee is, in effect, in business for himself; he may take personal time at his own convenience, and may accelerate or decelerate his work pace without being affected by or affecting others. Some persons in supervisory capacities state a preference for the paced line (or the group situation) since they feel this better controls the application of the employee to his job. Our experience does not support this contention.

Versatility of skills. The enlarged job, to varying degrees, provides to the employee multiple skill experiences which thereby makes the employee more valuable to the company and to himself. The broadening of experience and skill of the operator, through the learning of the enlarged job, gives him productive potential on a wider variety of kinds of work than he would secure through assignment to a non-enlarged work situation.

Personal satisfaction. Invariably the operator on an enlarged job enjoys certain factors which are not evident to the same degree on other jobs. He can see his production as a completed unit; he knows what it does, what its purpose is, and he has checked its quality. He takes an interest in his job since his ability makes itself evident in the product of his work. All this has a direct bearing upon his general morale and sense of responsibility. These factors have, in our opinion, genuine significance in light of the fact that the level of education continues to rise, and with it there is an increasing need to make work meaningful. The individual character of the enlarged job is, in certain respects, responsive to these needs.

Limitations

Job complexity. There is a limit in terms of complexity beyond which the enlargement of a job ceases to be practical. The complexity may be measured in the length of time of the complete cycle of production, the variety of skills required, and the technical character of the testing to be done. Job enlargement should not be perceived as a move to return to the idea of the master craftsman who built an entire product, although in theory at least, such might be the case in certain situations. It is, rather, the enlargement of work to the point at which the advantages noted above are at their maximum. We do recognize, however, the limitation of skills and cycle times.

Space and handling. Multiple setups or work stations for the same job require multiple units of space as well as duplicate containers, material handling aids, and the like. If the job has any reasonable degree of stability, this limitation is reduced. Even under optimum conditions of stability there are practical limitations to the ratio of space required to output secured when comparing the enlarged job design to the paced and fragmented job design.

Process limitations. Certain operations or processes do not lend themselves to enlargement, particularly where the operator is not in control of the operation as he is in the case of a completely manual assembly operation. Conveyorized furnaces, automatic plating equipment, and some specialized machine operations are examples. Even in these situations it would be a mistake to rule out completely the possibility of capturing certain of the advantages of job enlargement by modification of the job content or job design. Some factors such as setup, inspection and routine care of equipment may be considered here. The principal point of this limitation is to note that enlargement is controlled in certain respects by the character of the work to be done and the equipment required to perform that work.

Limitations imposed by components. An almost self-evident limitation is that imposed by the size, weight or special characteristic of the components to be used in the work. Such special characteristics would include toxicity, temperature, or other special limitations. These limitations are usually self-evident, and are almost always related to special processes or quality requirements.

Cost of equipment. Individual work stations for enlarged jobs require for each such station a complete complement of equipment, tools and fixtures. Where the production level is such that several such stations would be required, there is then duplication of such equipment at each station. Since each operator is performing several operations within the enlarged job cycle and since he will not use all tools constantly, there is a higher percentage of total time during which a given item will be idle than would be the case if the same tool were on a paced line with fragmented work assignments and a high degree of repetitive work at each work position. In our own application of job enlargement, this limitation has not proved to be a limiting factor. However, it is quite apparent that in some situations, such multiple setup of work stations could raise some questions because of the costs involved.

Absenteeism. An employee working on an enlarged job, as noted elsewhere in this paper, has acquired multiple skills required for the job and certain versatility in the nature of his work. Such skills, while not in themselves necessarily complicated, often do require a somewhat longer learning time for the total job than in the case of a single operation or small group of operations characteristic of a job on a paced line. The skills require learning, and of equal importance is the sequence and significance of each step in the enlarged job which now has a larger total content and a longer time cycle than the individual job on the paced line. In view of these considerations, the unplanned absence of a qualified operator working on an enlarged job can pose some problems in that a replacement is not always immediately available, and a substitute employee on the job will usually require somewhat longer time to become fully effective. It has been our experience, however, that this limitation is no more of a problem than many of the other unforeseen production problems that occur from time to time.

Conclusions

In this paper, we have described our approach to job enlargement. We have explained our reasons for exploring this subject, and told how we tested our preliminary conclusions by means of actual installations. We have described some of the background activities which we believe have been helpful and have presented some case 'notes' which describe our experience. We have also listed some of the advantages and limitations which we see in job enlargement.

We believe that certain conclusions can be drawn from our experience up to this time:

1. The actual installation of job enlargement to shop situations has been encouraging, and the results have demonstrated the benefits

which we had anticipated. There have been problems requiring revision and modification, but we are confident that the beneficial results have far outweighed any problems experienced to date.

2. Job enlargement offers definite opportunities to enhance the meaning of work through greater involvement of the operator, to favorably affect quality and cost, and to provide an opportunity for greater job satisfaction for the man on the job and his supervisor.

3. Successful experience with job enlargement requires positive interest and understanding on the part of all involved, whether directly or indirectly and including middle and upper management. Successful experience also requires unreserved support and involvement. We believe that it is not advisable to proceed with any job enlargement installation if there are reservations or questions unresolved on the part of any person who has a responsible role to play in connection with such installation.

4. Successful experience with job enlargement requires thorough technical preparation on layout, methods, facilities and aids. In several instances, we set up a trial work station to test the technical aspects before taking the new job into the shop.

5. Successful experience requires early and meaningful involvement of the operator. After all, he is the one who will work at this job, and his ideas, suggestions and requests should be taken into consideration. We found it well worth while to have the operator 'try out' the enlarged setup, and then to secure his ideas for possible use before the job was considered to be in production on even a preliminary basis.

6. Successful experience requires close attention and follow-up by supervision and staff during the early days of the installation. This job design is not just another job, but a totally new idea. Failure to attach importance, interest and attention to it greatly increases the probability of unnecessary misunderstandings and problems. It may even permit the job to get started in a manner not planned for or intended in the first place.

21 J. Richard Hackman and Edward E. Lawler III

Employee Reactions to Job Characteristics

Excerpts from J. R. Hackman and E. E. Lawler III, 'Employee reactions to job characteristics', *Journal of Applied Psychology*, vol. 55, 1971, pp. 265–86.

Strategy of the present research

The conceptualization presented [in Reading 12] provides the basis for the present empirical research on the relationships among job characteristics; individual differences in need strength; and employee motivation, satisfaction, performance and absenteeism on the job. In particular, the research to be reported here follows the strategy steps listed below:

1. Measures of the following six job dimensions were developed: (a) variety, the degree to which a job requires employees to perform a wide range of operations in their work and/or the degree to which employees must use a variety of equipment and procedures in their work; (b) autonomy, the extent to which employees have a major say in scheduling their work, selecting the equipment they will use, and deciding on procedures to be followed; (c) task identity, the extent to which employees do an entire or whole piece of work and can clearly identify the result of their efforts; (d) feedback, the degree to which employees receive information as they are working which reveals how well they are performing on the job; (e) dealing with others, the degree to which a job requires employees to deal with other people (either customers, other company employees, or both) to complete the work; (f) friendship opportunities, the degree to which a job allows employees to talk with one another on the job and to establish informal relationships with other employees at work.

The latter two dimensions were included to permit exploration of the impact of the interpersonal characteristics of job design. These dimensions were adapted with very minor revision from the task attributes 'required interaction' and 'optional interaction' proposed by Turner and Lawrence (1965). They are not, however, directly relevant to the conceptualization about job-based work motivation proposed above, and no specific predictions regarding them were made. Thirteen different jobs were described on these six dimensions by the researchers, by employees who worked on the jobs, and by members of the management of the telephone company in which the research was carried out.

2. A measure was developed which was expected, on an *a priori* basis, to reflect the level of employee desire for the satisfaction of higher order needs.

3. Based on the mean scores of the employees on the measure of need strength, predictions were made regarding the expected relationships between the job characteristics as measured by the four core dimensions and the dependent variables: satisfaction, performance and absenteeism. Relevant data were collected from 208 employees, and correlations between each of the four core dimensions and each of the dependent measures were computed.

4. The theory outlined above indicates that how a job is experienced or perceived by an individual employee should determine his reactions to it, rather than the objective characteristics of the job. This possibility can be examined by analyzing the relationship between the characteristics of a single job (as they are perceived by employees) and the behavioral and attitudinal reactions of individuals who hold that job. By restricting the scope of the analysis to individuals working on the same job, it is possible to rule out objective differences in jobs as an explanation for obtained empirical relationships – and, thereby, to address the possibility that the perceived characteristics of jobs affect employees in the same general fashion as do objectively measured characteristics. Therefore, relationships between perceived job characteristics and the dependent variables of interest were computed separately for employees who worked on each of the thirteen objectively different jobs included in the study, and these relationships were compared to those obtained in the overall analyses involving all subjects of the study (S) and all thirteen jobs.

5. The theory implies that satisfaction, performance, and attendance should be highest when all four of the core dimensions are present. [. . .]

The importance of having all four core dimensions present was tested by comparing the dependent variable scores of employees who saw their jobs as moderately high on all four core dimensions both with the scores of employees who saw their jobs as high on some dimensions and low on others, and with the scores of employees who saw their jobs as moderately low on all four dimensions.

6. The theory states that individual differences in desire for higher order need satisfactions should moderate the relationships between job characteristics and the dependent variables. In order to test this possibility, relationships were computed separately and compared for the third of the employees highest on desire for higher order need satisfaction and for those employees lowest on desire for higher order need satisfaction.

7. Finally, exploratory analyses were made of the relationships between the two interpersonal job dimensions (dealing with others, and friendship opportunities) and the dependent variables.

Method

Research setting and subjects

The research was carried out in an eastern telephone company, and focused on employees who worked on thirteen different jobs in the plant and traffic departments of the company. The jobs were selected so as (a) to include several varieties of operators, installers, central office repairmen, and cable splicers; (b) to range widely in complexity and in the level of employee skill required; and (c) to be located in both rural and urban settings.

Data were collected from 208 employees and sixty-two supervisors. Employees in the traffic department (about one-third of the sample) were female; all plant department employees were male.

Procedure

All data were collected on site at each of the thirteen job locations. [. . .]

At each location, the following five procedural steps were followed (although the order of the steps sometimes varied because of local circumstances).

1. Local second- or third-level management was visited to obtain permission to collect data from employees working on a particular job. When permission was secured (it was never denied), the managers were interviewed about the general nature of the job as they perceived it.

2. First-level supervisors on the local job were interviewed about the nature of the job and employees' reactions to it and were given a questionnaire which tapped the supervisors' perceptions of the employee job in a format similar to that used for obtaining the employees' own job perceptions.

3. Employees working on the job were observed and interviewed informally. These observations and interviews were conducted by two researchers and continued until the researchers felt that they were no longer obtaining substantial new information about the job. Observation typically lasted approximately one working day. Ratings of the job characteristics by the researchers were made on the basis of these observations and interviews.

4. A questionnaire was administered to a sample of fifteen to twenty employees on the job. The questionnaire took between half-an-hour and one hour to complete and usually was administered to employees in groups of three or four. The general nature of the research was explained to each group of employees before they began work on the questionnaire, although the hypotheses of the study and the dependent variables to be analyzed were not mentioned. It was emphasized to each individual that participation was voluntary, and a few individuals did decline to participate. In addition, employees were told that putting their names on the questionnaires, while desirable for research purposes, also was voluntary. About 10 per cent of the employees who participated declined to give their names.

5. Ratings of the performance of those employees who had taken the questionnaire and provided their names were made by first-line supervisors. Absence data were collected later from company records. [. . .]

Instruments and measures

The various measures used in the research are summarized below. [. . .] The measures include: (a) Job descriptions: variety, autonomy, task identity, feedback, dealing with others, and friendship opportunities. Descriptions were made by employees, by supervisors, by the researchers using the Turner–Lawrence procedures, and by the researchers subjectively after job observations and interviews. Because there was generally high convergent validity among the four sets of job descriptions, and because the conceptual basis of the study suggests that jobs as experienced by employees should be most directly causal of employee reactions to their jobs, the employee job descriptions are used in the analyses to be reported in subsequent sections. (b) Level of higher order need strength of employees: a summary score of employee reactions to twelve need strength items. (c) Employee reactions to their jobs and work. Questionnaire-derived measures of: the amount of intrinsic motivation experienced by employees, and the focus of their motivation; general job satisfaction; personal job involvement; and twelve specific satisfactions or dissatisfactions with the job or the work situation. (d) Rated performance effectiveness of employees, in terms of quantity of work produced, work quality, and overall performance effectiveness. (e) Absenteeism, measured by the number of occasions an employee was absent during a twelve-month period.

Results
General relationships between job characteristics and employee reactions

According to the conceptual position outlined earlier, the nature of the relationships between job characteristics and employee reactions to their work (including satisfaction, performance and absenteeism) will depend upon the need states of the employees. In particular, it was predicted that, if employees are desirous of higher order need satisfactions, there should be a positive relationship between the four core dimensions (variety, autonomy, task identity and feedback) and motivation, satisfaction, performance and attendance.

The mean score of the 208 telephone company employees on the twelve-item scale indicative of higher order need strength was 6·01. Given that the maximum possible score on the scale is 7·0, it would appear that the employees who participated in the present research had strong higher order needs, or at least that they felt it was

Table 1 General relationships between job characteristics and employee reactions

	Core dimension				Interpersonal dimension	
Dependent variable	Variety	Autonomy	Task identity	Feedback	Dealing with others	Friendship opportunities
Level of intrinsic motivation	0·32*	0·30*	0·16*	0·18*	0·07	0·09
Focus of motivation						
Taking personal responsibility	0·14*	0·12*	0·19*	0·06	0·08	0·05
Doing large quantities of work	−0·10	−0·12	0·01	0·02	0·06	−0·17
Doing high quality work	0·16*	0·12*	0·13*	0·10	0·04	0·12*
Rated performance						
Quantity	−0·03	0·13*	0·05	0·00	−0·02	−0·18
Quality	0·17*	0·16*	0·07	0·02	−0·11	0·02
Overall effectiveness	0·20*	0·26*	0·11*	−0·03	−0·07	−0·09
General job satisfaction	0·38*	0·39*	0·20*	0·28*	0·17*	0·21*
Job involvement	0·24*	0·22*	0·12*	0·24*	0·03	0·16*
Absenteeism (number of times absent)	0·02	−0·14*	−0·22*	−0·10	0·01	−0·05

Specific satisfaction items						
Self-esteem obtained from job	0·32*	0·32*	0·15*	0·35*	0·15*	0·27*
Personal growth and development	0·36*	0·34*	0·14*	0·31*	0·11*	0·29*
Prestige of job inside company	0·30*	0·25*	0·15*	0·35*	0·14*	0·28*
Amount of close supervision received	0·31*	0·35*	0·13*	0·30*	0·07	0·16*
Independent thought and action	0·53*	0·62*	0·25*	0·15*	0·00	0·25*
Security	0·22*	0·27*	0·19*	0·39*	0·15*	0·28*
Pay	0·04	0·05	0·04	0·34*	0·25*	0·24*
Feeling of worthwhile accomplishment	0·29*	0·32*	0·28*	0·42*	0·23*	0·31*
Participation in job-related decisions	0·28*	0·27*	0·20*	0·34*	0·12*	0·25*
Development of close friendships	0·25*	0·12*	0·09	0·29*	0·09	0·47*
Promotion	0·17*	0·20*	0·15*	0·34*	0·21*	0·19*
Respect and fair treatment from boss	0·19*	0·26*	0·22*	0·35*	0·14*	0·24*

Note $N = 208$

* $p < 0.05$ (one-tailed test)

appropriate to express high desires for these need satisfactions. Therefore, generally positive relationships would be expected between job descriptions on the four core dimensions and the dependent variables.

Correlations between the six job description measures obtained from employees and the scores of employees on the dependent variable measures are presented in Table 1. Results are discussed below separately for the four core dimensions and the two interpersonal dimensions.

Core dimensions: toward internal motivation

In general, positive relationships were obtained between the four core dimensions and dependent measures indicative of motivation, satisfaction, performance, and attendance.

Performance motivation and actual performance. The higher jobs are on the core dimensions, the more employees tend to report feeling internal pressures to take personal responsibility for their work and to do high quality work. And, in fact, when jobs are described as being higher on variety, autonomy, and task identity, employees are rated as doing higher quality work and as being generally more effective performers on the job. [. . .]

The data suggest, moreover, that 'doing well' is interpreted in the job context as having much more to do with high quality performance than producing large quantities of work. The core dimensions do not relate either to felt pressure for high quantity production, or to the actual quantity of work which is produced. [. . .]

General satisfaction, job involvement, and absenteeism. The core dimensions are, as expected, strongly and positively related to overall job satisfaction and to the degree that employees feel personally involved in their work. It is not, therefore, surprising to find that employees whose jobs are seen as high on the core dimensions tend to have better absence records as well. Work apparently is a satisfying place to be for employees with jobs high on the four core dimensions, and one way they behaviorally demonstrate this is by coming to work regularly.

Specific satisfactions. Nearly all of the specific satisfaction items were significantly positively correlated with the descriptions of jobs

n the core dimensions. This is to be expected from the fact that the
ore dimensions relate substantially to overall job satisfaction.
. . .]

The four specific satisfaction items most strongly related to the
core dimensions are, in descending order: (a) The opportunity for
independent thought and action in my job. (b) The feeling of
worthwhile accomplishment in my job. (c) The opportunity for
personal growth and development in my job. (d) The self-esteem
and self-respect a person gets from being in my job. [. . .]

It appears, as expected, that the four core dimensions seem to be
most strongly related to the satisfaction of higher order needs.
. . .]

Two interpersonal dimensions

[. . .] The two interpersonal dimensions do not relate very consistently or strongly either to employee affective responses to the
job, or to their actual work performance. There is no significant
relationship between the dimension 'dealing with others' and any
measure of motivation, performance or absenteeism.

Relationships involving the dimension 'friendship opportunities' also are generally negligible. The dimension does not relate to
the level of intrinsic motivation employees report, or to any
measure of performance or absenteeism. [. . .]

Within-job relationships between job dimensions and
employee reactions

It was proposed earlier that job design factors affect employee
attitudes and behavior because of their impact on the perceptions
employees have of their jobs. This may be represented schematic-
ally as follows:

Objective job   1   Perceived job   2   Work attitudes
characteristics   →   characteristics   →   and behavior

Employee perceptions of their jobs have substantial convergence
with the assessments of objective job characteristics made by the
researchers and by company supervisors. If it is assumed that
the assessments by the researchers and supervisors do reflect the
'objective' character of the jobs, these data strongly suggest that
employee job perceptions are based (at least in major part) on

objective job characteristics – the first link in the chain. Results reported in Table 1 and discussed immediately above show that employee job perceptions also are related to work attitudes and behavior – the second link in the chain. However, these latter analyses are based on job descriptions provided by employees who worked on thirteen different jobs – jobs which have been shown to vary substantially on the six job dimensions. [. . .]

By examining the relationships between employee perceptions of their jobs and the dependent variables separately for workers on each of the thirteen jobs, it is possible to determine if perceptual factors, largely uncontaminated by objective between-job differences, bear a significant relationship to the dependent variables. [. . .]

Thirteen matrices of relationships were obtained by correlating job descriptions and dependent variables separately for employees working on each of the thirteen jobs. The median of the thirteen correlations between each job dimension and each dependent variable was selected. [. . .]

As expected, the median within-job correlations generally are consistent with the correlations computed across all employees and jobs. The order of magnitude of the median within-job correlations, also as expected, is lower than that of the correlations based on data from all employees. These results suggest, therefore, that employees' perceptions of their jobs are of central importance in affecting job attitudes and behaviors, but that the major determinant of such perceptions is the objective make-up of the job itself.

Exploration of condition for enhancing motivation and satisfaction

Results presented in the preceding discussion indicate that when jobs are high on the core dimensions, employees who have strong desires for higher order need satisfaction will be highly motivated and well satisfied on the job. In the following discussion, two analyses will be reported which extend these findings and provide additional documentation of the conditions which seem necessary to enhance employee motivation and satisfaction through job design.

Must jobs be high on all four core dimensions?

The theory on which the present research is based specifies that when jobs are high on the core dimensions, employees have the opportunity to find out (feedback) that they personally (autonomy) have accomplished something meaningful (task identity and variety) when they perform well. The implication of this assertion is that, for maximum motivation, jobs should be high simultaneously on all four of the core dimensions.

To test this possibility, S's were partitioned into three groups: (a) those who described their jobs as being above the sixtieth percentile on all four core dimensions; (b) those who described their jobs as being below the fortieth percentile on all four core dimensions; and (c) the majority of S's, who typically described their jobs as being high on some of the core dimensions and low on others. A one-way, missing-data, unequal N analysis of variance was used to compare the mean scores of employees in the three groups on each of the dependent variables. Means and F ratios are presented in Table 2.

Results are consistent with those reported in Table 1 and, in addition, tend to be more substantial in magnitude and more statistically reliable. It was expected that when jobs were described as high on all four core dimensions: (a) experienced pressures to take personal responsibility for one's work and to do high quality work would be high, (b) intrinsic motivation would be high, (c) rated performance quality and overall performance effectiveness would be high, (d) job satisfaction and involvement would be high, and (e) absenteeism would be low. All of these expectations were borne out substantially and statistically significantly, except for the one involving absenteeism. While absenteeism was lowest when jobs were seen as high on all four core dimensions, differences among the three groups were not statistically significant. [. . .]

Does high order need strength moderate obtained relationships?

It has been maintained throughout this article that jobs which are high on the core dimensions should be motivating only to individuals who are desirous of the intrinsic rewards that the jobs provide, namely, higher order need satisfactions.

The analysis reported in this section tests the possibility that S's differing in higher order need strength do in fact show differential

Table 2 Comparison of jobs described as high on all core dimensions, high on some core dimensions, and low on all core dimensions

		Dependent variable $\bar{X}$		
Dependent variable	F ratio	Jobs low on all core dimensions[a]	Jobs high on some core dimensions[b]	Jobs high on all core dimensions[c]
Level of intrinsic motivation	13·72**	5·28	5·99	6·46
Focus of motivation				
Taking personal responsibility	6·08**	5·90	6·40	6·88
Doing large quantities of work	0·24	5·48	5·17	5·29
Doing high quality work	3·04*	6·00	6·20	6·71
Rated performance				
Quantity	0·15	5·19	5·23	5·39
Quality	3·36*	4·97	5·57	5·89
Overall effectiveness	3·40*	5·14	5·54	5·94
General job satisfaction	28·97**	3·78	4·99	6·21
Job involvement	18·40**	2·30	2·94	4·43
Absenteeism (no. of times absent)	1·62	3·11	2·70	2·00

Specific satisfaction items

Self-esteem obtained from job	27·06**	3·33	6·00
Personal growth and development	24·45**	3·43	6·00
Prestige of job inside company	21·65**	3·24	5·59
Amount of close supervision received	15·97**	3·57	5·65
Independent thought and action	31·66**	3·24	6·35
Security	9·75**	4·52	6·24
Pay	2·95	3·38	4·47
Feeling of worthwhile accomplishment	35·59**	3·05	6·41
Participation in job-related decisions	21·09**	2·81	5·29
Development of close friendships	9·56**	4·14	5·65
Promotion	13·98**	3·24	5·47
Respect and fair treatment from boss	14·64**	4·14	6·24

[a] $N = 21$

[b] $N = 170$

[c] $N = 17$

* $p < 0.05$ (one-tailed test)

** $p < 0.01$ (one-tailed test)

responsiveness to jobs high on the core dimensions, despite the generally high mean of all S's on the need strength measure. Correlations between each of the core dimensions and the dependent variables were computed separately for those employees whose higher order need strength scores were in the top one-third of the distribution of scores for all S's, and for those employees whose scores were in the bottom one-third of the same distribution. The mean higher order need strength score for the employees in the top third was 6·78, and the mean score for employees in the bottom third was 5·09. Since 5·09 is still one full point above the midpoint of the scale, it was expected that even for these 'low' need strength employees, relationships between the core dimensions and the dependent variables would be in the positive direction, but lower in magnitude than the relationships for S's in the top third of the distribution. [. . .]

For variety, autonomy and, to a lesser extent, feedback, the expectation of a differential relationship was confirmed. Relationships between these job dimensions and the dependent variables are larger, and often strikingly so, for the S's with high higher order need strength than for S's with moderate higher order need strength. Further, the correlations for higher need strength employees are typically larger than those reported in the general analysis involving all S's, and the correlations based on the lower need strength S's are typically lower than the general relationships. [. . .]

. . . it would be expected from the theory that differences between high and low need strength employees should be maximized when jobs are moderately high on all four core dimensions. [. . .]

To examine the validity of this argument, therefore, the product score (Variety × Autonomy × Task Identity × Feedback) described earlier was correlated with the dependent variables separately for the third of S's highest in higher order need strength and for the third of S's lowest in higher order need strength. Since the product score reflects the degree to which a job is seen as being simultaneously high on all four core dimensions, substantial differences would be expected in the magnitude of correlations obtained for high versus low need strength employees. Results are presented in Table 3.

Again, obtained relationships were much higher for S's who

Table 3 Moderating effect of higher order need strength for jobs high on all four core dimensions

Dependent variable	High need strength	Low need strength
Level of intrinsic motivation	0·54*	0·23*
Focus of motivation		
Taking personal responsibility	0·37*	0·12
Doing large quantities of work	−0·09	−0·01
Doing high quality work	0·21*	0·12
Rated performance		
Quantity	0·07	−0·04
Quality	0·23*	0·02
Overall effectiveness	0·15	0·05
General job satisfaction	0·48*	0·40*
Job involvement	0·45*	0·28*
Absenteeism (number of times absent)	−0·26*	−0·08
Specific satisfaction items		
Self-esteem obtained from job	0·54*	0·13[a]
Personal growth and development	0·57*	0·16[a]
Prestige of job inside company	0·50*	0·26*
Amount of close supervision received	0·48*	0·27*
Independent thought and action	0·70*	0·45*[a]
Security	0·49*	0·25*[a]
Pay	0·27*	0·09
Feeling of worthwhile accomplishment	0·59*	0·32*[a]
Participation in job-related decisions	0·44*	0·37*
Development of close friendships	0·54*	−0·19[a]
Promotion	0·45*	0·08[a]
Respect and fair treatment from boss	0·48*	0·20*[a]

Note: $N = 67$ in each group.

[a] The difference between the correlations for high need strength S's and for low need strength S's is significant at $p < 0·05$.

*$p < 0·05$ (one-tailed test).

were high in relevant need strength than for S's low in need strength for nearly all of the measures of motivation, satisfaction and performance. The difference between the correlations for high and low need strength S's was tested for statistical significance, and these results are included in the table. Even though most of the correlations were positive (because of the relatively high mean need strength for even the 'low' need strength employees), a number of pairs of correlations were significantly different from one another. All in all, the data make a strong case for the moderating effect of individual higher order need strength in determining the effects of job characteristics on employee behavior and attitudes at work.

Discussion and implications
Job design and individual differences

The results of this study suggest that there are important interdependencies among the characteristics of individuals and the characteristics of jobs which must be taken account of in the development of any full understanding of the impact of various kinds of job designs. Both the advocates of a 'scientific management' approach to job design (make the work routine, simple and standardized) and the more recent supporters of 'job enlargement' (make the work complex, challenging, and demanding of individual responsibility and decision making) appear to have attached insufficient importance to individual–job interactions in determining affective and behavioral reactions to jobs. Those of the scientific management persuasion, for example, have tended to assume that the typical employee will be content, if paid judiciously for his cooperation, to work on jobs which provide little or no opportunity for personal feelings of accomplishment or achievement. Those of the job enlargement school, on the other hand, have tended to assume that most employees are desirous of such opportunities and will work hard and effectively when they have a job which provides them. The present research suggests that, depending on the characteristics of the workers involved, both points of view would lead to job design practices which are appropriate some of the time and inappropriate other times. [. . .]

Use of perceived characteristics

One of the major conceptual and methodological problems which pervades studies of task and job effects on behavior has to do with the differences between task materials as they exist in objective reality and as they are perceived by individual performers. Tasks and jobs are invariably redefined by the individuals who perform them, sometimes deliberately and sometimes without full awareness by the performers of the changes or re-emphases that are being made. Further, it is the redefined task rather than the objective task which the individual tries to perform, and thus only those aspects of tasks or jobs which are actually perceived or experienced by a performer can have an impact on his performance and attitudes. This would seem to argue for the use of task and job characteristics as described by the performers themselves in research aimed at ascertaining the effects of these characteristics on performance. Yet when such subjective assessments are used, many of the important conceptual and methodological advantages associated with the use of independently and objectively described independent variables are lost.

There are at least two strategies for dealing with this problem in research on task and job effects on behavior. One, which was used in the present research, is to employ subjective assessments of the tasks or jobs by the performers themselves, but simultaneously to develop means of determining the relationship between these assessments and others, including objective measures when possible. [. . .]

A second strategy for dealing with the re-definition problem has been proposed by Hackman (1970). [. . .] In essence, this strategy suggests that the redefinition process should be viewed as the first stage of the performance process itself, and the redefined task should be conceived of as a potentially measurable intervening variable in the causal chain between the objective task input and the dependent variables of interest (e.g. performance, satisfaction). Just as individual differences in need strength have been shown in this research to moderate the effects of job characteristics on employee behavior and attitudes, so would individual needs, values and goals be expected to interact with the objective task or job in influencing task redefinition. [. . .]

Nature of the four core dimensions

The results of the present research show that, in general, employees with moderately high desires for higher order need satisfaction tend to work harder and be more satisfied when they perceive their jobs as being relatively high on the four core dimensions. In addition, it was shown that for the most favorable outcomes, jobs need to be at least moderately high on all four of the dimensions. [. . .]

Interpersonal components of jobs

The two job dimensions reflective of the interpersonal components of jobs (dealing with others, and friendship opportunities) did not relate to employee work motivation or performance. The dimensions did relate positively to certain kinds of satisfaction, but the relationships were not as substantial as those involving the four core dimensions.

According to the conceptualization on which the present study is based, the degree to which jobs require interpersonal activities should relate to work motivation only when (a) workers have high desires for the satisfaction of social needs, and (b) working hard on the job can lead to the satisfaction of these needs. Even those jobs which scored relatively high on the two interpersonal dimensions (e.g. some operators' jobs) fail to meet the latter criterion. Operators reported in fact that they could obtain social satisfactions best when they were not 'working hard' by company standards (i.e. completing a large number of calls), since when the load of calls was heavy they had little or no time for meaningful interpersonal activities with either customers or fellow employees. [. . .]

Implications for organizational practice

Standard organizational selection and placement procedures attempt to match the skills and abilities of a prospective employee with the skill requirements of the job for which he is being considered. The results of the present research suggest that it may be equally critical for long-term organizational effectiveness to achieve a match between the psychological makeup of the prospective employee and the psychological demands and opportunities of the job. In particular, the present results suggest that individuals who desire higher order need satisfaction will be likely to contribute most effectively to organizational goals (and simultaneously to satisfy their own needs) if they are placed on jobs which are high on the four core dimensions. Other employees of course, who may be neither desirous of higher order need satisfactions nor capable of dealing with complex jobs requiring considerable autonomy, would be ineffective on such jobs and dissatisfied with them.

It appears from research cited earlier in this article that many organizations err rather consistently by designing jobs which are too low on the core dimensions. The present study supports this conclusion. It suggests that there are many workers who want to obtain more higher order need satisfactions from their work, but few who are overwhelmed by the psychological demands of their jobs. The implication of this argument, of course, is that organizations might be well advised to consider redesigning many of their jobs.

When job enlargement is carried out, the question often arises whether the changes should be toward horizontal enlargement (i.e. increasing the number of different things an employee does) or toward vertical enlargement (i.e. increasing the degree to which an employee is responsible for making most major decisions about his work) or both. Lawler (1969) has reviewed the literature regarding the effects of vertical and horizontal job enlargement and concludes that simultaneous enlargement in both directions may be optimal in most cases. The results of the present study provide some support for this contention. Only if a job is enlarged vertically is an employee likely to feel personally responsible for his work outcomes; and only if a job has some amount of horizontal enlargement is he likely to experience his work as meaningful – although it should be kept in mind that too much horizontal enlargement apparently can cause problems. Simultaneous vertical and horizontal enlargement should increase the likelihood that a redesigned job will be high on all four of the core dimensions.

It should be re-emphasized in conclusion, however, that while jobs appear to be highly potent in determining employee motivation and satisfaction, there is no single best way to design a job. Instead, the results of the present research suggest that the substantial motivational potential of jobs can be realized only when the psychological demands and opportunities of jobs mesh well with the personal needs and goals of employees who work on them. This kind of matching can be developed through selection and placement of employees, through job redesign, or (perhaps optimally) by attempting to fit people to jobs and jobs to people simultaneously and continuously as both the organization and the characteristics of its employees change over time.

References

HACKMAN, J. R. (1970), 'Tasks and task performance in research on stress', in J. E. McGrath (ed.), *Social and Psychological Factors in Stress*, Holt, Rinehart & Winston.

LAWLER, E. E., III (1969), 'Job design and employee motivation', *Personnel Psychology*, vol. 22, pp. 426–35.

TURNER, A. N., and LAWRENCE, P. R. (1965), *Industrial Jobs and the Worker*, Harvard University Graduate School of Business Administration.

Part Six
Work-System Studies

The five Readings included in this section present empirical
evidence for the facilitative effects of autonomous work group
behaviors in the design of work roles. This concept of role
rather than job emphasizes the importance of job environment
characteristics that are directly related to the production process.

The first paper (Reading 22) reviews some of the more
important studies in work systems, and provides a transition
between the Job Content studies prevalent in the United States
during the 1960s and the Role (or work) Content studies
undertaken primarily in Great Britain during the same period.
In this selection, Davis emphasizes that enrichment in both
Job Content and Role Content are compatible in designing
work that is more motivating and more productive.

Some of the British studies, by now classics, of the
1950s–1960s have not been included, since they are so widely
available, and their more important findings have been
summarized by Davis (Reading 22). The Readings included,
strongly influenced by the earlier British developments, are
very recent empirical studies dealing with emerging issues in the
development of job designs, i.e. process (advanced) technology
jobs, the impact of technology on organization change and
work groups, and the characteristics of autonomous groups.

Engelstad (Reading 23) makes explicit socio-technical systems
analysis – in particular, the potent analytic tool for the design
of work systems involving regulation and control of complex
variables.

Susman (Reading 24) and Gulowson (Reading 25) contribute
to our understanding of autonomous work groups – one in

automated or process technology and the other in older, conventional technological settings.

Taylor (Reading 26) presents quantitative evidence for the greater incidence of autonomous work groups in high technology settings. Previous references to this phenomenon have been either theoretical propositions, or more subjective case studies. Reading 26 also presents evidence that planned change in the direction of further autonomous group structure is markedly facilitated by a modern high technology setting. These findings suggest that expanding role content will recur more often in the post-industrial than in the industrial era.

22 Louis E. Davis

The Design of Jobs

L. E. Davis, 'The design of jobs', *Industrial Relations*, vol. 6, 1966, pp. 21–45.

Job design means specification of the contents, methods and relationships of jobs in order to satisfy technological and organizational requirements as well as the social and personal requirements of the job-holder.

For the purposes of discussion only, specification of job contents can be divided into two categories: (a) physical-environment and physiological requirements, and (b) organization, social and personal requirements. An extensive body of knowledge exists on the first category and is assiduously applied in designing plant environment, work methods, equipment and tools, and in fitting the physical work demand to the capabilities of workers. No conflict exists over the application of this physiological and ergonomic knowledge for it does not require any models of human behavior in complex organizations. Man's responses to the physical environments and work tasks are studied at the microscopic level with man taken as a machine element, albeit a human one, in the system. The objectives are either adjustment of man, as by training, or adjustment of environment or technology, as by design of tools, equipment, and dials and machine controls for rapid and error-free operation or to suit particular human capabilities, such as those of older workers.

On the side of organizational, social and personal requirements, what is the state of job design today? There is a large discrepancy between available knowledge and practice, although – paradoxically, perhaps – there is much evidence that management faithfully keeps abreast of developments in job and organization design research. The thinking of many a management today appears to be not unlike that of an old farmer who went to a lecture delivered by a county agent to a group of small farmers in a remote rural area about a new development in farming that would increase crop yield. When asked by the county agent whether he would use the new development, the old-timer said, 'I won't – I already know how to farm better than I am doing.'

Managements are well aware that there now exists a considerable body of evidence which challenges accepted organizational and job design practices. Experimental and empirical findings, for instance, indicate that imposed pacing of work is detrimental to output and to quality, yet paced work is common and is considered to be desirable (Conrad, 1955, and Davis, 1966). There is extensive evidence concerning the positive effects of group reward systems in achieving an organization's primary objectives. There is also considerable evidence of the effects of variety of job content and of task assignments that permit social relationships and communication patterns to develop, all of which enhance performance and personal satisfaction on the job (Davis and Werling, 1960; Davis, 1957; Davis, Canter and Hoffman, 1955; Richardson and Walker, 1948). Yet in a very few instances do we find application of such findings to job designs.

The incentive to apply job design knowledge must be presumed to be strong, for the very simple reason that there are gains to be made all round – for the organization in productivity, quality, and costs of performance, and for workers in personal satisfactions. On the other hand, inhibitions against application are formidable. The status quo bristles with institutional barriers in the form of established personnel policies, job evaluation plans, union relationships and contracts, supervisory practices at all levels, and, not least, managerial practices. All of these barriers are perpetually present, prompting the manager to choose the path of least resistance and to do as little as the situation compels, that is, to satisfy the obvious needs of technology. At a deeper level, the status quo is reinforced by more basic and pervasive inhibitions which again and again lead the manager to fall back on time-honored, but inappropriate and unrealistic models which are based on unsupported dogma or on popular clichés regarding human behavior in productive organizations.

The practical consequences are inconsistent and incompatible job designs, as well as *ad hoc* use of piecemeal research results. With minor modifications, there is still a strong commitment to the proposition that meeting the requirements of the technology (process, equipment) will yield superior job performance, measured by organizationally relevant criteria, and a deep-seated conviction that the same performance will *not* be achieved if technological requirements are not given exclusive consideration. Requirements such as communication, group formation, personality development, decision-making, and control are seen as marginal at best, and at worst as opposed to the satisfaction of technological requirements. This fictitious conflict reveals the poverty of present conceptualization of human behavior in productive organizations and helps to maintain the dominance of technological requirements as exclusive determinants of job contents and relationships.

Models of human behavior

Models and concepts of individual–organization relationships and of human behavior in productive organizations have a history almost as long as that of Western civilization. However, only two have been historically influential in their contribution to purposeful job design. Both were handed down to us by late eighteenth century economists – the ubiquitous model of man as an economic animal and the concept of the division of labor. The former has provided the rationale for our present reward systems, as well as for our concentration on monetary rewards as the only ones suitable for consideration. The division-of-labor concept provided the basis for specialization and, as a result, for our existing job and organization structures. Based on these approaches, organizations were able to make immediate use of an untutored and unskilled work force. To the extent that lack of education and skill are still the main characteristics of a work force, the concept has utility, even if there are secondary costs in the form of reduced contribution on the part of individuals and the need for a coordination apparatus.

During the late nineteenth century, a series of models were developed; all of them derived from the mechanistic model of human behavior in which man's role was conceived to be that of an element or cog in a complex production system dominated by costly equipment. In mechanical systems, elements must be completely designed if they are to function. When transposed to human effort, this requirement states that initiative and self-organization are not acceptable, for they may increase system variability and the risk of failure. (Incidentally, the question raised today of whether workers are responsible or irresponsible appears not to have entered into consideration.) The result was rigidly specified task assignments and complete job descriptions indicating the specific behaviors desired and their organizational and temporal bounds. The drive to achieve reduced sources of variability encouraged the development of the concept of minimum skill requirements for task performance. Given highly specialized or fractionated jobs consisting of few minimally skilled tasks, skills could be rapidly acquired with short training. That man might engage in behavior other than that specifically required by the system was never part of the conceptual framework of the mechanistic model. To ensure successful outcomes, reward systems were designed that provided reinforcement only for the precisely specified behaviors desired. To be sure, many of these principles were applied without conscious design and in the euphoric atmosphere of applying science to complex organizations.

The more recent models of individual–organization relationships which have undergirded the evolution of job design can be classified into four groups. The oldest of these is the minimum interaction model, under which there is a minimal connection between the individual and the organization in terms of skill, training, involvement, and complexity of his contribution, in return for maximum flexibility and independence on the part of the organization in using its manpower. In other words, the organization strives for maximum interchangeability of personnel (with minimum training) to reduce its dependence on availability, ability, or motivation of individuals. This model has been the basis for the development of twentieth century industrial relations practices and for modern personnel management. In application, it frequently takes the form of the work-flow or process-flow model of job design. In this model the material or information processes are in themselves the job content, or determine it.

Evolving from and tied to the minimum interaction model is the welfare model, which gives nodding recognition to the inadequacy of the 'economic man' theory. Without disturbing job and organization structures, it attempts to build extra-role and extra-job associations and, hopefully, loyalties to the organization. It places great faith in the prospect that meaningful social relationships can be built with fellow workers and supervisors outside the immediate production framework, which continues to operate on the basis of the restricted role of the individual and of minimum organizational interaction. In applying the model, organizations bubble with programs that provide fun and games for workers after hours, company newspapers that jolly workers along to make them feel part of the organization, extra-job rewards, profit shares, etc.

The third group of models grew out of the shock of the Hawthorne studies and is characterized by emphasis on leadership and personal relations. Growth of awareness that there are informal leaders and groups, and that groups have social standards and norms, led to the development of the human relations movement. If informal leaders and groups exist, no matter what the formal organization description indicates, then management had better get busy, either to capture these or provide leadership patterns and personal relations that go some way toward reconciling the informal and formal structures. Having been built on these objectives, the human relations movement is now seriously hampered by restricting itself to them. Its narrow approach, which completely overlooks job content and the interaction between social, organizational and technological requirements, was bound to produce the limited success it has achieved thus far.

The last and most recent group of models grew directly out of the impact of social and behavioral science research. Results of various studies provide information on self-selected aspects of the whole man at work in an organization. In most instances, the studies are piecemeal approaches which nibble at the edges of the central problems of job design, the role of the individual in a productive organization, and his control over the functions performed. Most of these approaches unfortunately assume that job content is not a significant variable or is so fixed by the needs of technology that it is not worth examining, since it cannot be altered in any event. Only ignorance of technology can lead to such a conclusion. Within this group are such approaches as sensitivity development; group–member participation, and status and personality development; communication; and even job enlargement, whatever that may be. The unfortunate consequence is a series of competing fads, one continually replacing the other as offering the true answer.

Recent job design studies

Job design research is relatively new, having originated only in the last decade. More recently, a few industrial firms have begun to manipulate some job contents and configurations. The first such experiment that was reported took place in the late forties in a large US electronics firm which undertook a series of job changes in the form of job enlargement (Richardson and Walker, 1948). The changes were instituted as a part of management industrial relations policy.

What characterizes the difference between job design research and personnel, industrial psychological, and sociological studies? Job design studies take technology as an operant variable and, as a consequence, are concerned with the interaction between personal, social, and organization needs and technology as manifested in jobs. The other studies take technology as given and therefore do not consider it as a variable to be examined. Job design studies can be classified into two groups, both based on field experiments: those carried out in the United States under the name of job design and those carried out in England, where they are known as socio-technical systems studies. The former studies have sought to manipulate the configuration of technology, as interpreted in task designs and assignments making up jobs, and to determine what variations are possible and what the effects of these are on personal, social and organization variables. The latter studies have approached jobs and organization configurations from the direction of social psychology, modifying technological configurations of tasks to permit the development of social structure in support of functions and objectives of work groups. Both types of studies are concerned with jobs and organizations as socio-technical systems.

In presenting a brief review of results available, numerous informal reports known to the author, based on experiences of firms with various job configurations, will not be used. Published reports only will be examined. This may make the number of formal and informal job design studies appear to be smaller than it is in fact. Reports have appeared about operator jobs consisting of repetitive manual tasks and maintenance jobs organized around traditional crafts. Four studies of operator jobs taken from different technologies are presented: two studies of assembly-line jobs from the pharmaceutical and home appliance industries, a study of machine-tender jobs in the textile industry, and a study of pit-face jobs in coal mining. One study of maintenance craft jobs in the chemical industry will be discussed. The first experimental field study of supervisory job design was recently reported, and the results are presented here to permit comparison with worker-level jobs. The studies presented are intended to indicate the multi-dimensionality of the job design problem and the pervasiveness of its influence on quantity and quality of output, costs, and job satisfactions.

Operator, assembly line: pharmaceutical
appliance manufacture[1]

This study was the first controlled experiment on the shop floor to manipulate the configuration of technology as interpreted in task design and assignment as jobs. It followed a national survey of the methods used and decisions reached in designing jobs by specifying their contents and structure (Davis, Canter and Hoffman, 1955). The study revealed that neither clearly developed theories of job specification nor design principles were available and that job design decisions were based on the very narrow criterion of minimizing immediate costs of an operation as interpreted through minimum unit operation time. It was also found that the job design process took place after the basic production process had been planned and separate operations in the production sequence were being developed. No methods for evaluating the effectiveness of job designs were found to exist.

Designers of jobs satisfied the criterion of minimum cost (or immediate cost) of operations by application of the following precepts or guides:

1. Specification of the content of individual tasks comprising a job to
(a) achieve specialization of skills;
(b) minimize skill requirements;
(c) minimize learning time or worker training time;
(d) equalize and permit the assignment of a full workload;

1. Davis and Canter (1956).

(e) provide for worker satisfaction (no specific criteria for job satisfaction were in use);

(f) conform to the requirements of equipment or facilities layout and, where they exist, of union restrictions on work assignment.

2. Combining individual tasks into specific jobs to achieve

(a) maximum specialization by limiting both the number of tasks in a job and variations in tasks;

(b) maximum repetitiveness;

(c) minimum training time.

The specific purpose of the assembly-line worker study was to explore the conditions under which improvement in productivity could be expected from changes in job content. The major criteria used to evaluate the effectiveness of the modifications were quantity and quality of output. Worker attitudes and satisfaction were also measured.

A manufacturing department producing a line of similar small plastic appliances in a unionized West Coast firm was the setting of the study. Over the years the department's activities and organization had been subjected to careful and detailed study, reflecting the latest in manufacturing engineering practices. The product had been made on an assembly line, where the operations, at which twenty-nine of the department's thirty-five women worked, were carefully specified and minutely divided. The worker's average experience on these jobs was four-and-a-half years. The rest of the people were engaged in material preparation and removal, inspection, and supply. A similar department in the company was used as a control group to permit monitoring of the presence of plantwide changes which might affect employee attitudes, practices and performance. The investigation centered around the jobs on the assembly line, and modifications were introduced through the department manager.

In the pre-existing Line Job Design each worker performed one of the nine operations, spaced at stations along the conveyor line required to assemble the appliance. Defective parts were rejected when necessary as part of each operation. Job rotation from hard to easy stations and vice versa took place every two hours. The operations were similar in skill requirements and technological content. Pacing eliminated responsibility for productivity, and job rotation, with the grouping of work stations for identical operations, practically eliminated individual responsibility for quality of work performed.

Two experimental job designs were compared with the pre-existing design:

1. Group Job Design: here the conveyor (and pacing) was eliminated and workers rotated among nine individual stations using a batch method of assembly. Other conditions were the same as for the pre-existing design.

2. Individual Job Design: all nine operations, final inspection, and securing of materials were combined into one job and performed by workers at individual work stations.

The results supported the hypothesis that greater variety of tasks and responsibility for methods, quality, pacing, and product completion leads to higher productivity, quality and satisfaction. The average hourly output over a period of consecutive days on the original or Line Job Design was taken as a productivity index of 100, and the quality over the period was taken as reported in per cent of defects per lot. Under the Group Job Design (no pacing by conveyor) the productivity index fell to an average of 89, while quality improved, with defects falling from an average of 0·72 per cent to 0·49 per cent per lot. After only six days on the Individual Job Design, the average productivity index rose slightly above the original Line average. Quality improved fourfold with defects per lot falling to 0·18 per cent.

In summary, the Individual Job Design

1. Provided a slight improvement in output.

2. Brought about a large improvement in quality, although quality levels were very high originally.

3. Increased the flexibility of the production process.

4. Permitted identification of individuals having deficiencies in productivity and quality.

5. Reduced external service and control functions in the department, e.g. material delivery, inspection.

6. Developed a more favorable attitude toward individual responsibility, individual work rate, effort expenditure, distribution

of work load, and making whole units. After experience with the Individual Job Design, workers disliked the lack of personal responsibility characteristic of the Line Job Design.

Operator, assembly line: home appliance manufacture[2]

Enlargement of assembly-line jobs was undertaken recently by a midwestern home laundry manufacturing firm which sought to improve workers' attitudes toward work and to increase output and quality. The company felt it might have gone beyond the 'optimum' division of labor on its assembly lines, so that increased costs of nonproductive work and line-balance delay might have exceeded the savings of fractionation. To the company job enlargement meant providing jobs that involved an increased number and variety of tasks, self-determination of pacing, increased responsibility for quality, increased discretion for work methods, and completion of a part- or sub-assembly. For a number of years the company had been pursuing a deliberate program of transferring work from progressive assembly lines to single-operator work stations; this transfer permitted study of the effects of enlarged jobs on workers' performance and attitudes.

Over a five-year period, fourteen bench assembly jobs had been established. Thirteen of these were from elements previously performed on assembly lines. One of the jobs was pump assembly, in which six operators each doing six work elements on an assembly line had required 1·77 minutes to complete a unit. This was transformed into one job having thirty-five elements requiring 1·49 minutes per assembly, including inspection. Costs for pump assembly were reduced $2000 annually. The other thirteen jobs were similarly enlarged, with their average allowed time changed from 0·78 to 3·15 minutes and average number of work elements from nine to thirty-three. They showed an average decrease in rejects from 2·9 to 1·4 per cent and a slight average decrease in output efficiency from 138 to 126 per cent.

Social interaction opportunities and actual work interaction showed sharp reductions in bench work. This may have resulted largely from the creation of independent jobs. The indications were that conditions were not very favorable for developing stable informal groups among the workers on enlarged jobs.

2. Conant and Kilbridge (1965).

The attitudes and preferences of workers having experience on both line and bench work were examined by questionnaire. Enlarged bench jobs were preferred 2 to 1 over assembly-line jobs. There were no preferences associated with personal characteristics. All of the attributes of the enlarged jobs were liked; except for social interaction and short learning time, all of the attributes of the line jobs were disliked. Preference for self-pacing was the reason given in half of the cases for liking bench jobs. Where line work was preferred, no single reason was given; rather it was less disliked than bench work.

This study demonstrates that there may be an 'optimum' division of labor on assembly lines. The authors make a case for job enlargement based on reduction of costs of nonproductive work and line-balance delays. It is unfortunate that these reductions were permitted to mask worker contributions to output flowing from enlarged job design. The results indicate strong contributions in the form of greatly improved quality of output and increased worker satisfaction with their jobs. These are gains for the company, perhaps otherwise unobtainable, along with savings in labor costs and greater production flexibility.

Operator, machine tender: textile weaving[3]
The third operator study indicates the impact of the organizational component of job design on the productivity of work groups. A socio-technical systems study in an Indian textile mill revealed the poor consequences of job designs which center only about worker–machine allocations and lead to inhibition of interaction of workers. The field study took place in a mill which had recently been intensively studied by engineers for the purpose of laying out equipment and assigning work loads based on careful time measurements of all of the job components. After installation of the layout and work assignments, the mill still failed to produce at satisfactory productivity and quality levels. The job designs required twelve specialist activities to operate the equipment assigned to a weaving room containing 240 looms.

1. A weaver tended approximately thirty looms.
2. A battery filler served about fifty looms.

   3. Rice (1953).

3. A smash-hand tended about seventy looms.

4. A gater, cloth carrier, jobber, and assistant jobber were each assigned to 112 looms.

5. A bobbin carrier, feller-motion fitter, oiler, sweeper, and humidification-fitter were each assigned to 224 looms.

The occupational tasks were all highly interdependent, and the utmost coordination was required to maintain continuity of production. However, the worker–machine assignments and consequent organizational grouping produced an interaction pattern which militated against continuity of production. The interaction resulting from work assignment brought each weaver into contact with five-eighths of a battery filler, three-eighths of a smash-hand, one-quarter of a gater, and one-eighth of a bobbin carrier.

After study of travel and communication patterns, the jobs were redesigned so that all of the workers who were interdependent were made part of the same work group. Work groups were organized so that a single group was responsible for the operation and maintenance of a specific bank of looms. Geographic division rather than functional division of the weaving room produced interaction patterns which made for regularity of relationships among individuals whose jobs were interrelated, and they could be held responsible for their production. As a result of these changes, efficiency rose from an average of 80 per cent to 95 per cent, and damage dropped from a mean of 32 per cent to 20 per cent after sixty working days. In the adjacent part of the weaving shed, where job design changes were not made, efficiency dropped to 70 per cent and finally rose to 80 per cent, while damage continued at an average of 31 per cent.

Operator, miner: coal mining[4]
This is one of the earliest long-term socio-technical systems studies of a complex organization. Its uniqueness lies in the fact that mining technology and its physical environment sharply displayed the effect of organization design on socio-psychological relations, an effect which in other technologies is frequently masked by compensatory management action. Quite aside from

4. Trist, Higgin, Murray and Pollock (1963) and Trist and Bamforth (1951).

mechanical devices, individual skill, or wage payment systems, the design of the organization, in its effect on all participants, is found to be a major factor contributing to system performance and personal satisfaction. During the study, coal mining was first carried out under an older nonmechanized technology with a traditionally developed organization structure and then under a newer technology which operated under one and subsequently under another organizational design.

The pre-mechanization, or single-place coal mining, technology was based on a pair of miners (with occasional reinforcements) making up a simple small-group organization structure. Work was done with hand tools and required great energy expenditure; performance depended on intimate knowledge of the mine and working conditions. Members of a group were self-selected and were multi-skilled, all-round workers performing the entire cycle of extraction as a joint undertaking. The group performed without supervision in dispersed, self-contained locations, was paid as a group, and developed high adaptability to local working conditions. Management was represented in the work area by a minor official who performed various services, including safety inspection and setting wage incentive payments. This system was effective because each work group had developed responsible autonomy and because the entire production system was slow, requiring little coordination at the coal face.

The successor to the single-place system was a partially mechanized technology, the maximum mechanization level possible at the time for low seam conditions in British mines. The first organization design introduced, known as the conventional long-wall system, reflected in its organizational design and occupational roles the prevailing outlook of mass production engineering. Mine output depended on completion of a working cycle, which consisted of preparing an area for coal extraction, using machinery to dig the coal out of the face, and removing the coal with the aid of conveyors. Cycle activities were divided into seven specialized tasks, each carried out by a different task group. Each of the tasks had to be completed in sequence and on schedule over three working shifts. On each of the shifts, one or more task groups performed their work, provided that the preceding tasks had been completed. The filling tasks, for coal removal, were the most onerous, and incompletion frequently impeded the work cycle, reducing output. Having been assigned a specialized task and an ostensibly equal work load, each worker was paid an incentive to perform his task without reference to the other tasks of workers in his or other groups.

The outgrowth of this organization design was the development of isolated task groups, each with its own customs, agreements with management, and payment arrangements related to its own interests. Coordination between men and groups on different shifts and control of work had to be provided entirely from outside, by the management. To be effective, control had to be coercive, which was both unsuitable for, and impracticable in, the high-risk coal-face environment. Management lacked the means to weld the individual task groups into an integrated team for performance of the cycle as a whole, and intergroup self-coordination could not develop. The inability to develop work-team relationships resulted in hostility and conflict among workers, and between them and management. Each worker and task group viewed the assigned task in isolation, which indeed is how it existed. When mine conditions were bad or prior work was not completed, the individual could not cope and resorted to waiting for management to take corrective action and to absenting himself in frustration and self-protection. The lowest level of management in the mine spent most of its time in emergency action over technical breakdowns, systems disfunctioning, and bargaining with workers over special payment for abnormal tasks.

The second organizational design, known as the composite longwall method, was introduced to overcome the deficiencies of the conventional design. Composite design was aimed at providing an organization structure suitable for maintaining continuity and for achieving early conclusion of a work cycle requiring more than one shift for completion. Although the same activity groups were maintained, the overall group, comprised of the successive task groups of the three-shift cycle, developed into a corporate whole. This was aided by setting goals for the performance of the entire cycle and making inclusive payments to the group as a whole for the completion of all the tasks in the cycle, plus an incentive for output. Such payment placed responsibility on the entire group for all operations, generating the need for individuals performing different tasks over interdependent phases of the cycle to inter-relate. Equal earnings required equal contributions from the cycle group's members, which led to the spontaneous development of interchangeability of workers according to need. Interchangeability required development of multi-skilled face workers and permitted sharing the common fund of underground skill and identity.

The method of work employed in each shift was directed at maintaining task continuity. Each shift picked up where the previous shift had left off and, when an activity group's main task was done, redeployed itself to carry on with the next task even if this meant starting a new cycle. All of the required roles were internally allocated to members by the work group as it developed responsible autonomous behavior. Opportunity for equalizing good and bad work times was thus afforded. Teams as a whole also worked out their own systems for rotating tasks and shifts, thereby taking over regulation of deployment. Each team was of sufficient size to make enough men available to fill the roles that arose on each shift.

The autonomous cycle group thus integrated the differentiated activities of longwall mining by internal control through self-regulating mechanisms. By contrast, the integration practices used in conventional longwall mining were those of indirect ex-ternal control through specialization of tasks with fixed assign-ments, wage incentive bargaining for each task, and skimpy attempts at direct supervision. Although the study was performed in British coal mines, the differences in concept between the two approaches characterize the present ambivalence on the part of US management over the application of managerial authority. The attempts, so widely recommended, to apply 'human relations–participative supervisorial methods' are likely to be ineffective, for they are inappropriate when used for external control purposes. Task and organization designs, compatible with technology, that permit the development of autonomous group functioning are very likely to be determinants for delineating the appropriate boundaries between authoritarian managerial action and internal control by participative self-regulatory mechanisms.

Some objective indicators of the appropriateness of composite organization for longwall mining were changes in absence rates, cycle progress, and productivity. Face-work places many stresses on miners, particularly when difficulties arise. Changing tasks, shifts, or work places helps reduce stress. Table 1 shows the variety of work experiences possible under each organization. Where changing or sharing of difficult tasks was not possible, there was increased withdrawal or absence from work. Table 2 shows the difference in absence rates. It may be inferred that absence rates had an effect on cycle progress and productivity which are shown in Tables 3 and 4.

Table 1 **Variety of work experience**

| | Averages for whole team | |
| | Conventional | Composite |
Aspect of work experience	longwall	longwall
Main tasks	1·0	3·6
Different shifts	2·0	2·9
Different activity groups	1·0	5·5

Source: Trist *et al.* (1963, p. 122).

Table 2 **Absence rates**

| | Percentage of possible shifts | |
| | Conventional | Composite |
Reason for absence	longwall	longwall
No reason given	4·3	0·4
Sickness and other	8·9	4·6
Accident	6·8	3·2
Total	20·0	8·2

Source: Trist *et al.* (1963, p. 123).

Table 3 **State of cycle progress at end of filling shift**

| | Percentage of cycles | |
| | Conventional | Composite |
State of cycle progress	longwall	longwall
In advance	0	22
Normal	31	73
Lagging	69	5
All cycles	100	100

Source: Trist *et al.* (1963, p. 124).

Table 4 Productivity as percentage of estimated face potential

	Conventional longwall	Composite longwall
Without allowance for haulage system efficiency	67	95
With allowance	78	95

Source: Trist *et al.* (1963, p. 125).

Maintenance craftsmen: chemical manufacture[5]

Modification of job content and organization units of general maintenance craftsmen was undertaken by a West Coast branch plant of a national industrial chemical manufacturing company. Local management was seeking to improve productivity, to respond to worker demands for more creative activities and for opportunities for closer identification with the job, and to eliminate jurisdictional disagreements among the various crafts. After the program was under way for about two and a half years, a study of the effects was undertaken to identify job content and job perception factors correlated with quantitative criteria of effective performance, i.e. that which minimizes total costs of production.

Prior to the change, each operating department had had its own maintenance crew that looked after 60 to 75 per cent of its needs. The remainder was supplied by central crafts shops. When a centralized maintenance department was organized – introducing planning, scheduling, and work under control – skill and function enlargement for general maintenance and repair workers was decided upon. The jobs of workers in the maintenance shops remained unchanged, being specialized to a single craft. The jobs of the newly designated maintenance repairmen were enlarged to include general welding, layout and fabrication, pipe fitting, boilermaking, equipment installation, and dynamic machine repair. The additional skills were acquired by means of a formal on- and off-the-job training program. Jobs were reclassified and wages increased accordingly. To support the broad-spectrum repairmen, two specialist classifications were introduced to per-

5. Davis and Werling (1960).

form special welding and machine repair. Two classes of specialist instructors were created to increase skills and develop new methods. Perhaps crucial to the entire undertaking was the presence of a strong industrial union and a long history of mutual trust and respect in union–management relations.

The changes in organization and enlargement of jobs produced positive results shown in a number of criteria of operational effectiveness, namely, quantity and quality of output, costs, and personal relationships and reactions. Prior to the changes, the company's total maintenance labor costs had moved upward, paralleling the national index. After reorganization and job enlargement, they fell from an index of 130 to 110 in two years (1954 = 100), while the national index continued to rise from 110 to 120. The labor costs of the enlarged maintenance repairmen, considered separately, fell from an index of 90 to 65 over the same period. When the index of performance (output/direct labor costs) was examined, the production departments showed no change over the period, while the maintenance repairmen showed an increase from 150 to 230. Total employment in the firm was reduced from an index of 100 to 95. The ratio of complaints about product quality and packaging to orders shipped, which is an indirect measure of quality, fell from an index of 100 to 55 over the same period.

To identify job content and job perception factors correlated with performance criteria, a questionnaire was administered based on hypotheses concerning the effect on worker performance of job content and relationships (see Davis, 1957). Questions reflected such variables as sequential relation of job duties and size of technological process segment included in jobs; inclusion in job of supply and inspection tasks and of final and completion activities; control over work content, rate and quality; communication with related work stations; extent of decision-making and participation in improvement activities; perception of value of contribution and of role in work group and organization; identification with product and process; feedback on quality and quantity of performance; measures of performance and incentives or rewards. The questionnaires were anonymously answered during working hours by 223 workers in seven departments. The remaining eleven employees, in the eighth department, were unavailable and did not participate.

Two analyses were made. The first identified job factors associated with criterion variables, and the second examined the questionnaire responses which distinguished the enlarged jobs from the others in the plant. The criteria used reflected the total cost of performance concept previously proposed as the inclusive criterion for measuring effectiveness, which includes quantity and quality of output, departmental operating costs, and absences. Because grievances and employee turnover were almost non-

Summary of job factors associated with performance criteria

Criterion variable *(performance indicator)*	Job factors
1. Improvement in quality of output	Fully specified work assignment and work rate
2. Reduction in operating costs	Full work assignment
3. Mean quality of output	1. Perception of job as being important
	2. Identification of high quality needs; independence as to control of quality; identification of high performance with success in company
	3. Self control of organization of work, including rate; high evaluation of fellow workers
	4. Peer communication
4. Improvement in quantity of output	1. Full work assignment and some independence as to variety and rate of work; wide job knowledge
	2. Specified work assignment and independence as to preparatory activities
	3. Relates success to management fairness; minimal standards of performance; specified work rate
5. Absence rate	1. Wide job knowledge
	2. Full work assignment consisting of production activities
	3. Full work assignment

existent and transfers took place by union–management agreement, neither was used as a criterion. A summary of job factors associated (correlated at the 5 per cent level or better) with performance criteria is given below. The criterion variables 'Improvement in quantity of output' and 'Reduction in operating costs' correlated 0·759 ($p = 0·05$), and both correlated 0·964 ($p = 0·01$) and 0·777 ($p = 0·05$) respectively with 'absence rate'. No suitable explanation of intercorrelation with absence rate was available. The average absence rate was approximately 2 per cent.

Workers with enlarged higher skill jobs were concerned with the importance of their jobs, control over job content and work methods, high variety of assignments, special training, responsibility for quality, and performance of preparatory activities. The responses of this group indicate that they were concerned with matters to which management attaches great importance, which may foreshadow the development of identity in objectives between workers on enlarged jobs and management. They indicated that they wished to make contributions to improvements of operations, related company success to their own, related their own advancement to better skills and performance, identified learning of new skills as a positive value of the job, and indicated readiness to accept additional duties to help improve their own and group performance. The negative responses of this group dealt with lack of variety of assignments and lack of control over work in process, and indicated that company, supervision and management ranked low on what was liked about jobs. Attitudes of enlarged jobholders toward performance were positive and so was their responsiveness to management goals, which seemed to have developed in spite of negative attitudes toward company, management and supervision.

Supervisor: aircraft instruments repair and manufacture[6]

The design of supervisory jobs is also plagued by poor models of individual–organization relationships and of human behavior in productive organizations. It is further complicated by the supervisor's conflicting objectives *vis-à-vis* workers and management, by the conflict between the supervisor's management objectives and his superior's, by his uncertainty over behavior required for effective leadership, by the implied threat to his status and effec-

6. Davis and Valfer (1965a and 1965b).

tiveness inherent in the authoritarian–participation conflict, and by the ambiguity that exists over the discharge of his responsibility. For purposes of design of supervisory jobs there is a general lack of information and data apart from some generalities concerning leadership behavior.

The management of the industrial facility of a large West Coast military installation introduced modifications in organization and in duties, responsibilities, and authority of some first-line supervisors, as part of a planned experimental field study directed by a University of California research team. The primary function of the facility was to overhaul, repair and test military aircraft and their components. With the exception of the senior executives, all of its 5900 employees were civilians, of whom 3800 were in line functions. The study was confined to eleven shops, the basic (first level) organization units, in which the sensing, power and control accessories of aircraft systems were overhauled, repaired and tested. The shops, each under a supervisor, employed from twelve to thirty craftsmen and processed many sub-types of relatively homogeneous types of equipment, such as flight instruments.

The study was intended to test the primary hypothesis that higher economic productivity (lower total cost) and greater need satisfaction for all members of a work group will result when the supervisor's authority and responsibility is increased by giving him direct control over all operational and inspection functions required to complete and determine final acceptance of the products or services assigned to his work group. A response mechanism model was developed which postulated that changes in a supervisor's performance result from intervening sequential changes in his perceptions, attitudes, motivations, and consequent behavior toward tasks and toward other members of the organization. Intervening criteria reflecting perceptions, attitudes and behavior toward others were developed; questionnaires and interviews were used as measuring instruments. Changes in supervisors' task behaviors were assessed by random activity sampling and job content inventory.

Two modifications in supervisors' jobs were introduced separately into a number of experimental shops. Control shops matched to these as to type of work, style of supervision, worker skills, and past performance were used.

The treatments were as follows:

1. Product Responsibility treatment provided supervision of all functions required to complete the products processed in a shop. It was introduced into two experimental shops with two control shops.

2. Quality Responsibility treatment added inspection to the functions required to complete a product, including authority for final quality acceptance of products. It was introduced into four experimental shops with three control shops.

The Product Responsibility treatment moved two experimental shops from their initial or functional organizational state to the second or product organizational state. In the initial state, the functions of overhaul and repair, calibrate and test, and quality acceptance were each performed by different groups. In the second state all functions required to complete its products, with external quality acceptance, were performed by one work group. The differences in functions between the first and second states were technically complex, requiring the acquisition of additional knowledge and skills by supervisors and workers.

The Quality Responsibility treatment moved four experimental shops from the second to the third organizational state of full responsibility for product completion, including quality acceptance. The tasks added in the third state were largely replicative and only trivially different from those performed by the shops in their initial (second) state. The major differences were in the explicit delegation of responsibility for quality and authority to perform quality acceptance. For this purpose quality control inspectors were withdrawn from the experimental shops and their authority for product acceptance was transferred to the shop supervisors, who, not long afterward, transferred the authority to key workers.

Proper evaluation of the treatment responses required that the pre-existing organizational environment be completely delineated, particularly since the expected effects were generated through supervisors of units which tended to become more autonomous as a result of the treatments. This environment was one of known overall demand for products and services, varying in the short run and requiring a highly skilled work force. Such skilled workers were in limited supply in the area, making it difficult, if not impossible, to rely on hiring as a means of adding workers to a unit to suit immediate needs. This situation generated manpower-maintenance goals directed at conserving manpower in preparation for meeting overall known demand requirements under 'emergency' (short-run) conditions. Goal conflicts could and did arise between this real goal of supervisors and such usual and stated goals of top management as efficiency and cost reduction. In implementing its goals, management reviewed each supervisor's performance every three months by comparing the productivity, quality and costs of his shop against a standard. Based on this review and planned quarterly work load, a supervisor would expect to have workers added or removed from his shop for the next calendar quarter. When unplanned increases in work load occurred, a supervisor could request, and received, additional workers transferred from other shops. Whether these were the workers he wanted, or may even previously have lost, can be left to conjecture.

If supervisors responded positively to the treatments, they were expected to achieve changes in the objective criteria of cost reduction and quality improvement, satisfying management's stated goals without violating their own real goal of manpower-maintenance. Achievement of improvement in productivity was not expected since this might have resulted in a loss of manpower, constituting a negative incentive to the supervisor in maintaining the capability of his shop to meet anticipated fluctuating work load.

The study lasted for twenty-four months. During the first nine months data were collected on all of the criterion variables for operation of the eleven shops in their initial states. After the experimental treatments were introduced into six shops, data on objective criteria were collected for six months and data on intervening criteria were collected for fifteen months. The results of the study can be summarized as follows.

Personnel costs in the form of absenteeism, grievances, transfers, injuries, etc., were not significantly affected by the treatments. It is difficult to evaluate whether the nonsensitivity was specific to the treatments or to the short duration of the study. Historically, personnel costs were markedly low and unchanging in the organization and this pattern continued into the post-change period.

The treatment which enlarged the responsibility and authority of the supervisors and the operational functions of their organizational units resulted in the following changes in objective criteria:

Criteria	Product Responsibility (technically complex change)	Quality Responsibility (technically trivial change)
1. Compatible with supervisors' goal:		
(a) Quality	Significant improvement	No significant change, but indications of improvement
(b) Costs	No change	Significant improvement
2. Incompatible with supervisors' goal:		
(a) Productivity	No change	No change

As can be seen, those objective performances improved that were compatible with the supervisors' goal of manpower maintenance.

Supervisor behavior became more autonomous and more oriented to the technical problems of producing the product and to worker training. The treatments shortened the quality and process information feedback loops to workers and concentrated dispersed functional authority. In moving toward technological aspects of management, giving more time to planning, inspection, control, etc., supervisors did so at the expense of management of men. This change in management style appeared to be salutary as judged by positive worker attitudes.

Positive attitudes of workers and supervisors were enhanced, indicating satisfaction of personal needs in the direction of developing individuals who were contributing to the organization's viability or health. The major response perceptions and attitudes were:

Treatment	Favorable	Unfavorable
Product Responsibility (technically complex change: new tasks and skills required)	1. Greater autonomy 2. Less limiting internal structure 3. Greater skill for workers in long run 4. Greater product control 5. Increased information flow to workers	1. Loss of man-orientation 2. Loss of concern for worker 3. Low rate of transfer of treatment tasks and responsibilities 4. Low delegation
Treatment	Favorable	Unfavorable
Quality Responsibility (technically trivial change: addition of inspection and authority for product acceptance)	1. Greater authority 2. Greater autonomy 3. Greater concern for worker 4. Higher rate of transfer of treatment tasks and responsibilities to workers 5. Reduced conflict with staff group 6. Increased information flow to workers	1. Loss of man-orientation 2. Greater internal structure 3. Low delegation

Conclusions

The studies reviewed here lend support to the general model of responsible autonomous job behavior as a key facet of individual–organizational–technological relationships in productive organizations. Responsible behavior as defined here implies (a) acceptance of responsibility by the individual or group for the cycle of activities required to complete the product or service, (b) acceptance of responsibility for rate, quantity and quality of output, and (c) recognition of interdependence of the individual or group on others for effective progress of a cycle of activities. Similarly, autonomous behavior encompasses (a) self-regulation of work content and structure within the job, where the job is an assignment having inputs, facilities and outputs, (b) self-evaluation of performance, (c) self-adjustment to changes required by technological variability, and (d) participation in setting up of goals or objectives for job outputs.

Furthermore, the studies provide a partial demonstration of the positive effects on total performance of job and organization designs which lead to responsible autonomous job behavior, i.e. positive effects on objective organization performance, as well as on the attitudes, perceptions and satisfactions of members of the organization. Such designs also tend to maintain a production system in an on-going state of relative equilibrium. For example, in many of the studies total performance was found to have been enhanced substantially by job designs which provided compatibility among technological, organizational and personal requirements. This suggests that here, as elsewhere, the system approach leads to more effective designs of organizations and jobs. The component or piecemeal approach (so prevalent at present), which concentrates on job designs exclusively tailored to one component of the system, namely technology, tends to result in less than optimal total performance. While failing to achieve the output and quality levels possible, it imposes higher direct costs on management and workers alike, reflected in increased inspection, supervision, and absenteeism, coupled with reduced satisfactions, negative attitudes, and hostility.

That some processes or activities may be automated does not alter the fact that for the organization as a whole people are the prime agents for the utilization of technology in the interests of achievement of an organization's objectives. The model of responsible autonomous job behavior makes it both permissible and imperative to view personal requirements in the focus of job design activity. But if the model is to be used as a basis for job (and organization) design, then these non-modifiable personal requirements and the characteristics of their interactions with technology and the organization will have to be specified as design criteria aimed at achieving compatibility. Variations in design may result from interpretations of non-modifiable criteria and from the introduction of others.

Some of the job characteristics of importance to job and organization design have asserted their dominance in the studies reviewed. They can be classified into two types: (a) job content and structure characteristics, which reflect the interaction between personal and technological requirements, and (b) job environment characteristics, which reflect the interaction between personal and organizational requirements. Job content characteristics are concerned with the number and kinds of tasks and their interrelationships. Many of these are specific illustrations of the need for the development of a work role which provides comprehensiveness, i.e. the opportunity to perform all tasks required for product or process completion and at the same time imposes the responsibility and confers the authority for self-direction and self-regulation.

Improvement in total performance was thus frequently obtained when the scope of jobs included all tasks required to complete a part, product or service; when the job content included all four types of tasks inherent in productive work: auxiliary or service (supply, tooling), preparatory (set-up), processing or transformation, and control (inspection); when the tasks included in the job content permitted closure of the activity, if not product completion, permitting development of identity with product or process. Tangible gains in performance were also obtained by the introduction of task variety in the form of larger numbers and kinds of tasks and skills as well as more complex tasks. The characteristics of processing tasks which led to improved performance were self-regulation of speed of work and self-determination of work methods and sequence. Total performance also improved when control tasks were included in jobs, permitting outputs to be evaluated by self-inspection, and when product quality acceptance was within the authority of the jobholder.

The job environment characteristics that contributed to improvement in total performance were again those that supported the development of responsible autonomous job behavior. They indicate a job structure that permits social interaction among jobholders and communication with peers and supervisors, particularly when the maintenance of continuity of operation is required. A reward system that supports responsible autonomy was shown to provide gains beyond those of simple increases in task output.

Appropriate management behavior is, of course, required for

jobs having these characteristics. The behaviors called for are supportive in providing service, general planning of activities, and evaluation of results on the basis of organizationally meaningful objectives. They stand in contrast to present overly specific task planning and work measurement, obtrusive supervision, coercive external control, imposed external integration of specialized tasks, and external coordination of fractionated activities.

Certain important aspects of organizational design were also brought to light by the studies. Where small organizational units, or work groups, are required, group structures having the following features appeared to lead to improved performance: (a) group composition that permits self-regulation of the group's functioning, (b) group composition that deliberately provides for the full range of skills required to carry out all the tasks in an activity cycle, (c) delegation of authority, formal or informal, to the group for self-assignment of tasks and roles to group members, (d) group structure that permits internal communication, and (e) a group reward system for joint output. As regards the design requirements for larger organizational units with more complex interactions, it would be hazardous to draw any conclusions from the studies reviewed. Whether or not present extensive research will make a contribution to our understanding of the design requirements of large organizations is not yet clear.

Overall, it is obvious that we are only beginning to identify relationships among technology, organization and the individual which are capable of being translated into organization and job design recommendations. Nevertheless, it requires no very great powers of foresight to suggest that we are rapidly approaching the time when re-evaluation of management precepts and practices will have to take place. Many currently fashionable management programs are mere palliatives, addressed to patching up essentially inappropriate organization and job structures. Among these, the so-called worker communications programs, participation techniques directed at providing workers with 'feelings of importance', and human relations programs dealing with personal relationships and supervision (often in the abstract, outside the industrial or business context) do not stand up under objective scrutiny. Almost without exception their achievements fall short even of their own stated objectives.

In summary, changes in organization and job design similar to those reviewed are indicated, as are associated changes in management behavior. Whether and when they will take place cannot be forecast. Industrial and business history is replete with examples of the continuation of superannuated institutions and procedures.

References

CONANT, E. H., and KILBRIDGE, M. D. (1965), 'An interdisciplinary analysis of job enlargement: technology, costs and behavioral implications', *Industrial and Labor Relations Review*, vol. 18, October, p. 377.

CONRAD, R. (1955), 'Comparison of paced and unpaced performance at a packing task', *Occupational Psychology*, vol. 29, pp. 15–28.

DAVIS, L. E. (1957), 'Toward a theory of job design', *Journal of Industrial Engineering*, vol. 8, p. 305.

DAVIS, L. E. (1966), 'Pacing effects on manned assembly lines', *International Journal of Production Research*, vol. 4, p. 171.

DAVIS, L. E., and CANTER, R. R. (1956), 'Job design research', *Journal of Industrial Engineering*, vol. 7, p. 275.

DAVIS, L. E., CANTER, R. R., and HOFFMAN, J. F. (1955), 'Current job design criteria', *Journal of Industrial Engineering*, vol. 6, p. 5.

DAVIS, L. E., and VALFER, E. S. (1965a), 'Supervisor job design', proceedings of the Second International Congress on Ergonomics, *Ergonomics*, vol. 8, p. 1.

DAVIS, L. E., and VALFER, E. S. (1965b), 'Intervening responses to changes in supervisor job designs', *Occupational Psychology*, vol. 39, p. 171.

DAVIS, L. E., and WERLING, R. (1960), 'Job design factors', *Occupational Psychology*, vol. 34, p. 109.

RICE, A. K. (1953), 'Productivity and social organization in an Indian weaving shed', *Human Relations*, vol. 6, November, p. 297.

RICHARDSON, F. L. W., and WALKER, C. R. (1948), *Human Relations in an Expanding Company*, Labor and Management Center, Yale University.

TRIST, E. L., and BAMFORTH, K. W. (1951), 'Some social and psychological consequences of the longwall method of coal getting', *Human Relations*, vol. 4, February, pp. 3–38.

TRIST, E. L., HIGGIN, G. W., MURRAY, H., and POLLOCK, A. B. (1963), *Organizational Choice*, Tavistock.

23 Per H. Engelstad

Socio-Technical Approach to Problems of Process Control

P. H. Engelstad, 'Socio-technical approach to problems of process control', in F. Bolam (ed.), *Papermaking Systems and Their Control*, 1970, transactions of the Symposium held at Oxford, September, 1969, the British Paper and Board Makers' Association.

Synopsis

The Industrial Democracy Project in Norway is a long-term research sponsored jointly by the Confederation of Employers and the Trades Union Council. The field experiment reported took place in the chemical pulp department of an integrated papermill as one of a series of four experiments carried out in different industrial settings. Extensive task fragmentation and bureaucratization in modern industry have produced widespread feelings of alienation in the work force, owing to an increasing mismatch between technologically based task requirements and human needs. Emerging theories of socio-technical systems, including a list of psychological job requirements, offer a frame of reference for understanding these problems. Previous experience suggests that full commitment to productive aims can be achieved only under conditions that allow for a high level of self-regulation and learning. In process technology (including pulp and paper), the dependence relationships among the state characteristics of the materials form a complex network. In the present case, this resulted in uncontrolled variations being transmitted along the process. Having identified the optimum unit for experimentation, individual jobs were redesigned in order to facilitate group learning, which would permit the work groups to increase their control of the process. Results of the socio-technical analyses before and after the experiment are reported and reference is made to the *variance matrix* technique.

Introduction

This paper describes a concrete experiment conducted by a team of social scientists in the Hunsfos pulp and paper mill during 1964–67 under the supervision of the author. This is part of the research team's complete program for which Professor Einar Thorsrud (Work Research Institutes, Oslo) and Professor Fred E. Emery (Human Resources Centre, Tavistock Institute of Human Relations, London) have been responsible. The study is one of the four experiments carried out in different industries under the so-called Industrial Democracy Project, an action research program sponsored jointly by the Norwegian Federation of Employers (NAF) and the Trades Union Council of Norway (LO).[1]

The primary objective of this program was, through a systematic redesign of jobs, to improve the conditions whereby men could exercise more discretion and have greater influence over their own work situation. To achieve these goals, however, neither party was willing to sacrifice the rising standard of living resulting from economic growth in industry.

Existing evidence indicated that one could reduce the feeling of alienation and release human resources in the company if jobs could be constructed either in accordance with the well-known principle of job enlargement or with the more promising model of partly autonomous work groups. The changes required were expected to be primarily related to the type of technology involved, taking for granted that the changes were in accordance with basic constraints imposed by the psychological needs of job-holders (see the next section and Appendix 1).

The research task was conceived of as twofold. Firstly, to give practical demonstrations of new principles of job design and, secondly, to encourage the diffusion of possible results that were found useful. In the following, we shall confine ourselves to the first task in general and to the experiment at Hunsfos in particular.[2] Consequently, it should be noted that, although this one field experiment might properly illustrate the socio-technical approach as such, a full evaluation of the results achieved by this research program requires the four field experiments to be considered as a whole. [. . .]

1. Thorsrud and Emery (1969).
2. The other field experiments were carried out in a wire-drawing department at Christiania Spigerverk, Oslo, in a department for assembling electrical panels at Nobo, Trondheim and in a fertilizer plant at Norsk Hydro, Porsgrunn.

The socio-technical approach

Improved production control in industry has hitherto very much been looked upon as a question of finding the best technical solution to the problem, whereas organizational factors were not taken so much into consideration, particularly during the design phase. This takes for granted that people, within their physical capacities, will be able to cope with and adapt to whatever type of task structures and variances they are left with. This procedure has led to a compartmentalization of the organization. Hence, many of the artificial segregations of crafts advocated by the trades unions are also reflections of traditional management practices. To our mind, it appears evident that these procedures must have resulted in sub-optimum solutions for the socio-technical system as a whole, since the reliability of the total system in this case will be decided by its weakest link. It should be noted that, with the general development towards automation, the location and character of the socio-technical interface will change, though such an interface will always persist at some level of an enterprise. Furthermore, in a period when almost everyone in society receives an increasingly higher education, it appears to be a paradox that the jobs, in particular at the lower levels in industry, still tend to be rigidly delineated, offering little scope for variation, learning and joint problem solving and decision-making.

The socio-technical approach is based on organizational thinking that, within the unavoidable constraints of the technology, encourages as far as possible local initiative and responsible autonomy.

In our terms of reference, enterprises and their subsystems are considered as open socio-technical systems. Hence, like other living systems, they are open to matter–energy–information exchanges with an environment. Without trying to go more deeply into any of the principles that are a consequence of the open system characteristics of the enterprise, the following may be listed as being of particular relevance to the present project.[3]

1. The primary task of a manager is to control the boundary conditions of his unit.

3. For a condensed presentation of the principles of systems theory referred to, see the Introduction in Emery (ed.) (1969).

2. The goals of an open system can be understood only as special forms of interdependence between the system and its environment.

3. The goal state has the characteristics of a steady state, which requires (a) a constancy of direction and (b) a tolerable rate of progress.

4. Steady state can be achieved only through leadership and commitment.

5. The basic regulation of open systems is self-regulation.

6. As individuals have open system properties, the enterprise must allow its members a sufficient measure of autonomy.

It is well known that motivations and attitudes of job-holders are decided not only by external rewards and sanctions but also by certain intrinsic characteristics of the tasks. Hence, empirical evidence suggests that workers prefer tasks[4]:

1. Of a substantial degree of wholeness (that is, which show a strong *gestalt*).

2. Where the individual has control over the materials and the processes involved.

These requirements have been further translated into a set of psychological job requirements (Appendix 1).

The co-existence of a social and a technical system involve a coupling of two part-systems, each independently governed by its own laws, towards a common goal. As the contributions of these systems are essentially complementary, special attention must be paid to the interdependencies between them.

The two systems are primarily coupled through the reciprocal allocation of tasks to work roles, each of which is able to form systems of a higher order. Existing evidence shows that, when units' tasks were small, job enlargement has been a useful organizational model (Thorsrud and Emery, 1969). In the English coalmines, where a number of tasks exceed the one man/one shift unit, it appeared that technological requirements as well as human needs could be adequately met by an autonomous work group (Herbst, 1962; Trist, Higgin, Murray and Pollock, 1963). The same principles of job design have later been applied also in the textile industry (Rice, 1958). In these cases, the problem of identifying

4. Emery (1959).

naturally bounded areas (in the sense that they had a high potential for self-regulation) was relatively easy. This task is considerably more difficult in an integrated pulp and paper technology where:

1. The dependence relationships of process variables form a complex network along the process.

2. The continuity of production, the level of throughput and the restricted buffer capacities in the process, to be effective, require that the disturbance control sequences be operated at appropriate speeds.

In order to identify units that would optimally meet these requirements, a method of analysis based on task structure has been developed. The so-called *matrix of variances*, which is based on the dependence relationship between state characteristics of the material, has been useful in identifying natural clusters of variances that are to be allocated within the same organizational unit (Appendix 2).

Finally, conditions for self-regulation can be improved by various changes in the social and the technical systems. This is best illustrated by our case material.

Hunsfos pulp and papermill

This account is an abstracted and rewritten version of a much more detailed report on the Hunsfos experiment, 1964–5, written for another purpose (Engelstad, Emery and Thorsrud, 1969). Further reference to this report will not be made in the following.

The Hunsfos mill is situated in a small community, about ten miles north of the industrial seaport of Kristiansand, in the very south of Norway. The rural surroundings as well as the tidiness of the workplaces contribute to the general impression of a friendly atmosphere when one is visiting the site.

Since the end of the last century, the company has been the major employer in the community and, even in 1963, employed almost 50 per cent of its adult male working population. About 80 per cent of the Hunsfos labor force of 900–1000 had close links with the community and the mill through their families, often employed by Hunsfos for three generations. The personal relationships at work are stable and closely linked to the religious, political and economic life of the community. The workers and foremen have been recruited mainly from the local district; the managers and most of the technical staff have moved in from other parts of the country. Hunsfos has a strongly professional management, respected both within the industry and within the plant, also a local union leadership with effective working relations with the central union headquarters in Oslo.

The company is one of five integrated papermills in Norway that offer the full range of the major technologies – mechanical pulping, chemical pulping and papermaking. Of the approximate total of 80 mills in the country, Hunsfos ranks fifth in terms of total sales. In 1964, the mill converted 200,000 m. of timber to 20,000 tons of mechanical woodpulp and 34,000 tons of chemical pulp. This again resulted in a total output of 65,000 tons of paper. The production covers a wide range of qualities within the sectors of magazine, packaging and fine papers. Total sales, of which 85 per cent were exported, came close to 80 million N.Cr.

The economic situation of the pulp and paper industries in Norway has been difficult for years, and Hunsfos during the last ten years, in order to meet the challenge, has carried out two large reconstructions and investment programs.

In 1959, the company, as the first one in Europe, introduced the magnesium bisulphite process in order economically to exploit the firs and hardwoods that, combined, are more prevalent than spruce in the south of Norway. Soon afterwards, fully continuous running, based on a four-shift schedule, was introduced to maximize plant utilization. A number of technical improvements have been effected, including the reconstruction of some of the paper-machines. This has allowed the company gradually to change its paper grades toward qualities of a higher converting value.

Selection of the chemical pulp department for experimenting

In September 1964, the management and the trades union at Hunsfos agreed to have the research team find a suitable area in the plant to introduce new principles of job design experimentally. From a research point of view, sites would be acceptable only in so far as they would have:

1. Process technology characteristics.

2. A high potential for diffusing possible results to the company as a whole.

Initially, this left us a choice among wood preparation, mechanical and chemical pulping, stock preparation and papermachines. Interviews with employees covering all levels of responsibility in these areas of production provided a detailed picture of the role system and how the technical interdependencies were coped with by role interrelations. The attitudes expressed by the employees were taken as clues to the fit or lack of fit of the social and technical systems.

A matrix of variances, based on the dependence relationships between state characteristics of the materials in different parts of the process, was constructed in close cooperation with some of the process technologists. Our focal concern, unlike that of the design engineer, however, was with those variances arising from the technical system that required responses from the organization of individuals if the production goals were to be achieved. The matrix helped us to identify where these variances arose in the technological process and where in the subsequent stages of production they could be identified, communicated or acted upon. The matrix was worked out in close cooperation with technologists in the company. Our analysis also entailed working over historical records of plant operations, estimating cost/benefit ratios for possible changes in different parts of the mill and collecting labor force statistics that would indicate social costs incurred by different departments.

It was agreed to start the experiment in the chemical pulp department. Taking into consideration such factors as the dependence structure of the variances in the materials, the spatio-temporal aspects of the process, potential input/output measurements and certain variables in the social system, this department appeared to be a naturally bounded socio-technical unit with a relatively high potential for self-regulation. It appeared also to be an optimum choice, because:

1. The department showed an opening for significant improvement in that some of the variances in the timber, if not coped with in the chemical pulping, could be met in the papermaking only by downgrading the quality (and economic value) of the paper. (To a much lesser extent, mechanical pulping had the same effect.)

2. Located in between the wood preparation and the papermill,

changes in the mode of chemical pulp operations would exert maximum leverage on these parts.

3. Local leadership on the management as well as on the union side appeared to be sufficiently capable and willing. This we expected would offset the resistance to change that might be expected from the senior operators (ten out of fifteen of whom were over fifty years of age) and from some of the men who were apt to stick to their viewpoints or to seek isolation.

Tasks arising from the technical system
The chemical pulp process

I shall describe only those aspects of the technology that were found to be of particular importance for this experiment.

The technical system of the chemical pulp department consists of five converting processes carried out in different, but adjacent areas – boiling, screening and bleaching and the preparation of boiling acid and of bleaching liquids. Chips of spruce, fir and hardwood are boiled separately in large digesters with acid magnesium bisulphite. (In the wood, the two major components of lignin and cellulose form a rigid three-dimensional structure.) Under the right conditions of acid concentration, temperature, pressure, time, etc., the lignin is dissolved and the cellulose fibres are released. The fibres, together with other undissolved material, are washed and prepared for further separation in the screening section; the lignin and the used boiling liquid go to waste.

Fresh acid magnesium bisulphite is drawn from a buffer tank, to which acid is continuously fed after it has been prepared from magnesium oxide and sulphur dioxide in a separate section.

A complex system of screens raises the homogeneity and purity of the fibres by removing unboiled wood particles (knots, splinters, etc.), small fibre fragments (fines), as well as sand, bark, resin and other impurities. From the screening section, the spruce pulp goes to buffer storage as unbleached pulp, whereas the fir and hardwood are transferred to the bleaching floor.

The bleaching liquid, prepared from chlorine and sodium hydroxide in a separate section, is used mainly to dissolve residual lignin still attached to the fibres and coloring them. The three pulps together with the mechanical woodpulp constitute the major inputs to the papermill.

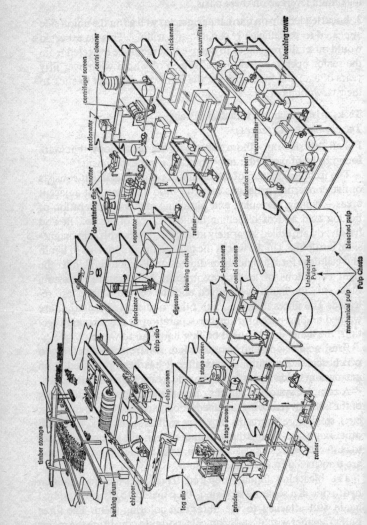

Figure 1 The chemical pulp department

Variances in the technical system

The following groups of variances arising from the system's technology were of particular relevance to be controlled by the social system:

1. The use of fir as one of the raw materials had led to serious pitch problems, which were only partly brought under control. Whenever sticky resin accumulated on the screens or in the bleaching equipment, extensive cleaning was required.

2. Since the growing and storage conditions of the timber vary a great deal, some of these input variances would be transmitted along with the flow of materials and, if not controlled, would reduce the paper quality.

3. The conversion of spruce, fir and hardwood batches in the same equipment induced additional variances, owing to pitch contamination one with the other and the mixing of fibres of different wood species.

4. The variances resulting from mechanical breakdowns had been extreme during the period after the introduction of the bisulphite method, but, by 1965, they had been reduced to a near-normal level.

Key characteristics of operator tasks

These are:

1. The individual part-processes were by themselves relatively complex and demanding. Spatially separate from each other, the present level of their performance could be sustained with a limited number of contacts with other areas. Hence, they appeared to form a strong *gestalt* by themselves.

2. In addition to the cluster of internal interdependencies, however, a number of important relationships still existed between the part-processes and across shifts. For example, the boiling and the bleaching operations were interdependent in terms of removing the lignin from the fibres, and the sixteen-hour cycle between filling and emptying each of the four boilers required close co-operation and contact across shifts. Hence, the naturally bounded unit tasks clearly exceeded the traditional one man/one shift type of work role.

3. Finally, it became evident in this case, as in others, that the requirements of the technology were not fully known and predictable. As previously indicated, the pitch problem was far from being fully understood and the variances in raw material made it impossible to predict what problems the operators at any time would have to tackle. Moreover, the properties of the technical equipment would change somewhat over a period. This implies that the designated process control standards were arbitrary ones based on current knowledge. Hence, they ought to be adjusted to the extent that the changing properties of the technical system caused a relocation of the optimum point for some of the process variables. For example, the evolutionary operation technique is based on this fact (Box, 1957).

The response resources in the social system
Formal organization

The department organization included seven shift positions and four shift teams, plus one daytime worker preparing the bleaching agents. A senior operator was charged with the responsibility for each of the other four part-processes. These men belonged to the highest of two formally recognized status levels. There were also a boiler assistant, a screener assistant and a reserve on each shift who, together with the daily worker, made up the second grade of operators.

In supporting roles outside the department were two laboratory technicians providing data for process control. In case of mechanical breakdowns or pitch troubles, the operators had to rely on maintenance men and cleaning people being called in from other areas by the foreman. Special contact man positions had been set up to facilitate communications between maintenance and operations.

Four shift foremen (plus one assistant foreman to cover absentees) were responsible for the chemical and mechanical pulping, even though the two processes were not technically interdependent. The levels above the shift foremen included the general foreman, the production engineer, the pulpmill manager and the general manager.

It should be noted that the number of operator positions is strictly prescribed in the central agreement between the employer and the trades union. This arrangement, having a long tradition in the Norwegian pulp and paper industry, is specific to this industry. This had undoubtedly added to the tendency of a strict delineation of work between individual job-holders, a well-known result of traditional job design in industry. Being of crucial importance to the problems of self-regulation and process control in this kind of technology, this point will be further explored in what follows.

Wages and bonus

The total wage of the operator includes hourly pay, shift allowances, regular overtime, additional hours and production bonus. Generally speaking, the complexity of this arrangement makes it difficult for the average man to see any direct connection between his efforts and his wage packet.

In accordance with this, the production bonus was based on the number of batches produced, even though the papermachines used to be the bottleneck in the production line. Thus, by leaving out the quality aspects of the pulp, which the operators could influence and by which alone *they* could facilitate the production of the papermachine, the production bonus, though paid out on a group basis, could not in fact function as a group goal. This is of particular significance, since management (at that time, extremely anxious to build up the quality reputation of the company in the market) could through a quality bonus have effectively translated such a quality-oriented policy into operational terms at the lower levels in the organization.

Of particular interest also are the additional hours, a form of extra pay earned by the men for odd jobs done in addition to their permanent tasks and within their regular working hours. This exemplifies one of the measures used by management in order to cope with the lack of flexibility on the shop floor, to be considered in the following section.

Segregation of operator jobs

Since 1961, the total manning had been gradually reduced through natural turnover, the major part of which used to occur in the spring. Recruitment was done mainly therefore through the annual intake of holiday reserves for the summer months. Operator training was, in keeping with the tradition in the industry, limited by the notion of one man/one job. Hence, when a man had been permanently selected for one department, further advancements would be confined to the more recognized jobs in the same area.

The segregation of jobs and lack of overlapping skills in the permanent shift teams had made the work organization increasingly unable to cope with the existing variances as the number of stand-ins in the general manpower pool was gradually reduced. In the chemical pulp department, for instance, one multi-skilled reserve had been introduced on each shift in order to stand in for absentees and otherwise to help out with odd jobs. Even if it had functioned, however, this arrangement would probably have proved inadequate to solve the flexibility problem on the shop floor. As it was, the lack of balance between the higher skill requirements for this key position in the shift groups and, on the other hand, the pay, security and working conditions offered, resulted in a disturbingly high turnover among the reserves.

Traditionally – and not only in the pulp and paper industry – management has seen apparent advantages in strict delineation and specification of individual jobs. The time needed for training is short and the supervisory control is strengthened through a clear definition of what each worker is accountable for. The workers for their part will tend to react to this system by interpreting the job specification as the maximum they owe rather than the minimum.

Beyond the first line of defence established by the union, the men make out of the job specification and customary practice a second line of defence against management. Moreover, within the welter of expectations about what is mine and what is yours, the men create a pecking order among themselves based on who gets the cosier jobs and who gets the less attractive ones.

Consequently, while the individual jobs may be lacking in intrinsic satisfaction, because of this rigid definition and segregation, they gain psychological significance because of what are merely relative advantages. As the men come to base their judgement of themselves and others on their ability to seize these relative advantages, they become stronger defenders of this system of job design than would be warranted by the built-in limitations for self-fulfilment.

As an example of this insidious trend, our *post hoc* analysis of the records revealed that one of the four digesters was a particularly good piece of equipment for pulping a certain wood. This we found was not public knowledge. In discussion, however, we found that one of the boilermen had already discovered this long ago and kept it to himself. This suggested to us at least that the lack of learning in the department was due not only to a *laissez-faire* attitude or feeling of uncertainty among the men, but that the system failed to encourage the men to share self-acquired knowledge, as they did not regard themselves as integrated members of a group.

Operator responses to task requirements

Our analysis of tasks and attitudes showed that, among the first three psychological requirements (Appendix 1), these jobs lacked mainly in the interest, excitement and self-enhancement that comes from being able to learn to do one's task better. Knowledge of results appeared adequate so long as learning was inhibited. The degree of variety and demand and the scope for personal control were higher than is usually found in industrial jobs and felt to be so by the operators.

This explained the relatively high level of job satisfaction expressed in interviews with senior operators and older workers, who had little reason to want to change in order to participate in a more comprehensive learning process that might disturb some of the privileges they had obtained. The more dependent nature of the assistant jobs and the particular situation of the reserves explain the lower level of satisfaction expressed by the second grade operators.

Interaction of operator roles with foreman and management roles

The position of the shift foreman in the chemical pulp department was introduced as a management response to increasing variances and planning problems arising after the changeover to the magnesium bisulphite method. This was in accordance with the traditional approach to organizational problems on the shop floor. These include such measures as specifying individual jobs in more detail, strengthening the hand of the supervisor, calling in specialists, introducing a new level in the organization, etc. In this case, a short-term solution was achieved at the cost of a more serious long-term problem.

Recruited from among the best operators, the foremen would only with extensive training succeed in forming a leadership and planning position clearly ranking above and essentially complementary to the operating group. Familiar with operator work and lacking the means and self-confidence to lift himself to a new level, the foreman tended to focus his attention primarily within the work group rather than on controlling its boundary conditions. Hence, the foreman had developed the practice of being constantly on the move as a troubleshooter within the department; he would then do most of the unpredictable tasks that the operators were reluctant to carry out without special compensations (see remarks on additional hours), perceiving such tasks as falling outside their own strictly defined jobs.

The behavior of the foreman then became part of a vicious circle of job segregation by reducing the job content and thereby further limiting the learning and growth potentials of the operators. As the first level of management was in this way lowering itself in order to complete the tasks within its particular area of command, so each higher level was correspondingly pulled down to fill out what was then lacking in control and coordination. The adverse consequences of such work organization at the floor level will easily affect all levels of management, a fact typically found in large organizations. Even at Hunsfos, these tendencies were evident. By filling in for their subordinates, the managers and foremen were subtly redefining their own jobs in a way that reinforced the tendencies of the men on the shop floor not to show more initiative than was demanded by the traditional job design. Thus, the vicious circle was established.

Conditions for optimum control by self-regulation

When the goals and purposes of an enterprise are operationalized on different levels in the organization, it is not arbitrary which of the factors – throughput, quality, material, labor, etc. – are given the highest priority in the ongoing optimization processes on each level. According to the theory of open systems, the choice of priorities will depend on conditions outside as well as inside the enterprise. Hence, at Hunsfos, we felt that key problems of optimization on the two lowest levels of the socio-technical system were the following:

1. *Process control* to achieve for each product a given set of quality specifications minimizing machine hours, cost of material, labor cost, etc. Among the cost factors, primary attention is usually paid to machine utilization.

2. *Production planning* to achieve optimum allocation of products and orders for market requirements as well as production costs. Whereas the individual customer would vary in terms of quality demands, time of delivery, etc., machine down-time would depend on the size of the orders, the production sequence of products, etc.

The two activities are obviously interdependent and complementary, yet the latter area potentially contains tasks for which a new type of supervision could develop.

For the process control function, this type of technology requires that it matches an extended interdependency network, as well as meeting the demands for immediate responses in the social system. This implies that the control sequences have to be explored in detail. Generally speaking, a self-regulating production system requires at least the following components:

1. *A production unit* that converts a specific input material into a specific output.

2. *An output standard* against which the output of the production unit can be judged at any time.

3. *A measuring device* that can detect deviations from the target output standard and feed the information back to a 'brain' unit.

4. *A 'brain' unit* that can translate the information received into a new set of operational instructions, appropriate to returning the production performance to the target, while also taking the momentary input characteristics into consideration.

5. *An operation unit* capable of carrying out the operational instructions.

6. *An input standard* (usually identical with the output standard of the preceding production unit) against which the input can be judged and a feedforward to the 'brain' unit of information about momentary deviations.

Applied to man/machine systems, this classification implies that human elements to some extent will be part of the control sequence either by performing the component tasks or by transmitting information between the components. The effectiveness of the feedback loops will therefore depend on:

1. The properties of the components.
2. The transmission of information.

Firstly, considering the qualitative aspect of pulp production, we found that, among the output criteria most relevant to process control, only degree of digestion, brightness and tearing strength were measured systematically by the laboratory technicians. Cleanliness was judged subjectively from special test sheets, but factors such as pitch and homogeneity were too expensive or difficult for regular measuring. While there were no measurements on the quality of the input chips, information about pH value and percentage of sulphur dioxide in the acid were available. The use of standards and control limits were rarely based on statistical calculations. Because of the great variances observed in some of the quality measurements of individual batches, it was difficult to reveal long-term trends in the process control. The lack of feedback on this level reduced possibilities for continuous learning and control. With some improvements, we felt that these measurements might form the basis of a temporary bonus that would make potential group goals visible to the operators. Since the measurement requirements were insufficiently met for us to bring such aspects as throughput, yield, waste or material costs directly into the experiment, we shall only note in passing that the lack of measuring devices for dry weight and moisture content of the chips in the boilers restricted further learning among the boilermen.

Secondly, in order to keep the feedback loops as short as possible, we suggest that information and decisions be brought to the lowest organizational level for meeting the requirements for skill and responsibility, also that they kept within the fewest work roles that the constraints imposed by the technology and the means communication would allow for. Hence, the well-known benefits of specialization and centralization, which tend to extend the information flows across special barriers (work roles, skill differences, levels in the organization, etc.), must be weighted not only against the obvious costs, incurred by delays and misinterpretations of the information, but also against the loss of task motivation and job satisfaction that pertain to tasks of a substantial degree of wholeness (a strong *gestalt*) and allowing the men themselves a sufficient measure of control over the materials and processes (see the second section).

As a consequence, the segregation of individual operator jobs and the division of labor among operator, laboratory technicians, cleaners, maintenance men and the supervisory levels were not necessarily optimum in terms of the total control requirements of the chemical pulp department.

A practical example of an inadequate feedback loop was test sheets showing the degree of cleanliness of the unbleached pulp, against which the screening performance was judged. These sheets were prepared by the laboratory workers about one hour after the screening of a new batch had begun. Instead of returning these sheets immediately to the screener, who could then correct the ongoing process according to the information given, the sheets were formerly sent to the foreman and some of the supervisors in other departments. Since the foreman was frequently away from his office, the feedbacks to the operators were often delayed. This is a very obvious case, because there was neither a question of the workers' ability to interpret the information embodied in the test sheets nor any doubts that the other departments would also benefit by a change in this feedback procedure. The critical factor was the speed of the feedback.

Considering the technical means of communication, it appeared that telephones were missing at some critical points and that the system of written information could be improved upon.

Finally, since it was evident that optimum conditions for control could be achieved only if the flow of information matched the technical interdependencies of the process, the actual communication network among operators was analysed before and after the experiment (see summary of analyses and results).

Program for redesign of jobs

Based on the previous analysis, it was assumed that an optimum socio-technical system in the chemical pulp department could be achieved only if:

1. The men as a group took greater reponsibility for the operation of the department as a whole.

2. They were enabled and initially encouraged to increase their understanding and control of the processes.

Consequently, increased autonomy for extended groups (across shifts) was a plausible name for the principle forming the basis of the experiment. The method of introducing change was to be step-by-step problem solving by small groups consisting of a representative from the workers, supervisors and management. Among the prerequisites for the development of partly autonomous work groups were:

1. Specification of the group's boundaries in relation to the environment (adjacent units).

2. Clarification and definition of what had to be measured in terms of quality and quantity of raw materials and services both received and delivered by the group as well as specification of quality control limits for the various criteria.

3. A proper incentive, such as a bonus, which could stimulate the groups to cooperate.

The following specific measures were to be introduced in order to support the group arrangement:

1. Training the operators to make them as far as possible qualified for all tasks within the department.

2. Allocation of a special repairman to the operator group to cope with smaller breakdowns requiring immediate attention.

3. Setting up an information center on the shop floor where measurements and other information were quickly available so that everyone would be aware of the current situation in the department. (If necessary, statistical methods would have to be employed.)

4. Arranging suitable conditions for department employees to meet in smaller or larger groups when necessary.

5. Installation of telephones in each department section.

6. Electing a group representative on each shift to facilitate communications.

The process of change

The changes suggested in the program were accepted by the management and by the majority of the workers in the department.

Gradually, but not without resistance on the part of some of the men concerned, the various measures were introduced with support from top management and from the union. In addition, operator training was linked to job rotation for the assistants, attempts were made to retrain the foremen and certain technical improvements were introduced in the bleaching. At the same time, the initiative in the socio-technical change process in the department was transferred from the research team to a project action committee (with one representative each for management, for the foremen and for the operators), then to the department management. Finally, by January 1966, with the introduction of a marginal group bonus paid on cleanliness, tearing strength, degree of digestion and brightness, the new basis for operator participation was established.

The subsequent years of 1966 and 1967 can (in terms of our dependent variable, the level of personal participation) be divided for analytical purposes into a search, a growth and a stagnation phase. Hence, abnormal variances in the timber inputs initiated a search among the men for new means of process control.

With a return to normal inputs before the summer 1966, the results of the above effects, combined with the effects of the change in job design, had made the men experience a situation that allowed them to exercise more discretion. In 1967, however, the project did not get the necessary attention from the management, which at that time had to concentrate their efforts on market problems and a technical reconstruction program. As will be seen, pulp quality reached a peak in the growth phase and thereafter stabilized at a higher level than before the experiment. Space allows only for a brief summary of the key points in the analysis and the major conclusions.

Summary of analyses and results

The experiment was designed in such a way that pulp quality as measured by the bonus would be the best single index of operator performance. It is agreed within the company that a general improvement in pulp qualities has been achieved (Table 1). This applies to the bleached pulps in particular. In line with this, the number of extremely bad batches have also been reduced during the experiment. For the majority of the individual quality variables (for each pulp), there appears to be some correspondence between quality achieved and the changes in the conditions for operator participation.

Table 1 Average quality bonus per week and per batch across all types of timber related to half-year periods of the experiment

Period	Average/week	Average/batch
First half-year	100 per cent	100 per cent
Second half-year	145 per cent	140 per cent
Third half-year	124 per cent	137 per cent
Fourth half-year	124 per cent	123 per cent

This broad picture of the bonus trend is confirmed by the more detailed breakdown on pulp qualities.

Before inferring too much from these broad indices, we had to explore whether:

1. The improved quality was achieved at excessive costs.
2. The improved quality was due to improved performance on the group level.
3. There was some evidence that the men took a greater interest in their work.
4. The improvement could have occurred without the men changing their approach to the job.
5. The men themselves perceived the new situation as favorable.

Taking these points in turn:

1. There is no evidence that quality has been achieved at the expense of an increased consumption of material resources. The major costs (fibre, yield, chemicals and machine utilization) that had shown decreasing trends before the experiment, continued to fall during the experiment (Table 2). There is, in fact, some indication that the experiment may have contributed to an increase in yield. It was agreed that manpower should be kept constant during the experiment.

Table 2 Measures of cost of various materials before and during the experiment

Materials	Nine-month period before experiment	Twelve-month period during experiment	Percentage improvement
Magnesium oxide per ton of pulp	106·0	91·0	14·0
Chlorine per ton of pulp	87·3	73·5	15·8
Sulphur dioxide per ton of pulp	128·0	123·0	3·9
Pulp yield per m³ timber	100·0	103·8	3·8

2. The improved control of pulp quality can to a large extent be ascribed to the men who as a group assumed greater responsibility.

(a) The quality development of the main product (fir pulp), which goes through all steps in the process, also the bleaching, shows a clear improvement in cleanliness and tearing strength (Table 3). At the same time, the changes in the kappa number show that the boilermen have changed their strategy from overcooking to undercooking, whereas the changes in brightness shows that the bleachers have moved from underbleaching to overbleaching (Engelstad, Emery and Thorsrud, 1969).

Table 3 Bonus as a percentage of the theoretical maximum for purity and tearing strength

Quality dimension	Type of wood	Phase		
		Search	Growth	Stagnation
Cleanliness (spots)	Fir	42	61	60
	Hardwood	45	53	53
	Spruce	3	21	10
Tearing strength	Fir	63	90	71
	Hardwood	76	96	93

The terms underbleaching and overbleaching are to be understood as relative to the given standards for kappa number and brightness, respectively. Nevertheless, these standards are arbitrary ones based on current knowledge and judgment about what would be required to achieve a given pulp quality with the available raw materials, technical equipment and labour force.

A detailed analysis of the situation revealed that the trends in pulp quality indicated could be explained only if the operators, on the basis of the new conditions established, had to some extent changed their attitudes towards the task and their way of working. From previously seeking to optimize within their own delineated work area, therefore, it appeared to be a change in orientation towards optimizing on department level, which required an increasing awareness of the technical interdependencies between the part-processes (for example, the removal of lignin in cooking and bleaching, respectively). In other words, the operators now tended to take responsibility as a group.

This conclusion was supported by measurable changes in the pattern of communications and the increased problem-solving activities in the work groups.

(b) Analysis of the communication data shows that the flows of information after the experiment match the technical inter dependencies in the process more closely than before (Engelstad, Emery and Thorsrud, 1969). At the same time, the men as a group have attained a higher level of autonomy. It also appears that the assistant operators have now become better integrated into the groups. Table 4 shows that the increased interaction in 1967 in all essentials refers to the substantial growth in inter-operator communication (+70 per cent).

(c) Concrete examples of operator participation in problem

Table 4 Number of contacts per shift before and after the experiment

Contact	1965	1967	Difference, per cent	1965, per cent	1967, per cent
Operator/operator	26·0	44·1	+70	25	34
Laboratory technician/operator	37·7	37·7	0	36	30
Foreman/operator	34·6	39·4	+14	33	31
Foreman/laboratory technician	7·6	6·7	+13	7	5
Total	105·9	127·9	+21	101	100

solving and decision making within the department during the experiments also indicate that the men have increased their capability to operate as a team.

3. The operators have, during the period of the experiment, contributed a number of suggestions for improvement of the technical equipment and the working condition in general, demonstrating an interest in the job that they previously had not shown (Table 5). At the same time, the operators have become more interested in problems of process control, timber utilization and costs.

Table 5 **Number of suggestions advanced and accepted in the operator meetings***

Date of meetings	Shifts	Acid	Boiling	Screening	Bleaching	Total
15th March 1966	3+4	5	5	11	3	24
25th March 1966 (additional)	1+2	1	9	3	3	16
August 1966	1+2+3+4	2	4	3	4	13
Total		8	18	17	10	53

* As a comparison, the company suggestion scheme had produced approximately one suggestion per year in the chemical pulp department for the period 1958–64.

4. Obviously, factors other than those included in the experimental design may have contributed to these improvements. It is unlikely, however, that the improved performance gained in the department during the experiment can be assigned to unilateral management actions (regardless of operator response) either in terms of the technical improvements introduced or in terms of the directives given. Indications of this were the lack of pressure from the men before the experiment for improvements in equipment or instrumentation and the fact that, when management's major concern in the summer 1966 turned to input costs, this had no effect on the strategies being followed by the operators in the department. As far as our evidence goes, the improved control, the increase in operator suggestions and other changes in group activities were primarily due to the voluntary efforts of the men.

5. No doubt the experiment as it developed in 1966 caused many operators to build up considerable expectations, and the feelings

of disappointment that were brought out in some of the interviews clearly refer back to the fact that the project was in 1967 only half-heartedly followed up in the department because of other priorities. Unfortunately, at this crucial point in the experiment, new measures necessary to sustain growth in the desired direction, that many had hoped for, were not introduced. In accordance with the logic of systems, it is unlikely that changes in a part will be sustained over an extended period if the changes are not reciprocated by sufficient adjustments in the total system (Angyal, 1941, pp. 243–61). Within areas where permanent learning has taken place or new technological conditions have been established, however, the socio-technical system in the department appears to have reached a new level of functioning. This applies to pulp quality, operator skill and the degree of flexibility in the shift teams.

Further developments in the company

The preconditions for a work group or department to assume the increased responsibility conveyed by a higher level of group autonomy are that (a) critical variances in the process can be brought under control, and (b) the change in job design and operator roles is sufficiently supported by adjustments in tasks and roles of the foreman and of the management. Changes in tasks and roles on department level, however, in the long run require adjustments on company level as well. In practice, this implies that the new principles of job design must be integrated into the objectives, policy and style of management, to guide the activities at all levels in the organization. In principle, a part of a system influences other parts only through its effects on the total system.

Accordingly, during the autumn of 1966 and the spring of 1967, experiences from the chemical pulp department produced discussions of company policies among the top management. It was decided to follow up the project within the company with a new experiment in the papermill, where a team of operators would run two of the papermachines without shift foremen. The changes in job design that were introduced in 1968 have otherwise mainly corresponded to those in the chemical pulp department, but the initiative in the change process has consistently been carried by the parties concerned through a temporary project action committee. The first six months' agreement about experimentation was extended for another six months. Nine months after the jobs had been redesigned, one could ascertain definite growth in commitment to the new way of working among operators and management. The operating team had then showed that they were able to utilize their machinery in a very flexible way, even without shift supervision, and the productivity trend proved very satisfactory.

Finally, by 1969, the company had decided on a three-year plan for redesigning the organization that will include:

1. Comprehensive operator training for multiple skills and increased technical insight.

2. Doing away with shift supervision of the old type. (By 1964, it had been an explicit policy to strengthen the hand of the foreman.)

3. The introduction of a management philosophy that encourages local problem-solving activities.

In particular, on the basis of what we have seen in the fourth field experiment at Norsk Hydro, we believe that this way of working will lead to a self-sustaining learning process that will improve the reliability of the human component in the process of control as a whole.

Appendix 1
Psychological job requirements

1. The need for the content of a job to be reasonably demanding in terms other than sheer endurance, yet providing a minimum of variety (not necessarily novelty).

2. The need for being able to learn on the job (which implies standards and knowledge of results) and go on learning. Again, it is a question of neither too much nor too little.

3. The need for some minimum area of decision-making that the individual can call his own.

4. The need for some minimum degree of social support and recognition in the work place.

5. The need to be able to relate what one does and what one produces to one's social life.

6. The need to feel that the job leads to some sort of desirable future.

Appendix 2

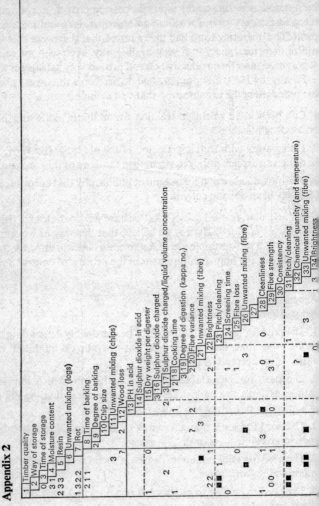

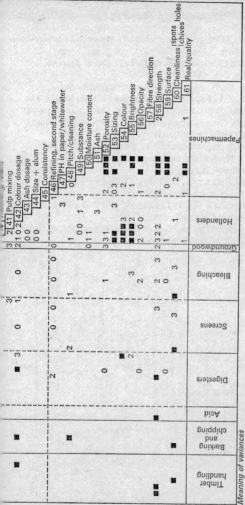

Meaning of variances
0- of theoretical interest only
1- of little practical importance
2- of medium practical importance
3- of great practical importance

Matrix of variances

References

ANGYAL, A. (1941), *Foundations for a Science of Personality*, Harvard University Press.

BOX, G. E. P. (1957), 'Evolutionary operation – a method for increasing industrial productivity', *Applied Statistics*, vol. 6, no. 1, pp. 3–22.

EMERY, F. E. (1959), *Characteristics of Socio-Technical Systems*, Tavistock Institute, doc. 527.

EMERY, F. E. (ed.) (1969), *Systems Thinking*, Penguin Books.

ENGELSTAD, P. H., EMERY, F. E., and THORSRUD, E. (1969), *The Hunsfos Experiment*, Work Research Institute, Oslo, mimeographed.

GUEST, R. H. (1957), 'Job enlargement: a revolution in job design', *Personnel Administration*, vol. 20, March/April, pp. 12–15.

HERBST, P. G. (1962), *Autonomised Group Functioning*, Tavistock.

RICE, A. K. (1958), *Productivity and Social Organization: The Ahmedabad Experiment*, Tavistock.

THORSRUD, E., and EMERY, F. E. (1969), *Mot on ny bedriftsorganisasjon*, Tanum, Forlag, Oslo.

TRIST, E. L., HIGGIN, G. W., MURRAY, H., and POLLACK, A. B. (1963), *Organisational Choice*, Tavistock.

WALKER, C. M. (1950), 'The problem of the repetitive job', *Harvard Business Review*, vol. 28, no. 3, pp. 54–8.

24 Gerald I. Susman

The Impact of Automation on Work Group Autonomy and Task Specialization

G. I. Susman, 'The impact of automation on work group autonomy and task specialization', *Human Relations*, vol. 23, 1970, pp. 567–77.

One consequence of increased automation is its effect on the patterns of interaction among workers. While some types of automation lead to decreased interaction among workers (Faunce, 1958), other types, namely continuous process production, appear to lead to an increase in interaction. Several writers have pointed out that the integration of many machine processes into larger units creates, at times, the need for a number of workers to be in frequent contact (Crossman, 1960; Blauner, 1964). One such group is composed of workers whose primary responsibility is the continued operation of an automated flow-process. It is about such groups that this paper is concerned. What will be discussed is the effect of changes in interaction patterns created by automation on the rigid job descriptions and evaluation schemes that have traditionally characterized industrial work.

In non-automated settings, tasks have been traditionally assigned by formal job description. This was possible for at least two reasons. Tasks could be broken down and assigned on the basis of the discrete sensorimotor and manipulative skills necessary to perform them. Secondly, the work-in-process between two job assignments could be temporally and spatially separated and regulated. As different jobs required varying degrees of training and education for satisfactory performance, evaluation schemes designed for each job arose as bases for rewarding superior performance and for allocating organization rewards. Training and skill differences provided the basis for differences in pay, differences in discretion over the use of organization resources and in opportunities for advancement to higher positions.

However, in continuous flow production, the skills of an operator are observational and interpretive rather than sensorimotor and manipulative (Crossman, 1960). Furthermore, his interdependence with team members, supervisors and staff is based on the need for rapid information exchange rather than exchange of materials. The newly created requirements are not readily divisible into discrete activities. The primary requirements are to interpret stimuli, make adjustments, and when appropriate provide relevant information. This is a continual process and a team member is assigned 'responsibility' to maintain his contribution as an integral part of an information-regulation feedback process. This new role for the operator has created demands for which rigid job descriptions become a hindrance to the effective and efficient accomplishment of work. The reasons for this will be discussed below. Davis (1962) has commented that rigid job descriptions have hampered the development of job assignments to suit the new automation. He predicted that one of the persistent problems confronting labor and management will be the need to consider new agreements which permit increased freedom of assignment.

The following section will provide a framework for discussing the requirements for effective operator performance and for work group structure in continuous flow production. Propositions are presented which follow from the framework. A field study is then presented with data to support the propositions.

Open systems and environmental uncertainty

In this paper the work group is treated as a member of a class of open systems (see Von Bertallanfy, 1956). Models of open systems have been formulated and tested at many different levels of analysis and considerable knowledge has accumulated concerning the properties they exhibit (see Miller, 1963). By treating the small group as an open system, knowledge about systems of this type can be utilized to understand the behavior of industrial work groups. An open system, as opposed to a closed one, is in dynamic interaction with its environment. Elements in the environment can pass through system boundaries and interact with elements of the system itself. If technology is conceptualized as contributing to conditions present in the work group environment, then increased automation will very likely alter these conditions. Thus, propositions which relate environmental properties to organization structure can be applied to predict the specific impact which automation has on the work group.

In several of the manufacturing industries where automation, at present, has reached its most advanced stage, a small group of three to five members is responsible for the operation of an integrated set of process equipment and machinery. This manufacturing process is controlled by a closed-loop negative feedback which is more or less self-correcting. The men responsible for the operation of the equipment generally monitor a control panel to ensure that relevant machine variables do not exceed acceptable limits. This monitoring requires being alert to relevant cues and then to intervene at specific points when necessary. While the *total set* of activities which are to be performed by the work group are fairly well defined and routinized, the occasion for the performance of any *particular* activity depends on machine stimuli whose time of occurrence is highly uncertain.

On the basis of the preceding formulation, the work group can be conceived as a system whose environment consists of inputs which cross its boundary and whose occurrence in time is subject to high uncertainty. This conception of a group and its environment coincides with models found in the organization literature (March and Simon, 1958; Thompson, 1967). Propositions derived from these models are presented below which predict the manner in which an open system adapts to environmental uncertainty.

Uncertainty and autonomy

If a work group is assigned responsibility for a set of intervention points and these points are allocated to the members of the group in some manner, then the environmental uncertainty described above results in each member's task-relevant behavior being contingent upon the task-relevant behavior of the others, or in other words, being reciprocally interdependent.

Thompson (1967) presents the following propositions concerning reciprocal interdependence:

Proposition 1

Organizations seek to place reciprocally interdependent positions tangent to one another in a common group which is (a) local and (b) conditionally autonomous (p. 58).

Reciprocal interdependence requires frequent communication in order to coordinate efficiently and effectively. The costs involved in transferring the output of one member to another increase rapidly the longer the distance and the greater the frequency with which it must occur. Organizations, thus, tend to localize the interdependence within the smallest possible groups. Furthermore, since communication is less expensive by mutual adjustment among the members than by coordination at higher organization levels, the work group tends to be conditionally autonomous.

Proposition 1 is consistent with the theorizing and empirical findings of various researchers. Blauner (1964), for example, found that in the chemical and oil refining industries where automation is highly advanced, work groups reported greater autonomy in the manner in which they performed their tasks. Strauss (1963) and Whyte (1969) prescribe decentralization under situations where (a) subordinates are required to make novel decisions to meet rapidly changing situations, and (b) where it is relatively easy to measure whether a goal has been reached. March and Simon (1958) state the specification of quantity and quality of output as opposed to specification of activities is more likely when (a) the activity pattern is difficult to observe and supervise, (b) the quantity and quality of output are easily observed and supervised, (c) ... the relations between activity patterns and output are highly variable depending on circumstances of the individual situation that are better known to operatives than to supervisors and specialists.

Uncertainty and specialization

March and Simon (1958) discuss specialization within the context of environmental variability. They present the following propositions:

Proposition 2

The greater the specialization by sub-program, the greater the interdependence among organization sub-units (p. 159).

Proposition 3

The greater the elements of variability and contingency, the greater is the burden of coordinating activities that are specialized by process (p. 159).

Proposition 4

Process specialization will be carried furthest in stable environments and that under rapidly changing circumstances specialization will be sacrificed to secure greater self-containment of separate programs (p. 159).

If the terms used in these propositions are translated to apply at the level of the work group, then certain implications follow concerning the effects of automation on group structure. Specifically, under conditions of uncertainty, the efficiency derived from specialization is outweighed by the increased effectiveness of the multi-skilled worker. Rapid local adjustment to unexpected contingencies is hindered by rigid job descriptions which specify that only certain tasks are to be performed by the occupant of that position. Suppose, for example, a worker leaves the premises for a moment or is engaged in a particular activity. If the need for a specific action is required, too much time would be wasted if there were frequent jurisdictional problems over job boundaries. As such, it may be necessary to have the most available worker make the adjustment.

If the foregoing interpretation is correct, then it can be hypothesized that work groups which operate under the conditions of uncertainty described above will be found which are (a) conditionally autonomous, (b) consist of workers who are multi-skilled. The empirical existence of such groups under the stated conditions requires either (a) that the managements of technologically relevant firms explicitly recognize the advantages that multi-skilled, semi-autonomous groups have over alternative arrangements and organize them that way, or (b) that lacking explicit constraints to the contrary, these arrangements are allowed to develop informally. This arrangement which is a response to the task requirements is tacitly accepted by the first line supervision and operators. It is the latter of the two situations which is the setting for the field study reported below.

The field study
The research site

The research site selected was a small oil refinery in Southern California. An oil refinery was chosen because its technology has, almost from inception, possessed attributes of the highest stages of automation. Furthermore, Blauner (1964), in a study of oil and chemical workers, reports that workers find one source of satisfaction in the variety and novelty in the events of a particular work day. The pattern of work activity described for the oil refinery by Blauner is characteristic of one which would exist under temporal uncertainty of task activating stimuli. It is this property which is hypothesized to exist for most monitoring-type job assignments. Hopefully, the findings from this industry can be generalized to other industries which employ or are likely to employ in the near future highly automated process equipment.

The research population

This investigation is concerned with the activities of thirteen groups of three men each. While there is considerable overlap in membership due to the system of rotation used, a work group is considered a different unit of analysis when at least one of its three members changes.

A work group is composed of one stillman and two stillman helpers. These men work a twenty-four-hour, seven-day-a-week schedule. Each man works five days straight, has two days off, and then rotates to a new shift. The schedule is arranged so that the stillman's five days of work overlap the schedule of two stillman helpers. As a result, each stillman helper works three days with one stillman and two days with another. The total number of work groups created by this rotation system is thirteen.

Initial observations

The first clue that some degree of task allocation autonomy existed in the work groups was provided by the president of the company. In the initial interview the researcher asked the president for a list of job descriptions. The president said he could provide these, but that they were not rigidly adhered to. He said that he preferred that job descriptions remain flexible. It was explained that rigid job descriptions would discourage the workers' initiative to perform tasks that arose outside their formal job descriptions.

On the basis of field observations over the next few weeks, it appeared that in each work group the members were performing tasks that were not formally assigned to them. In addition, the tasks which were allocated were not the same for each work group member when he rotated into another group. It was decided that more careful data should be collected. A questionnaire was devised by which the allocations which were taking place in each work group could be identified.

Development of the work groups' task domain

A procedure was developed to determine the total set of tasks which the work group, as a whole, must perform. The group members were observed for eight-hour shifts at a time, and inquiries were made about activities as they were being performed. From the responses given to the researcher, a procedure for organizing this information was developed. Symbols were designated for decisions, activities and for task assignment.

A first draft of the diagram was mimeographed and handed out to the workers. An explanation of all symbols was included. They were requested to make any corrections in the diagram they thought necessary and then to return it. This procedure was repeated until the total set of decisions and activities was complete and no additional corrections were needed. As defined by the procedure, the total number of tasks for which each group is responsible is forty-four. A task is considered a complete unit if the activities which make it up are started and totally performed by the same man.

Task allocation

A questionnaire was constructed with the forty-four tasks listed in columns. Down the rows were listed the two other members with whom the respondent worked in at least one other work group. The respondent was requested to place a number (1–5) in the appropriate box which best represented the frequency with which he carried out a task when working in the group under consideration. The five point scale ranged from 'always performed' to 'never performed'. For the purpose to which the data would be put, it was decided that the scale of frequency would be dichotomized between not performed (responses 1 and 2) and performed (responses 3, 4 and 5).[1]

The questionnaire was administered to both management and workers. Management was requested to fill out the task allocations

1. 1 = never; 2 = seldom; 3 = occasionally; 4 = quite often; 5 = always.

Table 1 Discrepancies between formal task allocations and reported task allocations

	Number of not-assigned-performed tasks			Number of assigned-not-performed tasks
	O	O+O+QO QO		S+ NP +A
GR 1				
S1	7	11	12	1
H1	6	12	13	0
H2	1	1	2	3
GR 2				
S1	7	11	12	1
H1	5	12	12	0
H3	4	5	6	1
GR 3				
S1	7	11	12	1
H4	5	10	10	4
H3	4	5	6	6
GR 4				
S2	5	8	9	3
H5	2	2	2	1
H6	0	13	17	4
GR 5				
S2	5	8	9	3
H5	2	2	2	1
H2	1	1	2	3
GR 6				
S2	5	8	9	3
H1	5	12	12	0
H2	1	1	2	3
GR 7				
S3	2	5	6	0
H5	2	2	2	1
H6	0	12	17	4
GR 8				
S3	1	5	6	0
H7	7	13	13	1
H6	6	10	10	0
GR 9				
S3	2	5	6	0
H7	7	13	13	1
H8	6	10	10	0

GR 10				
S4	2	4	4	1
H7	4	9	10	1
H8	3	7	7	0

GR 13				
S5	11	11	11	3
H4	3	8	8	4
H3	2	2	3	6

GR 11				
S4	2	4	4	1
H9	9	11	11	2
H8	3	7	7	0

GR 12				
S4	2	4	4	1
H9	9	11	11	2
H4	3	8	8	3

O = occasionally   A = always   NP = never performed   QO = quite often   S = seldom which were formally assigned by official job description. The data from management were compared with those of group members.

Management's formal task allocation

The formal assignment of tasks, as reported by supervisory personnel, can be summarized as follows: stillmen were assigned to control board activities such as interpreting gauges and dials. They were to make adjustments as necessary in temperature, pressure and flow rates. They were also assigned to inspect certain equipment both inside and immediately outside the control room. Stillman helpers were assigned to tasks which required mobility in and around the physical plant. Their assigned tasks generally required some physical exertion such as ladder climbing and were more routine. Activities included valve turns, recording meter readings, performing routine quality tests and taking samples to the testing lab. The formal assignments could roughly be grouped so that stillmen assignments were more mental than physical, while the reverse was true for stillman helpers. For many of the stillman's cognitive activities, stillman helpers can be viewed, to use a somatic analogy, as skeletal-muscular extensions of them.

Job description and actual task allocation

Through field observation and informal interviews with both workers and management, it appeared that a discrepancy existed between management's formal task allocation and the allocations which took place within each work group. Table 1 presents data from the questionnaire which substantiate this observation and clarify the extent to which it takes place.

The data were derived by comparing management's reported formal allocation with workers' reported frequency of task performance. There are thirteen three-man groups. A stillman, S, and a stillman helper, H, are identified by an appropriate subscript. The number of tasks which are not in the formal job description but are, in fact, performed is presented in cumulative fashion in the first three columns after identification of a stillman or stillman helper. The number of tasks which are in the formal job description, but are never or seldom performed, is presented in the fourth column. These data provide confirmation of initial field observations that a discrepancy exists between management's formal task allocation and those taking place by workers. There are no groups in which the membership report perfect agreement with management's formal assignment. For stillmen, the number of not-assigned-performed tasks ranges from four to twelve. For stillman helpers the range is from two to seventeen.

In general, it appears that there is a tendency for a worker to have a task domain which is larger than is formally assigned. For both stillmen and stillman helpers the number of not-assigned-performed tasks is, with two exceptions, higher than the opposite category, assigned-not-performed.

These data support the hypothesis that in work groups of this type members are allowed conditional autonomy. However, these findings are necessary but not sufficient evidence of autonomy. In further support, it is noted that the data for management were collected from the level closest to the work groups. These personnel would be the most likely to make task assignments if such an arrangement existed. They reported in interviews, however, that they do not assign tasks and, in fact, would run into strong resistance if this were actually attempted.

Task allocation and redundance

Proposition 4 states that organizations whose environments are uncertain require the sacrifice of some specialization in order to reduce the difficulties of coordinating highly interdependent sub-units. For a work group whose environment consists of the un-certain temporal occurrence of stimuli to elicit task relevant behavior, effective performance requires that the task domain of each worker has some redundancy.

Table 2 presents data on the number of tasks which are reported as being performed by *all three members* of a work group.

Column 2 presents the number of tasks, out of the possible total of forty-four, for which all three group members report their frequency of performance as at least 'occasionally'. The third column presents the same category of tasks but applies the stricter performance criterion of at least 'quite often'. In the fourth column, the task identification numbers are presented in parentheses to demonstrate that different tasks are being reported as performed by all three group members.

These data provide support for Proposition 4. In these work

Table 2 Task domain redundancy

Group number	Number of tasks which all three members report as performed O, QO or A	QO or A	Task number	Group number	Number of tasks which all three members report as performed O, QO or A	QO or A	Task number
1	10	2	(6, 26)	8	18	5	(16, 17, 20, 24, 44)
2	12	2	(13, 41)	9	16	4	(15, 16, 20, 41)
3	10	1	(13, 41)	11	9	1	(16)
4	9	2	(2, 33)	12	10	1	(33)
5	8	3	(2, 5, 29)	13	10	1	(13)
6	8	3	(2, 5, 19)		13	1	(41)
7	10	3	(10, 13, 33)				

O = occasionally   A = always   QO = quite often

groups which are permitted the opportunity to allocate their own tasks, the tendency is to move away from the formal assignment to a condition where some redundancy exists. It was noted by the researcher that the tasks with performance redundancy were not with any regularity those formally assigned to stillmen or stillman helpers.

Discussion

The conditions under which these data were collected require that conclusions remain tentative. The data were originally collected to test a theory of status congruence (see Susman, 1970). As such, certain variables could not be controlled which are relevant to a test of the hypotheses (a and b above). While these data are consistent with and provide support for the hypotheses, it will be necessary to re-test at new research sites before firmer conclusions are drawn.

If these hypotheses continue to be supported, certain implications follow for the structuring of work groups under increased automation. To understand these implications, however, it is necessary to discuss the nature and level of skills required in automated technologies. It has been pointed out that except for the transition years during which there would be a bi-polarization of skill levels (machine tenders and feeders vs. operators), automation would result in a leveling of skill differences between job classifications (Fine, 1964; Faunce, 1968). While the absolute level of skills for those who remain in automated jobs is likely to increase, Faunce points out that 'the task of monitoring a panel of lights and gauges is basically the same, irrespective of the part of the production process involved or the types of end product being produced' (p. 163). Several case studies have shown that the elimination and re-combination of tasks in automated plants result in a decrease in the number of separate job classifications (Walker, 1957; Mann and Hoffman, 1960). Blauner (1964) concludes that 'continuous process technology . . . reverses the historic trend toward greater division of labor and specialization' (p. 143).

Another consequence of increased automation is that the interdependence between members makes it exceedingly difficult, if not impossible, to measure individual contributions to greater quality and quantity of product. This is particularly so when the product is measured by volume rather than by discrete units. All team members make a contribution to the continuation of the process. If one member fails in his responsibilities, all other team members' performances may be affected. This situation prevents separate job evaluation schemes from being very effective. Group evaluation schemes would appear to be a more effective means to measure performance.

It is suggested that differentiated formal positions in autonomous work groups may have negative consequences for work group performance. The data collected to test the status congruence hypothesis are instructive of this point. A questionnaire was administered to management and workers which requested a judgment of the skill required to perform adequately each of the forty-four tasks assigned to a work group. While respondents frequently expressed the opinion that none of the tasks required very much judgment and learning time was short, they could express an opinion of relative skill when asked. A five point scale of judged skill was used to rate each task. These judgments were combined in an index to determine the skill level of the set of tasks each worker reported he performed.

When data were correlated with peer judgments of status, the relationship between status and the index of task skill was positive for stillman and negative for stillman helpers. For stillmen, who, as a group, expressed in interviews a high degree of identification with company objectives, it was consistent that those with high status would be more likely to perform high skilled tasks. For stillman helpers, the negative relationship was interpreted to mean that when they were accorded high status they tended to perform simple tasks in order to have more time to engage in more valued activities. On the basis of field observations and interviews these more valued activities were found to be social affiliative ones.

The data concerning status congruence have been interpreted to mean that occupying a lower position in these work groups is related to less identification with managerial objectives.[2] This is

2 It should be pointed out that the much less average seniority of stillman helpers (12·3 years vs. 4·0 years) could also contribute to less identification with company objectives. However, lack of challenging work is probably a more important influence. Four years should be sufficient time for company identification – if it is going to occur at all – to become established.

evidenced by the manner in which tasks are allocated by stillman helpers. At this plant and in automated plants generally, management tries to hire personnel who have completed high school. It is generally admitted by management that high school graduation is not required for entry level jobs like stillman helpers. However, it is a hiring criterion because with promotion based primarily on seniority, stillman helpers will someday move up to the stillman position. While such hiring practices allow management to have a reserve of employees to fill vacant stillmen positions, those who are currently stillman helpers are assigned activities with little opportunity to test one's abilities and skills. Such a conclusion is an affirmative statement consistent with research findings of an inverse relationship between rank of occupation and intrinsic job satisfaction (Argyris, 1964; Gurin et al., 1960; Inkeles, 1960).

It is suggested that if group members have an equal opportunity to engage in all the tasks available, the lack of motivation among lower position occupants might be eliminated. Equal opportunity to perform all tasks is economically permissible if all work group members receive adequate training for all tasks. The refining superintendent and several group members expressed the opinion that of the tasks assigned even those requiring the most skill could be learned within a two-year period. The stillman helper with the least seniority had been there longer than that. It can be concluded that formal position differentiation in work groups of this type results in keeping those in the lower formal positions underskilled and this creates a loss of potential work group and company resources.

March and Simon (1958) have written that under conditions where activity is contingent upon events in the external environment, 'specific activities are not assigned to departments, but conditional responsibility for performance' (p. 27). They specify that responsibility will likely be assigned by time periods, 'not (to) exceed a day's work' (p. 27). This is the arrangement tacitly accepted by supervisors and workers at the refinery studied. Responsibility for the continued operation of the process equipment is what is required of workers during an eight-hour shift. The essential data which supervisors use for control purposes are volume of throughput and the breakdown of crude oil into desired percentages of products.

A more formal recognition of assignment by group responsibility rather than by specific task assignments may have the effect of making the work group itself a more effective source of work discipline. According to Blauner (1964) men perform up to standards because they do not want to let down their workmates (p. 179). This inner direction of work group behavior makes an elaborate system of external controls through rules and supervision unnecessary in the same way as do the internalized norms of workmanship in the professions and craft occupations.

References

ARGYRIS, C. (1964), *Integrating the Individual and the Organization*, Wiley.

BLAUNER, R. (1964), *Alienation and Freedom*, University of Chicago Press.

BRIGHT, J. R. (1958), 'Does automation raise skill requirements?', *Harvard Business Review*, vol. 36, July/August, p. 85.

CROSSMAN, E. R. F. W. (1960), *Automation and Skill*, Department of Scientific and Industrial Research, London.

DAVIS, L. E. (1962), 'The effects of automation on job design', *Industrial Relations*, vol. 2, no. 1.

FAUNCE, W. A. (1958), 'Automation in the automobile industry; some consequences for in-plant social structure', *American Sociological Review*, vol. 23, pp. 401–7.

FAUNCE, W. A. (1968), *Problems of an Industrial Society*, McGraw-Hill.

FINE, S. A. (1964), 'The nature of automated jobs and their educational and training requirements', *Human Science Research, Inc.*

GURIN, G., VEROFF, J., FELD, S. (1960), *Americans View Their Mental Health*, Basic Books.

INKELES, A. (1960), 'Industrial man; the relation of status to experience, perception and values', *American Journal of Sociology*, vol. 66, no. 1, pp. 1–31.

MANN, F. C., and HOFFMAN, L. R. (1960), *Automation and the Worker*, Holt, Rinehart & Winston.

MARCH, J. G., and SIMON, H. A. (1958), *Organizations*, Wiley.

MILLER, J. G. (1963), 'Living systems: basic concepts', *Behavioral Science*, pp. 193–237.

STRAUSS, G. (1963), 'Some notes on power equalization', in H. J. Leavitt (ed.), *Social Science Approaches to Organization*, Prentice-Hall.

SUSMAN, G. I. (1970), 'The concept of status congruence as a basis to predict task allocations in autonomous work groups', *Administrative Science Quarterly*, vol. 15, no. 2, pp. 164–75.

THOMPSON, J. D. (1967), *Organizations in Action*, McGraw-Hill.

Von Bertallanfy, L. (1956), 'General systems theory', *General Systems*, vol. 1, pp. 1–10.

Walker, C. R. (1957), *Toward the Automatic Factory*, Yale University Press.

Whyte, W. H. (1969), *Organizational Behavior: Theory and Application*, Irwin.

25 Jon Gulowsen

A Measure of Work-Group Autonomy

Excerpts from J. Gulowsen, *Selvstyrte Arbeidsgrupper*, (Autonomous Work Groups), Tanum Press, 1971, Oslo; translated by author.

The background of the investigation

When social scientists entered the Norwegian debate on industrial democracy, one of their first conclusions was that the kind of influence that employees could get through representation on the boards of directors of companies would not, in itself, change the quality of working life significantly for the ordinary worker. Emery and Thorsrud (1969) argued that the basis of participation should permit every employee to develop himself through his work and to take on responsibility. Other kinds of participation would be of little importance if this process did not occur.

Having reached this conclusion, the researchers began looking for job designs and work organizations making it more likely that human resources could develop in industry. The issue of autonomous work-groups soon arose. The Tavistock Institute, London, had reported experiments in the British coal mines, where the workers had organized themselves into composite workgroups and taken responsibility for production (Herbst, 1962; Trist *et al.*, 1963).

This form of work organization had positive consequences for the workers' self-development, for general satisfaction in the workplace, and for productivity. The findings in the coal mines were backed up by results from the United States (Davis, 1966) and India (Rice, 1958).

In fact, the miners and the other workers studied had developed ways of work organization that illustrated what democracy in the work-place might look like. With this as background, a team working at the Norwegian Work Research Institutes concentrated its attention on the concept of autonomous work-groups. The

eam started experiments in industrial plants where it tried to set
p autonomous work-groups. At the same time, the team studied
xisting work-groups that were autonomous in some respects.
he investigation considered the following questions:

. Are there any structural dependencies between areas where
ork-groups can have autonomy and where they cannot?

. What conditions must be satisfied if groups are to have auton-
my? The research team was primarily interested in conditions
mposed by technology, geography, wage systems, and local cul-
ure.

. Is the idea of autonomous work-groups in harmony with Nor-
egian work culture? It was assumed that ways of work contrary
o local customs probably could never obtain any significant diffu-
ion in industry.

his article will only treat the first issue, the others having been re-
orted elsewhere (Gulowsen, 1971).

No precise conceptual framework had been formulated when
he case studies were made. However, the choice of case studies
as not made completely without guidelines. The research team
hose to study groups with some kind of joint payment, and in
ome cases, groups having a composite work organization, since
t was believed that these factors contributed to the emergence of
ork-group autonomy.

Some central variables, such as group size and working relation-
hips within the groups, were not treated in this study. Neither
ere power relations in the organization and competence among
he group members. Furthermore, all the groups operated within
omparatively simple technologies, where innovations were not
articularly dramatic. Finally, the empirical material includes only
ight case studies, of which only four were performed by the
uthor. For these reasons, this study should be regarded as
ndicative rather than definitive.

Criteria of autonomy

he criteria of autonomy were developed on a theoretical basis
ndependent of, but following the collection of, the data for all
he case studies. The criteria were not based on the empirical
naterial in the cases, but were concerned with the 'what, where,

when, who, and how', of the groups' functions. Excluded were decisions regarding determination of norms, policy and doctrines, although such decisions would have central importance, e.g. in religious or political groups. Under these restrictions, the following criteria of autonomy were developed:

1. *The group can influence the formulation of its goals, including:*
   (a) *qualitative aspects* (in other words, what the group shall produce), *and*
   (b) *quantitative aspects.* Included in the quantitative aspects of production are two issues. The first is the influence of the group on production volume; the second is the influence of the group on the terms of payment and other sanctions: e.g. through direct negotiations between the group and the company management. It is suggested that Criterion 1(b) is satisfied only if the group can influence both issues. This presupposes that both parties enter into negotiations on equal terms.

2. *Provided that established goals governing relationships to the superordinate system are satisfied, the group can govern its own performance in the following ways:*
   (a) *The group can decide where to work.* This criterion is relevant only if it is possible to move both raw materials, means of production, and products; therefore, a social scientist, for example, has possibilities for autonomy that are excluded for a coal miner. None of the case studies covered here can be measured against this criterion.
   (b) *The group can decide when to work.* This criterion includes two issues. The first concerns the timing of different tasks, which is in fact a question of plans and methods and will be treated under Criterion 3. The second concerns the limitation of working hours. It is suggested that Criterion 2b is satisfied in any one of the following cases:
     (i) if the group can limit working hours for the group as a whole
     (ii) if the group can decide whether any of its members may leave work during the regular working hours;
     (iii) if the group decides if and when its members may work overtime.
   (c) *The group can decide which other activities it wishes to engage in.* This criterion is satisfied if the work-group can leave work or

take breaks on its own recognizance. It is also satisfied if the group members may do personal work or other tasks as long as they have satisfied the established goals of production.

3. The group makes the necessary decisions in connection with the choice of the production method. (Whether or not the individual worker may decide on his own work methods is a question of individual autonomy and is dealt with in Criterion 7.) It is suggested that Criterion 3 is satisfied if the work-group has total responsibility for the means of production, and the environment only performs boundary control. The simplest way to operationalize this criterion is as follows:

    (a) there exist obvious alternative methods;
    (b) outsiders do not interfere in the choice of method.
    The criterion is irrelevant if (a) is not satisfied.

4. The group makes its own internal distribution of tasks. As was the case for Criterion 3, this criterion is satisfied if:

    (a) there exist alternative task distributions (technological constraints and formal requirements may limit the possibilities);
    (b) outsiders do not interfere in the decision process.
    The criterion is irrelevant if (a) is not satisfied.

5. The group decides on its own membership. Three important categories of choice are possible:

    (a) the group selects and appoints new members;
    (b) the group expels unwanted members;
    (c) management chooses members, and the group has no means of sanctioning the choice.

It is suggested that the criterion is satisfied if either (a) or (b) describes the procedure. Whether the decisions are made in plenum or, e.g. by a local shop steward, is unimportant in this context.

6. The group makes its own decisions with respect to two crucial matters of leadership:

    (a) *The group decides whether it wants to have a leader with respect to internal questions, and – if it does – who this leader shall be.*
    (b) *The group decides whether it wants a leader for the purpose of regulating boundary conditions, and – if it does – who this leader shall be.*

Criteria 6a and 6b are operational in their existing format, and referred tests of satisfaction are not necessary.

Criteria 1–6 concern decisions on the group level. But there are also other kinds of decisions within work-groups. The individual worker can to some extent make decisions that concern himself and his own work situation. Therefore, the concept of autonomy is also relevant at the level of the individual. Particularly with respect to the choice of production methods, it is convenient to distinguish between the level of the individual and the level of the work-group. It therefore seems useful to add a seventh criterion of autonomy, although this one cannot be immediately compared with the others:

7. *The group members decide how the work operations shall be performed.* There are three important possibilities:

   (a) The worker determines his own method; the criterion is satisfied.

   (b) Some other person – for instance, a foreman or planner – decides; the criterion is not satisfied.

   (c) Technology leaves no important choices. This situation was well illustrated by Charles Chaplin in *Modern Times*. In this case, the criterion is considered to be irrelevant.

The case studies

The empirical material includes case studies of eight work-groups. Four of the case studies were performed by the author. The other four have been described in previous literature: the coal mining group (Herbst, 1962), two groups of lime-workers (Hegland and Nylehn, 1968), and the groups in an electrical panel-heater production department (Ødegaard, 1967; Qvale, 1968). Detailed treatment is given here only of those groups not described fully in other sources. The groups are considered in the order of their respective autonomy, as revealed by subsequent analysis.

The logging group

Together with the introduction of new and highly mechanized equipment in 1962, a new type of organization was established for a five-man logging crew at Meråker Brug. The group consisted of three *loggers* equipped with motorsaws and axes. Their job was to fell trees and remove their branches. Further, there was a *driver* who used a specialized tractor equipped with a powerful winch.

The tractor, which could penetrate almost any kind of terrain, collected from eight to twenty logs at a time with the winch and a cable, and pulled them from the cutting area to the production area. The fifth man in the group, the *cutter*, worked in the production area cutting logs to proper lengths. He sorted out the different sizes and placed them in different stacks using a motorsaw and a tractor with stacking equipment.

The logging crew worked in areas which are distant (two to five miles) from Meråker and quite separated from other crews. The cutting areas where the group worked were usually so large that the distance between the members of the group prevented co-operation with each other. The only exception was that the driver periodically had contact with each of the workers. However, the group had lunch together and travelled to and from work together.

The group was responsible to a forest inspector and a forest guard, who were both responsible for much larger areas. Thus, they had contact with the group only a few times a week. However, these were the two who determined the extent of the cutting areas for the group. The boundaries were always clear, and it was never difficult for the group to decide which trees to cut.

The group was paid at a joint piece-rate which was equally shared. The payment calculations were based on the quantity of timber cut of different qualities and the price per cubic foot of each quality. The piece-rates were negotiated beforehand between the group and the management. The quantity of the production was measured by officially appointed persons. These people measured the size of the logs after they were cut and sorted in the production area.

There were always negotiations about the payment terms before the group started working in a particular area. The results of these negotiations were valid as a contract between the group and the management as long as the group worked within the given area. This period usually lasted from five to seven weeks. The rates of payment within an area were primarily dependent on the quality of the forest and how well the ground was suited for transport of timber. When working conditions changed abruptly and unexpectedly while the group was in an area (for instance after an early or heavy snowfall), new negotiations were started to develop a fair pay-rate for the group.

This group never formally or informally appointed a leader; group members, therefore, usually acted jointly during the payment negotiations. It only happened once that the group and management could not agree on terms. Their respective unions then took over the negotiations and found an agreement acceptable to both parties.

Although the logging crew consisted of workers with clearly defined and non-overlapping tasks, it was still almost completely autonomous. When at work, it was almost totally independent of the management. Every man knew his job, and the management never interfered with the work. For example, the workers themselves decided whether to cut off branches with axe or motorsaw, and how best to transport the logs from the cutting area to the central area. Finally the group carried out an important change in work method without consulting the management, gathering felled trees in the cutting area in a more comfortable, but less efficient, way than that originally planned.

The group determined its own working hours. Management kept no records of working hours or absence, and the workers themselves decided when to start and when to finish work. As an example of their autonomy, the group ceased to work on Saturdays without asking management.

The group also had influence over its own composition. When the group originally started to work in 1962, all the candidates were asked if they were willing to accept the new kind of work organization. Each time new employees were engaged, management first selected a candidate, and then the group members were asked if they were willing to accept him. One of the reasons why this worked is possibly that Meråker is a comparatively small community. Therefore the group members were likely to know the different qualities of a candidate, and were able to judge whether he would fit into the group or not.

There is one factor that must not be overlooked when we try to understand what made the group so autonomous. Probably the most important reason is that loggers have by tradition been accustomed to autonomous work. Formerly, a logger often worked alone all day, and his work consisted of more operations than the work of any of the men in the group at Meråker. As a result, the loggers seem to have less autonomy and less composite jobs when they work in the group than they had had when each worked alone. Autonomy, thus, to some extent, was moved from the individual to the group, and the technological changes made the different tasks less differentiated.

The coal-mining group and the electrical panel-heater group

The study in the coal mines was made in England in the early 1950s (see Herbst, 1962). The group in the electrical panel-heater department is much more recent (1967–68), and reflects the experience of a group established in close cooperation with the research workers in the Norwegian participation experiment (Ødegaard, 1967; Qvale, 1968). Nevertheless, the analysis of the coal mining group and of the workers in the electrical panel-heater department showed that these groups had generally the same kinds of autonomy as did the logging group, although their decision-making processes, of course, were adapted to their differing situations.

Alfa Lime Works: the oven group and quarry group

The Alfa Lime Works, which produces calcinated or burnt lime for industrial purposes, employed a total of about twenty workers. Within this body of workers there were two groups, one comprising three quarriers and the other comprising four workers stationed near the lime-kiln (oven). Each of these groups was autonomous within certain fields.

The members of the two groups, together with a worker who was in charge of transport between the groups, were paid according to a joint piece-rate system. The system included sanctions to be used against those who did not conform to the regular working hours. However it did not include the level of the piece rate. This was settled between the management and the national union.

The production planning was done during daily morning meetings between the manager and the workers. These meetings included discussions of what kind of maintenance and cleaning jobs workers should do if the work load allowed it.

The technology was very simple, and the questions regarding method seldom seemed to cause any problems. However, there was no doubt that the groups and the group members had complete control in this field. They also determined how the different tasks should be divided among the members.

Neither of the groups had chosen any leader. The group of quarriers had a *pro forma* leader – a post required by the national safety regulations – but his leadership did not go beyond the question of safety.

The group members were themselves responsible for the recruitment of new members.

The rail-spring group

In an isolated corner of the implement department at Christiania Spigerverk, a group of four men made rail springs. These rail springs were used by the Norwegian State Railways to fix the tracks to the sleepers. The springs had been made in the same way using the same machinery for more than ten years.

Since the demand for the springs was quite large, it was possible to maintain a fairly steady production load most of the time. However, at times it was necessary to cut back production from the usual two shifts to one shift for periods of up to a few months. This was the situation at the time of the investigation.

Rail springs were made from steel plates fabricated in another department, which were delivered to the group in large quantities. The task of the group was first to shape the springs by punching, forming, and cutting operations. The springs were then automatically hardened and annealed. Finally they were inspected and packed ready to be delivered to the customer.

The work area of the group consisted of a corner of a large production bay. The major mechanical equipment belonging to the group consisted of two punch presses with heating furnaces, one cutting machine, and an automatic hardening and annealing furnace.

Two men operated each of the punch presses, one operated the cutting machine, and the fourth man inspected and packed. The punch press operators alternated working so that one man punched while the other filled his furnace with steel plates and regulated the heating. Following forming, the cutting machine operator cut off one end of the spring and placed it on the hardening and annealing furnace conveyor. Finally, the springs were inspected for a critical dimension and the acceptable pieces were packed.

The production was frequently interrupted, usually because of mechanical trouble in one of the furnaces. Quite often one of the steel plates became stuck because of uneven edges or because of errors in the feeding equipment. Then the worker operating that furnace tried to remedy the error himself, while the worker on the identical machine immediately took over the production. As a result, errors of this kind did not necessarily cause a slow-down in production. Other errors such as complete breakdown in one of the heating elements, or mechanical breakdown in one of the punch presses, made it necessary to get aid from a repairman, who was assigned to provide immediate help to the group when needed.

As a consequence, the group, to a very high degree, was dependent on a repairman, and the formal organization therefore built up in such a way that there was contact between the group and one special repairman below the foreman level. His connection with the group was so strong that he had to leave whatever job he was on when the group called for his help. It is estimated that the repairman spent from 25 per cent to 50 per cent of his time with the group.

The repairman often needed help to do his work, and the group itself decided how to organize this. Each week one group member was responsible for calling on and helping the repairman when necessary. The same man was responsible no matter which unit broke down, so when he was absent, the other workers rearranged themselves to carry on the complete production cycle. (This meant that one of the two punch presses would always be unattended in the case of larger repair jobs.) The group completely adjusted itself to those variations that cause changes in the production capacity. However, if there was complete breakdown, then the necessary changes in manning were taken care of by management.

The workers formed their own work pattern and established a completely composite organization. All workers managed all the tasks, and there was complete job rotation with circulation every hour. Job rotation was introduced by the workers because, they argued, it made work less monotonous. The workers themselves decided when, in case of mechanical breakdown, it was necessary to cut down the manpower from four to three workers, and made necessary changes without any orders.

As previously mentioned, one of the group members inspected

each of the rail springs before packing to check if a critical measurement on the spring was within the desired range. On-going quality control inspection also took place. Every hour a quality control inspector, whose work area covered the entire implement department, thoroughly inspected a sample of five randomly selected springs. The inspection results were used as a basis for adjusting the punching equipment and the conditions in the hardening and annealing furnace and not to accept or reject the product.

Since the repairman was the one who actually adjusted the punching equipment and thus in effect controlled many of the variables affecting the quality of the product, the work-group was almost without influence upon the quality of the springs. The work-group controlled most of the variables which determined the quantity of springs produced, while the quality control inspector and the repairman controlled the variables determining the quality of the product.

This was in harmony with the wage system. Payment was by group bonus based on quantity of output, which was controlled by the work-group. On the other hand, the quality, which the group could not influence, did not affect payment.

The production unit operated by the rail-spring group was characterized by unusually stable and indisputable boundary conditions. Their tasks included a complete production cycle. This was probably the main reason why the group was so little dependent on external leadership. In fact, although the group formally shared a foreman with other workers, they contacted him at most once a week. The foreman never involved himself in the work, but tried to regulate the external conditions to the benefit of the group. The group had no formal or informal internal leader, but seemed to manage internal questions together.

The group had less direct influence on recruitment than the logging crew. Nevertheless, they once demanded that the management discharge a group member whom the rest of the group found uncooperative. Although the group was very hesitant to do this, it shows that they had sufficient indirect participatory influence to avoid unwanted members. It is important in this context that the labour turnover was very low.

The group had very little autonomy outside the area indicated. Technology determined the tasks and work methods to such an extent that choice between alternative work methods seems irrelevant. The working hours had been agreed upon between the company and the trade union leaving no choice for any work-group in the company. Finally, management had the right to move people whenever they found that the production or the economic situation made it necessary.

The ferro-alloy group

The author also studied four work-groups around an electrical furnace making ferro-alloys. For the most part, these groups had autonomy and lacked autonomy in the same areas as did the rail-spring group, and it is unnecessary to describe them fully here. They are included in the matrix analysis, below.

The galvanizing group

The galvanizing group, also in the Christiania Spigerverk, was most typical of the groups reported for industrial organizations. Most readers will easily be able to think of groups with as little autonomy. Detailed description will therefore not be given, but only a suggestion about how the decisions were made in this group according to the criteria of autonomy.

Working hours and piece-rates were negotiated between the company and the local union. Production plans were determined by the planning department so the group could only make changes within the schedule of one shift. Depending on the workload, management could decide if it was necessary to increase or decrease the manpower, and who should be moved from one job to the other.

The work method was as often as not determined by the foreman. However, on night-shifts, the group had some influence on these questions. Internal leadership in the group was also decided on by the management. Thus all that was left entirely to the group members was to determine how each one of them should do his own job. The foreman never seemed to interfere in this decision.

Analysis

Analysis of the data followed completion of the case studies and development of the criteria of autonomy. Primary interest was placed in possible structural relationships between the criteria of autonomy. The Guttman Scaling Technique was found suitable

(Guttman, 1944), but before a matrix could be established, a few questions regarding the coding of the material had to be settled.

Decisions made at different system levels

When comparing different units, it is important to make sure that the units really are comparable. For example, the two groups engaged in lime production made some decisions within their respective groups, while others were made at the morning meetings, where the local manager was also present. It is of course possible to treat the morning meeting as a group, but one can clearly see that this group is not immediately comparable with the other groups. It might therefore look as if the morning meetings had comparatively little autonomy. To avoid this problem, the individual groups have been chosen as the units of analysis. Each of these groups is considered to be autonomous in those areas in which it has been able to actively influence the decisions at the morning meetings.

Measurement scale

It was convenient to use a scale with the following values when coding the material:

+ The group or individual members within the group make the decisions either without interference or in cooperation with outsiders. In the latter case, it is presupposed that the group has a right to have a say.

0 The question is irrelevant. Nobody makes the actual decision.

— The group has no right to have a say in the decision-making process.

The matrix

Once these rules were established, a matrix could be set up with the different groups along the one axis, and the criteria of autonomy along the other.

The criterion regarding the groups' right to determine where to work (2a) proved to be irrelevant for all the groups. It was therefore not included in the following analysis.

Sorting the groups according to how many criteria of autonomy they satisfied, and sorting the criteria of autonomy according to

Figure 1 The matrix

Groups	The group has influence on its qualitative goals	The group has influence on its quantitative goals	The group decides on questions of external leadership	The group decides what additional tasks to take on	The group decides when it will work	The group decides on questions of production method	The group determines the internal distribution of tasks	The group decides on questions of recruitment	The group decides on questions of internal leadership	The group members determine their individual production methods
	1a	1b	6b	2c	2b	3	4	5	6a	7
The logging group	−	+	+	+	+	+	+	+	+	+
The coal-mining group	−	+	+	+	+	+	+	+	+	+
The electrical panel-heater group	−	+	+	+	+	+	+	+	+	+
Alfa Lime Works, oven group	−	−	−	+	+	+	+	+	+	+
Alfa Lime Works, quarrier group	−	−	−	+	+	+	+	+	+	+
The rail-spring group	−	−	−	−	−	0	+	+	+	+
The ferro-alloy group	−	−	−	−	−	−	+	+	+	+
The galvanizing group	−	−	−	−	−	−	−	−	−	+

how many groups satisfied them, the following matrix was generated.

The matrix shows that the criteria of autonomy, according to these data, form a Guttman scale. According to Guttman, if this scale were not purely accidental, one should, probably be able to find some underlying variable. In order to find such a variable, consequences of decisions were studied.

In many cases, a fairly obvious underlying variable might be that the consequences of a decision were either 'great' or 'small'. This variable, however, is insufficiently precise to offer much additional meaning or illumination for the investigator. Therefore, it was decided to look at two somewhat richer aspects of decisions. Since consequences of decisions may last for long or short periods, it was natural to look first at the time span. How long does it take before an actual decision does not represent an important limitation for the system any longer? Second, since decisions may have impact on different system levels, the level of the system on which the decision had impact could be used as another variable.

Both the time span of the consequences of the decisions and the system level could be considered underlying variables according to these data. These conclusions are more precisely stated below.

Conclusions and hypotheses

The analysis shows that the criteria of autonomy are ordered along a Guttman scale. This suggests the conclusion that autonomy is a one-dimensional property within work groups. It therefore becomes realistic to talk about degree of autonomy. In spite of the fact that the data point toward a clear conclusion, however, the reader is reminded that the empirical material is somewhat scanty and that other dimensions such as group size, group competence and the kind of task have not been brought into consideration. On this tentative basis, the following hypotheses are proposed:

Hypothesis 1
Autonomy, as defined here, is a one-dimensional property. The different criteria of autonomy have a specific order, as shown in the matrix. This order may be termed the scale of autonomy. In order to reach a certain level on this scale, a group must satisfy all the criteria that precede it on the scale of autonomy.

Why is the property of autonomy one-dimensional? Two reasons exist which are probably mutually interdependent. They concern the time span and the level of decision making.

Hypothesis 2
Once a group has made a decision, it has committed itself on shorter or longer terms. A group cannot make decisions that bring it into a long-term commitment unless it also makes the decisions that commit it on shorter terms.

Hypothesis 3
Decisions are made on different system levels. No group can make decisions about questions on higher system levels unless it also makes the decisions on the lower system levels.

Hypotheses 2 and 3 will not both be correct unless there is a one-to-one correspondence between the system level of the decisions and the time-span of its consequences. The limitations of the data available in the case materials make it impossible to test these relationships empirically. If these hypotheses prove to be correct, they will obviously have impact on the development of shop-floor democracy.

One final consequence can be mentioned since it is heavily backed by other data found in the case studies. It seems beyond doubt that external conditions such as technology and layout, or payment, or planning systems will have impact on how a work-group will behave and what kinds of responsibility it can take on. Some of these external conditions seem to limit a group's possibility for having certain kinds of autonomy.

It is probable that autonomy with respect to decisions high on the scale presupposes autonomy with respect to all the decisions lower on the scale. This means that if one of the kinds of autonomy low on the scale is dependent on certain external conditions, all kinds of autonomy that are higher on the scale are equally dependent on those same conditions. To illustrate this, the hypotheses give us reason to believe that control or planning systems that leave no room for individual workers to make decisions about their own work methods will leave no room for any kind of group autonomy.

In conclusion, there seems to be a very important difference between the three most autonomous work groups and the other groups. The loggers, the coal miners and the groups in the electrical panel-heater department work on time limited contracts, which impose equal obligations on the management and on the groups. These contracts last for periods from one to three months. Within these periods management has no right permitting it to interfere with what the groups are doing, as long as the groups are producing according to the contract. As for the other groups, it is beyond doubt that their autonomy relies completely on the attitudes of the management. After the case studies were made, the research team observed that some groups lost their autonomy through changes in work supervision.

It is therefore suggested that the term 'autonomous work group' be reserved for groups that negotiate and operate under contracts which impose obligations on both parties for a certain time period. Other groups may be called 'relatively autonomous'.

References

DAVIS, L. E. (1966), 'The design of jobs', *Industrial Relations*, vol. 6, pp. 21–45.

EMERY, F. E., and THORSRUD, E. (1969), *Form and Content in Industrial Democracy*, Tavistock.

GULOWSEN, J. (1971), *Selvstyrte Arbeidsgrupper*, Tanum, Oslo.

GUTTMAN, L. A. (1944), 'A basis for scaling qualitative data', *American Sociological Review*, vol. 40.

HERBST, P. G. (1962), *Autonomous Group Functioning*, Tavistock.

HEGLAND, T. J., and NYLEHN, B. (1968), 'Adjustment of work organizations', in *Contributions to the Theory of Organizations*, Munksgaard, Copenhagen.

QVALE, T. U. (1968), '*Etterstudier ved NOBØ fabrikker*', Institute of Industrial and Social Research, Trondheim, Norway.

RICE, A. K. (1958), *Productivity and Social Organization: The Ahmedabad Experiment*, Tavistock.

ØDEGAARD, L. A. (1967), '*Feltforsøk ved NOBØ fabrikker*', Institute of Industrial and Social Research, Trondheim, Norway.

TRIST, E. L., HIGGIN, G. W., MURRAY, H., and POLLOCK, A. B. (1963), *Organizational Choice*, Tavistock.

26 James C. Taylor

Some Effects of Technology in Organizational Change

Excerpts from J. C. Taylor, 'Some effects of technology in organizational change', *Human Relations*, vol. 24, 1971, pp. 105–23.

Advanced technology appears, in general, to elicit new forms of work group structure and behavior. These behavioral effects of automation seem to produce favorable attitudes which may in turn strengthen those behaviors. It cannot be expected that these effects result wholly from behavioral constraints of the technology, but are conditioned by management decisions which facilitate adaptation to that technology.

Technological effects on employee behavior

A review of research literature over the past decade reveals that technology can affect organizational structure (Burns and Stalker, 1961; Blauner, 1964; Woodward, 1965; Harvey, 1968), work group behavior and productivity (Trist and Bamforth, 1951; Trist, Higgin, Murray and Pollock, 1963; Rice, 1958; Walker, 1957; Mann and Hoffman, 1960; Mann and Williams, 1959, 1962; Marrow, Bowers and Seashore, 1967), and group member attitudes as well (Mann and Hoffman, 1960; Turner and Lawrence, 1965; Walker, 1957). Further, much of this evidence supports the notion that sophisticated technology, or automation, influences group process in the direction of more democratic, autonomous and responsible activities.

Specifically, evidence in the literature reveals that the effects of modern technology on the nature of the work group are less equivocal than technological effects on other variables, such as individual skill requirements, intrinsic job satisfaction, or intergroup communication patterns. These work group effects are clearer in the case of blue-collar groups than in white-collar counterparts, although it will be maintained that this difference is probably more historically artifactual than qualitatively real. Detailed description in two cases of unplanned social change following technological change (Mann and Hoffman, 1960; Walker, 1957) shows that intra-group status differences in blue-collar settings were reduced and work roles became more interdependent under advanced technology. Evidence that this kind of effect on the blue-collar work group is a useful sort of target of planned social change is presented by researchers at London's Tavistock Institute (Trist and Bamforth, 1951; Rice, 1958, 1963; Trist et al., 1963). The Tavistock people state that more sophisticated technology can lead to a number of antithetical supervisory and work group behaviors, but that autonomous group functioning (multi-skilled workers, responsibility to allocate members to all roles, group mission and incentive, and task definition involving continuity) seems to have the best results and is a more natural outgrowth of the technological change itself. The Tavistock people make an important contribution in concluding that more sophisticated technology is a necessary condition in installing autonomous groups, but for best effect, that structure must be consciously installed (Trist et al., 1963, p. 293).

In discussing the autonomous group, and socio-technical systems, the Tavistock researchers describe a different and broader role for the supervisor from what is traditionally held. What is required is that as the group comes to control the production process, the formal supervisor shifts to a control of boundary conditions such as liaison, maintenance, and supply (Emery, 1959; Rice, 1963, p. 8). This is similar to observations of emerging supervisory behaviors noted by Walker (1957), by Mann and Hoffman (1960), and by Marrow et al. (1967). The easier technology makes it for both group and supervisor to evaluate results, the easier it becomes to supervise on the basis of results and the less likely is the autocratic management of work activities (Herbst, 1962, p. 8; Woodward, 1965, p. 225). It seems apparent that even though the pattern of actual supervisory activities differs from one industry or plant to another, the trend with advanced technology is in the direction of supervisors doing less in the way of traditional supervision, i.e. supervising the behaviors of subordinates, and attending to selection and training functions, and more in the direction of either acting as a facilitator and communications link for the work group or becoming more technically skilled operators themselves. [. . .]

It would seem that automation does, in fact, provide the potential or opportunity for enhanced worker discretion, responsibility, intra-work group autonomy, interdependence and cooperation. In fact, what seems to be happening is that lowest level jobs are taking over more of what are usually thought of as traditional supervisory tasks. [. . .]

Organizational change and subsystem interdependence

It is reasonable to postulate that there is a systemic interdependence among the subsystems of an organization. Changes cannot be affected in the technical system without repercussions in the social system. Katz and Kahn's open system theory in organizations (1966) relies on the relatedness of sub-units or parts of a system *vis-à-vis* the organization's environment (pp. 19–29). Parts of social systems, for example personal and role relationships within work groups, can be changed without prior change in technical systems or organizational structure, but (they maintain) the change in organizational behavior is only mild reform, not radical change (p. 424). By the same token, parts of technical systems can also be changed without undue stress on the other systems in the organization.

Katz and Kahn view systemic change as the most powerful approach to changing organizations. Systemic change involves change inputs from the environment which create internal strain and imbalance among system sub-units. It is this internal strain which is the potent cause of the behavioral adaptation of subsystems indirectly connected with the change input (pp. 446–8). However, values and motivations of organizational members change in a more evolutionary way. Katz and Kahn maintain these elements are not as immediately amenable to the influence of changed inputs as is organizational behavior (p. 446).

Guest (1962, p. 55), Mann and Hoffman (1960, p. 193), Marrow *et al.* (1967, p. 229), and Woodward (1965, p. 239), among others, implicitly support the notion of interrelatedness of subsystems and the importance of considering the derivative effect on the social system of significant changes in technology. Yet they all conclude from their evidence that an improvement in the technical system was not sufficient in itself to assure good performance via the existing social system.

Order and precedence of subsystem change

It seems established that when technological change is considerable, some effects on the social system must be recognized and planned for, but the question of coordination of change in these two systems is still unanswered. Is technical change the best way of achieving organizational change, or would it be more efficient to purposefully change the social system, following that by planned changes in the organizational technology, or to change both simultaneously?

Cultural anthropologists have long maintained that changes in technology historically lead to changes in attitudes, values and philosophies (Ogburn, 1957, 1962; White, 1959, p. 27). Some direct evidence for this position is found in the studies reviewed here. Burns and Stalker, for example, concluded that mechanistic and organic management systems were dependent variables to the rate of environmental change, i.e. technology and market situation. Trist *et al.* (1963, p. 293) state that change conditions for installing autonomous groups were more favorable under greater mechanization and low group cohesiveness. Even here, however, these authors discovered that when new equipment was installed, the existing social system could create forces of resistance to the full potential of the technology. The technical outsiders supervising the change were frequently unaware of the operator's responsibilities to the rest of the work cycle, and tended to isolate the machine activity (p. 273). This had effects of unfavourably disrupting the existing social system and making subsequent change difficult. Planning for this contingency was necessary. Guest (1962, pp. 52–3), and Marrow *et al.* (1967, p. 237) attribute direct behavioral effects to the relatively minor technological change made, but in both of these cases these changes were preceded by management succession. These can be considered cases of what Schon (1967) describes as 'innovation by invasion' – the old borrows what it can of the new, the new introduces change into the old, or the new displaces the old. In the open system notion of Katz and Kahn, this is systemic change representing organizational social system change via new inputs from the environment. In both of these cases also, changes in interpersonal relations were modified at the top of the organization coincident with the technological change at the bottom.

Precedence and hierarchical level. Argyris (1962), like Anshen (1962), suggests that production technology has little effect on higher management. Argyris continues that effective organizational change comes about by improving interpersonal competence directly at the top of the organization, while improving it at the bottom more indirectly through changes in technology and control systems (p. 282). This implies that the socio-technical system is the lower part of the whole organization unlike the total organization of Katz and Kahn's open system. The Tavistock group, although it makes excursions into the socio-technical nature of management systems (Miller and Rice, 1967; Trist *et al.*, 1963) is primarily concerned with the production system (e.g. crews of miners across shifts) as socio-technical systems. It is implicitly clear in these particular studies, however, that effective introduction of technological change for ultimate organizational change involved the upper ranks, either in a commitment to plan adequately for social system effects (Trist *et al.*) or in a commitment to the technological change itself as a method of improving social relationships (Guest; Marrow *et al.*).

Implications of sophisticated technology effects on social system change

Direct effect. The direct effects of modern technology on more satisfying and productive methods of working have been noted (Guest; Mann and Hoffman; Mann and Williams; Marrow *et al.*; Trist *et al.*; Turner and Lawrence; Walker). Although the evidence is not overwhelming, it appears that a properly planned technical change can lead directly and without additional inputs, albeit slowly, to increased job complexity, autonomous and responsible work group processes, more helpful supervision, and higher productivity. It was also found that at least for some workers these direct effects can lead to more positive job involvement, improved work-group relations, more favorable attitudes toward supervision, and pride in higher productivity. The implication here is that social change can proceed as a direct outcome of certain technological changes, but if this were the only way social change was affected, the outcome would be slow and limited by chance factors.

Indirect effects. Several of the studies reviewed here consider social change not only resulting from the new technology itself, but resulting from a planned social change input made possible, at least in part, by the mere disruption created by the technological change (Marrow *et al.*; Rice; Trist *et al.*; Williams and Williams, 1964). This kind of disruption has been labeled 'unfreezing' by Lewin (1951), or 'internal system strain' by Katz and Kahn. In both cases, the dynamic created is that of a force toward total system restructuring to find a new equilibrium. It seems that social system changes are possible without technological change, but organizations may not be able in themselves to provide the force necessary. Williams and Williams, for example, state that such changes are not possible without a catalyst like expenditure on technological change which creates stresses, forcing departments and units to compromise on objectives and abandon traditional routines and activities. Marrow *et al.* claim that their apparel factory was unable to unfreeze itself – heroic measures were needed to create enough disturbance to allow normal change processes to begin (1967, p. 232). Trist *et al.* maintain that even limited technological changes can create enough disruption if their potentiality for inducing social change is recognized (1963, p. 284).

The dynamic involved in the direct effect of technology on social system changes seems to be the constraints it applies to employee behavior. The dynamic of unfreezing, on the other hand, seems to be a freedom provided by the new technology to seek new ways of behaving. Internal system strain comes about then in the latter case in which employees' cognitive maps may not match managements' under these circumstances, or that the values of one department may not match those of another. Management awareness of such conditions, and planning for it, becomes important for the outcomes on the social system.

It seems clear that the combination of direct and indirect effects of technology on the social system provides the basis for concluding that technological change would best precede social change, if both were contemplated, in that it probably requires less time and elicits less resistance. This is true because technology not only disrupts or unfreezes, but imposes strict, nonhuman control on minimum behavior. Following the same logic, it would also seem that changes toward autonomous group structure would be facilitated where an advanced system of technology was already in place.

Technology, role constraints, and permanence of social change

There is no evidence to prove that any change strategy provides permanent effects. Schein (1961), in describing change by 'compliance' (where an individual's behavior changes because the situation forces him to change), suggests that coercion–compliance is only a method of changing behavior; attitudinal change need not follow. In fact, if acquisition of new attitudes is also via coercive-compliance, these attitudes will be temporary, if they obtain at all. On the other hand, he continues, if behavioral changes are coerced at the same time as unfreezing operations are undertaken, actual influence can be facilitated if the individual finds himself having to learn new attitudes to justify the kinds of behavior he has been forced to exhibit. These new attitudes should act then to maintain the new behaviors. This is exactly the outcome that Festinger's dissonance theory of attitude change would predict (Cohen, 1964, p. 82; Festinger, 1957, pp. 94–5; Insko, 1967, p. 219) – that counter-attitudinal role playing will result in consistency-producing attitude change and maintenance of coerced behaviors. Although the attitude change portion of this position has received consistent support in the psychological laboratory (Insko, pp. 219–23), there is no mention of it as an explanatory concept in field research around technological change, and no evidence for the predictions of behavioral maintenance. In fact, only two cases exist where attitudes in industrial work were found to change as a function of the relatively ambiguous condition of role change (Lieberman, 1956; Tannenbaum, 1957). As this coercion–compliance position has received little empirical support in the field, so has the other generic strategy – that of conversion (Bennis, 1966, pp. 170–71). 'Conversion' – the attempt by persuasion and influence to change the individual's cognitive or attitudinal set – is a more common strategy in affecting social system change in organizations (Sayles, 1962).

Thus, it appears that although the evidence exists for asserting that planning for social change should, where possible, take place around technological change, it is not unambiguous. It seems that when technological changes are undertaken first, especially when the social effects are considered, the noticeable effects of change behavior will be manifested earlier. It is not at all clear, however, whether one sort of change strategy will work better with people of varied backgrounds, or will have more permanent effects via changed attitudes and satisfactions acting to maintain new behaviors.

Implications from the literature

It is not advanced here that the social system in an organization cannot be changed directly by appeals to members to alter the way they believe and behave, coupled with attempts to train members in the skills necessary to behave differently. In fact, it is assumed that such direct changes can be affected. An interesting question to ask, however, is what facilitating effects are manifest where the members affected by direct social change attempts exist in a modern system of production technology – where: (a) behavioral constraints may exist in the direction of greater worker discretion, responsibility, interdependence, and cooperation; (b) where some residual effects of 'unfreezing' may still exist in the direction of search for new ways of behaving *vis-à-vis* the modern technology; and (c) where the permanence of the technological constraints on behavior and the unfreezing effects may combine to change attitudes as well as behavior. Such facilitating effects seem reasonable to hypothesize, given the data reported in the literature described above. The question is not whether direct social change attempts can be effective, but rather, whether the existence of modern, sophisticated technology can enhance the results of such change efforts.

The study
Hypotheses

The purpose of the present study was to test several notions of those described above regarding the effects of sophisticated technology, or automation, on job-related behaviors in work groups. It tested three specific hypotheses: *first*, that sophisticated technology, in and of itself, is associated with more autonomous and participative group process; *second*, that sophisticated technology will facilitate planned-change efforts directed toward increasing participative group process; and *third*, that the change toward participative group process will be more permanent when the change is facilitated by technology than when it is not.

The literature reviewed above implied that automation has within it certain built-in constraints for lowered supervision, and increased intra-group communication and responsibility. If this is true, then the introduction of such technology should lead to such changes in member social behavior. If such a system is aided in social change by a consultant or change agent, he can help the change process if he urges those behaviors which turn out to be compatible with the new technological system. That the resultant organizational changes will be more permanent than those brought about by the exhortations of management or a consultant alone, can be explained in two ways. First, the technical system and its constraints are permanent. Second, as Festinger and others have shown, constrained counter-attitudinal behavior is one of the most important precursors of attitude change, ultimately making the new behaviors even more resistant to fluctuation than they otherwise would be.

The studies of technological effects mentioned above, and others like them, are mostly case studies. They have not quantitatively measured the effects of technology on group process. In addition, no longitudinal or quantitative studies of the facilitating effects of technology on planned social change programs are recorded. The present study dealt with both of these aspects, plus some assessment of the casual strength of changed behaviors on attitudes as well.

Methodology

This study used the responses of over 1000 persons in 140 non-supervisory work groups employed by a large petroleum refinery. Respondents completed paper and pencil questionnaires dealing with supervisory and peer leadership, work-group behaviors, satisfactions, and other job-related matters. These questionnaires were completed by respondents on three separate occasions over a period of twelve months.

A planned-change program aimed toward more participative management was introduced following the initial survey.

Finally, the judgements of some in-plant people were used to obtain evaluations of the sophistication of work-group production technology. These evaluations were obtained retroactively, using judgmental questionnaires with several in-plant judges who were familiar with the technological characteristics of the groups they evaluated.

The analytic design involved controlling for sophistication of technology, and examination of the survey results of group responses to questionnaire variables measuring participative leadership, group behavior and satisfaction.

Independent variable. The planned social change program is an implicit independent variable in this study. This change program involved an attempted change in management values and behaviors in the direction of Likert's 'System IV' (Likert, 1967). 'System IV' relies on a theory of organization and management in which high value is placed on total organizational commitment to joint decision-making, participation, openness, trust and confidence, mutual influence, and the sharing of organizational goals and mission. These planned changes, it was felt, would be compatible with the assumed forces inherent in advanced technology.

Consultants from the University of Michigan introduced this planned change program. This effort began following the first questionnaire administration, and prior to the second one. It involved using the by-group results of the survey as a self-help diagnostic tool and specially developed training programs as well. Consultants made themselves available to individual supervisors who wished help in using the data with which they were provided. On the basis of the survey data, and other observations, the consultants proceeded to develop training programs for use with various levels and groups within the company. Since the consultants attempted uniform diffusion of inputs throughout the lower level ranks in the refinery, this independent force was assumed constant.

The measure of sophistication of technology was considered both an independent variable and a conditioning variable in this study. As an independent variable, the effects of technology on pre-change levels of leadership, group process and satisfaction were examined. As a conditioning variable, the effects of technology on rate of change in these variables, and on causal priorities among them following the change program were examined.

Sophistication of technology was assessed using a questionnaire instrument constructed to measure the qualities of *standard materials input, throughput, mechanization,* and *output control* for each work group. These three technological constructs were measured using the following items:

1. *Sophistication of input*
Standardization of material or objects transformed by the work group.
Predictability of objects transformed in those characteristics important to the group.

2. *Sophistication of throughput*
The proportion of routine operations which are handled by machines.
Degree of nonhuman power, and automatic control of operations.
Extent to which machine is independent of the operator.

3. *Sophistication of output-control*
Absence of feedback by supervisor.
Degree supervisor provides feedback on request versus initiating feedback.
Speed of feedback.
Primary source of feedback (nonhuman versus human).

This instrument utilized the retrospective structured judgements of work groups on the nine scales by a small number of administrative people within the organization. These judges were asked to evaluate the groups for the time of the first survey, some eighteen months earlier. Since few technological changes had occurred in the intervening period, the task was relatively simple. Using this instrument in other organizations has revealed reasonable inter-rater and internal consistency reliability and discriminant validity for it (Taylor, 1971b).

Dependent variables. The survey instrument administered over time included over 100 items, some of which were used as single item estimates of constructs or concepts, others of which were combined into factorially derived mean score index variables and used as measures of other constructs. Five-unit Likert scale response alternatives were used in all questions. From this large set of variables, ten were used in the analysis for the present study. These variables fall into four classes: four areas of supervisory leadership; four areas of work group or peer leadership; work group behaviors; and satisfaction with the work group. These variables were measured using the following component questions:

1. *Supervisory leadership*. Measured by the following four mean score indices:

(a) Support; behavior which increases his subordinates' feeling of being worthwhile and important people. (Mean score index – three items.)

In the surveys this was measured by the following questions:

How friendly and easy to approach is your supervisor?

When you talk with your supervisor, to what extent does he pay attention to what you are saying?

To what extent is your supervisor willing to listen to your problems?

(b) Goal emphasis; behavior which stimulates an enthusiasm among subordinates for getting the work done. (Mean score index – two items.)

The survey used these items to measure this aspect of his behavior:

How much does your supervisor encourage people to give their best effort?

To what extent does your supervisor maintain high standards of performance?

(c) Work facilitation; behavior which helps his subordinates actually get the work done by removing obstacles and road-blocks. (Mean score index – three items.)

These items measured this form of behavior:

To what extent does your supervisor show you how to improve your performance?

To what extent does your supervisor provide the help you need so that you can schedule work ahead of time?

To what extent does your supervisor offer new ideas for solving job-related problems?

(d) Interaction facilitation; behavior which builds the subordinate group into a work team. (Mean score index – two items.)

These items were used to measure behavior of this kind.

To what extent does your supervisor encourage the persons who work for him to work as a team?

To what extent does your supervisor encourage people who work for him to exchange opinions and ideas?

2. *Peer (work group) leadership.* This was measured by survey questions and indices usually identical to those used to measure the manager's leadership. In this case, however, the questions are worded, 'To what extent are (do) persons in your work group . . .'

(a) *Support* (mean score index – three items):

Friendly and easy to approach?

Pay attention to what you're saying when you talk with them?

Willing to listen to your problems?

(b) *Goal emphasis* (mean score index – two items):

Encourage each other to give their best effort?

Maintain high standards of performance?

(c) *Work facilitation* (mean score index – three items):

Help you find ways to do a better job?

Provide the help you need so that you can plan, organize and schedule work ahead of time?

Offer each other new ideas for solving job-related problems?

(d) *Interaction facilitation* (mean score index – two items):

Encourage each other to work as a team?

Emphasize a *team* goal?

3. Work group activities

Work group team process (mean score index – three items): In your work group to what extent is work time used efficiently because persons in the work group plan and coordinate their efforts?

To what extent does your work group make good decisions and solve problems well?

To what extent do you feel that you and the other persons in your work group belong to a team that works together?

4. Satisfaction

With work group:

All in all, how satisfied are you with the persons in your work groups?

These items are similar to those used in other studies at the

Institute for Social Research and over time have revealed reasonable reliability and validity. The eight leadership variables are described in greater detail elsewhere (Bowers and Seashore, 1966; Taylor, 1971a).

These measures formed the basis of the dependent variables in the present study – the degree to which groups were originally participative and autonomous, and the extent to which they responded over time to the planned change program directed toward these ends.

Results

The data were first checked for the possible confounding effects of age, education, tenure with the company, and rural–urban upbringing of the respondents. It was determined that these variables had no measurable effect on any of the survey variables. Education of respondents was, however, found negatively related to the judgements of some of the technological characteristics for their groups, and related positively to some others. These effects of education were not unexpected, and were not corrected for in subsequent analyses.

The existence of interaction effects between sophistication of technology and the relationships among the dependent variables over time was noted. This interaction obviated any analysis technique using multiple linear regression in the estimation of causal priorities, or the relative strength of conditioning effects. As a consequence, the analyses took the somewhat cruder form of controlling for high and low levels of technological sophistication and examining the dependent variables for differences in mean scores, and differences in cross-lagged zero-order longitudinal correlations.

In order to keep the analysis simple, the data bases were combined such that groups with high sophistication of technological input, throughput and output scores could be compared with groups with low input, throughput and output scores. This total technology high-low design reduced the number of groups in each category, but still maintained reasonable N's for statistical purposes. The original 140 groups were reduced to sixty-eight using this design. Maximum N in the high category was forty-two groups. Maximum N in the low category was twenty-six groups.

Levels of education for the high group and the low group were not found significantly different from one another. What effects education had on the individual technological characteristics described earlier were effectively cancelled out using the total technology combination.

Table 1 presents data relevant to the first hypothesis – that advanced technology by itself can influence autonomous group process.

The differences between the mean scores for the high and low categories at time one clearly suggest that members of groups with high sophistication of production technology initially perceive higher levels of peer work facilitation, supervisory and peer interaction facilitation, and democratic group process in their groups, than did members of groups with low sophistication of technology. This is evidence that sophisticated technology in itself is associated with more autonomous group process.

Table 1 also presents evidence in support of the second hypothesis – that technology will facilitate planned change efforts directed toward greater autonomy and participation. Between time one, the first measure, and time three, the final measure, the high technology groups significantly increased their level of evaluation of supervisory and peer leadership in nearly all dimensions, while groups in the low technology category did not. It is interesting to note the only exception to this pattern in the high technology category, aside from satisfaction with the work group, is that of supervisory goal emphasis. If in fact these groups are becoming more autonomous, then *we should not expect* supervisory goal emphasis to increase as much as peer goal emphasis.

Figures 1 and 2 provide summary information in support of the second hypothesis.

Figure 1 presents the average means for *all four of the peer leadership variables* for high and low technology categories, compared with the combined four variables for the whole refinery ($n = 2200$, NGPs $= 350$). It is clear from this figure that the high technology groups start higher in peer leadership and increase faster than either the low technology groups, or the refinery as a whole.

Figure 2 uses the same data bases, but presents average means of *the four supervisory leadership variables*. Once again, it is clear that

Table 1 Mean score differences on dependent variables between groups in the categories of high and low sophistication of technology; and within these categories over time

Dependent variables	High Technology Means Time$_3$	Time$_1$	Diff. $t_3 - t_1$	Low Technology Means Time$_3$	Time$_1$	Diff. $t_3 - t_1$	Differences High$_1$–Low$_1$	High$_3$–Low$_3$
Supervisory support	4·16	3·92	0·24*	4·10	4·14	−0·04	−0·22	0·06
Supervisory goal emphasis	4·08	3·94	0·14	3·85	3·75	0·10	0·19	0·23*
Supervisory work facilitation	3·66	3·45	0·21*	3·39	3·20	0·19	0·25	0·27*
Supervisory interaction facilitation	3·92	3·64	0·28*	3·43	3·23	0·20	0·41*	0·49†
Peer support	4·01	3·83	0·18*	3·94	4·03	−0·07	−0·20	0·07
Peer goal emphasis	3·74	3·55	0·19*	3·48	3·44	0·04	0·11	0·26†
Peer work facilitation	3·75	3·47	0·28†	3·19	3·11	0·08	0·36*	0·56†
Peer interaction facilitation	3·65	3·37	0·28†	2·87	2·68	0·19	0·69†	0·78†
Group process	3·84	3·68	0·16*	3·33	3·17	0·16	0·51†	0·51†
Satisfaction with work group	4·38	4·38	0·00	4·22	4·22	0·00	0·16	0·16

* $p < 0.05$.
† $p < 0.01$.

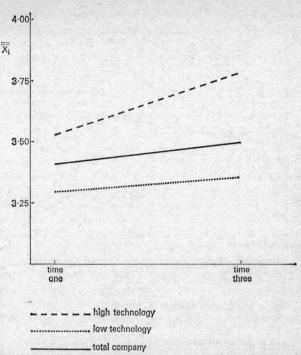

Figure 1 Combined peer leadership mean score change over time for high and low technology groups compared with total company

the high technology groups start higher and increase faster than either of the other comparison groups.

The data in Figure 3 help in examining the third hypothesis – that permanence of the change toward autonomous group process is greater in the high technology condition. This was done by examining the degree to which attitudes toward the social system changed to conform with the new behavior. Partial assessment of these effects was obtained using cross-lagged analysis of average zero-order correlations, while controlling for high and low technology.

Cross-lagged analysis allows for an estimation of causal priorities of dependent variables measured early in the study on those variables measured later. Since only general notions of causality

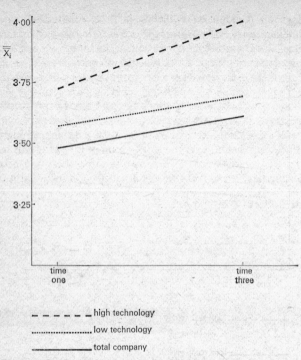

Figure 2 Combined supervisory leadership mean score change over time for high and low technology groups compared with total company

were desired, average correlations among the major variables were used. This manipulation had the advantage of much simplifying an otherwise bewildering array of data. It also had the disadvantage of lower precision, and the inability to legitimately utilize tests of statistical significance. The advantage of clarity, however, was deemed to outweigh the disadvantages on both counts.

Figure 3 presents the dominant chains of causal priority among the dependent variables for the three measurement periods separately for high and low technology. In order to simplify the figure, cases of reciprocal causality are not shown in favor of presenting only recursive, or more intransitive causal chains.

Before reviewing Figure 3 for the effects on satisfaction with the work group, it should be recalled from Table 1 that satisfaction did not increase at all for either high or low technology over time. Original levels of satisfaction were quite high for both groups, and remained so during the period of the study. In spite of this, Figure 3 suggests that satisfaction takes a key position in the causal matrix.

In the high technology condition peer leadership (probably our best indicator of autonomous group process) time two, is clearly the recipient of causal influence of the time one variables: group process, satisfaction, and of course, itself. Nothing strongly influences satisfaction with the work group at time two. But by time three, consolidations in time two group process and peer leadership have led to realignments in satisfaction such that it is

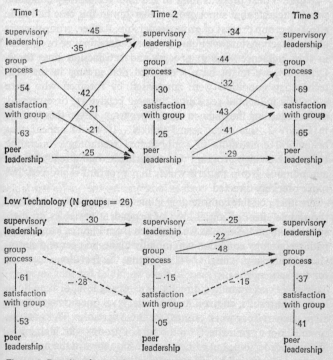

Figure 3 Results of cross-lag causal analysis refinery data

higher in groups which were more autonomous at time two. Thus, we may tentatively conclude that changes in group behavior, under the high technology condition, tend to maintain themselves via changes toward more consonant attitudes over time.

In the low technology condition, originally *lower* group process tends to lead to *higher* satisfaction at time two, and this in turn has a slight inverse causal influence on group process time three. It may be said that this situation reflects the lesser constraints on behavior for autonomous group process and little motivation for changing toward it. *Lower* group process time one produces *higher* satisfaction, which in turn has a slight perseverative effect on low group process time three, where technological sophistication is low.

Figure 3 also presents data in the high technology condition which suggests that supervisory leadership in this case had little effect on group process or group leadership. Rather, group process and satisfaction time one influence peer leadership time two, which in turn influenced group process and satisfaction time three. Originally, we might have speculated that groups in the high technology condition were supervised by foremen who were especially influential regarding the new behaviors, or especially active regarding the planned change program. Given these results in Figure 3, this effect seems unlikely. It would appear that behavioral constraints of sophisticated technology, operating before the change program was undertaken, had already set the autonomous group pattern which that program reinforced and more precisely directed.

Another possible confounding influence on these data might be the simple effect of initial level of dependent variables on their subsequent gain. Since, as we have seen from Figures 1 and 2, the high technology condition was initially higher in peer and supervisory leadership, it might be claimed that this fact alone accounts for the subsequent increases in these variables for that category. This effect was examined directly by assessing level of time three leadership results, controlling for initial level (medium-split over all nonsupervisory work groups) for these variables. This analysis revealed not a 'gain effect' on the part of groups with high initial levels of leadership; but rather, a regression toward the mean for groups with initially high, and initially low leadership scores.

Technology, it seems, by itself accounts for the greater gain over time in the high technology condition.

Conclusions and implications

We may conclude, with respect to the first hypothesis tested here, that technological sophistication in this refinery does have a measurable association with democratic and autonomous group process. These static relationships do not inexorably lead to statements of causality, but it seems more likely that pre-change levels of autonomous group process and peer leadership, were caused by, rather than caused, the advanced technology. This, of course, does not rule out a possible third variable leading to pre-change levels in both technology and leadership. If it exists, however, its form is not evident in the data collected here; for example, age and tenure were found unrelated to either technology or the dependent variables.

In regard to the second hypothesis, the implications are less equivocal. It would appear quite undeniable that the social change program was facilitated in groups with more sophisticated technology. Although the present design was not balanced to test all possible alternatives in examining efficiency in *organizational change*, it was suitable to test the hypothesis as presented. We cannot conclude that in larger organizational change, which includes changes in *both* social and technical systems, that change will be faster or greater where technical change precedes social change, than it will where social change precedes technical change. We can say, however, that the existence of technological sophistication better precedes social change than either a marked lack of sophistication in technology, or more average or moderate conditions of system technology would. This evidence, in addition to that presented in the introduction to the present paper, lends strength to the position that disruptive inputs from the organizational environment, in the service of social change, would more likely be technological than social in nature.

The results examined in the test of the third hypothesis in turn reinforce this conclusion. Traditionally, we have approached social change as an attempt to change attitudes directly – with varying degrees of success (subjectively assessed). Results in the present study strongly suggest that attitude change is better approached *indirectly* via more impersonal and compelling changes in behavior.

One final, and more general, implication may be drawn from the results of this study and others like it. These findings tend to suggest that the proposed management systems of such people as Argyris, Likert, McGregor and others may reflect a *Zeitgeist* stimulated by the advances in the industrial world. That is, the ideas advanced by these theorists may be most suitable for organizations in the present technological vanguard. As technology continues to advance, these ideas of participative management will have more meaning and application. The cultural-lag theories of anthropologists, such as William Ogburn, form a suitable model in this regard. Such theories state that cultural values and philosophies are not the first to change in cultural development, but the last – invariably following changes in technology.

References

ANSHEN, M. (1962), 'Managerial decisions', in J. T. Dunlop (ed.), *Automation and Technological Change*, American Assembly, Columbia University.

ARGYRIS, C. (1962), *Interpersonal Competence and Organizational Effectiveness*, Irwin–Dorsey.

BENNIS, W. G. (1966), *Changing Organizations*, McGraw-Hill.

BLAUNER, R. (1964), *Alienation and Freedom*, University of Chicago Press.

BOWERS, D. G., and SEASHORE, S. E. (1966), 'Predicting organizational effectiveness – with a four-factor theory of leadership', *Administrative Science Quarterly*, vol. 11, pp. 238–63.

BURNS, T., and STALKER, G. M. (1961), *The Management of Innovation*, Tavistock.

COHEN, A. (1964), *Attitude Change and Social Influence*, Basic Books.

EMERY, F. E. (1959), 'Characteristics of socio-technical systems', unpublished manuscript, Tavistock Institute.

FESTINGER, L. (1957), *A Theory of Cognitive Dissonance*, Stanford University Press.

GUEST, R. H. (1962), *Organizational Change: The Effect of Successful Leadership*, Dorsey Press.

HARVEY, E. (1968), 'Technology and the structure of organizations', *American Sociological Review*, vol. 33, pp. 247–59.

HERBST, P. G. (1962), *Autonomous Group Functioning*, Tavistock.

INSKO, C. A. (1967), *Theories of Attitude Change*, Appleton-Century-Crofts.

KATZ, D., and KAHN, R. L. (1966), *The Social Psychology of Organizations*, Wiley.

LEWIN, K. (1951), *Field Theory in Social Science*, Harper.

LIEBERMAN, S. (1956), 'The effects of changes in role in the attitudes of role occupants', *Human Relations*, vol. 9, pp. 385–402.

LIKERT, R. (1967), *The Human Organization: Its Management and Value*, McGraw-Hill.

MANN, F. C., and HOFFMAN, L. R. (1960), *Automation and the Worker*, Henry Holt.

MANN, F. C., and WILLIAMS, L. K. (1959), 'Organizational impact of white collar automation', *Industrial Relations Research Association, Proceedings*.

MANN, F. C., and WILLIAMS, L. K. (1962), 'Some effects of changing work environment in the office', *Journal of Social Issues*, vol. 18, no. 3, pp. 90–101.

MARROW, A. J., BOWERS, D. G., and SEASHORE, S. E. (1967), *Management by Participation*, Harper & Row.

MILLER, E. J., and RICE, A. K. (1967), *Systems of Organization*, Tavistock Institute.

OGBURN, W. F. (1957), in F. R. Allen, H. Hart, D. C. Miller and W. F. Ogburn (eds.), *Technology and Social Change*, Appleton-Century-Crofts.

OGBURN, W. F. (1962), 'National policy and technology', in C. R. Walker (ed.), *Modern Technology and Civilization*, McGraw-Hill.

RICE, A. K. (1958), *Productivity and Social Organization: The Ahmedabad Experiment*, Tavistock Institute.

RICE, A. K. (1963), *The Enterprise and Its Environment: A System Theory of Management Organization*, Tavistock Institute.

SAYLES, L. R. (1962), 'The change process in organizations: an applied anthropology analysis', *Human Organization*, vol. 21, no. 2, pp. 62–7.

SCHEIN, E. H. (1961), 'Management development as a process of influence', *Industrial Management Review*, vol. 2, pp. 59–77.

SCHON, D. A. (1967), *Technology and Change*, Delta Books.

TANNENBAUM, A. S. (1957), 'Personality change as a result of an experimental change of environmental conditions', *Journal of Abnormal and Social Psychology*, vol. 55, pp. 404–6.

TAYLOR, J. C. (1971a), 'An empirical examination of a four-factor theory of leadership using smallest space analysis', *Organizational Behavior and Human Performance*, vol. 6, pp. 249–66.

TAYLOR, J. C. (1971b), *Technology and Planned Organizational Change*, Institute for Social Research.

TRIST, E. L., and BAMFORTH, K. W. (1951), 'Some social and psychological consequences of the longwall method of coal getting', *Human Relations*, vol. 4, pp. 3–38.

TRIST, E. L., HIGGIN, G. W., MURRAY, H., and POLLOCK, A. B. (1963), *Organizational Choice*, Tavistock Institute.

TURNER, A. N., and LAWRENCE, P. R. (1965), *Industrial Jobs and the Worker*, Harvard University Press.

WALKER, C. R. (1957), *Toward the Automatic Factory*, Yale University Press.

WHITE, L. A. (1959), *The Evolution of Culture*, McGraw-Hill.

WILLIAMS, L K., and WILLIAMS, B. C. (1964), 'The impact of numerically controlled equipment on factory organization', *California Management Review*, vol. 7, no. 2, pp. 25–34.

WOODWARD, J. (1965), *Industrial Organization: Theory and Practice*, Oxford University Press.

Part Seven
The Future and Job Design

This concluding section ends on the note that what we now know about the nature of jobs and work is not enough to predict job design in the future. As Davis points out in both papers, we must recognize the new forces in society at large.

In the first paper (Reading 27), the probable effects of future production technology as 'stochastic' rather than 'deterministic' is developed, and the nature of future organizational forms is predicted from this. Reading 28 examines current trends in work ethic and values among those segments of the population that are historically underemployed, or disenfranchised, as well as those currently opting out of the traditional system of jobs and work.

27 Louis E. Davis

The Coming Crisis for Production Management:
Technology and Organization

Excerpts from L. E. Davis, 'The coming crisis for production
management: technology and organization', *International Journal of
Production Research*, vol. 9, 1971, pp. 65–82.

Introduction

Events cast their shadows before them. Already, we can discern
changes in our environment more than sufficient to show that
Western industrial society is in transition from one historical era
to another. It is the purpose of this paper to indicate that the
environmental characteristics of the post-industrial era will lead
to crisis and massive dislocation unless adaptation occurs. The
anticipated consequences will be greatest, at first, for the production industries, because they stand at the confluence of changes
involving technology, social values, the economic environment,
organizational design, job design and the practices of management.

Managers, as rational leaders, will seek to avoid these consequences by altering the forms of institutional regulation and control. It is a secondary purpose of this paper to describe some ways
in which managers are already beginning this process. Specifically,
examples will be given from the research results and organizational
experiments of an international coalition of English, American
and Norwegian researchers whose reports are referred to throughout this paper. [. . .]

The post-industrial challenge
Changes in society

In recent years, changes in Western societal environments have
been reflective of a rising level of expectations concerning material,
social and personal needs. The seeming ease with which new
(automated) technology satisfies material needs, coupled with the
provision of subsistence-level support for its citizens by society,
has stimulated a growing concern on the part of the individual over

his relationship to work, its meaningfulness and its value – i.e. a concern for the quality of work life (see Davis, 1970a). In the US, questioning of the relationship between work and satisfaction of material needs is widespread through the ranks of university students, industrial workers and minority unemployed. The viability of the belief, already described, that individuals may be used to satisfy the economic goals of organizations is being seriously questioned. It appears that people may no longer let themselves be used; they wish to see some relationship between their own work and the social life around them, and they wish some desirable future for themselves in their continuing relationship with organizations. No longer will workers patiently endure dehumanized work roles in order to achieve increased material rewards.

Among university students these expectations are leading to refusals to accept jobs with major corporations, in favour of more 'socially oriented' institutions – an unfortunate loss of talented people. Even the unemployed are refusing to accept dead-end demeaning jobs (see Doeringer, 1969), appearing to be as selective about accepting jobs as are the employed about changing jobs. There appear to be means, partly provided by society, for subsisting in minority ghettos without entering the industrial world. For industrial workers there is a revival of concern with the once-buried question of alienation from work, job satisfaction, personal freedom and initiative, and the dignity of the individual in the work place. Although on the surface the expressed concern is over the effects of automation on job availability and greater sharing in wealth produced, restlessness in unions, their failure to grow in the non-industrial sectors and the frequent overthrow of union leaders are all indicators, in the US, of a changing field that stems from the increasingly tenuous relationship between work and satisfaction of material needs.

Another factor impelling social change is the continuously rising level of education that Western countries provide, which is changing the attitudes, the aspirations, and the expectations of major segments of society (see Bell, 1967). Future trends are already visible in California, where almost 50 per cent of young people of college and university age are in school and where one-third of all the scientists and engineers in the US are employed.

Changes in technology

One of the forces driving the transition into the post-industrial era is the growing application of automated, computer-aided production systems. This development is bringing about crucial changes in the relationship between technology and the social organization of production – changes of such magnitude that the displacement of men and skills by computers is reduced to the status of a relatively minor effect.

The most striking characteristic of sophisticated, automated technology is that it absorbs routine activities into the machines, creating a new relationship between the technology and its embedded social system; the humans in automated systems are interdependent components required to respond to *stochastic*, not deterministic, conditions – i.e. they operate in an environment whose 'important events' are randomly occurring and unpredictable. Sophisticated skills must be maintained, though they may be called into use only very occasionally. This technological shift disturbs long-established boundaries between jobs and skills and between operations and maintenance. It has also contributed to a shift in the working population from providing goods to providing personal and societal services. As may be expected, there is a shift from blue-collar to white-collar work in clerical, technical and service jobs. At all levels of society, individuals find that they must change their careers or jobs over time.

Still further, the new technology requires a high degree of commitment and autonomy on the part of workers in the automated production processes (see Davis, 1970b). The required degree of autonomy is likely to be in serious conflict with the assumptions and values held within the bureaucratic technostructure (see Galbraith, 1967).

Another feature is that there are in effect two intertwined technologies. The primary technology contains the transformations needed to produce the desired output. It is machine- and capital-intensive. The secondary technology contains the support and service activities, such as loading and unloading materials, tools, etc. It is labour-intensive and its variances are capable of stopping or reducing throughput, but enhancing the secondary technology will not enhance the primary technology and its throughputs.

Although it poses new problems, highly sophisticated technology possesses an unrecognized flexibility in relation to social systems. There exists an extensive array of configurations of the technology that can be designed to suit the social systems desired, within limits. This property disaffirms the notion of the 'technological imperative' widely held by both engineers and social scientists. It places the burden on managers, hopefully aided by social scientists, to elucidate the characteristics of their particular social system suitable to the evolving post-industrial era. [. . .]

In production systems, stochastic events have two characteristics: unpredictability as to time and unpredictability as to nature. For economic reasons, they must be overcome as rapidly as possible, which imposes certain requirements on those who do the work. First, the workers must have a large repertoire of responses because the specific intervention that will be required is not known. Second, they cannot depend on supervision because they must respond immediately to events that occur irregularly and without warning. Third, they must be committed to undertaking the necessary tasks on their own initiative.

This makes a very different world, in which the organization is far more dependent on the individual (although there may be fewer individuals). From the point of view of the organization, the chain of causation is:

1. If the production process collapses, the economic goals of the organization will not be met.

2. If appropriate responses are not taken to stochastic events, the production process will collapse.

3. If the organization's members are not committed to their functions, the appropriate responses will not be made.

4. Commitment cannot be forced or bought; it can only arise out of the experiences of the individual with the quality of life in his working situation, i.e. with his job.

5. Therefore, automated industries seek to build into jobs the characteristics that will develop commitment on the part of the individual. The major characteristics are those of planning, self-control, self-regulation, i.e. of autonomy (see Davis, 1966).

A comparison between an industry that is highly automated and one that is not demonstrates these differences very clearly. In the oil-refining industry, the tasks that remain to be performed are almost entirely control and regulation, and the line between supervisor and worker is tenuous. The construction industry, on the other hand, still retains prominent roles for man as a source of energy and tool guidance, and supervision (often at several levels) mediates all system actions. Industrial relations officers in the oil industry are proud of their 'advanced and enlightened' personnel practices. And indeed, these practices may be accurately described as enlightened. But they were not adopted for the sake of their enlightenment. They were adopted because they are a necessary functional response to the demands of process technology.

Here is the point at which both the social and the technological forces can be seen working toward the same end, for 'job characteristics that develop commitment' and thus promote the economic goals of the highly automated organization are exactly those that are beginning to emerge as demands for 'meaningfulness' from the social environment – participation and control, personal freedom and initiative.

Nor is this linking of the two threads confined to industries that are as highly automated as oil and chemicals. Most industries are neither all automated nor all conventional; they utilize a mix of the two modes of production. If an industry has some employees whose jobs are designed to meet the requirements of automated technology, then the enhanced quality of their work life is visible to all the employees of the organization, creating demands by all employees for better, more meaningful jobs. It becomes very difficult to maintain a distinction in job design solely on the basis of a distinction in technological base.

Changes in economic organization

Developments in technology are interrelated with changes in economic organization. The scale of economic units is growing, stimulated by the developments of sophisticated production technology and organized knowledge leading to new products. In turn this is leading to new arrangements in the market, stimulating the development of higher-order interactions.

The organized use of knowledge brings about constant product innovation and for firms in electronics, aerospace, computers, information processing, etc., a new phenomenon in market relationship appears. Such firms are continually in the process of re-defining their products and their futures – an exercise that reflects back on their internal organization structures and on the response flexibility of their members. Within these companies, there is an observable shift to high-talent personnel and to the development of strategies of distinctive competence, stores of experience, and built-in redundance of response capabilities.

The consequences of these changes

A pervasive feature of the post-industrial environment is that it is taking on the quality of a turbulent field (see Emery and Trist, 1965). Turbulence arises from increased complexity and from the size of the total environment. It is compounded by increased inter-dependence of the environment's parts and the unpredictable connections arising between them as a result of accelerating but uneven change. The area of relevant uncertainty for individuals and organizations increases and tests the limits of human adapt-ability; earlier forms of adaptation, developed in response to a simpler environment, appear to suffice no longer. The turbulent environment requires that boundaries of organizations be extended into their technological, social and economic environments. The organization needs to identify the causal characteristics of the environments so that it can develop response strategies. The pro-duction organization, in particular, must provide a structure, a style of management and jobs so designed that adaptation can take place without massive dislocation. [. . .]

The post-industrial opportunity

Although the presence of the features outlined in the previous section indicates that we are already well launched into the post-industrial era, Trist (1968) finds that we suffer from a cultural lag – the absence of a culture congruent with the identifiable needs of post-industrialism. Furthermore, in the turbulent environmental texture of the post-industrial era, the individual organization, city, state, or even nation – acting alone – may be unable to meet the demands of increasing levels of complexity. Resources will have to be pooled; there will be a need for more sharing, more trust and more cooperation.

Seldom does society have a second chance to redress deep-seated errors in social organization and members' roles; however, the opportunity may now be at hand to overcome alienation and provide humanly meaningful work in socio-technical institutions (see Fromm, 1968, and Emery, 1967). The development, over a period of nearly twenty years, of a body of theory (see Emery, 1969) concerned with the analysis and design of interacting technological and social systems has furthered the examination of questions of organization and job design in complex environments, too long considered to be exclusively an art form. The diffusion of knowledge about applications of these theories is itself changing the environment of other organizations. The concepts were first developed in Britain (see Emery and Trist, 1960) and followed by developments in the United States and recently in Norway, Canada and Sweden. They are far from having come into common practice. Their most comprehensive application is taking place in Norway, on a national scale, as a basis for developing organizational and job design strategies suitable to a democratic society.

Briefly, socio-technical systems theory rests on two essential premises. The first is that in any purposive organization in which men are required to perform the organization's activities, there is a joint system operating, a *socio-technical* system. When work is to be done, and when human beings are required actors in the performance of this work, then the desired output is achieved through the actions of a social system as well as a technological system. Further, these systems so interlock that the achievement of the output becomes a function of the appropriate joint operation of both systems. The operative work is 'joint' for it is here that the socio-technical idea departs from more widely held views – those in which the social system is thought to be completely dependent on the technical system. The concept of joint optimization is proposed, which states that it is impossible to optimize for overall performance without seeking to optimize jointly the correlative independent social and technological systems.

The second premise is that every socio-technical system is embedded in an environment – an environment that is influenced by a culture and its values, an environment that is influenced by a set of generally acceptable practices, an environment that permits certain roles for the organisms in it. To understand a work system or an organization, one must understand the environmental forces that are operating on it. Without this understanding, it is impossible to develop an effective job or organization. This emphasis on environmental forces suggests, correctly, that the socio-technical systems idea falls within the larger body of 'open system' theories. What does this mean? Simply, that there is a constant interchange between what goes on in a work system or an organization and what goes on in the environment; the boundaries between the environment and the system are highly permeable, and what goes on outside affects what goes on inside. When something occurs in the general society, it will inevitably affect what occurs in organizations. There may be a period of cultural lag, but sooner or later, the societal tremor will register on the organizational seismographs.

Significantly, socio-technical systems theory provides a basis for analysis and design overcoming the greatest inhibition to development of organization and job strategies in a growing turbulent environment. It breaks through the long-existing tight compartments between the worlds of those who plan, study and manage social systems and those who do so for technological systems. At once it makes nonsensical the existing positions of psychologists and sociologists that in purposive organizations the technology is unalterable and must be accepted as a given requirement. Most frequently, therefore, only variables and relationships not influenced by technology are examined and altered. Without inclusion of technology, which considerably determines what work is about and what demands exist for the individual and organization, not only are peripheral relations examined but they tend to become disproportionately magnified, making interpretation and use of findings difficult, if not impossible. Similarly, it makes nonsensical the 'technological imperative' position of engineers, economists and managers who consider psychological and social requirements as constraints and at best as boundary conditions of technological systems. That a substantial part of technological system design includes social system design is neither understood nor appreciated. Frightful assumptions, supported by societal values, are made about men and groups and become built into machines and processes as requirements.

Socio-technical systems analysis provides a basis for determining appropriate boundaries of systems containing men, machines, materials and information. It considers the operation of such systems within the framework of an environment that is made an overt and specific object of the socio-technical study. It concerns itself with spontaneous reorganization or adaptation, with control of system variance, with growth, self-regulation, etc. These are aspects of system study that will become increasingly important as organizations in the post-industrial era are required to develop strategies that focus on adaptability and commitment. For these reasons, socio-technical systems analysis is felt to offer one of the best current approaches to meeting the post-industrial challenge.

The final section of this paper presents some selective aspects of socio-technical theory and application in greater detail. Wherever possible, actual field studies using the socio-technical approach are cited to support and illustrate the discussion.

Results of organizational and job design research

A number of developments, including on-site organizational experiments, lend strong support to the prospects of successfully developing suitable strategies of organization for the post-industrial era. In general, successful outcomes are measured by various objective criteria dependent on the finding of an accommodation between the demands of the organization and the technology on the one hand, and the needs and desires of people on the other, so that the needs of both were provided for. A summary report of US and English empirical studies appeared in Davis (1966).

The studies sought to find conditions in organization structure and job contents leading to cooperation, commitment, learning and growth, ability to change, and improved performance. The findings can be summarized under four categories of requirements: responsible autonomy, adaptability, variety and participation. When these factors were present, they led to learnings and behaviors that seemed to provide the sought-for organization and job response qualities. These studies lend support to the general model of responsible autonomous job and group behavior as a key facet in socio-technological relationships in production organizations.

By autonomy is meant that the content, structure and organization of jobs are such that individuals or groups performing those jobs can plan, regulate and control their own worlds. [. . .]

The results obtained indicated that when the attributes and characteristics of jobs were such that the individual or group became largely autonomous in the working situation, then meaningfulness, satisfaction and learning increased significantly, as did wide knowledge of process, identification with product, commitment to desired action and responsibility for outcomes. These supported the development of a job structure that permitted social interaction among job-holders and communication with peers and supervisors, particularly when the maintenance of continuity of operation was required. Simultaneously, high performance in quantity and quality of product or service outcomes was achieved. This has been demonstrated in such widely-different settings as the mining of coal (reported by Trist *et al.*, 1963), the maintenance of a chemical refinery, and the manufacture of aircraft instruments (reported by Davis and Werling, 1960, and Davis and Valfer, 1966).

The second requirements category, which has mainly been the province of psychologists, is concerned with 'adaptation'. The contents of the job have to be such that the individual can learn from what is going on around him, can grow, can develop, can adjust. Slighted, but not overlooked, is the psychological concept of self-actualization or personal growth, which appears to be central to the development of motivation and commitment through satisfaction of higher order intrinsic needs of individuals. The most potent way of satisfying intrinsic needs may well be through job design (see Lawler, 1969). Too often jobs in conventional industrial organizations have simply required people to adapt to restricted, fractionated activities, overlooking their enormous capacity to learn and adapt to complexity. [. . .]

Where the socio-technical system was so designed that the necessary adaptive behavior was facilitated, positive results in economic performance and in satisfactions occurred at all levels in the organization, as demonstrated in studies in oil refineries, automated chemical plants, pulp and paper plants (see Thorsrud and Emery, 1969), and aircraft instrument plants (see Davis, 1966).

The third category is concerned with variety. Man, surely, has always known it, but only lately has it been demonstrated that part of what a living organism requires to function effectively is a variety of experiences. If people are to be alert and responsive to their working environments, they need variety in the work situation. Routine, repetitious tasks tend to extinguish the individual. He is there physically, but not in any other way; he has disappeared from the scene. Psychologists have also studied this phenomenon in various 'deprived environments'. Adult humans confined to 'stimulus-free' environments begin to hallucinate. Workers may respond to the deprived work situation in much the same way – by disappearing (getting them back is another issue). Variety in industrial work has been the subject of study and controversy for fifty years. Recently, considerable attention has focused on the benefits to the individual and the organization of enlarging jobs to add variety (see Herzberg, 1966, and Davis, 1957).

There is another aspect of the need for variety that is less well-recognized in the industrial setting today, but that will become increasingly important in the emergent technological environment. The cyberneticist, Ashby (1960), has described this aspect of variety as a general criterion for intelligent behavior of any kind. To Ashby, adequate adaptation is only possible if an organism already has a stored set of responses of the requisite variety. This implies that in the work situation, where unexpected things will happen, the task content of a job and the training for that job should match this potential variability.

The last category concerns participation of the individual in the decisions affecting his work. Participation in development of job content and organizational relations, as well as in planning of changes, was fundamental to the outcomes achieved by the studies in Norway (see Thorsrud and Emery, 1969) and in the aircraft instrument industry (see Davis, 1962; 1966). Participation plays a role in learning and growth and permits those affected by changes in their roles and environments to develop assessments of the effects. An extensive literature on the process and dynamics of change (see Bennis, 1966) supports the findings of the field studies.

In a pioneering study, Lawrence and Lorsch (1967) examined the effects of uncertainty in technology and markets on the structure, relationship and performance of organizations. They found that where uncertainty is high, influence is high, i.e. if the situation becomes increasingly unpredictable, decision-making is forced down into the organization where the requisite expertise for daily decisions resides. Under environments of uncertainty, influence and authority are more evenly distributed; organizations become 'polyarchic'. Under environments of certainty or stability, organizations tend to be relatively less democratic, with influence, authority and responsibility centralized. These findings were derived from studies of firms in contrasting certain and uncertain environments.

Another category, which goes beyond the four and was implicit in them, concerns the total system of work. In the field studies, if tasks and activities within jobs fell into meaningful patterns, reflecting the interdependence between the individual job and the larger production system, then enhanced performance satisfaction and learning took place. In socio-technical terms, this interdependence is most closely associated with the points at which variance is introduced from one production process into another. When necessary skills, tasks and information were incorporated into the individual or group jobs, then adjustments could be made to handle error and exceptions within the affected subsystem; failing that, the variances were exported to other interconnecting systems. (In 'deterministic' systems, the layer on layers of supervisors, buttressed by inspectors, utility men, and repairmen, etc., absorb the variances exported from the work-place.)

These organizational experiments indicate that individuals and organizations can change and adapt to turbulent environments. Nonetheless, in moving into the post-industrial era, considerable learning is still needed about building into the organizational milieu the capability for continuing change. A number of studies have indicated that, if spontaneous and innovative behaviors are to result, conditions will have to be developed to bring about internalization of organizational goals (see Katz and Kahn, 1966). Such internalization exists at the upper levels of organizations, but (except in the Norwegian experiments) is found in the lower levels only in voluntary organizations.

Conclusion

In the post-industrial era, current organization structures will become increasingly dysfunctional. If strategies of survival are to be developed, advanced societies, particularly the managers of their industrial and business organizations, will have to accept the obligation to examine existing assumptions and face the value issues regarding men and technology raised by the evolving environments. Existing jobs and organizations will have to undergo reorganization to meet the requirements for a continuing high rate of change, new technologies and changing aspirations and expectations. These undertakings will be wrenching for institutions and individuals. Providing prescriptions would be presumptuous, but some organizations, joined by socio-technical researcher-consultants, seem to be well into the process.

References

ASHBY, W. R. (1960), *Design for a Brain*, Wiley.

BELL, D. (1967), 'Notes on the post-industrial society: I and II', *Public Interest*, Nos. 6 and 7.

BENNIS, W. G. (1966), *Changing Organisations*, McGraw-Hill.

DAVIS, L. E. (1957), 'Toward a theory of job design', *Journal of Industrial Engineering*, vol. 8, p. 305.

DAVIS, L. E. (1962), 'The effects of automation on job design', *Industrial Relations*, vol. 2, p. 53.

DAVIS, L. E. (1966), 'The design of jobs', *Industrial Relations*, vol. 6, p. 21.

DAVIS, L. E. (1970a), 'Restructuring jobs for social goals', *Manpower*, vol. 2, p. 2.

DAVIS, L. E. (1970b), 'Job satisfaction – a sociotechnical view', *Industrial Relations*, vol. 10.

DAVIS, L. E., and VALFER, E. S. (1966), 'Studies in supervisory job design', *Human Relations*, vol. 17, p. 339.

DAVIS, L. E., and WERLING, R. (1960), 'Job design factors', *Occupational Psychology*, vol. 28, p. 109.

DOERINGER, P. B. (1969), 'Ghetto labor markets and manpower', *Monthly Labor Review*, vol. 55.

EMERY, F. E. (1967), 'The next thirty years: concepts, methods and anticipations', *Human Relations*, vol. 20, p. 199.

EMERY, F. E. (1969), *Systems Thinking*, Penguin Books.

EMERY, F. E., and TRIST, E. L. (1960), 'Socio-technical systems' in C. W. Churchman and M. Verhulst (eds.), *Management Sciences, Models and Techniques*, vol. 2, Pergamon, p. 83.

EMERY, F. E., and TRIST, E. L. (1965), 'The causal texture of organizational environments', *Human Relations*, vol. 18, p. 21.

FROMM, E. (1968), *The Revolution of Hope: Toward a Humanised Technology*, Harper & Row, ch. 5.

GALBRAITH, J. K. (1967), *The New Industrial State*, Houghton–Mifflin.

HERZBERG, F. (1966), *Work and the Nature of Man*, World.

KATZ, D., and KAHN, R. L. (1966), *Social Psychology of Organisations*, Wiley, p. 345.

LAWLER, E. E. (1969), 'Job design and employee motivation', *Personnel Psychology*, vol. 22, p. 426.

LAWRENCE, P. R., and LORSCH, J. H. (1967), *Organisation and Environment*, Harvard University Press.

THORSRUD, E., and EMERY, F. (1969), *Moton ny bedriftsorganisasjon*, Tanum, Forlag, Oslo, ch. 6.

TRIST, E. L. (1968), *Urban North America, The Challenge of the Next Thirty Years – A Social Psychological Viewpoint*, Town Planning Institute of Canada.

TRIST, E. L., et al. (1963), *Organizational Choice*, Tavistock.

28 Louis E. Davis

Readying the Unready: Post-Industrial Jobs

Excerpts from L. E. Davis, 'Readying the unready: post-industrial jobs', *California Management Review*, vol. 13, 1971, no. 4, pp. 27-36.

United States attempts to bring some significant population segments into the economic and social mainstream have so far failed, partly because they were based on a succession of short-lived, inappropriate manpower models. Two factors affecting the texture of societal environment were overlooked: the technology our society uses to provide products and services, and the presence of societal enclaves differing in culture, skills, income, industrial experience and political status. These factors are related, and manpower policy that ignores them is doomed to fail.

Speeded by changes in social values and developments in technology, the industrial era is showing many signs of coming to a close. The transition into the post-industrial era is discernible in the development of automated technology for goods production, computer technology for provision of services, a tenuous relationship between work and economic production, and the development of new meanings for work and for relationships within and between working organizations.

We should now devote attention to an orderly transition into a post-industrial society. But in the midst of industrial nations there are still pre-industrial enclaves of the unemployed, untutored, unskilled, and unsophisticated, and on the international level there are economically underdeveloped nations among highly industrialized ones.

The objective of much government and private effort is to provide the means of introducing members of these enclaves into productive society. Most of the many transition programs assume that entrance into the economic mainstream leads to entrance into the social mainstream. This is more than a simple equating of economic status with social status. It reflects deeply held beliefs that participation in the economic activities of society serves social and psychological needs and provides the basis for political status. Business, industry and government agencies attempt to induct and train, giving men opportunities to prove themselves on the job. However, government agencies may be overly eager to have the unemployed trained and placed on jobs that may be short-lived. Choosing effective means for merging the unprepared into the economic mainstream presents the problems here discussed.

Many modes of preparing the unskilled for productive activities will be required. The focus here is on those using on-the-job learning and experience (excluding apprenticeship). The on-the-job mode requires that the unprepared be inducted into the work organization in a rapid and orderly fashion, which often means that entry jobs have to be designed *de novo* or by fractionating existing jobs so that they provide progressive learning stages. Job restructuring can provide the means for stepwise learning, but the job segments must be appropriately designed and progression through the segments must be a function of performance rather than of promotion or advancement based on available openings.

A newly developed theoretical framework provides help in understanding the requirements of job restructuring. The concepts were first sketched out nearly twenty years ago in Britain, and Norway has recently employed them as the substructure for a comprehensive program of labor–management relations, but they have yet to come into common practice in the United States. My colleagues and I are employing them as the basis of extensive reorganization of advanced industries. Briefly, one fundamental premise of this school of thought says that in any purposive organization in which men perform the organization's activities, there is a joint system operating – called, in the newly developing language of this theoretical framework, a socio-technical system. When human beings are required actors in the performance of work, the desired output is achieved through the actions of a social system as well as a technological system. Further, these systems so interlock that achievement of the output becomes a function of the appropriate joint operation of both systems. The operative word is 'joint', for it is here that the socio-technical idea departs from more widely held views – those in which the social system is thought to be dependent on the technical system.

The bearing on the question at hand is this: if the needs of the individual (which underlie the functioning of the social system) are not satisfied, then there will be no effective outcome from any program of job restructuring to provide entry and immediate follow-on jobs.

A second premise supporting the socio-technical concept is that every system is embedded in an environment and is influenced by a culture and its values. [. . .]

This, too, bears on the question of job restructuring. It says that programs will fail if they focus on the restructuring of jobs without giving due attention to the societal environment in which the jobs are embedded. Moreover, such programs will fail if they are not addressed to the emergent post-industrial environment whose dimensions are now becoming visible. [. . .]

Three meanings of job restructuring

Neither society, the organization, nor the individual is free to ascribe its own meaning to the concept of job restructuring; their differing slants on the concept (like the three sectors themselves) are and must be mutually interdependent. No matter how noble are society's objectives for a program of job restructuring, that program must meet the needs of both an organization and an individual.

Societal goals embedded in the concept of job restructuring are to get unskilled individuals into productive work, to help them acquire skills, and to provide a viable future for them. This listing begins to set some requirements for the outcome of any program of job restructuring.

Society's objectives must also take into account a finding by Clark (1967) in his study of the black ghetto:

The roots of the multiple-pathology in the dark ghetto are not easy to isolate. They do not lie primarily in unemployment. In fact, if all its residents were employed it would not materially alter the pathology of the community. More relevant is the status of the jobs held . . . more important than merely having a job, is the kind of job it is.

But the organization is also a partner in restructuring; it has a set of needs that it wants to satisfy, and the meaning of restructuring must address itself to these.

1. Management may see job restructuring as a way of coping with a labor shortage. 'Demand' or 'structural' explanations aside, it is clear that the economy is currently exhibiting both unemployment and labor shortages. To organizations, job restructuring may mean the ability to fulfill production requirements with available workers.

2. The organization has economic objectives and restructuring must contribute to them. On the basis that today's unskilled and untutored do not contribute adequately to an organization's economic goals, the federal government may partially repay the estimated deficit. This is probably a short-run situation – at least for the American economy.

3. The organization wants its members to adapt and cooperate, learning what is necessary and taking appropriate actions to maintain the productive system in a steady state. The organization will expect this behavior of workers holding restructured jobs. More importantly, it will require that job restructuring for some of the work force does not affect adversely the adaptiveness and cooperativeness of other workers whose jobs are not restructured.

Individuals also have requirements and aspirations that affect job restructuring. The first two of these are similar to society's aspirations: entry into gainful occupation and acquisition of skills. Further, the tasks that are performed have to be meaningful to the individual, and the role he performs must be meaningful within the organization. Obviously, the term 'meaningful' is conceptual shorthand, glossing over the many questions of satisfaction and status that are examined later.

Finally, the restructured jobs must offer some prospects for a desirable future career. The idea of a career at the working level is novel over most of the industrial world. Accustomed to thinking of jobs as entities in themselves, both managements and unions have lost the sense of the dynamics of working life – the expected progression from stage to stage of development. For many workers there are no dynamics – there is only one job over a lifetime. There is no 'career' in the sense of an evolution of the individual matched by an evolution of the work that he does. Job restructuring, particularly if concentrated at the entry level, may be analogous to preparing a man to walk off the edge of a cliff; he is well organized to take the first step, and after that there isn't anything else. The literature – indeed, the whole industrial culture of Western civilization, the United States included – takes the job as a discrete entity, independent of the idea of a career or even of a simple job progression other than promotion.

Trends to static separation

Specialization of work roles is as old as Western history. Western man specialized his work in relation to a particular product, technology, or material, or because he had to acquire certain skills and wanted to grasp them in a certain way.

Although the jobs created by this trend were, for the most part, highly specialized, they were also highly skilled. But, beginning about 1790, the trend toward specialization took a different turn. New power sources required factories where people could be brought together to do their work. The steam engine determined the placement of machines which, in turn, determined the placement of people; [and] [. . .] a new kind of specialization of labor, by specialization of tasks [was created], in which jobs were deliberately broken down so that unskilled people could do them.

In fact, almost anything that can be said about the 'modern' industrial practice of breaking down jobs can be found in Babbage's book, *On the Economy of Machinery and Manufactures*, which was written in 1835 and reflected twenty years of experience.[1]

In the United States, around 1890, Frederick W. Taylor rediscovered Babbage and created an approach called 'scientific management', which is the basis of industrial practice in the United States today.[2] [. . .]

Scientific management, as developed by Taylor, can be called the machine theory of organization, and is characterized by the following elements:

1. The man and his job are the essential building blocks of an organization; if the analyst gets these 'right' (in some particular but unspecified way), then the organization will be correctly defined.

1. See Reading 1 of the present volume [Ed.].
2. See Reading 2 of the present volume [Ed.].

2. Man is an extension of the machine, useful only for doing things that the machine cannot.

3. The men and their jobs – the individual building blocks – are to be glued together by supervisors who will absorb the uncertainties of the work situation. Furthermore, these supervisors need supervisors, and so on, *ad infinitum*, until the enterprise is organized in a many-layered hierarchy. In bureaucratic organizations, the latter notion ultimately leads to situations in which a man can be called a 'manager' solely because he supervises a certain number of people.

4. The organization is free to use any available social mechanisms to enforce compliance and ensure its own stability.

5. Job fractionation is a way of reducing the costs of carrying on the work by reducing the skill contribution of the individual who performs it. Man is simply an extension of the machine, and the more you simplify the machine (whether it's a living or nonliving part), the more you lower costs.

To talk of job restructuring now – at the beginning of the 1970s – is to evoke this whole dismal history. People have seen this used to get work done cheaply. They have seen it used to control many kinds of workers, and now a number of kinds of professionals. The success of current programs of job restructuring will depend on overcoming or averting the problems that were created by similar movements in history, and this, in turn, will depend on the correctness with which such programs assess the emerging environment, both changes on the social side and in the technology.

Environmental nature and effects

What are some of the forces operating in the social and technological environments? What can be predicted about the short-run future? What effect should these forces have on programs of job restructuring?

Socially, there seems to be a collapse of Western society's basic proposition about the relationship between work and the satisfaction of material needs. The 'Protestant ethic' says that man is put into the world to work; to satisfy his basic needs, he has to work hard because the environment is hostile and demands difficult, extended endeavor. This is now being very seriously questioned by

American youth, by industrial workers, and (to our great surprise) by the unemployed, although they question it in widely differing ways. People see technology as being capable of providing for material needs without any real effort on anybody's part. Whether this is an accurate or inaccurate perception is, perhaps, irrelevant. It is partly accurate and will grow more accurate over time.

This change implies that the use of individuals to satisfy the economic goals of an organization is no longer a viable social value. People will not let themselves be used. They want other things out of the work situation than the material reward. They want to see some relationship between their own work and the social life that goes on around them and to see some desirable future for themselves in a continuing relationship with the organization.

This change is already explicit in the words of college students about their work expectations. They say, 'We want a chance to participate and to control; we want a chance to make a contribution to developing more meaning in what we do.' And they carry these words into action, turning down jobs that would put their feet under the corporation board in favor of jobs with the Peace Corps or as members of Nader's Raiders.

That the unemployed may be saying this as well is seen in a study of the Boston area by Doeringer (1969, p. 55), which indicates that the unemployed seem to be as selective about accepting jobs as the employed are in changing jobs, because there are means – partly provided by society – for the jobless to subsist in the ghetto.

In short, many people in the United States are newly concerned about the quality of working life, about alienation from work, about job satisfaction, about personal freedom and initiative, and about the dignity of the individual in the work place. These questions are now arising because the relationship between work and the satisfaction of material needs is becoming more tenuous.

Another factor is that continuously rising levels of education are changing the attitudes, aspirations and expectations of many members of our society. Although the focus here is on the United States, I offer an example from Norway because it illustrates so strikingly the connection between education and work expectations.

A few years ago the Norwegian government decided to extend the school-leaving age of children by one year because education was an important requirement for the future society. Very soon Norway's important maritime industry was seriously threatened by an inability to recruit new workers. Before the school-leaving age was extended, about 80 per cent of the boys were willing to go to sea; afterwards, only 15 per cent sought seafaring careers. They wanted a different kind of life because the extra schooling had had an impact on them. (A creative solution was found by shifting from a focus on maritime jobs to one on careers.)

Other social forces in the environment might be mentioned. There is the drive toward professionalization; people want to be identified with activities of a professional nature, and we find a movement to provide a dignity for work that is analogous to that exhibited by the professions. The issue of appropriate labor-management relations, as now narrowly defined, has pretty well been settled. Consequently, labor unions are having some difficulty expanding their membership, keeping old members loyal, attracting new members, and so on.

What of the technological side? The most significant aspect of technological development is generally (and somewhat vaguely) called 'automation'. This means that there are devices in productive work systems that can be programmed to do routine tasks, sense outcomes, adjust machines if necessary, and continue the work process.

Man once had three roles to play in the production process, two of which have been preempted by machines. Man's first role was as an energy supplier, but since the advent of steam and electricity this role is now practically nonexistent in the United States. Man's second role was as a guider of tools. This is essentially what is meant by the term 'skill' – the trained ability to guide tools or manipulate machines or materials – and this role for man is increasingly being programmed into machines. The third contribution remains: man as regulator of a working situation or system, an adjuster of difficulties. Under automation, man's work in the physical sense has disappeared. The notion of skill in the conventional sense has disappeared. What is left are two kinds of skills related to regulation – skills in monitoring and diagnostics, and skills in the adjustment of processes.

This shift in the role of man unites the forces emergent in the social and technological environments in the following way. In conventional work the transformation system can be described as 'deterministic'. What is to be done, when it is to be done, and how it is to be done are all specifiable. The whole of Taylor's scientific management movement was based on the fundamental idea that the world was deterministic.

In the presence of sophisticated or automated technology, the deterministic world disappears into the machine. Only two kinds of functions are left for man: deterministic tasks for which machines have not yet been devised, and control of stochastic events – variability and exceptions. For example, in modern banks where third-generation computers are already in use, human functions fall very neatly into these two categories. There are people carrying pieces of paper from one machine to the next (because there is no machine for carrying paper). And there are people handling the indeterminate, randomly occurring situations with which the self-regulating capacities of the computer cannot cope.

In a production system, stochastic events have two characteristics. They are unpredictable as to time and nature. For economic reasons they must be overcome as rapidly as possible. These characteristics impose certain requirements on workers. First, they must have a large repertoire of responses, because the specific thing that will happen is not known. Second, they cannot depend on supervision because they must respond immediately to events that occur irregularly and without warning; they must be *committed* to undertaking the necessary tasks on their own initiative.

This makes a very different world, in which the organization is far more dependent on the individual (although there may be fewer individuals). [. . .]

Most industries are neither all automated nor all conventional. If an industry has some employees whose jobs are designed to meet the requirements of automated technology, then the characteristics of those jobs are visible to, and desired by, all the employees of the industry, and it becomes very difficult to maintain a distinction in job design solely on the basis of a distinction in technological base.

Job design suggestions

A considerable amount of formal and informal experimentation with job and organization design has occurred in the past twenty years in business and industry. Most of the experiments have been done in the United States, Norway and England. They are usually reported in highly specialized publications, and only occasionally in general, widely read journals. So far, researchers are talking to researchers and rarely to managers or union officials.

The research results point to three categories of job requirements, the first of which concerns the matter of 'autonomy' – jobs so designed that those performing them can regulate and control their own work worlds. They can decide when they are doing well or poorly, and they can organize themselves to do what is needed. Management's function is to specify the outcomes desired. Autonomy implies the existence of multiple skills, either within a single person (the French call such a person the 'polyvalent craftsman') or within the work group. Autonomy also implies self-regulation and self-organization, a radical notion in the industrial world of the United States. Further, it implies that those working will be managed or evaluated on the basis of outcomes rather than on conformity to rules.

Nevertheless, the research shows that when the attributes of jobs are such that autonomy exists in the working situation, the result is high meaning, high satisfaction, and high outcome performance. This has been demonstrated in such widely different settings as coal mining (Trist *et al.*, 1963), chemical refinery maintenance (Davis and Werling, 1960), and aircraft instrument manufacture (Davis and Valfer, 1966).

The second category concerns 'adaptation'. The elements of the job have to be such that the individual can learn from what is going on around him, can grow, can develop, can adjust. All living organisms adapt or they cease to exist, and man's every act is adaptive. Too often, jobs created under scientific management principles have overlooked that people adapt or learn and, in fact, that the organization needs them to adapt. (In automated technology, the very role of the individual depends on *his adaptability and his commitment*, because nobody is around at the specific instant to tell him what to do.) Unintentionally overlooked is that the job is also a setting in which personal psychic and social growth of the individual takes place. Such growth can be facilitated or blocked, leading to distortions having costs for the individual, the organization, and society.

Where the job and technology are designed so that adaptive behavior is facilitated, positive results occur at all levels in the organization, as demonstrated in studies of oil refineries (Hill, 1971), automated chemical plants (Thorsrud and Emery, 1969, ch. 6), pulp and paper plants (Thorsrud and Emery, 1969, ch. 4; Engelstad, 1970), and aircraft instrument plants (Davis, 1966).

The third research category concerns 'variety'. If people are to be alert and responsive to their working environments, they need variety in the work situation. Science began to get some notion of this after the Second World War, when research began on radar watchers. Radar watchers sit in a darkened room, eyeing blips on the radar screen that appear in random patterns. Eventually this blurs into a totally uniform background for the individual, and precisely when the important 'foreign' signal appears, the watcher has become incapable of attending to it. Psychologists have also studied this phenomenon in various 'deprived environments'. Monkeys raised in restricted environmental conditions do not develop into normal adult primates. Adult humans confined to 'stimulus-free' environments begin to hallucinate. Workers may respond to the deprived work situation in much the same way.

Specifically, what do the experiments say about the restructuring of jobs? All jobs, even fractionated jobs, should contain categories of activity that are important to the individual's development of self-organization and self-control in the work situation. There are preparatory tasks, transformation tasks, control tasks, and auxiliary tasks in a work process. Preparatory tasks, as the name implies, get the worker ready to do the work required. Transformation tasks cover the main productive activity. Control tasks give the individual short-loop feedback about how he is doing. (In many cases, this means that people may have to become their own inspectors, to carry out the requirements of providing themselves with feedback.) Auxiliary tasks include getting supplies, disposing of materials, and so on; they may provide relief from other more stressful tasks. If possible, a job ought to contain at least these components in order to incorporate autonomy.

To promote adaptability, the job – given objectives set by the organization – should permit the individual to set his own standards of quantity and quality of performance and to obtain knowledge of results over time (long-loop feedback). Within the context of the conventional industrial culture, this notion is taken to be either heretical or quaint. But research suggests that if overall goals are specified, people will respond appropriately, will determine what is right and wrong, and will work at meeting the goals.

To incorporate variety, the job should contain a sufficiently large number and kind of tasks. Some companies recognize at least one aspect of this need for variety. For instance, in very flat, unvarying situations, such as assembly lines, companies may rotate people through jobs to provide them with variety. This is an artificial mechanism, but it probably does keep workers from falling asleep at the switch. [. . .]

[Another] specification for the design of restructured jobs goes beyond autonomy, adaptation, and variety into the study of the total system of work: the tasks within a job should fall into a meaningful pattern reflecting the interdependence between the individual job and the larger production system. In sociotechnical terms, this interdependence is most closely associated with the points at which variance is introduced from one production process into another. The variance may arise from human action, from defects in the raw materials, or from malfunction of the equipment. A job must contain tasks and incorporate skills that permit the individual to cope with these variances. If the job does not provide this, the worker cannot control his own sphere of action; worse, he is forced to export variance to other interconnecting systems. In deterministic systems, the layers of supervision, buttressed by various inspectors, utility and repair men, and the like, absorb the variances exported from the workplace.

A related specification is that the tasks within the job ought to build and maintain the interdependence between individuals and the organization. This may occur through communication, through informal groups (if these are appropriate), and through cooperation between individuals. The tasks within the job and the jobs themselves ought to be seen as permitting relationships between individuals, permitting rotation, and encouraging the social support of one individual for another, particularly in stressful work situations. Otherwise, one gets isolation of the individual and conflict in the work situation.

Finally, the job should provide the basis on which an individual can relate his work to the community. Ask many American workers what they do and they will say, 'Oh, I work for Company X.' This is a good signal that the person either does not know or cannot explain the meaning of his work; it is merely some unspecified and unlocated portion of activity in a featureless landscape called 'the company'. This perception can have very serious consequences for his performance and for the satisfactions he derives.

The job-holder

The general requirements of job design also suggest some new ways of looking at job-holders. First, the job-holder ought to have some minimal area of decision-making that he can call his own. If he is to adapt and to achieve an autonomous working relationship, the content of his tasks ought to be sustained and bounded by recognition of the authority and responsibility required to perform them. However, in tightly interconnected systems and those with high variance, the extension of responsibility and control to encompass the interconnections is a particular requirement of job and organization design.

Second, the content of a job ought to be reasonably demanding of the individual in other than simply physical ways. This is related in part to growth and to learning, to the idea that jobs ought to provide for at least some minimum variety of activity, and to the idea that they should be related to the environment.

One of the problems in modern industrial life is to cope in a meaningful way with individual growth. Promotions are the only mechanism in wide use. Promotion assumes that a man is moved to another and better job. But in fact, the content of a given job held by a given man may be continually changing. That the same job should be different for people who have been working at it for a long time than it is for a beginner is simply not accepted. The whole standardization movement - represented by standardization of occupations and published job descriptions – is antithetical to this possibility and works against it.

To close this topic, a real example is offered in which some of these job specifications were applied. In 1968, the Director of the Institute for Work Research in Norway asked me and a colleague from the Tavistock Institute of Human Relations, London, to aid in an interesting experiment (Thorsrud and Emery, 1969, ch. 5). A company in Norway was in the process of designing an automated chemical fertilizer plant. They asked if jobs could be designed solely on the basis of the blueprints of the factory before it was built or staffed. In that way, as the physical plant was going up, they could begin to prepare the organization and the jobs and skills of the people who would man the plant when it was finished. The plant has now been in operation for over two years, with remarkable success.

The engineers had designed the plant so that the work to be done (monitoring, diagnosing, and adjusting, there being no physical work done in the plant other than maintenance) would be carried out in three monitoring or control rooms, in front of control panels. The equipment was so sophisticated that it required only one man in each control room. For three work shifts, this would have required nine men. (Other miscellaneous functions brought the total work force to sixteen men, excluding maintenance workers.) Based on the theoretical grounds reviewed above, the research team wished to avoid a situation in which people would work in isolation. But to put two men in a control room would have been economically inefficient. Therefore, totally new jobs were created by combining the maintenance and control functions. As the completed plant now operates, at least two men are based in each control room, alternately leaving it to perform maintenance tasks. They support each other, and the new job design also brings feed-back from the plant by means other than the instruments on the control panels. For the company, this meant that maintenance men had to learn chemistry, and chemical operators had to learn maintenance skills. But totally different jobs were developed than had ever existed before. Looking at any of the previous job histories would have revealed none of this. It had to come out of the theory rather than out of past practice. And it has been extremely successful.

To adduce another Norwegian example – an American ocean-going tanker has fifty-seven men; new Norwegian tankers have fifteen men. The difference is that between conventional and automated technology. The engineers who designed these Norwegian ships and their automated equipment learned that they could construct almost any kind of arrangement if they knew what kind of social system was wanted on board the ship.

Unexamined questions of policy

All of the foregoing provides a background against which to examine some questions of policy for job restructuring. The first concerns the existing job definitions and job boundaries that are cast in concrete in agreements between unions and managements, in state and federal civil service commissions, in personnel policies, and in a multitude of other ways. What will be required to break these molds? Simply to go to an employer with a proposal for job restructuring is, in many instances, to go to only half of the essential power. The union is the other half. Federal and state governments have contributed to the rigid stance of both halves by institutionalizing jobs and job descriptions. Jobs can be made infinitely better than they are. Jobs can be restructured for entry purposes and for advancement. But the issue must be made a matter of public and private policy, arrived at by open discussion.

The second policy question concerns the commitment to career development (in the sense it has been used throughout this paper), and not specifically to the individual job or to training for the individual job. A career-development approach was employed when the Norwegian maritime industry, in concert with government and labor, solved its recruitment problem. To get boys to go to sea, the maritime industry built career chains reaching out in both directions beyond the work on shipboard itself. Pretraining equips the boy to work on merchant ships and tankers for a number of years. Then the work and training aboard ship are designed to prepare him for later functions ashore. The man's entire working life is viewed as a continuum, his service at sea is an integral part of this continuum, achieving economic objectives for the maritime industry and preparatory, developmental objectives for the seaman.

American industry has ignored the issue of career development, except for professionals, and its omission is as detrimental to individuals within the mainstream of our productive society as it is to individuals seeking entry to it. Furthermore, planning programs that concentrate on a single entry level do violence to the job-design requirements discussed. The job designer, free to examine an entire logical sequence of activities, might find that some activities in the present entry-level job belonged in a higher stage, and that some in higher stages belonged at the entry level. In short, job restructuring has the potential of improving the whole range of industrial and service jobs (Paul, Robertson and Herzberg, 1969) but only if commitment to the concept of career progression becomes a matter of public concern.

A third matter of public policy concerns the quality of working life. This matter goes beyond mere satisfaction with working conditions and directly to the essential involvement of individuals in the working world. As noted above, many younger people – who are in the next working generation – quite clearly feel that they need not work to live. But it remains unclear whether this is a response to work itself, or to the negative aspects of work as it is organized in American culture.

The following additional questions also require consideration:

1. How flexible must an organization become in permitting individuals to pass through it to some level at which they can stabilize and perform usefully? There is a gain to flexibility, but there is also a cost, and the trade-offs will have to be worked out with the organizations involved.

2. What advantages might be gained from an alteration of on- and off-the-job continued learning? America has only begun to scratch the surface with the manpower programs it has developed so far.

3. What commitment should organizations make to job changes that facilitate the acquisition of knowledge and skills?

Finally, job restructuring should not be reduced to simplification.

Summary

Many planners behave as if one way of putting a job together were as good as any other. It may be possible to cut a skill in two and give half to man *A* and half to man *B*. But if that cut destroys any meaning in the work, the job designer had better spare the surgery.

Taking apart a job is very much analogous to disassembling a clock or dissecting an animal: in a clock or an animal, there is an ordered relationship among parts; in jobs, there is an ordered relationship of the individual tasks to the functioning of the whole sociotechnical system. If the needs of individuals for meaningfulness are at issue, then the results of taking apart a job and reconstructing it become very serious indeed. New job structures that are created must be relevant to the social outcomes that are required.

There should also be an ordered set of relationships through which an individual progresses to arrive at a job that is viable and meaningful, and that has continuity for him and for the organization. This notion of different jobs as stages in a chain has to be made explicit in any program for job restructuring. The employer must develop a chain of jobs from the entry point into the mainstream of his productive system, so that individuals can arrive at some desirable future. Acquiring skills is a transitional act in a person's life. It is unreasonable to expect a person to remain in transition for twenty years, or even two years. He must be able to get to some level, and this level must be specified.

Technology today is so rich in potential variations and arrangements that design decisions can depend almost exclusively on the social side of the situation. Machinery and tools can be organized in a variety of ways that will achieve the same economic objectives. The real question is, what social objectives are to be satisfied ? Any program for job restructuring must first define its social objectives with respect to the organization, the individual, and the whole society.

References

CLARK, K. B. (1967), 'Explosion in the ghetto', *Psychology Today*, September.

DAVIS, L. E. (1966), 'The design of jobs', *Industrial Relations*, vol. 6, p. 21. [See Reading 22.]

DAVIS, L. E., and VALFER, E. S. (1966), 'Studies in supervisory job design', *Human Relations*, vol. 19, no. 4, p. 339.

DAVIS, L. E., and WERLING, R. (1960), 'Job design factors', *Occupational Psychology*, vol. 28, p. 109.

DOERINGER, P. B. (1969), 'Ghetto labor markets and manpower problems', *Monthly Labor Revew*, March, p. 55.

HILL, P. (1971), *Towards a New Management Philosophy*, Gower Press.

PAUL, W. J., ROBERTSON, K. B., and HERZBERG, F. (1969), 'Job enrichment pays off', *Harvard Business Review*, vol. 47, p. 61. [See Reading 19.].

THORSRUD, E., and EMERY, F. E. (1969), *Mot on ny Bedriftsorganisjon*, Tanum.

ENGELSTAD, E. (1970), *Teknologi og Sosial Forandring på Arbeidsplassen* (*Hunsfos Experiment*), Tanum.

TRIST, E. L. (1963), *Organizational Choice*, Tavistock.

Job Design in the Wider Context

Einar Thorsrud

Job Design in the Wider Context

This book has been an attempt to look back over several streams of development that have led to presently existing concepts about the design of jobs. Viewing the whole development from this vantage point, I believe that two points stand out: First, the concepts described are fundamentally connected to, and carry great potential for, improvements in the quality of working life and society in the future. Second, the concepts are in a state at present that is both tenuous and fragile; they are insufficiently diffused, and their wider application depends in part on other, broader streams of development that lie outside the control of job designers.

Job design may degenerate into a mere gimmick if it is not part of both a comprehensive new policy concerning the use and development of human resources and a comprehensive new philosophy of management (Hill, 1971). But as a corollary – and illustrating the inherent interdependence of these three factors – the most advanced policies and philosophies cannot impinge on real life unless we learn more about job design and apply it better. The relationship between man and his work is basic to his relationships to himself and to his fellow men. If we cannot improve these basic relationships, I doubt very much whether we can even turn our attention to more global problems.

As I attempt to look into the future, I see three strands of development that may unite and emerge in the form of a new pattern. The first concerns the values of the younger generation and the necessary effect of those values and expectations on the character of institutions. The second concerns the kinds of models – involving new perceptions and appreciations – that are being applied to the study of man in institutions. The third concerns the directions from which general changes in institutional values can be expected

to emerge, and the ways in which such value changes can b
effected. The successful emergence of the new pattern depends
further, on the ability of institutions to learn, to grow, and to foste
individual growth of their individual members. Below, I offer ;
very brief description of the process by which (I hope) the nev
pattern may create itself.

The rising generation

Widespread discontent and alienation, particularly among th
younger generation, may crystallize into a new consciousness and
willingness to stop the state of affairs observable in over-indus
trialized societies. In such societies, mechanistic and reductionis
technocratic principles of job design are used to build meaningles
jobs, with little opportunity for learning and for participation i
decision-making. These job characteristics lead to a lack of soci;
support and attenuated relationships between the job and th
outside world and between the present and the future. Purel
economic rewards then reinforce the instrumental behavior of me
at work. After some time, the workers come to behave accordin
to the model of man underlying the technocratic principles of jo
design. A self-fulfilling hypothesis has been applied, and furthe
jobs are designed that are even more meaningless, that offer les
learning, less participation in decision-making, and so on. In man
countries, the younger generation is simply not willing to accep
these kinds of jobs and the vicious circle in job design will have t
stop.

The application of new models

Analysis of the crucial steps leading to this vicious circle ma
in fact, disclose the key to a higher quality of working life, for th
process can be changed into one of self-perpetuating learning an
growth. As before, a set of self-fulfilling hypotheses may be pi
into effect, but in this case embodying other values and othe
models of man than those underlying technocratic job design.

Widened jobs (jobs that are enlarged or enriched may be the fir
step. Such jobs would demand more than sheer endurance an
would offer some real personal meaning. (In terms of the ne
model, this step views man as *more capable*.)

Improved conditions for continuous learning can thus be built into jobs through increased variation, greater control of inputs and outputs at the boundary of the task, and involvement in problem-solving on the job (thus viewing man as more teachable).

Involvement in coordination and decision-making can be reinforced through problem-solving and learning.

Social support and mutual respect can be built into jobs through overlapping tasks, joint planning, participation, and feedback of results on the individual as well as on the group and organizational levels (viewing man as *more responsible*).

Meaningful relations between the job and the outside world can be developed if the above four steps have been taken. They are, of course, not sufficient conditions for such a positive relationship to be seen, but they are necessary.

A more desirable future, both on the job and in the wider institutional and societal setting, can be experienced if the above steps are taken. Promotions and pay increases cease to be the only improvements possible. The steps and the process described may build a set of conditions for continuous organizational development as a learning process.

It may be observed that this learning process is based on a set of hypotheses about the nature of man that may be of the self-fulfilling variety. This is exactly what they are supposed to be. The difference is that other values and other models of man are built into these hypotheses than the ones underlying technocratic job design. Some people may ask if we are aware of the possible Hawthorne effect involved in establishing these hypotheses. The answer is yes. If the Hawthorne effect really works, why not use it? But let us use it systematically and on a large scale; let us make explicit why and how we use it.

The emergence of new values

Experiments in job design and organizational development such as are suggested above all will not be sufficiently diffused unless they are undertaken in institutional settings. This means that they will have to be correlated with overall changes in values that are probably emerging in industrial societies. It means that we must be aware of changes in power structures.

If we can believe the vast literature dealing with the next thirty years, such changes are on their way. Some social critics deny that there are any signs of the industrial power structure changing from within, and that it will have to be broken down from outside if new structures are to emerge. This prediction is, I think, both incorrect and unrealistic. at least as far as the western European scene is concerned. It is often based on data used for predictions in economically underdeveloped countries. It overlooks the possible effects of a redefinition of capital and reallocation of resources in mixed economics. It overlooks the possible effects of professional management and institutional leadership. It also oversimplifies the future consequences of growth, which has lately become, to some extent, a bad word.

Growth can mean 'more of the same things produced the same way as before' – in which case we shall soon face global disaster. But growth can also mean different things produced with the same or less consumption of energy and with less waste than today. In that case, there is no contradiction between growth and structural changes in society. In fact, I suspect that structural changes cannot be achieved unless an optimal rate of growth can be achieved in those organizations and institutions involved. The optimal rate and type of growth will not be the same in different types of environments (Emery and Trist, 1965). In stable and rather passive environments, one-dimensional, quantitative growth can in some cases still be optimal for the larger system. In reactive or turbulent environments such as those we find in highly industrialized societies, growth in the form of differentiation is more likely to be functional for the global system. My point is that growth cannot be discarded if we want to look at the redesign of jobs and organizations as a learning process, as indicated above.

The prospects for change

Are there any strong signs that institutions and organizations can learn? What would it in fact mean if they did? In a small way, the Norwegian Industrial Democracy project has for ten years used a strategy of research and development based on institutional learning (Emery and Thorsrud, 1969). In spite of all types of difficulties, it has been possible to develop a number of field experiments. Diffusion is taking place slowly in Scandinavian industry and perhaps more rapidly in Norwegian shipping and some sectors of education.

The relationships among institutional learning, individual learning, and job design were emphasized by the Norwegian Trade Union Council and the Confederation of Employers, which, with the assistance of social scientists, formulated in 1962 a joint research and development program for industrial democracy. The following postulates were used as starting points:

The manner in which employees participate in the work-life of their companies is critical for the use they make of formal mechanisms for representation and consultation, and also for their attitudes, apathy or constructive interest, dissatisfaction, or satisfaction.

The bulk of the scientific evidence suggests that the more the individual is enabled to exercise control over his task, and to relate his efforts to those of his fellows, the more likely he is to accept a positive commitment. This positive commitment shows in a number of ways, not the least of which is the release of that personal initiative and creativity which constitute the basis of a democratic climate.

However, there is no simple technique that can be applied in all industrial conditions to bring about these changes. Thus, while job enlargement has proved effective for some conditions, it would be inappropriate in others; the development of autonomous work groups has been effective for some conditions, but likewise would be ineffective in others. The important point is that the kinds of change required are likely to be related to the kind of technology involved.

From these postulates and from the work of F. E. Emery at the Tavistock Institute in England and L. E. Davis in the United States, certain principles (Emery and Thorsrud, 1969) were derived for the design of jobs:

(a) *Optimum variety of tasks within the job.* Too much variety can be inefficient for training and production as well as frustrating for the worker. However, too little can be conducive to boredom or fatigue. The optimum amount would be that which allows the operator to take a rest from the high level of attention or effort in a demanding activity while working at another and, conversely, allows him to stretch himself and his capacities after a period of routine activity.

(b) *A meaningful pattern of tasks that gives to each job the semblance of a single overall task*. The tasks should be such that, although involving different levels of attention, degrees of effort, or kinds of skill, they are interdependent. That is, carrying out one task makes it easier to get on with the next or gives a better end-result to the overall task. Given such a pattern, the worker can help to find a method of working suitable to his requirements and can more easily relate his job to those of others.

(c) *Optimum length of work cycle*. Too short a cycle means too much finishing and starting; too long a cycle makes it difficult to build up a rhythm of work.

(d) *Some scope for setting standards of quantity and quality of production and a suitable feedback of knowledge of results*. Minimum standards generally have to be set by management to determine whether a worker is sufficiently trained, skilled, or careful to hold the job. Workers are more likely to accept responsibility for higher standards if they have some freedom in setting them and are more likely to learn from the job if there is feedback. They can neither effectively set standards nor learn if there is not a quick enough feedback of knowledge of results.

(e) *The inclusion in the job of the auxiliary and preparatory tasks*. The worker cannot and will not accept responsibility for matters outside his control. In so far as the preceding criteria are met, the the inclusion of such 'boundary tasks' will extend the scope of the worker's responsibility for and involvement in the job.

(f) *The tasks included in the job should entail some degree of care, skill, knowledge, or effort that is worthy of respect in the community*.

(g) *The job should make some perceivable contribution to the utility of the product for the consumer*.

(h) *Provision for 'interlocking' tasks, job rotation, or physical proximity where there is a necessary interdependence of jobs.* At a minimum this helps to sustain communication and to create mutual understanding between workers whose tasks are interdependent, and thus lessens friction, recriminations, and 'scapegoating'. At best this procedure will help to create work groups that enforce standards of cooperation and mutual help.

(i) *Provision for interlocking tasks, job rotation, or physical proximity where the individual jobs entail a relatively high degree of stress.*

(j) *Provision for interlocking tasks, job rotation, or physical proximity where the individual jobs do not make an obvious perceivable contribution to the utility of the end-product.*

(k) *Where a number of jobs are linked together by interlocking tasks or job rotation they should as a group:*

  (i) have some semblance of an overall task which makes a contribution to the utility of the product;
  (ii) have some scope for setting standards and receiving knowledge of results;
  (iii) have some control over the 'boundary tasks'.

(l) *Provision of channels of communication so that the minimum requirements of the workers can be fed into the design of new jobs at an early stage.*

(m) *Provision of channels of promotion to foreman rank, which are sanctioned by the workers.*

Predictions for change

The redesign of jobs and organizations can be seen as a learning process only if it includes a search for entirely new ways of dealing with the organization of work and the allocation of resources on all levels, including workers and staff as well as management. The values and objectives behind the experiments to be undertaken must be expressed in concrete conditions for change and operational criteria for evaluation. Initially, these experiments will need protection within the present power structure, but after evaluation on local and higher levels, the process of change must become self-sustaining. This means that the institution must provide enough time and resources to enable the new forms of organization to take root and stand out as viable demonstrations.

When this has occurred, local demonstrations, with the support of leading institutions, will have to survive on their own merits. They must survive on the basis of the human values they represent and not only because they work in practice. (Of course, they must also work in practice so that those who participate can be reinforced to go on learning and developing, not only in their work but also in their private life.) Institutions must be willing and able to use experiments to test and establish the new relationships among themselves and their members. (Companies and unions, schools and welfare institutions, governments and voluntary associations will tend to block each other from change unless new alternatives can be tested out experimentally.)

In the preceding few pages, I have suggested a mechanism by which the job design concepts elaborated in this book may be implemented – a possible process for achieving their full potential and for avoiding their degeneration into a set of hollow terms in a specialized jargon. If this process is in fact to occur, two kinds of supportive instrumentalities are necessary.

The first needs to work at the local level, providing institutional matrices within which the new management philosophy can function, within which job designs reflecting the new management philosophy can emerge, and within which a new set of relationships among all the members of an organization can manifest itself. At this level, jobs designed in accordance with the new concepts will be performed in the real world, viable in themselves and observable by other organizations and by the community.

The second supportive instrumentality needs to work at national and international levels, providing to institutional leaders an expression of meaningful social support for the new kinds of jobs and relationships and for their testing, reinforcement, and diffusion.

With support of these two kinds, we may look forward to an experimental renewal of existing organizations and institutions – a renewal that spreads from discrete foci and leads gradually toward a more effective consonance of most institutions with the broad framework of emerging social values.

References

EMERY, F. E., and TRIST, E. L. (1965), 'The casual texture of organizational environments', *Human Relations*, vol. 18, p. 21.
EMERY, F. E., and THORSRUD, E. (1969), *Form and Content in Industrial Democracy*, Tavistock.
HILL, P. (1971), *Towards a New Philosophy of Management*, Gower Press.

Further Reading

Work in the industrial era

M. Crozier, *The World of the Office Worker*, University of Chicago, 1971.

J. Gooding, 'Blue collar blues on the assembly line', *Fortune*, July 1970, pp. 68–71.

J. Gooding, 'It pays to wake up the blue collar worker', *Fortune*, September 1970, pp. 132–5.

H. L. Sheppard and N. Q. Herrick, *Where Have All the Robots Gone?*, Upjohn Institute for Employment Research, 1971.

C. R. Walker, 'The problem of the repetitive job', *Harvard Business Review*, May 1950, vol. 28, no. 3, pp. 54–58.

C. R. Walker and R. H. Guest, *The Man on the Assembly Line*, Harvard University Press, 1952.

Automation, and the effects of modern technology on work

A. D. Little, Inc., *Analysis of Automation Potential by means of Unit Operations*, US Department of Labor, 1965.

R. Blauner, *Alienation and Freedom*, University of Chicago Press, 1964.

T. Burns and G. M. Stalker, *The Management of Innovation*, Tavistock, 1961.

J. Chadwick-Jones, *Automation and Behavior*, Wiley, 1969.

E. R. F. W. Crossman, *Taxonomy of Automation: State of Arts and Prospects*, Organisation for Economic Cooperation and Development, European Conference on Manpower Aspects of Automation and Technical Change, Zurich, 1–4 February, 1966.

L. E. Davis and P. H. Engelstad, 'Unit operations in socio-technical systems: analysis and design', *Tavistock Institute of Human Relations*, doc. no. T.894, 1966.

F. E. Emery, 'Report on a theoretical study of unit operations', Human Resources Centre, *Tavistock Institute of Human Relations*, doc. no. T.900, October 1966.

B. Gardell, *Alienation and Mental Health in the Modern Industrial Environment*, Proceedings from W.H.O. Symposium: Society, Stress and Disease, no. 1, Stockholm, April 1970.

P. G. Herbst, 'Socio-technical unit design', Human Resources Centre, *Tavistock Institute of Human Relations*, doc. no. T.899, October 1966.

I. Hoos, *Automation in the Office*, Public Affairs Press, 1961.

F. C. Mann and L. K. Williams, 'Organizational impact of white collar automation', *Proceedings of the Eleventh Annual Meeting, Industrial Relations Research Association*, 1959.

E. Mumford, 'Clerks and computers', *Journal of Management Studies*, 1965, vol. 2, pp. 138–52.

C. Perrow, *Organizational Analysis: A Sociological View*, Wadsworth, 1970; also Tavistock, 1970.

C. R. Walker, *Toward the Automatic Factory*, Yale University Press, 1957.

L. K. Williams and B. C. Williams, 'The impact of numerically controlled equipment on factory organization', *California Management Review*, 1964, vol. 7, no. 2, pp. 25–34.

J. Woodward, *Industrial Organization: Theory and Practice*, Oxford University Press, 1965.

Job enlargement

R. Centers and D. E. Bugental, 'Intrinsic and extrinsic job motivations among different segments of the working population', *Journal of Applied Psychology*, 1966, vol. 50, pp. 193–7.

E. H. Conant and M. D. Kilbridge, 'An interdisciplinary analysis of job enlargement: technology, costs, and behavioral implications', *Industrial and Labor Relations Review*, April 1965, vol. 18, no. 3.

R. H. Guest, 'Job enlargement – a revolution in job design', *Personnel Administration*, March 1957, vol. 20, no. 2, pp. 13–14.

C. L. Hulin and M. R. Blood, 'Job enlargement, individual differences and worker responses', *Psychological Bulletin*, 1968, vol. 69, pp. 41–55.

E. E. Lawler, 'Job design and employee motivation', *Personnel Psychology*, 1969, vol. 22, pp. 426–35.

J. M. Shepard, 'Functional specialization and work attitudes', *Industrial Relations*, 1969, vol. 8, pp. 185–94.

Job enrichment

L. E. Davis and E. S. Valfer, 'Intervening responses to changes in supervisor job designs', *Occupational Psychology*, July 1965, vol. 39, no. 3, pp. 171–89.

L. E. Davis and R. Werling, 'Job design factors', *Occupational Psychology*, April 1960, vol. 34, no. 2, pp. 109–132.

R. N. Ford, *Motivation Through The Work Itself*, American Management Association, Inc., 1969.

F. K. Foulkes, *Creating More Meaningful Work*, American Management Association, Inc., 1969.

H. R. Koplan, C. Tausky and B. S. Bolaria, 'Job enrichment', *Personnel Journal*, October 1969, pp. 791–8.

J. R. Maher, *New Perspectives in Job Enrichment*, Litton Educational Publishing Co. Inc., 1971.

M. S. Myers, *Every Employee A Manager*, McGraw–Hill, 1970.

H. M. F. Rush, *Job Design for Motivation*, Report no. 55, Conference Board Inc., 1971.

Current developments

F. E. Emery, 'Democratization of the work place', *Manpower and Applied Psychology*, 1966, vol. 1, no. 2, pp. 118–29.

F. E. Emery, 'The next thirty years: concepts, methods and anticipations', *Human Relations*, 1967, vol. 20, no. 3, pp. 197–237.

F. E. Emery and E. L. Trist, 'The causal texture of organizational environments', *Human Relations*, 1965, vol. 18, pp. 21–32.

R. L. Kahn, D. Wolfe, R. Quinn, J. D. Snoek and R. Rosenthal, *Organizational Stress*, Wiley, 1964.

D. Katz and R. L. Kahn, *The Social Psychology of Organizations*, Wiley, 1966.

D. J. Levinson, 'Role, personality, and social structure in the organizational setting', *Journal of Abnormal and Social Psychology*, 1959, vol. 58, pp. 170–80.

E. J. Miller, 'Technology, territory, and time: the internal differentiation of complex production systems', *Human Relations*, 1959, vol. 12, pp. 243–72.

L. W. Porter, 'Job attitudes in management: 1. Perceived deficiencies in need fulfilment as a function of job level', *Journal of Applied Psychology*, 1963, vol. 47, pp. 141–8.

E. L. Trist, 'Urban North America – the challenge of the next thirty years: a social psychological viewpoint', *Plan*, Journal of the Town Planners Institute of Canada, 1970, vol. 10, no. 3, pp. 3–20.

L. von Bertalanffy, *Robots, Men and Minds*, Braziller, 1967.

J. Woodward, *Industrial Organization: Behavior and Control*, Oxford University Press, 1970.

Cost criteria for design of jobs

M. O. Alexander, 'Investments in people', *Canadian Chartered Accountant*, July 1971, pp. 38–45.

R. L. Brummet, E. G. Flamholtz and W. C. Pyle, 'Human resource accounting: a tool to increase managerial effectiveness', *Management Accounting*, August 1969, vol. 51, no. 1, pp. 12–15.

W. C. Pyle, 'Accounting system for human resources', *Innovation*, 1970, no. 10, pp. 46–55.

W. C. Pyle, 'Human resource accounting', *Financial Analysts Journal*, September–October 1970, pp. 69–78.

W. C. Pyle, 'Monitoring human resources – "on line"', *Michigan Business Review*, 1970, vol. 22, no. 4, pp. 19–32.

Socio-technical systems

L. E. Davis and E. S. Valfer, 'Studies in supervisory job design', *Human Relations*, 1966, vol. 19, no. 4, pp. 339–52.

F. E. Emery, E. Thorsrud and K. Lange, 'Field experiments at Christiania Spigerverk', *the Industrial Democracy Project, report no. 2 on phase B*, Institute for Industrial Social Research in cooperation with Tavistock Institute of Human Relations.

F. E. Emery and E. L. Trist, 'Socio-technical systems', *Management Sciences, Models and Techniques*, 1960, vol. 2, pp. 83–97.

P. G. Herbst, *Autonomous Group Functioning*, Tavistock, 1962.

P. G. Herbst, *Socio-Technical Theory and Design*, Tavistock, 1972.

P. Hill, *Towards a New Philosophy of Management*, Gower Press.

J. Marek, K. Lange and P. H. Engelstad, 'Wire mill of the Christiania Spegerverk', *The Industrial Democracy Project, report no. 1, phase B*, Norwegian Technological University, June 1964.

E. J. Miller and A. K. Rice, *Systems of Organization*, Tavistock, 1967.

A. K. Rice, *Productivity and Social Organization: The Ahmedabad Experiment*, Tavistock, 1958.

L. F. Smyth, P. H. Engelstad and H. van Beinum, 'Report on the pilot study in the crude distilling unit no. 2 at Stanlow Refinery', Tavistock Institute of Human Relations, doc. no. T.980, 1967.

G. I. Susman, 'The concept of status congruence as a basis to predict task allocation in autonomous work groups', *Administrative Science Quarterly*, 1970, vol. 15, pp. 164–75.

J. C. Taylor, *Technology and Planned Organizational Change*, Institute for Social Research, 1971.

E. Thorsrud, 'Policy making as a learning process', *Work Research Institutes*, A.I. Doc., June 1970.

E. Thorsrud, 'Socio-technical approach to job design and organizational development', *Management International Review*, 1968, vol. 8, pp. 120–31.

E. L. Trist, 'A socio-technical critique of scientific management', paper contributed to the Edinburgh Conference on the Impact of Science and Technology, Edinburgh University, May, 1970, pp. 24–6.

E. L. Trist and K. W. Bamforth, 'Some social and psychological consequences of the longwall method of coal getting', *Human Relations*, 1951, vol. 4, pp. 3–38.

E. L. Trist, G. W. Higgin, H. Murray and A. B. Pollock, *Organizational Choice*, Tavistock, 1963.

H. van Beinum, *The Morale of the Dublin Busmen*, Tavistock Institute of Human Relations, 1966.

Industrial democracy

Editor's note: Readings on industrial democracy are provided to indicate an old development emphasizing redistribution of power and control in work organizations. The implied assumption is that new broad roles for workers will result and that the workplace will be democratized. It remains, however, that jobs in such systems will still have to be designed. The Norwegian Industrial Democracy development, however, is proceeding from the workplace upward.

I. Adizes, *Industrial Democracy: Yugoslav Style*, Free Press, 1971.

F. H. Blum, *Work and Community*, Routledge & Kegan Paul, 1968.

H. A. Clegg, *A New Approach to Industrial Democracy*, Blackwell, 1960.

F. E. Emery and E. Thorsrud, *Form and Content in Industrial Democracy*, Tavistock, 1969.

A. Flanders, R. Pomeranz and J. Woodward, *Experiment in Industrial Democracy*, Faber & Faber, 1968.

E. Jaques, *The Changing Culture of a Factory*, Tavistock, 1951.

J. Kolaja, *Workers Councils: The Yugoslav Experience*, Tavistock, 1965.

J. Kolaja, *A Polish Factory: A Case Study of Workers' Participation in Decision Making*, University of Kentucky Press, 1960.

F. G. Lesieur, *The Scanlon Plan*, Massachusetts Institute of Technology, Industrial Relations Section, 1958.

C. Pateman, *Participation and Democratic theory*, Cambridge University Press, 1970.

T. U. Qvale, 'The industrial democracy project in Norway', International Industrial Relations Association, Geneva, September 1970.

E. Rhenman, *Industrial Democracy and Industrial Management*, Tavistock, 1968.

E. Thorsrud, 'A strategy for research and social change in industry: a report on the industrial democracy project in Norway', *Social Science Information*, 1970, vol. 9, no. 5, pp. 65–90.

E. Thorsrud and F. E. Emery, 'Industrial conflict and industrial democracy', *Operational Research and the Social Sciences*, International Conference – Cambridge 14–18 September 1964.

Acknowledgements

Permission to reproduce the Readings in this volume is acknowledged to the following sources:

Harper & Row, Publishers Inc.
Mr Daniel Bell
Prentice-Hall Inc.
McGraw-Hill Inc.
Journal of Industrial Engineering
Industrial Relations Research Association
American Psychological Association
Tavistock Institute of Human Relations and
Professor Hans van Beinum
Harvard Business Review
Division of Research, Harvard Business School
American Psychological Association
Industrial Relations
Tavistock Institute of Human Relations and Dr F. E. Emery
Administrative Science Quarterly
Journal of Industrial Engineering
McGraw-Hill Inc.
Industrial Relations
Harvard Business Review
Bureau of Labor & Management, University of Iowa,
Mr P. Stewart and Mr J. Biggane
American Psychological Association
Industrial Relations
The British Paper & Board Makers' Association
Plenum Publishing Corporation
Tanum Press
Plenum Publishing Corporation
The International Journal of Production Research
California Management Review

Author Index

Subject Index